# PORTUGUESE
## V O C A B U L A R Y

### FOR ENGLISH SPEAKERS

# ENGLISH-
# PORTUGUESE

The most useful words
To expand your lexicon and sharpen
your language skills

## 9000 words

# Portuguese vocabulary for English speakers - 9000 words

Andrey Taranov

T&P Books vocabularies are intended for helping you learn, memorize and review foreign words. The dictionary is divided into themes, covering all major spheres of everyday activities, business, science, culture, etc.

The process of learning words using T&P Books' theme-based dictionaries gives you the following advantages:

Correctly grouped source information predetermines success at subsequent stages of word memorization

Availability of words derived from the same root allowing memorization of word units (rather than separate words)

Small units of words facilitate the process of establishing associative links needed for consolidation of vocabulary

Level of language knowledge can be estimated by the number of learned words

T&P Books Publishing
www.tpbooks.com

ISBN: 978-1-78071-308-3

This book is also available in E-book formats.
Please visit www.tpbooks.com or the major online bookstores.

# PORTUGUESE VOCABULARY
## for English speakers

T&P Books vocabularies are intended to help you learn, memorize, and review foreign words. The vocabulary contains over 9000 commonly used words arranged thematically.

- Vocabulary contains the most commonly used words
- Recommended as an addition to any language course
- Meets the needs of beginners and advanced learners of foreign languages
- Convenient for daily use, revision sessions, and self-testing activities
- Allows you to assess your vocabulary

### Special features of the vocabulary

- Words are organized according to their meaning, not alphabetically
- Words are presented in three columns to facilitate the reviewing and self-testing processes
- Words in groups are divided into small blocks to facilitate the learning process
- The vocabulary offers a convenient and simple transcription of each foreign word

### The vocabulary has 256 topics including:

Basic Concepts, Numbers, Colors, Months, Seasons, Units of Measurement, Clothing & Accessories, Food & Nutrition, Restaurant, Family Members, Relatives, Character, Feelings, Emotions, Diseases, City, Town, Sightseeing, Shopping, Money, House, Home, Office, Working in the Office, Import & Export, Marketing, Job Search, Sports, Education, Computer, Internet, Tools, Nature, Countries, Nationalities and more ...

# &P BOOKS' THEME-BASED DICTIONARIES

## e Correct System for Memorizing Foreign Words

quiring vocabulary is one of the most important elements of learning a
eign language, because words allow us to express our thoughts, ask
estions, and provide answers. An inadequate vocabulary can impede
mmunication with a foreigner and make it difficult to understand a book or
vie well.

e pace of activity in all spheres of modern life, including the learning of modern
guages, has increased. Today, we need to memorize large amounts of
ormation (grammar rules, foreign words, etc.) within a short period. However, this
es not need to be difficult. All you need to do is to choose the right training
terials, learn a few special techniques, and develop your individual training
tem.

ving a system is critical to the process of language learning. Many people fail to
cceed in this regard; they cannot master a foreign language because they fail to
ow a system comprised of selecting materials, organizing lessons, arranging
w words to be learned, and so on. The lack of a system causes confusion and
entually, lowers self-confidence.

P Books' theme-based dictionaries can be included in the list of elements
eded for creating an effective system for learning foreign words. These
tionaries were specially developed for learning purposes and are meant to help
dents effectively memorize words and expand their vocabulary.

## nerally speaking, the process of learning words consists of three
## in elements:

Reception (creation or acquisition) of a training material, such as a word list

Work aimed at memorizing new words

Work aimed at reviewing the learned words, such as self-testing

three elements are equally important since they determine the quality of work
d the final result. All three processes require certain skills and a well-thought-out
proach.

w words are often encountered quite randomly when learning a foreign language
d it may be difficult to include them all in a unified list. As a result, these words
nain written on scraps of paper, in book margins, textbooks, and so on. In order
systematize such words, we have to create and continually update a "book of
w words." A paper notebook, a netbook, or a tablet PC can be used for these
poses.

This "book of new words" will be your personal, unique list of words. However, it will only contain the words that you came across during the learning process. For example, you might have written down the words "Sunday," "Tuesday," and "Friday." However, there are additional words for days of the week, for example, "Saturday," that are missing, and your list of words would be incomplete. Using a theme dictionary, in addition to the "book of new words," is a reasonable solution to this problem.

### The theme-based dictionary may serve as the basis for expanding your vocabulary.

It will be your big "book of new words" containing the most frequently used words of a foreign language already included. There are quite a few theme-based dictionaries available, and you should ensure that you make the right choice in order to get the maximum benefit from your purchase.

Therefore, we suggest using theme-based dictionaries from T&P Books Publishing as an aid to learning foreign words. Our books are specially developed for effective use in the sphere of vocabulary systematization, expansion and review.

Theme-based dictionaries are not a magical solution to learning new words. However, they can serve as your main database to aid foreign-language acquisition. Apart from theme dictionaries, you can have copybooks for writing down new words, flash cards, glossaries for various texts, as well as other resources; however, a good theme dictionary will always remain your primary collection of words.

### T&P Books' theme-based dictionaries are specialty books that contain the most frequently used words in a language.

The main characteristic of such dictionaries is the division of words into themes. For example, the *City* theme contains the words "street," "crossroads," "square," "fountain," and so on. The *Talking* theme might contain words like "to talk," "to ask," "question," and "answer".

All the words in a theme are divided into smaller units, each comprising 3–5 words. Such an arrangement improves the perception of words and makes the learning process less tiresome. Each unit contains a selection of words with similar meanings or identical roots. This allows you to learn words in small groups and establish other associative links that have a positive effect on memorization.

The words on each page are placed in three columns: a word in your native language, its translation, and its transcription. Such positioning allows for the use of techniques for effective memorization. After closing the translation column, you can flip through and review foreign words, and vice versa. "This is an easy and convenient method of review – one that we recommend you do often."

Our theme-based dictionaries contain transcriptions for all the foreign words. Unfortunately, none of the existing transcriptions are able to convey the exact nuances of foreign pronunciation. That is why we recommend using the transcriptions only as a supplementary learning aid. Correct pronunciation can only be acquired with the help of sound. Therefore our collection includes audio theme-based dictionaries.

## e process of learning words using T&P Books' theme-based
## :tionaries gives you the following advantages:

You have correctly grouped source information, which predetermines your success at subsequent stages of word memorization

Availability of words derived from the same root (lazy, lazily, lazybones), allowing you to memorize word units instead of separate words

Small units of words facilitate the process of establishing associative links needed for consolidation of vocabulary

You can estimate the number of learned words and hence your level of language knowledge

The dictionary allows for the creation of an effective and high-quality revision process

You can revise certain themes several times, modifying the revision methods and techniques

Audio versions of the dictionaries help you to work out the pronunciation of words and develop your skills of auditory word perception


ǝ T&P Books' theme-based dictionaries are offered in several variants differing in number of words: 1.500, 3.000, 5.000, 7.000, and 9.000 words. There are also tionaries containing 15,000 words for some language combinations. Your choice lictionary will depend on your knowledge level and goals.

ǝ sincerely believe that our dictionaries will become your trusty assistant in rning foreign languages and will allow you to easily acquire the necessary :abulary.

# TABLE OF CONTENTS

# PRONUNCIATION GUIDE

| Letter | Portuguese example | T&P phonetic alphabet | English example |
|---|---|---|---|
| a | patinadora | [a] | shorter than in ask |
| ã | capitão | [ɑ̃] | nasal [a] |
| b | cabriolé | [b] | baby, book |
| b [1] | acabar | [β] | between b and v |
| c [2] | contador | [k] | clock, kiss |
| c [3] | injector | [s] | silent [s] |
| c [4] | ambulância | [s] | city, boss |
| ç | comemoração | [s] | city, boss |
| ch | champanha | [ʃ] | machine, shark |
| d | diário | [d] | day, doctor |
| e | expressão | [ɛ], [ɛ:] | habit, bad |
| e | grau científico | [e] | elm, medal |
| e | nove | [ə] | driver, teacher |
| f | fonética | [f] | face, food |
| g [5] | língua | [g] | game, gold |
| g [6] | estrangeiro | [ʒ] | forge, pleasure |
| gu [7] | fogueiro | [g] | game, gold |
| h [8] | hélice | [h] | silent [h] |
| i [9] | bandeira | [i] | shorter than in feet |
| i [10] | sino | [i] | shorter than in feet |
| j | juntos | [ʒ] | forge, pleasure |
| k [11] | empresa-broker | [k] | clock, kiss |
| l | bolsa | [l] | lace, people |
| lh | escolher | [ʎ] | daily, million |
| m [12] | menu | [m] | magic, milk |
| m [13] | passagem | [ŋ] | English, ring |
| n | piscina | [n] | name, normal |
| nh | desenho | [ɲ] | canyon, new |
| o [14] | escola de negócios | [o], [ɔ] | drop, baught |
| o [15] | ciclismo | [u] | book |
| p | prato | [p] | pencil, private |
| qu [16] | qualidade da imagem | [kv] | square, quality |
| qu [17] | querosene | [k] | clock, kiss |
| r | forno | [r] | rice, radio |
| r | resto | [ʁ] | fricative r |
| s [18] | sereia | [s] | city, boss |
| ss | passado | [s] | city, boss |

| ter | Portuguese example | T&P phonetic alphabet | English example |
|---|---|---|---|
| | explosivo | [z] | zebra, please |
| | rede de lojas | [ʃ] | machine, shark |
| | tordo | [t] | tourist, trip |
| | truta | [u] | book |
| | voar | [v] | very, river |
| | savana | [β] | between b and v |
| 2 | cow-boy | [u] | book |
| | bruxa | [ʃ] | machine, shark |
| | exercício | [gz] | exam, exact |
| | display | [j] | yes, New York |
| | amizade | [z] | zebra, please |
| | giz | [ʃ] | machine, shark |

## Combinations of letters

| | | | |
|---|---|---|---|
| | embraiagem | [ja] | Kenya, piano |
| 27 | estado-maior | [jɔ] | New York |
| 28 | arroio | [ju] | youth, usually |
| 29 | aniversário | [ju] | youth, usually |
| | ciumento | [ju] | youth, usually |
| , um | fungo, algum | [ʊn] | soon |
| im | cinco, sim | [ĩ] | meeting, evening |
| , em | cento, sempre | [ẽ] | nasal [e] |

## Comments

usually between vowels
before a, o, u and consonants
before b, d, p, t
in front of e, i
before a, o, u and consonants
before e, i
before e, i
at the beginning of words
unstressed between vowel and consonant
elsewhere
in loanwords only
before vowels and b, p
before consonants and in em, im
stressed
unstressed, before a, e and in do, dos, o, os)
before a, o and ü
before e and i
at the beginning of a word

[19] between vowels
[20] at the end of a word
[21] usually between vowels
[22] in loanwords only
[23] between vowels
[24] in ex- before a vowel
[25] between vowels
[26] at the end of a word
[27] stressed, after vowels
[28] unstressed, after vowels
[29] unstressed, after consonants

# BBREVIATIONS
## ;ed in the vocabulary

| | | |
|---|---|---|
| | - | about |
| j | - | adjective |
| v | - | adverb |
| m. | - | animate |
| adj | - | attributive noun used as adjective |
| l. | - | for example |
| :. | - | et cetera |
| n. | - | familiar |
| n. | - | feminine |
| m. | - | formal |
| nim. | - | inanimate |
| sc. | - | masculine |
| th | - | mathematics |
| l. | - | military |
| | - | noun |
| | - | plural |
| )n. | - | pronoun |
| | - | somebody |
| g. | - | singular |
| } | - | something |
| ux | - | auxiliary verb |
| | - | intransitive verb |
| vt | - | intransitive, transitive verb |
| | - | transitive verb |
| | | |
| | - | masculine noun |
| | - | feminine noun |
| ɔl | - | masculine plural |
| ( | - | feminine plural |
| f | - | masculine, feminine |
| | - | pronominal verb |

# BASIC CONCEPTS

## Basic concepts. Part 1

### 1. Pronouns

| | | |
|---|---|---|
| I, me | eu | ['eu] |
| you | tu | [tu] |
| he | ele | ['ɛlə] |
| she | ela | ['ɛlɐ] |
| we | nós | [nɔʃ] |
| you (to a group) | vocês | [vɔs'eʃ] |
| they (masc.) | eles | ['ɛləʃ] |
| they (fem.) | elas | ['ɛlɐʃ] |

### 2. Greetings. Salutations. Farewells

| | | |
|---|---|---|
| Hello! (fam.) | Olá! | [ɔl'a] |
| Hello! (form.) | Bom dia! | [bõ d'iɐ] |
| Good morning! | Bom dia! | [bõ d'iɐ] |
| Good afternoon! | Boa tarde! | [b'oɐ t'ardə] |
| Good evening! | Boa noite! | [b'oɐ n'ojtə] |
| to say hello | cumprimentar (vt) | [kũprimẽt'ar] |
| Hi! (hello) | Olá! | [ɔl'a] |
| greeting (n) | saudação (f) | [sɐudɐs'ãu] |
| to greet (vt) | saudar (vt) | [sɐud'ar] |
| How are you? (form.) | Como vai? | [k'omu v'aj] |
| How are you? (fam.) | Como vais? | [k'omu v'ajʃ] |
| What's new? | O que há de novo? | [ukə a də n'ovu] |
| Bye-Bye! Goodbye! | Até à vista! | [ɐt'ɛ a v'iʃtə] |
| See you soon! | Até breve! | [ɐt'ɛ br'ɛvə] |
| Farewell! | Adeus! | [ɐd'euʃ] |
| to say goodbye | despedir-se (vp) | [dəʃpəd'irsə] |
| So long! | Até logo! | [ɐt'ɛ l'ɔgu] |
| Thank you! | Obrigado! -a! | [ɔbrig'adu -ɐ] |
| Thank you very much! | Muito obrigado! -a! | [m'ujtu ɔbrig'adu -ɐ] |
| You're welcome | De nada | [də n'adɐ] |
| Don't mention it! | Não tem de quê | [n'ãu tẽj də k'e] |

| as nothing | De nada | [də n'adɐ] |
| cuse me! (fam.) | Desculpa! | [dəʃk'ulpɐ] |
| cuse me! (form.) | Desculpe! | [dəʃk'ulpɐ] |
| excuse (forgive) | desculpar (vt) | [dəʃkulp'ar] |
| apologize (vi) | desculpar-se (vp) | [dəʃkulp'arsɐ] |
| apologies | As minhas desculpas | [ɐʃ m'iɲɐʃ dəʃk'ulpɐʃ] |
| sorry! | Desculpe! | [dəʃk'ulpɐ] |
| orgive (vt) | desculpar (vt) | [dəʃkulp'ar] |
| okay! | Não faz mal | [n'ãu faʃ m'al] |
| ase (adv) | por favor | [pur fev'or] |
| n't forget! | Não se esqueça! | [n'ãu sə əʃk'esɐ] |
| rtainly! | Certamente! | [sɛrtem'ẽtə] |
| course not! | Claro que não! | [kl'aru kə n'ãu] |
| ay! (I agree) | De acordo! | [əʃt'a bẽj] |
| at's enough! | Basta! | [b'aʃtɐ] |

## How to address

| cuse me! | Desculpe ... | [dəʃk'ulpɐ] |
| ter, sir | senhor | [səɲ'or] |
| am | senhora | [səɲ'orɐ] |
| s | rapariga | [ʀɐpɐr'igɐ] |
| ung man | rapaz | [ʀɐp'aʒ] |
| ing man (little boy) | menino | [mən'inu] |
| s (little girl) | menina | [mən'inɐ] |

## Cardinal numbers. Part 1

| ero | zero | [z'ɛru] |
| ne | um | [ũ] |
| vo | dois | [dojʃ] |
| ree | três | [treʃ] |
| ur | quatro | [ku'atru] |
| ve | cinco | [s'ĩku] |
| ix | seis | [s'ejʃ] |
| even | sete | [s'ɛtə] |
| ight | oito | ['ojtu] |
| ine | nove | [n'ɔvə] |
| ten | dez | [dɛʒ] |
| eleven | onze | ['õzə] |
| twelve | doze | [d'ozə] |
| thirteen | treze | [tr'ezə] |
| fourteen | catorze | [kɐt'orzə] |
| fifteen | quinze | [k'ĩzə] |

| 16 sixteen | dezasseis | [dəzɐsˈɐjʃ] |
| 17 seventeen | dezassete | [dəzɐsˈɛtə] |
| 18 eighteen | dezoito | [dəzˈojtu] |
| 19 nineteen | dezanove | [dəzɐnˈɔvə] |

| 20 twenty | vinte | [vˈĩtə] |
| 21 twenty-one | vinte e um | [vˈĩtə i ˈũ] |
| 22 twenty-two | vinte e dois | [vˈĩtə i dˈojʃ] |
| 23 twenty-three | vinte e três | [vˈĩtə i trˈeʃ] |

| 30 thirty | trinta | [trˈĩtə] |
| 31 thirty-one | trinta e um | [trˈĩtə i ˈũ] |
| 32 thirty-two | trinta e dois | [trˈĩtə i dˈojʃ] |
| 33 thirty-three | trinta e três | [trˈĩtə i trˈeʃ] |

| 40 forty | quarenta | [kuɐrˈẽtə] |
| 41 forty-one | quarenta e um | [kuɐrˈẽtə i ˈũ] |
| 42 forty-two | quarenta e dois | [kuɐrˈẽtə i dˈojʃ] |
| 43 forty-three | quarenta e três | [kuɐrˈẽtə i trˈeʃ] |

| 50 fifty | cinquenta | [sĩkuˈẽtə] |
| 51 fifty-one | cinquenta e um | [sĩkuˈẽtə i ˈũ] |
| 52 fifty-two | cinquenta e dois | [sĩkuˈẽtə i dˈojʃ] |
| 53 fifty-three | cinquenta e três | [sĩkuˈẽtə i trˈeʃ] |

| 60 sixty | sessenta | [səsˈẽtə] |
| 61 sixty-one | sessenta e um | [səsˈẽtə i ˈũ] |
| 62 sixty-two | sessenta e dois | [səsˈẽtə i dˈojʃ] |
| 63 sixty-three | sessenta e três | [səsˈẽtə i trˈeʃ] |

| 70 seventy | setenta | [sətˈẽtə] |
| 71 seventy-one | setenta e um | [sətˈẽtə i ˈũ] |
| 72 seventy-two | setenta e dois | [sətˈẽtə i dˈojʃ] |
| 73 seventy-three | setenta e três | [sətˈẽtə i trˈeʃ] |

| 80 eighty | oitenta | [ojtˈẽtə] |
| 81 eighty-one | oitenta e um | [ojtˈẽtə i ˈũ] |
| 82 eighty-two | oitenta e dois | [ojtˈẽtə i dˈojʃ] |
| 83 eighty-three | oitenta e três | [ojtˈẽtə i trˈeʃ] |

| 90 ninety | noventa | [nuvˈẽtə] |
| 91 ninety-one | noventa e um | [nuvˈẽtə i ˈũ] |
| 92 ninety-two | noventa e dois | [nuvˈẽtə i dˈojʃ] |
| 93 ninety-three | noventa e três | [nuvˈẽtə i trˈeʃ] |

## 5. Cardinal numbers. Part 2

| 100 one hundred | cem | [sˈẽj] |
| 200 two hundred | duzentos | [duzˈẽtuʃ] |
| 300 three hundred | trezentos | [trəzˈẽtuʃ] |

| four hundred | quatrocentos | [kuatrus'ẽtuʃ] |
| five hundred | quinhentos | [kiɲ'ẽtuʃ] |
| six hundred | seiscentos | [sɐjʃs'ẽtuʃ] |
| seven hundred | setecentos | [sɛtəs'ẽtuʃ] |
| eight hundred | oitocentos | [ojtus'ẽtuʃ] |
| nine hundred | novecentos | [nɔvəs'ẽtuʃ] |
| one thousand | mil | [mil] |
| two thousand | dois mil | [d'ojʃ mil] |
| three thousand | três mil | [tr'eʃ mil] |
| ten thousand | dez mil | [d'ɛʒ mil] |
| hundred thousand | cem mil | [sẽj mil] |
| ion | um milhão | [ũ miʎ'ãu] |
| on | mil milhões | [mil miʎ'ojʃ] |

## Ordinal numbers

| (adj) | primeiro | [prim'ɐjru] |
| ond (adj) | segundo | [səg'ũdu] |
| d (adj) | terceiro | [tərs'ɐjru] |
| rth (adj) | quarto | [ku'artu] |
| (adj) | quinto | [k'ĩtu] |
| h (adj) | sexto | [s'ɐʃtu] |
| enth (adj) | sétimo | [s'ɛtimu] |
| hth (adj) | oitavo | [ojt'avu] |
| th (adj) | nono | [n'onu] |
| th (adj) | décimo | [d'ɛsimu] |

## Numbers. Fractions

| ction | fração (f) | [fras'ãu] |
| half | um meio | [ũ m'ɐju] |
| third | um terço | [ũ t'ersu] |
| quarter | um quarto | [ũ ku'artu] |
| eighth | um oitavo | [ũ ojt'avu] |
| tenth | um décimo | [ũ d'ɛsimu] |
| thirds | dois terços | [d'ojʃ t'ersuʃ] |
| e quarters | três quartos | [treʃ ku'artuʃ] |

## Numbers. Basic operations

| traction | subtração (f) | [subtras'ãu] |
| ubtract (vi, vt) | subtrair (vi, vt) | [subtrɐ'ir] |

| division | divisão (f) | [diviz'ãu] |
| to divide (vt) | dividir (vt) | [divid'ir] |

| addition | adição (f) | [ɐdis'ãu] |
| to add up (vt) | somar (vt) | [sum'ar] |
| to add (vi, vt) | adicionar (vt) | [ɐdisjun'ar] |
| multiplication | multiplicação (f) | [multiplikɐs'ãu] |
| to multiply (vt) | multiplicar (vt) | [multiplik'ar] |

## 9. Numbers. Miscellaneous

| digit, figure | algarismo, dígito (m) | [algɐr'iʒmu], [d'iʒitu] |
| number | número (m) | [n'umɐru] |
| numeral | numeral (m) | [numɐr'al] |
| minus sign | menos (m) | [m'enuʃ] |
| plus sign | mais (m) | [m'ajʃ] |
| formula | fórmula (f) | [f'ɔrmulɐ] |

| calculation | cálculo (m) | [k'alkulu] |
| to count (vt) | contar, calcular (vt) | [kõt'ar], [kalkul'ar] |
| to count up | fazer a contagem | [fɐz'er ɐ kõt'aʒẽj] |
| to compare (vt) | comparar (vt) | [kõpɐr'ar] |

| How much? | Quanto? | [ku'ãtu] |
| How many? | Quantos? -as? | [ku'ãtuʃ -ɐʃ] |
| sum, total | soma (f) | [s'omɐ] |
| result | resultado (m) | [ʀɐzult'adu] |
| remainder | resto (m) | [ʀ'ɛʃtu] |

| a few … | alguns … | [alg'ũʃ] |
| few (not many) | poucos, poucas | [p'okuʃ], [p'okɐʃ] |
| a little (~ tired) | um pouco … | [ũ p'oku] |
| the rest | resto (m) | [ʀ'ɛʃtu] |
| one and a half | um e meio | [ũ i m'eju] |
| dozen | dúzia (f) | [d'uziɐ] |

| in half (adv) | ao meio | [au m'eju] |
| equally (evenly) | em partes iguais | [ẽ p'artɐʃ igu'ajʃ] |
| half | metade (f) | [mɐt'adɐ] |
| time (three ~s) | vez (f) | [veʒ] |

## 10. The most important verbs. Part 1

| to advise (vt) | aconselhar (vt) | [ɐkõsɐʎ'ar] |
| to agree (say yes) | concordar (vt) | [kõkurd'ar] |
| to answer (vi, vt) | responder (vt) | [ʀɐʃpõd'er] |
| to apologize (vi) | desculpar-se (vp) | [dɐʃkulp'arsɐ] |
| to arrive (vi) | chegar (vi) | [ʃɐg'ar] |

| | | |
|---|---|---|
| ask (~ oneself) | perguntar (vt) | [pərgũt'ar] |
| ask (~ sb to do sth) | pedir (vt) | [pəd'ir] |
| | | |
| be (~ a teacher) | ser (vi) | [ser] |
| be (~ on a diet) | estar (vi) | [əʃt'ar] |
| | | |
| be afraid | ter medo | [ter m'edu] |
| be hungry | ter fome | [ter f'ɔmə] |
| be interested in ... | interessar-se (vp) | [ĩtərəs'arsə] |
| be needed | ser necessário | [ser nəsəs'ariu] |
| be surprised | surpreender-se (vp) | [surpriẽd'ersə] |
| be thirsty | ter sede | [ter s'edə] |
| | | |
| begin (vt) | começar (vt) | [kuməs'ar] |
| belong to ... | pertencer (vt) | [pərtẽs'er] |
| boast (vi) | gabar-se (vp) | [geb'arsə] |
| break (split into pieces) | quebrar (vt) | [kəbr'ar] |
| | | |
| call (for help) | chamar (vt) | [ʃem'ar] |
| can (v aux) | poder (v aux) | [pud'er] |
| catch (vt) | pegar (vt) | [pəg'ar] |
| change (vt) | mudar (vt) | [mud'ar] |
| choose (select) | escolher (vt) | [əʃkuʎ'er] |
| | | |
| come down | descer (vi) | [dəʃs'er] |
| come in (enter) | entrar (vi) | [ẽtr'ar] |
| compare (vt) | comparar (vt) | [kõper'ar] |
| complain (vi, vt) | reclamar (vi) | [ʀəklem'ar] |
| | | |
| confuse (mix up) | confundir (vt) | [kõfũd'ir] |
| continue (vt) | continuar (vt) | [kõtinu'ar] |
| control (vt) | controlar (vt) | [kõtrul'ar] |
| cook (dinner) | preparar (vt) | [prəper'ar] |
| | | |
| cost (vt) | custar (vt) | [kuʃt'ar] |
| count (add up) | contar (vt) | [kõt'ar] |
| count on ... | contar com ... | [kõt'ar kõ] |
| create (vt) | criar (vt) | [kri'ar] |
| cry (weep) | chorar (vi) | [ʃur'ar] |

## The most important verbs. Part 2

| | | |
|---|---|---|
| deceive (vi, vt) | enganar (vt) | [ẽgen'ar] |
| decorate (tree, street) | decorar (vt) | [dəkur'ar] |
| defend (a country, etc.) | defender (vt) | [dəfẽd'er] |
| demand (request firmly) | exigir (vt) | [eziʒ'ir] |
| | | |
| dig (vt) | cavar (vt) | [kɐv'ar] |
| discuss (vt) | discutir (vt) | [diʃkut'ir] |
| do (vt) | fazer (vt) | [fɐz'er] |

| | | |
|---|---|---|
| to doubt (have doubts) | **duvidar** (vt) | [duvid'ar] |
| to drop (let fall) | **deixar cair** (vt) | [dɐjʃ'ar kɐ'ir] |
| | | |
| to excuse (forgive) | **desculpar** (vt) | [dɐʃkulp'ar] |
| to exist (vi) | **existir** (vi) | [eziʃt'ir] |
| to expect (foresee) | **prever** (vt) | [prɐv'er] |
| to explain (vt) | **explicar** (vt) | [ɐʃplik'ar] |
| | | |
| to fall (vi) | **cair** (vi) | [kɐ'ir] |
| to find (vt) | **encontrar** (vt) | [ẽkõtr'ar] |
| to finish (vt) | **terminar** (vt) | [tɐrmin'ar] |
| to fly (vi) | **voar** (vi) | [vu'ar] |
| to follow ... (come after) | **seguir ...** | [sɐg'ir] |
| to forget (vi, vt) | **esquecer** (vi, vt) | [ɐʃkɛs'er] |
| to forgive (vt) | **perdoar** (vt) | [pɐrdu'ar] |
| | | |
| to give (vt) | **dar** (vt) | [dar] |
| to give a hint | **dar uma dica** | [dar 'umɐ d'ikɐ] |
| | | |
| to go (on foot) | **ir** (vi) | [ir] |
| to go for a swim | **ir nadar** | [ir nɐd'ar] |
| to go out (from ...) | **sair** (vi) | [sɐ'ir] |
| to guess right | **adivinhar** (vt) | [ɐdiviɲ'ar] |
| | | |
| to have (vt) | **ter** (vt) | [ter] |
| to have breakfast | **tomar o pequeno-almoço** | [tum'ar u pɐk'enu alm'osu] |
| to have dinner | **jantar** (vi) | [ʒɐ̃t'ar] |
| to have lunch | **almoçar** (vi) | [almus'ar] |
| | | |
| to hear (vt) | **ouvir** (vt) | [ov'ir] |
| to help (vt) | **ajudar** (vt) | [ɐʒud'ar] |
| to hide (vt) | **esconder** (vt) | [ɐʃkõd'er] |
| to hope (vi, vt) | **esperar** (vt) | [ɐʃpɐr'ar] |
| to hunt (vi, vt) | **caçar** (vi) | [kɐs'ar] |
| to hurry (vi) | **estar com pressa** | [ɐʃt'ar kõ pr'ɛsɐ] |

## 12. The most important verbs. Part 3

| | | |
|---|---|---|
| to inform (vt) | **informar** (vt) | [ĩfurm'ar] |
| to insist (vi, vt) | **insistir** (vi) | [ĩsiʃt'ir] |
| to insult (vt) | **insultar** (vt) | [ĩsult'ar] |
| to invite (vt) | **convidar** (vt) | [kõvid'ar] |
| to joke (vi) | **fazer piadas** | [fɐz'er pj'adɐʃ] |
| | | |
| to keep (vt) | **guardar** (vt) | [guɐrd'ar] |
| to keep silent | **ficar em silêncio** | [fik'ar ẽ sil'ẽsiu] |
| to kill (vt) | **matar** (vt) | [mɐt'ar] |
| to know (sb) | **conhecer** (vt) | [kuɲɐs'er] |
| to know (sth) | **saber** (vt) | [sɐb'er] |
| to laugh (vi) | **rir** (vi) | [ʀir] |

| iberate (city, etc.) | libertar (vt) | [libərt'ar] |
| ike (I like ...) | gostar (vt) | [guʃt'ar] |
| ɔok for ... (search) | buscar (vt) | [buʃk'ar] |
| ɔve (sb) | amar (vt) | [em'ar] |
| | | |
| ɲake a mistake | errar (vi) | [ɛʀ'ar] |
| ɲanage, to run | dirigir (vt) | [diriʒ'ir] |
| ɲean (signify) | significar (vt) | [signifik'ar] |
| ɲention (talk about) | mencionar (vt) | [mɛ̃siun'ar] |
| ɲiss (school, etc.) | faltar a ... | [falt'ar e] |
| ɲotice (see) | perceber (vt) | [pərsəb'er] |
| | | |
| ɔbject (vi, vt) | objetar (vt) | [ɔbʒɛt'ar] |
| ɔbserve (see) | observar (vt) | [ɔbsərv'ar] |
| ɔpen (vt) | abrir (vt) | [ebr'ir] |
| ɔrder (meal, etc.) | pedir (vt) | [pəd'ir] |
| ɔrder (mil.) | ordenar (vt) | [ordən'ar] |
| ɔwn (possess) | possuir (vt) | [pusu'ir] |
| | | |
| ɔarticipate (vi) | participar (vi) | [pertisip'ar] |
| ɔay (vi, vt) | pagar (vt) | [peg'ar] |
| ɔermit (vt) | permitir (vt) | [pərmit'ir] |
| ɔlan (vt) | planear (vt) | [plɛnj'ar] |
| ɔlay (children) | brincar, jogar (vi, vt) | [brĩk'ar], [ʒug'ar] |
| | | |
| ɔray (vi, vt) | rezar, orar (vi) | [ʀəz'ar], [ɔr'ar] |
| ɔrefer (vt) | preferir (vt) | [prəfər'ir] |
| ɔromise (vt) | prometer (vt) | [prumət'er] |
| ɔronounce (vt) | pronunciar (vt) | [prunũsj'ar] |
| ɔropose (vt) | propor (vt) | [prup'or] |
| ɔunish (vt) | punir (vt) | [pun'ir] |
| | | |
| ead (vi, vt) | ler (vt) | [ler] |
| ecommend (vt) | recomendar (vt) | [ʀəkumɛ̃d'ar] |
| efuse (vi, vt) | negar-se (vt) | [nəg'arsə] |
| egret (be sorry) | lamentar (vt) | [ləmɛ̃t'ar] |
| | | |
| ent (sth from sb) | alugar (vt) | [elug'ar] |
| epeat (say again) | repetir (vt) | [ʀəpət'ir] |
| eserve, to book | reservar (vt) | [ʀəzərv'ar] |
| un (vi) | correr (vi) | [kuʀ'er] |

## 3. The most important verbs. Part 4

| ɕave (rescue) | salvar (vt) | [salv'ar] |
| ɕay (~ thank you) | dizer (vt) | [diz'er] |
| ɕcold (vt) | repreender (vt) | [ʀəpriɛ̃d'er] |
| ɕee (vt) | ver (vt) | [ver] |
| ɕell (vt) | vender (vt) | [vɛ̃d'er] |
| ɕend (vt) | enviar (vt) | [ẽvj'ar] |

| | | |
|---|---|---|
| to shoot (vi) | **atirar** (vi) | [ətir'ar] |
| to shout (vi) | **gritar** (vi) | [grit'ar] |
| to show (vt) | **mostrar** (vt) | [muʃtr'ar] |
| to sign (document) | **assinar** (vt) | [əsin'ar] |
| to sit down (vi) | **sentar-se** (vp) | [sẽt'arsə] |
| to smile (vi) | **sorrir** (vi) | [suʀ'ir] |
| | | |
| to speak (vi, vt) | **falar** (vi) | [fəl'ar] |
| to steal (money, etc.) | **roubar** (vt) | [ʀob'ar] |
| to stop (please ~ calling me) | **cessar** (vt) | [səs'ar] |
| to stop (for pause, etc.) | **parar** (vi) | [pər'ar] |
| to study (vt) | **estudar** (vt) | [əʃtud'ar] |
| to swim (vi) | **nadar** (vi) | [nəd'ar] |
| | | |
| to take (vt) | **pegar** (vt) | [pəg'ar] |
| to think (vi, vt) | **pensar** (vt) | [pẽs'ar] |
| to threaten (vt) | **ameaçar** (vt) | [əmiəs'ar] |
| to touch (with hands) | **tocar** (vt) | [tuk'ar] |
| to translate (vt) | **traduzir** (vt) | [trəduz'ir] |
| to trust (vt) | **confiar** (vt) | [kõfj'ar] |
| to try (attempt) | **tentar** (vt) | [tẽt'ar] |
| to turn (~ to the left) | **virar** (vi) | [vir'ar] |
| | | |
| to underestimate (vt) | **subestimar** (vt) | [subəʃtim'ar] |
| to understand (vt) | **compreender** (vt) | [kõpriẽd'er] |
| to unite (vt) | **unir** (vt) | [un'ir] |
| | | |
| to wait (vt) | **esperar** (vi, vt) | [əʃpər'ar] |
| to want (wish, desire) | **querer** (vt) | [kər'er] |
| to warn (vt) | **advertir** (vt) | [ədvərt'ir] |
| to work (vi) | **trabalhar** (vi) | [trəbəʎ'ar] |
| to write (vt) | **escrever** (vt) | [əʃkrəv'er] |
| to write down | **anotar** (vt) | [ənut'ar] |

## 14. Colors

| | | |
|---|---|---|
| color | **cor** (f) | [kor] |
| shade (tint) | **matiz** (m) | [mət'iʒ] |
| hue | **tom** (m) | [tõ] |
| rainbow | **arco-íris** (m) | ['arku 'iriʃ] |
| | | |
| white (adj) | **branco** | [br'ãku] |
| black (adj) | **preto** | [pr'etu] |
| gray (adj) | **cinzento** | [sĩz'ẽtu] |
| | | |
| green (adj) | **verde** | [v'erdə] |
| yellow (adj) | **amarelo** | [əmər'ɛlu] |
| red (adj) | **vermelho** | [vərm'əʎu] |
| blue (adj) | **azul** | [əz'ul] |

| | | |
|---|---|---|
| t blue (adj) | azul claro | [ɐz'ul kl'aru] |
| k (adj) | cor-de-rosa | [kor də ʀ'ozɐ] |
| nge (adj) | cor de laranja | [kor də lɐr'ãʒɐ] |
| et (adj) | violeta | [viul'etɐ] |
| wn (adj) | castanho | [kɐʃt'ɐɲu] |
| | | |
| den (adj) | dourado | [dor'adu] |
| ery (adj) | prateado | [prɐtj'adu] |
| | | |
| ge (adj) | bege | [b'ɛʒɐ] |
| am (adj) | creme | [kr'ɛmɐ] |
| quoise (adj) | turquesa | [turk'ezɐ] |
| rry red (adj) | vermelho cereja | [vɐrm'eʎu sɐr'eʒɐ] |
| c (adj) | lilás | [lil'aʃ] |
| nson (adj) | carmesim | [kɐrmɐz'ĩ] |
| | | |
| t (adj) | claro | [kl'aru] |
| k (adj) | escuro | [əʃk'uru] |
| ght, vivid (adj) | vivo | [v'ivu] |
| | | |
| ored (pencils) | de cor | [də kor] |
| or (e.g., ~ film) | a cores | [ɐ k'orɐʃ] |
| ck-and-white (adj) | preto e branco | [pr'etu i br'ãku] |
| in (one-colored) | de uma só cor | [də 'umɐ sɔ kor] |
| lticolored (adj) | multicor, multicolor | [multik'or], [multikul'or] |

## 5. Questions

| | | |
|---|---|---|
| o? | Quem? | [kẽj] |
| at? | Que? | [ke] |
| ere? (at, in) | Onde? | ['õdɐ] |
| ere (to)? | Para onde? | [p'ɐrɐ 'õdɐ] |
| m where? | De onde? | [də 'õdɐ] |
| en? | Quando? | [ku'ãdu] |
| y? (What for?) | Para quê? | [p'ɐrɐ ke] |
| y? (reason) | Porquê? | [purk'e] |
| | | |
| at for? | Para quê? | [p'ɐrɐ ke] |
| w? (in what way) | Como? | [k'omu] |
| at? (What kind of ...?) | Qual? | [ku'al] |
| ich? | Qual? | [ku'al] |
| | | |
| whom? | A quem? | [ɐ kẽj] |
| out whom? | De quem? | [də kẽj] |
| out what? | Do quê? | [du ke] |
| h whom? | Com quem? | [kõ kẽj] |
| | | |
| w many? | Quantos? -as? | [ku'ãtuʃ -ɐʃ] |
| w much? | Quanto? | [ku'ãtu] |
| ose? | De quem? | [də kẽj] |

## 16. Prepositions

| | | |
|---|---|---|
| with (accompanied by) | com | [kõ] |
| without | sem | [sẽj] |
| to (indicating direction) | a, para | [ɐ], [p'ɐɾɐ] |
| about (talking ~ ...) | sobre | [s'obɾə] |
| before (in time) | antes de ... | ['ãtəʃ də] |
| in front of ... | na frente de | [nɐ fɾ'ẽtə də] |
| | | |
| under (beneath, below) | sob, debaixo de ... | [sob], [dəb'ajʃu də] |
| above (over) | sobre, em cima de ... | [s'obɾə], [ẽ s'imɐ də] |
| on (atop) | sobre, em | [s'obɾə], [ẽ] |
| from (off, out of) | de | [də] |
| of (made from) | de | [də] |
| | | |
| in (e.g., ~ ten minutes) | dentro de | [d'ẽtru də] |
| over (across the top of) | por cima de ... | [pur s'imɐ də] |

## 17. Function words. Adverbs. Part 1

| | | |
|---|---|---|
| Where? (at, in) | Onde? | ['õdə] |
| here (adv) | aqui | [ɐk'i] |
| there (adv) | lá, ali | [la], [ɐl'i] |
| | | |
| somewhere (to be) | em algum lugar | [ɛn alg'ũ lug'ar] |
| nowhere (not anywhere) | em lugar nenhum | [ẽ lug'ar nəɲ'ũ] |
| | | |
| by (near, beside) | ao pé de ... | ['au pɛ də] |
| by the window | ao pé da janela | ['au pɛ də ʒɐn'ɛlɐ] |
| | | |
| Where (to)? | Para onde? | [p'ɐɾɐ 'õdə] |
| here (e.g., come ~!) | para cá | [p'ɐɾɐ ka] |
| there (e.g., to go ~) | para lá | [p'ɐɾɐ la] |
| from here (adv) | daqui | [dɐk'i] |
| from there (adv) | de lá, dali | [də la], [dɐl'i] |
| | | |
| close (adv) | perto | [p'ɛɾtu] |
| far (adv) | longe | [l'õʒə] |
| | | |
| near (e.g., ~ Paris) | perto de ... | [p'ɛɾtu də] |
| nearby (adv) | ao lado de | [au l'adu də] |
| not far (adv) | perto, não fica longe | [p'ɛɾtu], [n'ãu f'ikɐ l'õʒə] |
| | | |
| left (adj) | esquerdo | [əʃk'erdu] |
| on the left | à esquerda | [a əʃk'erdɐ] |
| to the left | para esquerda | [p'ɐɾɐ əʃk'erdɐ] |
| | | |
| right (adj) | direito | [dir'ejtu] |
| on the right | à direita | [a dir'ejtɐ] |

| English | Portuguese | IPA |
|---|---|---|
| he right | para direita | [p'ere dir'ejte] |
| ront (adv) | à frente | [a fr'ẽte] |
| ıt (as adj) | da frente | [de fr'ẽte] |
| ɔad (look ~) | para a frente | [p'ere a fr'ẽte] |
| ıind (adv) | atrás de ... | [etr'aʃ de] |
| n behind | por detrás | [pur detr'aʃ] |
| ɔk (towards the rear) | para trás | [p'ere tr'aʃ] |
| ɪdle | meio (m), metade (f) | [m'eju], [met'ade] |
| he middle | no meio | [nu m'eju] |
| he side | de lado | [de l'adu] |
| ɛrywhere (adv) | em todo lugar | [ãn t'odu lug'ar] |
| und (in all directions) | ao redor | ['au ʀed'ɔr] |
| n inside | de dentro | [de d'ẽtru] |
| newhere (to go) | para algum lugar | [p'ere alg'ũ lug'ar] |
| ɹight (directly) | diretamente | [dirɛtem'ẽte] |
| ɔk (e.g., come ~) | de volta | [de v'ɔlte] |
| n anywhere | de algum lugar | [de alg'ũ lug'ar] |
| n somewhere | de um lugar | [de ũ lug'ar] |
| tly (adv) | em primeiro lugar | [ẽ prim'ejru lug'ar] |
| ɔondly (adv) | em segundo lugar | [ẽ seg'ũdu lug'ar] |
| ɔdly (adv) | em terceiro lugar | [ẽ tɐrs'ejru lug'ar] |
| ɪdenly (adv) | de repente | [de ʀep'ẽte] |
| irst (adv) | inicialmente | [inisialm'ẽte] |
| the first time | pela primeira vez | [p'ele prim'ejrɐ v'eʒ] |
| g before ... | muito antes de ... | [m'ujtu 'ãteʃ de] |
| ɛw (over again) | novamente | [novɐm'ẽte] |
| good (adv) | para sempre | [p'ere s'ẽpre] |
| /er (adv) | nunca | [n'ũke] |
| ɑin (adv) | de novo | [de n'ovu] |
| /ɟ (adv) | agora | [ɐg'ɔre] |
| ɔn (adv) | frequentemente | [frekuẽtem'ẽte] |
| n (adv) | então | [ẽt'ãu] |
| ɛntly (quickly) | urgentemente | [urʒẽtem'ẽte] |
| ɹally (adv) | usualmente | [uzualm'ẽte] |
| the way, ... | a propósito | [ɐ prup'ɔzitu] |
| ɔsible (that is ~) | é possível | [ɛ pus'ivɛl] |
| ɔbably (adv) | provavelmente | [pruvavɛlm'ẽte] |
| ybe (adv) | talvez | [talv'eʒ] |
| ɔides ... | além disso, ... | [al'ẽj d'isu] |
| t's why ... | por isso ... | [pur 'isu] |
| ɔpite of ... | apesar de ... | [epez'ar de] |
| ɪnks to ... | graças a ... | [gr'aseʃ e] |
| at (pron.) | que | [ke] |

| that (conj.) | que | [kə] |
| something | algo | [algu] |
| anything (something) | alguma coisa | [alg'umɐ k'ojzɐ] |
| nothing | nada | [n'adɐ] |

| who (pron.) | quem | [kẽj] |
| someone | alguém | [alg'ẽj] |
| somebody | alguém | [alg'ẽj] |

| nobody | ninguém | [nĩg'ẽj] |
| nowhere (a voyage to ~) | para lugar nenhum | [p'ɐɾɐ lug'ar nəɲ'ũ] |
| nobody's | de ninguém | [də nĩg'ẽj] |
| somebody's | de alguém | [də alg'ẽj] |

| so (I'm ~ glad) | tão | [t'ãu] |
| also (as well) | também | [tãb'ẽj] |
| too (as well) | também | [tãb'ẽj] |

## 18. Function words. Adverbs. Part 2

| Why? | Porquê? | [purk'e] |
| for some reason | por alguma razão | [pur alg'umɐ ʀɐz'ãu] |
| because ... | porque ... | [p'urkə] |
| for some purpose | não se sabe para que | [n'ãu sə s'abə p'ɐɾɐ kə] |

| and | e | [i] |
| or | ou | ['ou] |
| but | mas | [mɐʃ] |
| for (e.g., ~ me) | para | [p'ɐɾɐ] |

| too (~ many people) | demasiado, muito | [dəmɐzi'adu], [m'ujtu] |
| only (exclusively) | só, somente | [sɔ], [sɔm'ẽtə] |
| exactly (adv) | exatamente | [ezatɐm'ẽtə] |
| about (more or less) | cerca de | [s'erkɐ də] |

| approximately (adv) | aproximadamente | [ɐprɔsimadɐm'ẽtə] |
| approximate (adj) | aproximado | [ɐprɔsim'adu] |
| almost (adv) | quase | [ku'azə] |
| the rest | resto (m) | [ʀ'ɛʃtu] |

| the other (second) | o outro | [u 'otru] |
| other (different) | outro | ['otru] |
| each (adj) | cada | [k'edɐ] |
| any (no matter which) | qualquer | [kualk'ɛɾ] |
| many (adv) | muitos, muitas | [m'ujtuʃ -ɐʃ] |
| much (adv) | muito | [m'ujtu] |
| many people | muitas pessoas | [m'ujtɐʃ pəs'oɐʃ] |
| all (everyone) | todos | [t'oduʃ] |
| in return for ... | em troca de ... | [ẽ tr'okɐ də] |
| in exchange (adv) | em troca | [ẽ tr'okɐ] |

| hand (made) | à mão | [a m'ãu] |
| dly (negative opinion) | é pouco provável | [ɛ p'oku pruv'avɛl] |
| bably (adv) | provavelmente | [pruvavɛlm'ẽtə] |
| purpose (adv) | de propósito | [də prup'ɔzitu] |
| accident (adv) | por acidente | [pur ɐsid'ẽtə] |
| y (adv) | muito | [m'ujtu] |
| example (adv) | por exemplo | [pur ez'ẽplu] |
| ween | entre | ['ẽtrə] |
| ong | entre, no meio de ... | ['ẽtrə], [nu m'ɐju də] |
| much (such a lot) | tanto | [t'ãtu] |
| ecially (adv) | especialmente | [əʃpəsjalm'ẽtə] |

# Basic concepts. Part 2

## 19. Weekdays

| | | |
|---|---|---|
| Monday | segunda-feira (f) | [səg'ũdɐ f'ejɾɐ] |
| Tuesday | terça-feira (f) | [t'ersɐ f'ejɾɐ] |
| Wednesday | quarta-feira (f) | [ku'art f'ejɾɐ] |
| Thursday | quinta-feira (f) | [k'ĩtɐ f'ejɾɐ] |
| Friday | sexta-feira (f) | [s'ɐʃtɐ f'ejɾɐ] |
| Saturday | sábado (m) | [s'abɐdu] |
| Sunday | domingo (m) | [dum'ĩgu] |
| | | |
| today (adv) | hoje | ['oʒə] |
| tomorrow (adv) | amanhã | [amɐɲ'ã] |
| the day after tomorrow | depois de amanhã | [dəp'ojʃ də amɐɲ'ã] |
| yesterday (adv) | ontem | ['õtẽj] |
| the day before yesterday | anteontem | [ãtj'õtẽj] |
| | | |
| day | dia (m) | [d'iɐ] |
| working day | dia (m) de trabalho | [d'iɐ də treb'aʎu] |
| public holiday | feriado (m) | [fəɾj'adu] |
| day off | dia (m) de folga | [d'iɐ də f'ɔlgɐ] |
| weekend | fim (m) de semana | [fĩ də sɐm'ɐnɐ] |
| | | |
| all day long | o dia todo | [u d'iɐ t'odu] |
| next day (adv) | no dia seguinte | [nu d'iɐ səg'ĩtə] |
| two days ago | há dois dias | [a d'ojʃ d'iɐʃ] |
| the day before | na véspera | [nɐ v'ɛʃpəɾɐ] |
| daily (adj) | diário | [dj'ariu] |
| every day (adv) | todos os dias | [t'oduʃ uʃ d'iɐʃ] |
| | | |
| week | semana (f) | [sɐm'ɐnɐ] |
| last week (adv) | na semana passada | [nɐ sɐm'ɐnɐ pɐs'adɐ] |
| next week (adv) | na próxima semana | [nɐ pr'ɔsimɐ sɐm'ɐnɐ] |
| weekly (adj) | semanal | [sɐmɐn'al] |
| every week (adv) | semanalmente | [sɐmɐnalm'ẽtə] |
| twice a week | duas vezes por semana | [d'uɐʃ v'ezəʃ p'ur sɐm'ɐnɐ] |
| every Tuesday | cada terça-feira | [k'adɐ tersɐ f'ejɾɐ] |

## 20. Hours. Day and night

| | | |
|---|---|---|
| morning | manhã (f) | [mɐɲ'ã] |
| in the morning | de manhã | [də mɐɲ'ã] |
| noon, midday | meio-dia (m) | [m'ɐju d'iɐ] |

| he afternoon | à tarde | [a t'ardə] |
|---|---|---|
| ening | noite (f) | [n'ojtə] |
| he evening | à noite | [a n'ojtə] |
| ht | noite (f) | [n'ojtə] |
| night | à noite | [a n'ojtə] |
| dnight | meia-noite (f) | [m'ɐjɐ n'ojtə] |
| | | |
| ond | segundo (m) | [səg'ũdu] |
| ute | minuto (m) | [min'utu] |
| ur | hora (f) | ['ɔrɐ] |
| f an hour | meia hora (f) | [m'ɐjɐ 'ɔrɐ] |
| arter of an hour | quarto (m) de hora | [ku'artu də 'ɔrɐ] |
| een minutes | quinze minutos | [k'ĩzə min'utuʃ] |
| hours | vinte e quatro horas | [v'ĩtɐ i ku'atru 'ɔrɐʃ] |
| | | |
| nrise | nascer (m) do sol | [nɐʃs'er du sɔl] |
| vn | amanhecer (m) | [ɐmɐɲəs'er] |
| ly morning | madrugada (f) | [mɐdrug'adɐ] |
| nset | pôr do sol (m) | [por du s'ɔl] |
| | | |
| ly in the morning | de madrugada | [də mɐdrug'adɐ] |
| s morning | hoje de manhã | ['ɔʒə də mɐɲ'ã] |
| norrow morning | amanhã de manhã | [amɐɲ'ã də mɐɲ'ã] |
| | | |
| s afternoon | hoje à tarde | ['ɔʒə a t'ardə] |
| he afternoon | à tarde | [a t'ardə] |
| norrow afternoon | amanhã à tarde | [amɐɲ'ã a t'ardə] |
| | | |
| ight (this evening) | hoje à noite | ['ɔʒə a n'ojtə] |
| norrow night | amanhã à noite | [amɐɲ'ã a n'ojtə] |
| | | |
| 3 o'clock sharp | às três horas em ponto | [aʃ treʃ 'ɔrɐʃ ẽ p'õtu] |
| out 4 o'clock | por volta das quatro | [pur v'ɔltɐ dɐʃ ku'atru] |
| 12 o'clock | às doze | [aʃ d'ozə] |
| | | |
| 20 minutes | dentro de vinte minutos | [d'ẽtru də v'ĩtɐ min'utuʃ] |
| an hour | dentro duma hora | [d'ẽtru d'umɐ 'ɔrɐ] |
| time (adv) | a tempo | [ɐ t'ẽpu] |
| | | |
| uarter of … | menos um quarto | [m'enuʃ 'ũ ku'artu] |
| nin an hour | durante uma hora | [dur'ãtɐ 'umɐ 'ɔrɐ] |
| ery 15 minutes | a cada quinze minutos | [ɐ k'ɐdɐ k'ĩzə min'utuʃ] |
| nd the clock | as vinte e quatro horas | [ɐʃ v'ĩtɐ i ku'atru 'ɔrɐʃ] |

## 1. Months. Seasons

| nuary | janeiro (m) | [ʒɐn'ɐjru] |
|---|---|---|
| oruary | fevereiro (m) | [fəvər'ɐjru] |
| rch | março (m) | [m'arsu] |
| ril | abril (m) | [ɐbr'il] |

| May | maio (m) | [m'aju] |
| June | junho (m) | [ʒ'uɲu] |

| July | julho (m) | [ʒ'uʎu] |
| August | agosto (m) | [ɐg'oʃtu] |
| September | setembro (m) | [sɐt'ẽbru] |
| October | outubro (m) | [ot'ubru] |
| November | novembro (m) | [nuv'ẽbru] |
| December | dezembro (m) | [dɐz'ẽbru] |

| spring | primavera (f) | [primɐv'ɛrɐ] |
| in spring | na primavera | [nɐ primɐv'ɛrɐ] |
| spring (as adj) | primaveril | [primɐvɐr'il] |

| summer | verão (m) | [vɐr'ãu] |
| in summer | no verão | [nu vɐr'ãu] |
| summer (as adj) | de verão | [dɐ vɐr'ãu] |

| fall | outono (m) | [ot'onu] |
| in fall | no outono | [nu ot'onu] |
| fall (as adj) | outonal | [oton'al] |

| winter | inverno (m) | [ĩv'ɛrnu] |
| in winter | no inverno | [nu ĩv'ɛrnu] |
| winter (as adj) | de inverno | [dɐ ĩv'ɛrnu] |

| month | mês (m) | [meʃ] |
| this month | este mês | ['eʃtɐ meʃ] |
| next month | no próximo mês | [nu pr'ɔsimu meʃ] |
| last month | no mês passado | [nu meʃ pɐs'adu] |

| a month ago | há um mês | [a ũ meʃ] |
| in a month | dentro de um mês | [d'ẽtru dɐ ũ meʃ] |
| in two months | dentro de dois meses | [d'ẽtru dɐ d'ojʃ m'ezɐʃ] |
| the whole month | durante todo o mês | [dur'ãtɐ t'odu u meʃ] |
| all month long | um mês inteiro | [ũ meʃ ĩt'ɐjru] |

| monthly (~ magazine) | mensal | [mẽs'al] |
| monthly (adv) | mensalmente | [mẽsalm'ẽtɐ] |
| every month | cada mês | [k'ɐdɐ meʃ] |
| twice a month | duas vezes por mês | [d'uɐʃ v'ezɐʃ pur meʃ] |

| year | ano (m) | ['ɐnu] |
| this year | este ano | ['eʃtɐ 'ɐnu] |
| next year | no próximo ano | [nu pr'ɔsimu 'ɐnu] |
| last year | no ano passado | [nu 'ɐnu pɐs'adu] |

| a year ago | há um ano | [a ũ 'ɐnu] |
| in a year | dentro dum ano | [d'ẽtru dũ 'ɐnu] |
| in two years | dentro de 2 anos | [d'ẽtru dɐ d'ojʃ 'ɐnuʃ] |
| the whole year | durante todo o ano | [dur'ãtɐ t'odu u 'ɐnu] |
| all year long | um ano inteiro | [ũ 'ɐnu ĩt'ɐjru] |

| ery year | cada ano | [k'edɐ 'ɐnu] |
| ual (adj) | anual | [ɐnu'al] |
| ually (adv) | anualmente | [ɐnualm'ẽtə] |
| mes a year | quatro vezes por ano | [ku'atru v'ezəʃ pur 'ɐnu] |
| e (e.g., today's ~) | data (f) | [d'atɐ] |
| e (e.g., ~ of birth) | data (f) | [d'atɐ] |
| endar | calendário (m) | [kɐlẽd'ariu] |
| f a year | meio ano | [m'ɐju 'ɐnu] |
| months | seis meses | [s'ɐjʃ m'ezəʃ] |
| ason (summer, etc.) | estação (f) | [əʃtɐs'ãu] |
| tury | século (m) | [s'ɛkulu] |

| e | tempo (m) | [t'ẽpu] |
| tant (n) | momento (m) | [mum'ẽtu] |
| ment | instante (m) | [ĩʃt'ãtə] |
| tant (adj) | instantâneo | [ĩʃtãt'ɐniu] |
| se (of time) | período (m) de tempo | [pər'iudu də t'ẽpu] |
| | vida (f) | [v'idɐ] |
| rnity | eternidade (f) | [etərnid'adə] |
| och | época (f) | ['ɛpukɐ] |
| | era (f) | ['ɛrɐ] |
| le | ciclo (m) | [s'iklu] |
| iod | período (m) | [pər'iudu] |
| n (short-~) | prazo (m) | [pr'azu] |
| future | futuro (m) | [fut'uru] |
| ure (as adj) | futuro | [fut'uru] |
| ct time | da próxima vez | [dɐ pr'ɔsimɐ veʒ] |
| past | passado (m) | [pɐs'adu] |
| st (recent) | passado | [pɐs'adu] |
| t time | na vez passada | [nɐ veʒ pɐs'adɐ] |
| er (adv) | mais tarde | [m'ajʃ t'ardə] |
| er (prep.) | depois | [dəp'ojʃ] |
| wadays (adv) | atualmente | [etualm'ẽtə] |
| w (adv) | agora | [ɐg'ɔrɐ] |
| nediately (adv) | imediatamente | [imədjatɐm'ẽtə] |
| on (adv) | logo, brevemente | [l'ɔgu], [brɛvɐm'ẽtə] |
| advance (beforehand) | de antemão | [də ãtəm'ãu] |
| ong time ago | há muito tempo | [a m'ujtu t'ẽpu] |
| ently (adv) | há pouco tempo | [a p'oku t'ẽpu] |
| stiny | destino (m) | [dəʃt'inu] |
| mories (childhood ~) | recordações (f pl) | [ʀəkurdɐs'ojʃ] |
| hives | arquivo (m) | [ɐrk'ivu] |

| during ... | durante ... | [du'rãtə] |
| long, a long time (adv) | durante muito tempo | [du'rãtə m'ujtu t'ẽpu] |
| not long (adv) | pouco tempo | [p'oku t'ẽpu] |
| early (in the morning) | cedo | [s'edu] |
| late (not early) | tarde | [t'ardə] |

| forever (for good) | para sempre | [p'ɐɾɐ s'ẽprə] |
| to start (begin) | começar (vt) | [kuməs'ar] |
| to postpone (vt) | adiar (vt) | [ɐdj'ar] |

| at the same time | simultaneamente | [simultɐniɐm'ẽtə] |
| permanently (adv) | permanentemente | [pərmɐnẽtəm'ẽtə] |
| constant (noise, pain) | constante | [kõʃt'ãtə] |
| temporary (adj) | temporário | [tẽpur'ariu] |

| sometimes (adv) | às vezes | [aʃ v'ezəʃ] |
| rarely (adv) | raramente | [ʀaɾɐm'ẽtə] |
| often (adv) | frequentemente | [frəkuẽtəm'ẽtə] |

## 23. Opposites

| rich (adj) | rico | [ʀ'iku] |
| poor (adj) | pobre | [p'ɔbrə] |

| ill, sick (adj) | doente | [du'ẽtə] |
| healthy (adj) | são | [s'ãu] |

| big (adj) | grande | [gr'ãdə] |
| small (adj) | pequeno | [pək'enu] |

| quickly (adv) | rapidamente | [ʀapidɐm'ẽtə] |
| slowly (adv) | lentamente | [lẽtɐm'ẽtə] |

| fast (adj) | rápido | [ʀ'apidu] |
| slow (adj) | lento | [l'ẽtu] |

| cheerful (adj) | alegre | [ɐl'ɛgrə] |
| sad (adj) | triste | [tr'iʃtə] |

| together (adv) | juntos | [ʒ'ũtuʃ] |
| separately (adv) | separadamente | [səpɐɾadɐm'ẽtə] |

| aloud (to read) | em voz alta | [ẽ vɔʒ 'altə] |
| silently (to oneself) | para si | [p'ɐɾɐ si] |

| tall (adj) | alto | ['altu] |
| low (adj) | baixo | [b'ajʃu] |

| deep (adj) | profundo | [pruf'ũdu] |
| shallow (adj) | pouco fundo | [p'oku f'ũdu] |

| | | |
|---|---|---|
| s | **sim** | [sĩ] |
| | **não** | [nãu] |
| tant (in space) | **distante** | [diʃt'ãtə] |
| arby (adj) | **próximo** | [pr'ɔsimu] |
| (adv) | **longe** | [l'õʒə] |
| arby (adv) | **perto** | [p'ɛrtu] |
| g (adj) | **longo** | [l'õgu] |
| ɔrt (adj) | **curto** | [k'urtu] |
| ɔd (kindhearted) | **bondoso** | [bõd'ozu] |
| l (adj) | **mau** | [m'au] |
| rried (adj) | **casado** | [kɐz'adu] |
| gle (adj) | **solteiro** | [sɔlt'ejru] |
| orbid (vt) | **proibir** (vt) | [pruib'ir] |
| ɔermit (vt) | **permitir** (vt) | [pərmit'ir] |
| ɟ | **fim** (m) | [fĩ] |
| ʒinning | **começo** (m) | [kum'esu] |
| (adj) | **esquerdo** | [əʃk'erdu] |
| ʼt (adj) | **direito** | [dir'ejtu] |
| t (adj) | **primeiro** | [prim'ejru] |
| t (adj) | **último** | ['ultimu] |
| ne | **crime** (m) | [kr'imə] |
| ʼishment | **castigo** (m) | [kəʃt'igu] |
| ɔrder (vt) | **ordenar** (vt) | [ɔrdən'ar] |
| ɔbey (vi, vt) | **obedecer** (vt) | [ɔbədəs'er] |
| ʼight (adj) | **reto** | [ʀ'ɛtu] |
| ʼved (adj) | **curvo** | [k'urvu] |
| ʼadise | **paraíso** (m) | [pɐɾɐ'izu] |
| l | **inferno** (m) | [ĩf'ɛrnu] |
| ɔe born | **nascer** (vi) | [nɐʃs'er] |
| ɟie (vi) | **morrer** (vi) | [muʀ'er] |
| ɔng (adj) | **forte** | [f'ɔrtə] |
| ak (adj) | **fraco** | [fr'aku] |
| (adj) | **idoso** | [id'ozu] |
| ʌng (adj) | **jovem** | [ʒ'ɔvẽj] |
| (adj) | **velho** | [v'ɛʎu] |
| v (adj) | **novo** | [n'ovu] |

| hard (adj) | duro | [d'uru] |
| soft (adj) | mole | [m'ɔlə] |

| warm (adj) | morno | [m'ornu] |
| cold (adj) | frio | [fr'iu] |

| fat (adj) | gordo | [g'ordu] |
| thin (adj) | magro | [m'agru] |

| narrow (adj) | estreito | [əʃtr'ejtu] |
| wide (adj) | largo | [l'argu] |

| good (adj) | bom | [bõ] |
| bad (adj) | mau | [m'au] |

| brave (adj) | valente | [vɐl'ẽtə] |
| cowardly (adj) | cobarde | [kub'ardə] |

## 24. Lines and shapes

| square | quadrado (m) | [kuɐdr'adu] |
| square (as adj) | quadrado | [kuɐdr'adu] |
| circle | círculo (m) | [s'irkulu] |
| round (adj) | redondo | [ʀəd'õdu] |
| triangle | triângulo (m) | [trj'ãgulu] |
| triangular (adj) | triangular | [triãgul'ar] |

| oval | oval (f) | [ɔv'al] |
| oval (as adj) | oval | [ɔv'al] |
| rectangle | retângulo (m) | [ʀɛt'ãgulu] |
| rectangular (adj) | retangular | [ʀɛtãgul'ar] |

| pyramid | pirâmide (f) | [pir'ɐmidə] |
| rhombus | rombo (m) | [ʀ'õbu] |
| trapezoid | trapézio (m) | [trɐp'ɛziu] |
| cube | cubo (m) | [k'ubu] |
| prism | prisma (m) | [pr'iʒmɐ] |

| circumference | circunferência (f) | [sirkũfər'ẽsiɐ] |
| sphere | esfera (f) | [əʃf'ɛrɐ] |
| ball (solid sphere) | globo (m) | [gl'obu] |
| diameter | diâmetro (m) | [dj'emətru] |
| radius | raio (m) | [ʀ'aju] |
| perimeter (circle's ~) | perímetro (m) | [pər'imətru] |
| center | centro (m) | [s'ẽtru] |

| horizontal (adj) | horizontal | [ɔrizõt'al] |
| vertical (adj) | vertical | [vərtik'al] |
| parallel (n) | paralela (f) | [pɐrɐl'ɛlɐ] |
| parallel (as adj) | paralelo | [pɐrɐl'ɛlu] |

| | linha (f) | [l'iɲɐ] |
| ɔke | traço (m) | [tr'asu] |
| ɑight line | reta (f) | [ʀ'ɛtɐ] |
| ve (curved line) | curva (f) | [k'urvɐ] |
| ɪ (line, etc.) | fino | [f'inu] |
| ɪtour (outline) | contorno (m) | [kõt'ornu] |

| ɜrsection | interseção (f) | [ĩtɐrsɛs'ãu] |
| ɪt angle | ângulo (m) reto | [ãgulu ʀ'ɛtu] |
| ɟment | segmento (m) | [sɛgm'ẽtu] |
| ːtor | setor (m) | [sɛt'or] |
| ɘ (of triangle) | lado (m) | [l'adu] |
| ɟle | ângulo (m) | [ãgulu] |

## 6. Units of measurement

| ight | peso (m) | [p'ezu] |
| gth | comprimento (m) | [kõprim'ẽtu] |
| ɪth | largura (f) | [lɐrg'urɐ] |
| ght | altura (f) | [alt'urɐ] |
| ɔth | profundidade (f) | [prufũdid'adɐ] |
| ume | volume (m) | [vul'umɐ] |
| ɑ | área (f) | ['ariɐ] |

| m | grama (m) | [gr'emɐ] |
| ligram | miligrama (m) | [miligr'emɐ] |
| ɔgram | quilograma (m) | [kilugr'emɐ] |
| | tonelada (f) | [tunɘl'adɐ] |
| ɪnd | libra (f) | [l'ibrɐ] |
| ɪce | onça (f) | ['õsɐ] |

| ter | metro (m) | [m'ɛtru] |
| limeter | milímetro (m) | [mil'imɘtru] |
| ɪtimeter | centímetro (m) | [sẽt'imɘtru] |
| ɔmeter | quilómetro (m) | [kil'ɔmɘtru] |
| ɘ | milha (f) | [m'iʎɐ] |

| ɪ | polegada (f) | [pulɘg'adɐ] |
| t | pé (m) | [pɛ] |
| ɪd | jarda (f) | [ʒ'ardɐ] |

| ɪare meter | metro (m) quadrado | [m'ɛtru kuɐdr'adu] |
| ːtare | hectare (m) | [ɛkt'arɐ] |

| ɪ | litro (m) | [l'itru] |
| ɟree | grau (m) | [gr'au] |
| t | volt (m) | [v'ɔltɐ] |
| ɔere | ampere (m) | [ãp'ɛrɐ] |
| sepower | cavalo-vapor (m) | [kɐv'alu vɐp'or] |
| ɪntity | quantidade (f) | [kuãtid'adɐ] |

| a little bit of ... | um pouco de ... | [ũ p'oku də] |
| half | metade (f) | [mət'adə] |
| dozen | dúzia (f) | [d'uziɐ] |
| piece (item) | peça (f) | [p'ɛsɐ] |

| size | dimensão (f) | [dimɐ̃s'ãu] |
| scale (map ~) | escala (f) | [əʃk'alɐ] |

| minimal (adj) | mínimo | [m'inimu] |
| the smallest (adj) | menor, mais pequeno | [mən'ɔr], [m'ajʃ pək'enu] |
| medium (adj) | médio | [m'ɛdiu] |
| maximal (adj) | máximo | [m'asimu] |
| the largest (adj) | maior, mais grande | [mɐj'ɔr], [m'ajʃ gr'ãdə] |

## 26. Containers

| jar (glass) | boião (m) de vidro | [boj'ãu də v'idru] |
| can | lata (f) | [l'atɐ] |
| bucket | balde (m) | [b'aldə] |
| barrel | barril (m) | [bɐʀ'il] |

| basin (for washing) | bacia (f) | [bɐs'iɐ] |
| tank (for liquid, gas) | tanque (m) | [t'ãkə] |
| hip flask | cantil (m) de bolso | [kãt'il də b'olsu] |
| jerrycan | bidão (m) de gasolina | [bid'ãu də gəzul'inɐ] |
| cistern (tank) | cisterna (f) | [siʃt'ɛrnɐ] |

| mug | caneca (f) | [kɐn'ɛkɐ] |
| cup (of coffee, etc.) | chávena (f) | [ʃ'avənɐ] |
| saucer | pires (m) | [p'irəʃ] |
| glass (tumbler) | copo (m) | [k'ɔpu] |
| wineglass | taça (m) de vinho | [t'asɐ də v'iɲu] |
| saucepan | panela (f) | [pɐn'ɛlɐ] |

| bottle (~ of wine) | garrafa (f) | [gɐʀ'afɐ] |
| neck (of the bottle) | gargalo (m) | [gɐrg'alu] |

| carafe | jarro, garrafa (f) | [ʒ'aʀu], [gɐʀ'afɐ] |
| pitcher (earthenware) | jarro (m) de barro | [ʒ'aʀu də b'aʀu] |
| vessel (container) | vasilhame (m) | [vɐziʎ'emə] |
| pot (crock) | pote (m) | [p'ɔtə] |
| vase | vaso (m) | [v'azu] |

| bottle (~ of perfume) | frasco, frasquinho (m) | [fr'aʃku], [frəʃk'iɲu] |
| vial, small bottle | frasco (m) | [fr'aʃku] |
| tube (of toothpaste) | tubo (m) | [t'ubu] |

| sack (bag) | saca (f) | [s'akɐ] |
| bag (paper ~, plastic ~) | saco (m) | [s'aku] |
| pack (of cigarettes, etc.) | maço (m) | [m'asu] |

| (e.g., shoebox) | caixa (f) | [k'ajʃɐ] |
| te | engradado (m) | [ẽgrɐd'adu] |
| sket | cesto (m), cesta (f) | [s'eʃtu], [s'eʃtɐ] |

## 7. Materials

| terial | material (m) | [metɐrj'al] |
| od | madeira (f) | [mɐd'ejrɐ] |
| oden (adj) | de madeira | [də mɐd'ejrɐ] |
| ss (n) | vidro (m) | [v'idru] |
| ss (as adj) | de vidro | [də v'idru] |
| ne (n) | pedra (f) | [p'ɛdrɐ] |
| ne (as adj) | de pedra | [də p'ɛdrɐ] |
| stic (n) | plástico (m) | [pl'aʃtiku] |
| stic (as adj) | de plástico | [də pl'aʃtiku] |
| ber (n) | borracha (f) | [buʀ'aʃɐ] |
| ber (as adj) | de borracha | [də buʀ'aʃɐ] |
| th, fabric (n) | tecido, pano (m) | [təs'idu], [p'ɐnu] |
| ric (as adj) | de tecido | [də təs'idu] |
| er (n) | papel (m) | [pɐp'ɛl] |
| er (as adj) | de papel | [də pɐp'ɛl] |
| dboard (n) | cartão (m) | [kɐrt'ãu] |
| dboard (as adj) | de cartão | [də kɐrt'ãu] |
| yethylene | polietileno (m) | [poliɛtil'enu] |
| ophane | celofane (m) | [səluf'ɐnə] |
| leum | linóleo (m) | [lin'ɔliu] |
| wood | contraplacado (m) | [kõtrɐplɐk'adu] |
| celain (n) | porcelana (f) | [pursəl'ɐnɐ] |
| celain (as adj) | de porcelana | [də pursəl'ɐnɐ] |
| y (n) | barro (f) | [b'aʀu] |
| y (as adj) | de barro | [də b'aʀu] |
| amics (n) | cerâmica (f) | [sər'emikɐ] |
| amic (as adj) | de cerâmica | [də sər'emikɐ] |

## 8. Metals

| tal (n) | metal (m) | [mət'al] |
| tal (as adj) | metálico | [mət'aliku] |
| y (n) | liga (f) | [l'igɐ] |

| gold (n) | ouro (m) | ['oru] |
| gold, golden (adj) | de ouro | [də 'oru] |
| silver (n) | prata (f) | [pr'atɐ] |
| silver (as adj) | de prata | [də pr'atɐ] |

| iron (n) | ferro (m) | [f'ɛʀu] |
| iron (adj), made of iron | de ferro | [də f'ɛʀu] |
| steel (n) | aço (m) | ['asu] |
| steel (as adj) | de aço | [də 'asu] |
| copper (n) | cobre (m) | [k'ɔbrə] |
| copper (as adj) | de cobre | [də k'ɔbrə] |

| aluminum (n) | alumínio (m) | [ɐlum'iniu] |
| aluminum (as adj) | de alumínio | [də ɐlum'iniu] |
| bronze (n) | bronze (m) | [br'õzə] |
| bronze (as adj) | de bronze | [də br'õzə] |

| brass | latão (m) | [lɐt'ãu] |
| nickel | níquel (m) | [n'ikɛl] |
| platinum | platina (f) | [plɐt'inɐ] |
| mercury | mercúrio (m) | [mɐrk'uriu] |
| tin | estanho (m) | [əʃt'ɐɲu] |
| lead | chumbo (m) | [ʃ'ũbu] |
| zinc | zinco (m) | [z'ĩku] |

# UMAN BEING

## uman being. The body

### 9. Humans. Basic concepts

| | | |
|---|---|---|
| man being | **ser** (m) **humano** | [ser um'ɐnu] |
| n (adult male) | **homem** (m) | ['ɔmẽj] |
| man | **mulher** (f) | [muʎ'ɛr] |
| ld | **criança** (f) | [krj'ãsɐ] |
| | **menina** (f) | [mən'inɐ] |
| / | **menino** (m) | [mən'inu] |
| nager | **adolescente** (m) | [ɐduleʃs'ẽtə] |
| man | **velhote, idoso** (m) | [vɛʎ'ɔtə], [id'ozu] |
| woman | **velhota** (f) | [vɛʎ'ɔtə] |

### 10. Human anatomy

| | | |
|---|---|---|
| anism | **organismo** (m) | [ɔrgɐn'iʒmu] |
| art | **coração** (m) | [kurɐs'ãu] |
| od | **sangue** (m) | [s'ãgə] |
| ery | **artéria** (f) | [ɐrt'ɛriɐ] |
| n | **veia** (f) | [v'ɐjɐ] |
| in | **cérebro** (m) | [s'ɛrəbru] |
| ve | **nervo** (m) | [n'ervu] |
| ves | **nervos** (m pl) | [n'ervuʃ] |
| tebra | **vértebra** (f) | [v'ɛrtəbrɐ] |
| ne | **coluna** (f) **vertebral** | [kul'unɐ vərtəbr'al] |
| mach (organ) | **estômago** (m) | [əʃt'omɐgu] |
| estines, bowel | **intestinos** (m pl) | [ĩtəʃt'inuʃ] |
| estine (e.g., large ~) | **intestino** (m) | [ĩtəʃt'inu] |
| er | **fígado** (m) | [f'igedu] |
| ney | **rim** (m) | [ʀĩ] |
| ne | **osso** (m) | ['osu] |
| eleton | **esqueleto** (m) | [əʃkəl'etu] |
| | **costela** (f) | [kuʃt'ɛlɐ] |
| ll | **crânio** (m) | [kr'ɐniu] |
| scle | **músculo** (m) | [m'uʃkulu] |
| eps | **bíceps** (m) | [b'isɛps] |

| triceps | triceps (m) | [tris'ɛʃ] |
| tendon | tendão (m) | [tẽd'ãu] |
| joint | articulação (f) | [ɐrtikules'ãu] |
| lungs | pulmões (m pl) | [pulm'ojʃ] |
| genitals | órgãos (m pl) genitais | ['ɔrg'ãuʃ ʒɐnit'ajʃ] |
| skin | pele (f) | [p'ɛlə] |

# 31. Head

| head | cabeça (f) | [kɐb'esɐ] |
| face | cara (f) | [k'arɐ] |
| nose | nariz (m) | [nɐr'iʒ] |
| mouth | boca (f) | [b'okɐ] |

| eye | olho (m) | ['oʎu] |
| eyes | olhos (m pl) | ['ɔʎuʃ] |
| pupil | pupila (f) | [pup'ilɐ] |
| eyebrow | sobrancelha (f) | [subrãs'eʎɐ] |
| eyelash | pestana (f) | [pəʃt'ɐnɐ] |
| eyelid | pálpebra (f) | [p'alpəbrɐ] |

| tongue | língua (f) | [l'ĩguɐ] |
| tooth | dente (m) | [d'ẽtə] |
| lips | lábios (m pl) | [l'abiuʃ] |
| cheekbones | maçãs (f pl) do rosto | [mɐs'ãʃ du ʀ'oʃtu] |
| gum | gengiva (f) | [ʒẽʒ'ivɐ] |
| palate | céu (f) da boca | [s'ɛu də b'ɔkɐ] |

| nostrils | narinas (f pl) | [nɐr'inɐʃ] |
| chin | queixo (m) | [k'ejʃu] |
| jaw | mandíbula (f) | [mãd'ibulɐ] |
| cheek | bochecha (f) | [buʃ'eʃɐ] |

| forehead | testa (f) | [t'ɛʃtɐ] |
| temple | têmpora (f) | [t'ẽpurɐ] |
| ear | orelha (f) | [ɔr'eʎɐ] |
| back of the head | nuca (f) | [n'ukɐ] |
| neck | pescoço (m) | [pəʃk'osu] |
| throat | garganta (f) | [gɐrg'ãtɐ] |

| hair | cabelos (m pl) | [kɐb'eluʃ] |
| hairstyle | penteado (m) | [pẽtj'adu] |
| haircut | corte (m) de cabelo | [k'ɔrtə də kɐb'elu] |
| wig | peruca (f) | [pɐr'ukɐ] |

| mustache | bigode (m) | [big'ɔdə] |
| beard | barba (f) | [b'arbɐ] |
| to have (a beard, etc.) | usar, ter (vt) | [uz'ar], [ter] |
| braid | trança (f) | [tr'ãsɐ] |
| sideburns | suíças (f pl) | [su'isɐʃ] |

| -haired (adj) | ruivo | [ʀ'ujvu] |
| y (hair) | grisalho | [gʁiz'aʎu] |
| d (adj) | calvo | [k'alvu] |
| d patch | calva (f) | [k'alve] |
| | | |
| ytail | rabo-de-cavalo (m) | [ʀabu də kɐv'alu] |
| gs | franja (f) | [fʁ'ãʒe] |

## 2.  Human body

| d | mão (f) | [m'ãu] |
| n | braço (m) | [bʁ'asu] |
| | | |
| jer | dedo (m) | [d'edu] |
| | dedo (m) | [d'edu] |
| mb | polegar (m) | [pulɐg'aʁ] |
| e finger | dedo (m) mindinho | [d'edu mĩd'iɲu] |
| l | unha (f) | ['uɲe] |
| | | |
| | punho (m) | [p'uɲu] |
| m | palma (f) da mão | [p'alme də m'ãu] |
| st | pulso (m) | [p'ulsu] |
| earm | antebraço (m) | [ãtɐbʁ'asu] |
| ow | cotovelo (m) | [kutuv'elu] |
| ulder | ombro (m) | ['õbru] |
| | | |
| | perna (f) | [p'ɛrne] |
| t | pé (m) | [pɛ] |
| e | joelho (m) | [ʒu'ɐʎu] |
| f (part of leg) | barriga (f) da perna | [bɐʀ'ige də p'ɛrne] |
| | coxa (f) | [k'oʃe] |
| l | calcanhar (m) | [kalkɐɲ'aʁ] |
| | | |
| dy | corpo (m) | [k'orpu] |
| mach | barriga (f) | [bɐʀ'ige] |
| est | peito (m) | [p'ɐjtu] |
| ast | seio (m) | [s'ɐju] |
| k | lado (m) | [l'adu] |
| k | costas (f pl) | [k'ɔʃtɐʃ] |
| er back | região (f) lombar | [ʀɐʒj'ãu lõb'aʁ] |
| ist | cintura (f) | [sĩt'ure] |
| | | |
| el | umbigo (m) | [ũb'igu] |
| tocks | nádegas (f pl) | [n'adɐgɐʃ] |
| tom | traseiro (m) | [trɐz'ɐjru] |
| | | |
| uty mark | sinal (m) | [sin'al] |
| hmark | sinal (m) de nascença | [sin'al də nɐʃs'ẽse] |
| oo | tatuagem (f) | [tɐtu'aʒẽj] |
| r | cicatriz (f) | [sikɐtr'iʒ] |

# Clothing & Accessories

## 33. Outerwear. Coats

| clothes | roupa (f) | [ʀ'opɐ] |
| outer clothes | roupa (f) exterior | [ʀ'opɐ əʃtərj'or] |
| winter clothes | roupa (f) de inverno | [ʀ'opɐ də ĩv'ɛrnu] |
| | | |
| overcoat | sobretudo (m) | [sobrət'udu] |
| fur coat | casaco (m) de peles | [kɐz'aku də p'ɛləʃ] |
| fur jacket | casaco curto (m) de peles | [kɐz'aku k'urtu də p'ɛləʃ] |
| down coat | colchão (m) de penas | [kɔlʃ'ãu də p'enɐʃ] |
| | | |
| jacket (e.g., leather ~) | casaco, blusão (m) | [kɐz'aku], [bluz'ãu] |
| raincoat | capa (f) | [k'apɐ] |
| waterproof (adj) | impermeável | [ĩpərmj'avɛl] |

## 34. Men's & women's clothing

| shirt | camisa (f) | [kɐm'izɐ] |
| pants | calças (f pl) | [k'alsɐʃ] |
| jeans | calças (f pl) de ganga | [k'alsɐʃ də g'ãgɐ] |
| jacket (of man's suit) | casaco (m) | [kɐz'aku] |
| suit | fato (m) | [f'atu] |
| | | |
| dress (frock) | vestido (m) | [vəʃt'idu] |
| skirt | saia (f) | [s'ajɐ] |
| blouse | blusa (f) | [bl'uzɐ] |
| knitted jacket | casaco (m) de malha | [kɐz'aku də m'aʎɐ] |
| jacket (of woman's suit) | casaquinho (m) | [kɐzɐk'iɲu] |
| | | |
| T-shirt | t-shirt, camiseta (f) | [t'iʃərt], [kɐmiz'ete] |
| shorts (short trousers) | calções (m pl) | [kals'ojʃ] |
| tracksuit | fato (m) de treino | [f'atu də tr'ejnu] |
| bathrobe | roupão (m) de banho | [ʀop'ãu də b'ɐɲu] |
| pajamas | pijama (m) | [piʒ'emɐ] |
| | | |
| sweater | suéter (m) | [su'ɛtɛr] |
| pullover | pulôver (m) | [pul'ovɛr] |
| | | |
| vest | colete (m) | [kul'etə] |
| tailcoat | casaca (f) | [kɐz'akɐ] |
| tuxedo | smoking (m) | [sm'okĩg] |
| uniform | uniforme (m) | [unif'ɔrmɐ] |

| rkwear | roupa (f) de trabalho | [ʀ'opɐ də treb'aʎu] |
| ɜralls | fato-macaco (m) | [f'atu mek'aku] |
| ɪt (e.g., doctor's smock) | bata (f) | [b'atɐ] |

## 5. Clothing. Underwear

| derwear | roupa (f) interior | [ʀ'opɐ ĩtərj'or] |
| ɯers | cuecas boxer (f pl) | [ku'ɛkɐʃ b'ɔksər] |
| ɪties | cuecas (f pl) | [ku'ɛkɐʃ] |
| dershirt (A-shirt) | camisola (f) interior | [kɐmiz'ɔlɐ ĩtərj'or] |
| ɔks | peúgas (f pl) | [pj'ugɐʃ] |

| htgown | camisa (f) de noite | [kɐm'izɐ də n'ojtɐ] |
| ʲ | sutiã (m) | [sutj'ã] |
| ɜe highs | meias 3/4 (f pl) | [m'ejɐʃ tr'eʃ ku'atru] |
| ɪts | meias-calças (f pl) | [m'ejɐʃ k'alsɐʃ] |
| ckings (thigh highs) | meias (f pl) | [m'ejɐʃ] |
| hing suit | fato (m) de banho | [f'atu də b'ɐɲu] |

## 6. Headwear

| | chapéu (m) | [ʃɐp'ɛu] |
| ora | chapéu (m) de feltro | [ʃɐp'ɛu də f'eltru] |
| ɜeball cap | boné (m) de beisebol | [bɔn'ɛ də b'ɛjzbɔl] |
| cap | boné (m) | [bɔn'ɛ] |

| ɜet | boina (f) | [b'ɔjnɐ] |
| ɔd | capuz (m) | [kɐp'uʃ] |
| ɪama hat | panamá (m) | [pɐnɐm'a] |
| tted hat | gorro (m) de malha | [g'oʀu də m'aʎɐ] |

| adscarf | lenço (m) | [l'ẽsu] |
| ɯen's hat | chapéu (m) de mulher | [ʃɐp'ɛu də muʎ'ɛr] |

| d hat | capacete (m) de proteção | [kɐpɐs'etɐ də prutɛs'ãu] |
| rison cap | bivaque (m) | [biv'akɐ] |
| ɯet | capacete (m) | [kɐpɐs'etɐ] |

| by | chapéu (m) de coco | [ʃɐp'ɛu də k'oku] |
| ʲ hat | chapéu (m) alto | [ʃɐp'ɛu 'altu] |

## 7. Footwear

| twear | calçado (m) | [kals'adu] |
| ɔle boots | botinas (f pl) | [but'inɐʃ] |
| ɜes (low-heeled ~) | sapatos (m pl) | [sɐp'atuʃ] |

| boots (cowboy ~) | botas (f pl) | [b'ɔtɐʃ] |
| slippers | pantufas (f pl) | [pãt'ufɐʃ] |

| tennis shoes | ténis (m pl) | [t'ɛniʃ] |
| sneakers | sapatilhas (f pl) | [sɐpɐt'iʎɐʃ] |
| sandals | sandálias (f pl) | [sãd'aliɐʃ] |

| cobbler | sapateiro (m) | [sɐpɐt'ejru] |
| heel | salto (m) | [s'altu] |
| pair (of shoes) | par (m) | [par] |

| shoestring | atacador (m) | [ɐtɐkɐd'or] |
| to lace (vt) | amarrar (vt) | [ɐmɐʀ'ar] |
| shoehorn | calçadeira (f) | [kalsɐd'ejɾɐ] |
| shoe polish | graxa (f) para calçado | [gɾ'aʃɐ p'ɐɾɐ kals'adu] |

## 38. Textile. Fabrics

| cotton (n) | algodão (m) | [algud'ãu] |
| cotton (as adj) | de algodão | [dɐ algud'ãu] |
| flax (n) | linho (m) | [l'iɲu] |
| flax (as adj) | de linho | [dɐ l'iɲu] |

| silk (n) | seda (f) | [s'edɐ] |
| silk (as adj) | de seda | [dɐ s'edɐ] |
| wool (n) | lã (f) | [lã] |
| woolen (adj) | de lã | [dɐ lã] |

| velvet | veludo (m) | [vɐl'udu] |
| suede | camurça (f) | [kɐm'ursɐ] |
| corduroy | bombazina (f) | [bõbɐz'inɐ] |

| nylon (n) | nylon (m) | [n'ajlɔn] |
| nylon (as adj) | de nylon | [dɐ n'ajlɔn] |
| polyester (n) | poliéster (m) | [poli'ɛstɛr] |
| polyester (as adj) | de poliéster | [dɐ poli'ɛstɛr] |

| leather (n) | couro (m) | [k'oru] |
| leather (as adj) | de couro | [dɐ k'oru] |
| fur (n) | pele (f) | [p'ɛlɐ] |
| fur (e.g., ~ coat) | de peles, de pele | [dɐ p'ɛlɐʃ], [dɐ p'ɛlɐ] |

## 39. Personal accessories

| gloves | luvas (f pl) | [l'uvɐʃ] |
| mittens | mitenes (f pl) | [mit'ɛnɐʃ] |
| scarf (muffler) | cachecol (m) | [kaʃɐk'ɔl] |
| glasses | óculos (m pl) | ['ɔkuluʃ] |

| ne (eyeglass ~) | armação (f) de óculos | [ɐrmɐsˈãu də ˈɔkuluʃ] |
| brella | guarda-chuva (m) | [guardɐ ʃˈuvɐ] |
| king stick | bengala (f) | [bẽgˈalɐ] |
| rbrush | escova (f) para o cabelo | [əʃkˈovɐ pˈɐrɐ u kɐbˈelu] |
|  | leque (m) | [lˈɛkə] |

| ktie | gravata (f) | [grɐvˈatɐ] |
| v tie | gravata-borboleta (f) | [grɐvˈatɐ burbulˈetɐ] |
| spenders | suspensórios (m pl) | [suʃpẽsˈɔriuʃ] |
| ndkerchief | lenço (m) | [lˈẽsu] |

| nb | pente (m) | [pˈẽtə] |
| rette | travessão (m) | [trɐvəsˈãu] |
| rpin | gancho (m) de cabelo | [gˈãʃu də kɐbˈelu] |
| kle | fivela (f) | [fivˈɛlɐ] |

| t | cinto (m) | [sˈĩtu] |
| ulder strap | correia (f) | [kurˈɐjɐ] |

| g (handbag) | bolsa (f) | [bˈolsɐ] |
| se | bolsa (f) de senhora | [bˈolsɐ də səɲˈorɐ] |
| ckpack | mochila (f) | [muʃˈilɐ] |

## 0. Clothing. Miscellaneous

| hion | moda (f) | [mˈɔdɐ] |
| vogue (adj) | na moda | [nɐ mˈɔdɐ] |
| hion designer | estilista (m) | [əʃtilˈiʃtɐ] |

| lar | colarinho (m), gola (f) | [kulɐrˈiɲu], [gˈɔlɐ] |
| cket | bolso (m) | [bˈolsu] |
| cket (as adj) | de bolso | [də bˈolsu] |
| eve | manga (f) | [mˈãgɐ] |
| nging loop | cabide (m) | [kɐbˈidə] |
| (on trousers) | braguilha (f) | [brɐgˈiʎɐ] |

| per (fastener) | fecho de correr (m) | [fˈeʃu də kurˈer] |
| tener | fecho (m), colchete (m) | [fˈeʃu], [kolʃˈetə] |
| ton | botão (m) | [butˈãu] |
| tonhole | casa (f) de botão | [kˈazɐ də butˈãu] |
| come off (ab. button) | cair (vi) | [kɐˈir] |

| sew (vi, vt) | coser, costurar (vi) | [kuzˈer], [kuʃturˈar] |
| embroider (vi, vt) | bordar (vt) | [burdˈar] |
| broidery | bordado (m) | [burdˈadu] |
| wing needle | agulha (f) | [ɐgˈuʎɐ] |
| ead | fio (m) | [fˈiu] |
| am | costura (f) | [kuʃtˈurɐ] |
| get dirty (vi) | sujar-se (vp) | [suʒˈarsə] |
| in (mark, spot) | mancha (f) | [mˈãʃɐ] |

| to crease, crumple (vi) | amarrotar-se (vp) | [emeʀut'arsə] |
| to tear (vt) | rasgar (vt) | [ʀeʒg'ar] |
| clothes moth | traça (f) | [tr'asə] |

## 41. Personal care. Cosmetics

| toothpaste | pasta (f) de dentes | [p'aʃte də d'ẽtəʃ] |
| toothbrush | escova (f) de dentes | [əʃk'ove də d'ẽtəʃ] |
| to brush one's teeth | escovar os dentes | [əʃkuv'ar uʃ d'ẽtəʃ] |

| razor | máquina (f) de barbear | [m'akine də berbi'ar] |
| shaving cream | creme (m) de barbear | [kr'ɛmə də berbj'ar] |
| to shave (vi) | barbear-se (vp) | [berbj'arsə] |

| soap | sabonete (m) | [sebun'etə] |
| shampoo | champô (m) | [ʃãp'o] |

| scissors | tesoura (f) | [təz'orə] |
| nail file | lima (f) de unhas | [l'ime də 'uɲəʃ] |
| nail clippers | corta-unhas (m) | [k'ɔrte 'uɲəʃ] |
| tweezers | pinça (f) | [p'ĩsə] |

| cosmetics | cosméticos (m pl) | [kuʒm'ɛtikuʃ] |
| face mask | máscara (f) | [m'aʃkere] |
| manicure | manicura (f) | [menik'urə] |
| to have a manicure | fazer a manicura | [fez'er e menik'urə] |
| pedicure | pedicure (f) | [pədik'urə] |

| make-up bag | bolsa (f) de maquilhagem | [b'olse də mekiʎ'aʒẽj] |
| face powder | pó (m) | [pɔ] |
| powder compact | caixa (f) de pó | [k'ajʃe də pɔ] |
| blusher | blush (m) | [bleʃ] |

| perfume (bottled) | perfume (m) | [pərf'umə] |
| toilet water (perfume) | água (f) de toilette | ['ague də tual'ɛtə] |
| lotion | loção (m) | [lus'ãu] |
| cologne | água-de-colónia (f) | ['ague də kul'ɔniə] |

| eyeshadow | sombra (f) para os olhos | [s'õbre p'ere uʃ 'ɔʎuʃ] |
| eyeliner | lápis (m) delineador | [l'apiʃ dəlinied'or] |
| mascara | máscara (f), rímel (m) | [m'aʃkere], [ʀ'imɛl] |

| lipstick | batom (m) | [b'atõ] |
| nail polish, enamel | verniz (m) de unhas | [vərn'iʒ də 'uɲəʃ] |
| hair spray | laca (f) para cabelos | [l'ake p'ere keb'eluʃ] |
| deodorant | desodorizante (m) | [dezɔdoriz'ãtə] |

| cream | creme (m) | [kr'ɛmə] |
| face cream | creme (m) de rosto | [kr'ɛme də ʀ'oʃtu] |
| hand cream | creme (m) de mãos | [kr'ɛme də m'ãuʃ] |

| i-wrinkle cream | creme (m) antirrugas | [krˈɛmə ãtiʀˈugeʃ] |
| / cream | creme (m) de dia | [krˈɛmə də dˈie] |
| ht cream | creme (m) de noite | [krˈɛmə də nˈojtə] |
| / (as adj) | de dia | [də dˈie] |
| ht (as adj) | da noite | [də nˈojtə] |
| | | |
| ιpon | tampão (m) | [tãpˈãu] |
| et paper | papel (m) higiénico | [pɐpˈɛl iʒjˈɛniku] |
| r dryer | secador (m) elétrico | [səkɐdˈor elˈɛtriku] |

## 2. Jewelry

| /elry | joias (f pl) | [ʒˈɔjɐʃ] |
| cious (e.g., ~ stone) | precioso | [prəsjˈozu] |
| lmark | marca (f) de contraste | [mˈarkɐ də kõtrˈaʃtə] |
| | | |
| ɟ | anel (m) | [ɐnˈɛl] |
| dding ring | aliança (f) | [ɐljˈãsɐ] |
| ιcelet | pulseira (f) | [pulsˈɐjɾɐ] |
| | | |
| rings | brincos (m pl) | [brˈĩkuʃ] |
| cklace (~ of pearls) | colar (m) | [kulˈar] |
| wn | coroa (f) | [kuɾˈoɐ] |
| ɪd necklace | colar (m) de contas | [kulˈar də kˈõtɐʃ] |
| | | |
| mond | diamante (m) | [diɐmˈãtə] |
| erald | esmeralda (f) | [əʒmərˈaldɐ] |
| ιy | rubi (m) | [ʀubˈi] |
| )phire | safira (f) | [sɐfˈiɾɐ] |
| arl | pérola (f) | [pˈɛrulɐ] |
| ber | âmbar (m) | [ˈãbar] |

## 3. Watches. Clocks

| tch (wristwatch) | relógio (m) de pulso | [ʀəlˈɔʒiu də pˈulsu] |
| l | mostrador (m) | [muʃtrɐdˈor] |
| ιd (of clock, watch) | ponteiro (m) | [põtˈɐjru] |
| tal watch band | bracelete (f) em aço | [brɐsɛlˈɛtə ɐn ˈasu] |
| tch strap | bracelete (f) em pele | [brɐsɛlˈɛtə ẽ pˈɛlə] |
| | | |
| tery | pilha (f) | [pˈiʎɐ] |
| )e dead (battery) | acabar (vi) | [ɐkɐbˈar] |
| change a battery | trocar a pilha | [trukˈar ɐ pˈiʎɐ] |
| ʿun fast | estar adiantado | [əʃtˈar ɐdiãtˈadu] |
| ʿun slow | estar atrasado | [əʃtˈar ɐtrɐzˈadu] |
| | | |
| ll clock | relógio (m) de parede | [ʀəlˈɔʒiu də pɐrˈedə] |
| ιrglass | ampulheta (f) | [ãpuʎˈetɐ] |

| | | |
|---|---|---|
| sundial | **relógio** (m) **de sol** | [ʀəl'ɔʒiu də sɔl] |
| alarm clock | **despertador** (m) | [dəʃpərted'or] |
| watchmaker | **relojoeiro** (m) | [ʀəluʒu'ejru] |
| to repair (vt) | **reparar** (vt) | [ʀəper'ar] |

# ood. Nutricion

## 4. Food

| | | |
|---|---|---|
| at | carne (f) | [kˈarnə] |
| cken | galinha (f) | [gɐlˈiɲɐ] |
| ing chicken | frango (m) | [frˈãgu] |
| ck | pato (m) | [pˈatu] |
| ose | ganso (m) | [gˈãsu] |
| ne | caça (f) | [kˈasɐ] |
| key | peru (m) | [pɐrˈu] |
| | | |
| k | carne (f) de porco | [kˈarnə də pˈorku] |
| al | carne (f) de vitela | [kˈarnə də vitˈɛlɐ] |
| hb | carne (f) de carneiro | [kˈarnə də kɐrnˈɐjru] |
| ef | carne (f) de vaca | [kˈarnə də vˈakɐ] |
| bit | carne (f) de coelho | [kˈarnə də kuˈeʎu] |
| | | |
| sage (salami, etc.) | chouriço (m) | [ʃorˈisu] |
| nna sausage | salsicha (f) | [salsˈiʃɐ] |
| con | bacon (m) | [bˈɐjkɐn] |
| m | fiambre (f) | [fjˈãbrə] |
| mmon (ham) | presunto (m) | [prɐzˈũtu] |
| | | |
| é | patê (m) | [pɐtˈe] |
| er | iscas (f pl) | [ˈiʃkɐʃ] |
| | | |
| d | toucinho (m) | [tosˈiɲu] |
| und beef | carne (f) moída | [kˈarnə muˈidɐ] |
| gue | língua (f) | [lˈĩguɐ] |
| | | |
| g | ovo (m) | [ˈovu] |
| gs | ovos (m pl) | [ˈovuʃ] |
| g white | clara (f) do ovo | [klˈarɐ du ˈovu] |
| g yolk | gema (f) do ovo | [ʒˈemɐ du ˈovu] |
| | | |
| h | peixe (m) | [pˈejʃə] |
| food | marisco (m) | [mɐrˈiʃku] |
| staceans | crustáceos (m pl) | [kruʃtˈasiuʃ] |
| iar | caviar (m) | [kavjˈar] |
| | | |
| b | caranguejo (m) | [kɐrãgˈeʒu] |
| imp | camarão (m) | [kɐmɐrˈãu] |
| ster | ostra (f) | [ˈɔʃtrɐ] |
| ny lobster | lagosta (f) | [lɐgˈoʃtɐ] |
| opus | polvo (m) | [pˈolvu] |

| squid | lula (f) | [l'ulə] |
| sturgeon | esturjão (m) | [əʃturʒ'ãu] |
| salmon | salmão (m) | [salm'ãu] |
| halibut | halibute (m) | [alib'utə] |

| cod | bacalhau (m) | [bəkeʎ'au] |
| mackerel | cavala (m), sarda (f) | [kev'alə], [s'ardə] |
| tuna | atum (m) | [ɐt'ũ] |
| eel | enguia (f) | [ẽg'iɐ] |

| trout | truta (f) | [tr'utə] |
| sardine | sardinha (f) | [sɐrd'iɲɐ] |

| pike | lúcio (m) | [l'usiu] |
| herring | arenque (m) | [ɐr'ẽkə] |

| bread | pão (m) | [p'ãu] |
| cheese | queijo (m) | [k'ɐjʒu] |

| sugar | açúcar (m) | [ɐs'ukar] |
| salt | sal (m) | [sal] |

| rice | arroz (m) | [ɐʀ'ɔʒ] |
| pasta | massas (f pl) | [m'asəʃ] |
| noodles | talharim (m) | [tɐʎɐr'ĩ] |

| butter | manteiga (f) | [mãt'ɐjgɐ] |
| vegetable oil | óleo (m) | ['ɔliu] |
| sunflower oil | óleo (m) de girassol | ['ɔliu də ʒires'ɔl] |
| margarine | margarina (f) | [mɐrgɐr'inɐ] |

| olives | azeitonas (f pl) | [ɐzejt'onɐʒ] |
| olive oil | azeite (m) | [ɐz'ɐjtə] |

| milk | leite (m) | [l'ɐjtə] |
| condensed milk | leite (m) condensado | [l'ɐjtə kõdẽs'adu] |
| yogurt | iogurte (m) | [iog'urtə] |

| sour cream | creme (m) azedo | [kr'ɛmə ɐz'edu] |
| cream (of milk) | nata (f) do leite | [n'atɐ du l'ɐjtə] |

| mayonnaise | maionese (f) | [majun'ezə] |
| buttercream | creme (m) | [kr'ɛmə] |

| cereal grain (wheat, etc.) | grãos (m pl) de cereais | [gr'ãuʃ də sɐrj'ajʃ] |
| flour | farinha (f) | [fɐr'iɲə] |
| canned food | conservas (f pl) | [kõs'ɛrvɐʃ] |

| cornflakes | flocos (m pl) de milho | [fl'ɔkuʃ də m'iʎu] |
| honey | mel (m) | [mɛl] |
| jam | doce (m) | [d'osə] |
| chewing gum | pastilha (f) elástica | [pɐʃt'iʎɐ el'aʃtikɐ] |

## 5. Drinks

| | | |
|---|---|---|
| ter | **água** (f) | ['aguɐ] |
| ʌking water | **água** (f) **potável** | ['aguɐ put'avɛl] |
| ʌeral water | **água** (f) **mineral** | ['aguɐ minər'al] |
| | | |
| (adj) | **sem gás** | [sẽj gaʃ] |
| bonated (adj) | **gaseificada** | [gɐziifik'adɐ] |
| ʌrkling (adj) | **com gás** | [kõ gaʃ] |
| | **gelo** (m) | [ʒ'elu] |
| ʌ ice | **com gelo** | [kõ ʒ'elu] |
| | | |
| ʌ-alcoholic (adj) | **sem álcool** | [sɛm 'alkuɔl] |
| t drink | **bebida** (f) **sem álcool** | [bəb'idɐ sɛn 'alkuɔl] |
| ʌl soft drink | **refresco** (m) | [Rəfr'eʃku] |
| ʌonade | **limonada** (f) | [limun'adɐ] |
| | | |
| ʌor | **bebidas** (f pl) **alcoólicas** | [bəb'idɐʃ alku'ɔlikəʃ] |
| ʌe | **vinho** (m) | [v'iɲu] |
| ʌte wine | **vinho** (m) **branco** | [v'iɲu br'ãku] |
| ʌ wine | **vinho** (m) **tinto** | [v'iɲu t'ĩtu] |
| | | |
| ʌeur | **licor** (m) | [lik'or] |
| ʌmpagne | **champanhe** (m) | [ʃãp'ɐɲə] |
| ʌmouth | **vermute** (m) | [vərm'utə] |
| | | |
| ʌisky | **uísque** (m) | [u'iʃkə] |
| ʌka | **vodca, vodka** (f) | [v'ɔdkɐ] |
| | **gim** (m) | [ʒĩ] |
| ʌnac | **conhaque** (m) | [kuɲ'akə] |
| ʌn | **rum** (m) | [Rũ] |
| | | |
| ʌfee | **café** (m) | [kɐf'ɛ] |
| ʌck coffee | **café** (m) **puro** | [kɐf'ɛ p'uru] |
| ʌfee with milk | **café** (m) **com leite** | [kɐf'ɛ kõ l'ejtə] |
| ʌpuccino | **cappuccino** (m) | [kaputʃ'inu] |
| ʌtant coffee | **café** (m) **solúvel** | [kɐf'ɛ sul'uvɛl] |
| | | |
| ʌ | **leite** (m) | [l'ejtə] |
| ʌktail | **coquetel** (m) | [kɔkət'ɛl] |
| ʌ shake | **batido** (m) **de leite** | [bɐt'idu də l'ejtə] |
| | | |
| ʌe | **sumo** (m) | [s'umu] |
| ʌato juice | **sumo** (m) **de tomate** | [s'umu də tum'atə] |
| ʌnge juice | **sumo** (m) **de laranja** | [s'umu də lɐr'ãʒə] |
| ʌhly squeezed juice | **sumo** (m) **fresco** | [s'umu fr'eʃku] |
| | | |
| ʌr | **cerveja** (f) | [sərv'ɐʒə] |
| ʌt beer | **cerveja** (f) **clara** | [sərv'ɐʒɐ kl'arɐ] |
| ʌk beer | **cerveja** (m) **preta** | [sərv'ɐʒɐ pr'etɐ] |
| | **chá** (m) | [ʃa] |

| black tea | chá (m) preto | [ʃa pr'etu] |
| green tea | chá (m) verde | [ʃa v'erdə] |

## 46. Vegetables

| vegetables | legumes (m pl) | [ləg'uməʃ] |
| greens | verduras (f pl) | [vərd'urəʃ] |

| tomato | tomate (m) | [tum'atə] |
| cucumber | pepino (m) | [pəp'inu] |
| carrot | cenoura (f) | [sən'orɐ] |
| potato | batata (f) | [bɐt'atə] |
| onion | cebola (f) | [səb'olɐ] |
| garlic | alho (m) | ['aʎu] |

| cabbage | couve (f) | [k'ovə] |
| cauliflower | couve-flor (f) | [k'ovə fl'or] |
| Brussels sprouts | couve-de-bruxelas (f) | [k'ovə də bruʃ'ɛləʃ] |
| broccoli | brócolos (m pl) | [br'ɔkuluʃ] |

| beetroot | beterraba (f) | [bətəʀ'abɐ] |
| eggplant | beringela (f) | [bərĩʒ'ɛlɐ] |
| zucchini | curgete (f) | [kurʒ'ɛtə] |
| pumpkin | abóbora (f) | [ɐb'ɔburɐ] |
| turnip | nabo (m) | [n'abu] |

| parsley | salsa (f) | [s'alsɐ] |
| dill | funcho, endro (m) | [f'ũʃu], ['ẽdru] |
| lettuce | alface (f) | [alf'asə] |
| celery | aipo (m) | ['ajpu] |
| asparagus | espargo (m) | [əʃp'argu] |
| spinach | espinafre (m) | [əʃpin'afrə] |

| pea | ervilha (f) | [erv'iʎɐ] |
| beans | fava (f) | [f'avɐ] |
| corn (maize) | milho (m) | [m'iʎu] |
| kidney bean | feijão (m) | [fɐjʒ'ãu] |

| pepper | pimentão (m) | [pimẽt'ãu] |
| radish | rabanete (m) | [ʀɐbɐn'etə] |
| artichoke | alcachofra (f) | [alkɐʃ'ofrɐ] |

## 47. Fruits. Nuts

| fruit | fruta (f) | [fr'utɐ] |
| apple | maçã (f) | [mɐs'ã] |
| pear | pera (f) | [p'erɐ] |
| lemon | limão (m) | [lim'ãu] |

| nge | laranja (f) | [ler'ãʒe] |
| awberry | morango (m) | [mur'ãgu] |
| | | |
| ndarin | tangerina (f) | [tãʒər'ine] |
| m | ameixa (f) | [em'ejʃe] |
| ach | pêssego (m) | [p'esegu] |
| icot | damasco (m) | [dem'aʃku] |
| pberry | framboesa (f) | [frãbu'eze] |
| eapple | ananás (m) | [enen'aʃ] |
| | | |
| nana | banana (f) | [ben'ene] |
| termelon | melancia (f) | [melãs'ie] |
| pe | uva (f) | ['uve] |
| ur cherry | ginja (f) | [ʒ'ĩʒe] |
| eet cherry | cereja (f) | [sər'eʒe] |
| lon | meloa (f), melão (m) | [məl'oe], [məl'ãu] |
| | | |
| pefruit | toranja (f) | [tur'ãʒe] |
| ocado | abacate (m) | [ebek'ate] |
| aya | papaia (f), mamão (m) | [pep'aje], [mem'ãu] |
| ngo | manga (f) | [m'ãge] |
| negranate | romã (f) | [ʀum'ã] |
| | | |
| currant | groselha (f) vermelha | [gruz'eʎe verm'eʎe] |
| ckcurrant | groselha (f) preta | [gruz'eʎe pr'ete] |
| oseberry | groselha (f) espinhosa | [gruz'eʎe əʃpiɲ'oze] |
| erry | mirtilo (m) | [mirt'ilu] |
| ckberry | amora silvestre (f) | [em'ore silv'eʃtre] |
| | | |
| sin | uvas (f pl) passas | ['uveʃ p'aseʃ] |
| | figo (m) | [f'igu] |
| e | tâmara (f) | [t'emere] |
| | | |
| anut | amendoim (m) | [emẽdu'ĩ] |
| nond | amêndoa (f) | [em'ẽdue] |
| lnut | noz (f) | [nɔʒ] |
| zelnut | avelã (f) | [evel'ã] |
| conut | coco (m) | [k'oku] |
| tachios | pistáchios (m pl) | [piʃt'aʃiuʃ] |

## 8. Bread. Candy

| nfectionery (pastry) | pastelaria (f) | [peʃteler'ie] |
| ad | pão (m) | [p'ãu] |
| okies | bolacha (f) | [bul'aʃe] |
| | | |
| ocolate (n) | chocolate (m) | [ʃukul'ate] |
| ocolate (as adj) | de chocolate | [də ʃukul'ate] |
| ndy | rebuçado (m) | [ʀebus'adu] |
| ke (e.g., cupcake) | bolo (m) | [b'olu] |

| cake (e.g., birthday ~) | **bolo** (m) **de aniversário** | [b'olu də ɐnivərs'ariu] |
| pie (e.g., apple ~) | **tarte** (f) | [t'artə] |
| filling (for cake, pie) | **recheio** (m) | [ʀəʃ'ɐju] |

| whole fruit jam | **doce** (m) | [d'osə] |
| marmalade | **geleia** (f) **de frutas** | [ʒəl'ɐjɐ də fr'utɐʃ] |
| waffle | **waffle** (m) | [w'ɐjfəl] |
| ice-cream | **gelado** (m) | [ʒəl'adu] |
| pudding | **pudim** (m) | [pud'ĩ] |

## 49. Cooked dishes

| course, dish | **prato** (m) | [pr'atu] |
| cuisine | **cozinha** (f) | [kuz'iɲɐ] |
| recipe | **receita** (f) | [ʀəs'ɐjtɐ] |
| portion | **porção** (f) | [purs'ãu] |

| salad | **salada** (f) | [sɐl'adɐ] |
| soup | **sopa** (f) | [s'opɐ] |

| clear soup (broth) | **caldo** (m) | [k'aldu] |
| sandwich (bread) | **sandes** (f) | [s'ãdəʃ] |
| fried eggs | **ovos** (m pl) **estrelados** | ['ɔvuʃ əʃtrəl'aduʃ] |

| cutlet (croquette) | **croquete** (m) | [kruk'etə] |
| hamburger (beefburger) | **hambúrguer** (m) | [ãb'urgɛr] |
| beefsteak | **bife** (m) | [b'ifə] |
| stew | **guisado** (m) | [giz'adu] |

| side dish | **conduto** (m) | [kõd'utu] |
| spaghetti | **espaguete** (m) | [əʃpɐg'etə] |
| mashed potatoes | **puré** (m) **de batata** | [pur'ɛ də bɐt'atɐ] |
| pizza | **pizza** (f) | [p'itzɐ] |
| porridge (oatmeal, etc.) | **papa** (f) | [p'apɐ] |
| omelet | **omelete** (f) | [ɔməl'ɛtə] |

| boiled (e.g., ~ beef) | **cozido** | [kuz'idu] |
| smoked (adj) | **fumado** | [fum'adu] |
| fried (adj) | **frito** | [fr'itu] |
| dried (adj) | **seco** | [s'eku] |
| frozen (adj) | **congelado** | [kõʒəl'adu] |
| pickled (adj) | **em vinagre** | [ẽ vin'agrə] |
| sweet (sugary) | **doce, açucarado** | [d'osə], [ɐsukɐr'adu] |
| salty (adj) | **salgado** | [salg'adu] |
| cold (adj) | **frio** | [fr'iu] |
| hot (adj) | **quente** | [k'ẽtə] |
| bitter (adj) | **amargo** | [ɐm'argu] |
| tasty (adj) | **gostoso** | [guʃt'ozu] |
| to cook in boiling water | **cozinhar em água a ferver** | [kuziɲ'ar ɛn 'aguɐ ɐ fərv'er] |

| cook (dinner) | fazer, preparar (vt) | [fez'er], [prəper'ar] |
| ry (vt) | fritar (vt) | [frit'ar] |
| heat up (food) | aquecer (vt) | [ɐkɛs'er] |

| salt (vt) | salgar (vt) | [salg'ar] |
| pepper (vt) | apimentar (vt) | [ɐpimẽt'ar] |
| grate (vt) | ralar (vt) | [ʀɐl'ar] |
| el (n) | casca (f) | [k'aʃkɐ] |
| peel (vt) | descascar (vt) | [dəʃkɐʃk'ar] |

## 0. Spices

| t | sal (m) | [sal] |
| ty (adj) | salgado | [salg'adu] |
| salt (vt) | salgar (vt) | [salg'ar] |

| ck pepper | pimenta (f) preta | [pim'ẽtɐ pr'etɐ] |
| pepper | pimenta (f) vermelha | [pim'ẽtɐ vɐrm'eʎɐ] |
| stard | mostarda (f) | [muʃt'ardɐ] |
| seradish | raiz-forte (f) | [ʀɐ'iʃ f'ɔrtə] |

| ndiment | condimento (m) | [kõdim'ẽtu] |
| ce | especiaria (f) | [əʃpəsiɐr'iɐ] |
| uce | molho (m) | [m'oʎu] |
| egar | vinagre (m) | [vin'agrə] |

| se | anis (m) | [ɐn'iʃ] |
| sil | manjericão (m) | [mãʒɐrik'ãu] |
| ves | cravo (m) | [kr'avu] |
| ger | gengibre (m) | [ʒẽʒ'ibrə] |
| iander | coentro (m) | [ku'ẽtru] |
| namon | canela (f) | [kɐn'ɛlɐ] |

| same | sésamo (m) | [s'ɛzɐmu] |
| y leaf | folhas (f pl) de louro | [f'oʎəʃ də l'oru] |
| orika | páprica (f) | [p'aprikɐ] |
| away | cominho (m) | [kum'iɲu] |
| fron | açafrão (m) | [ɐsɐfr'ãu] |

## 1. Meals

| d | comida (f) | [kum'idɐ] |
| eat (vi, vt) | comer (vt) | [kum'er] |

| akfast | pequeno-almoço (m) | [pɐk'enu alm'osu] |
| have breakfast | tomar o pequeno-almoço | [tum'ar u pɐk'enu alm'osu] |
| ch | almoço (m) | [alm'osu] |
| have lunch | almoçar (vi) | [almus'ar] |

| dinner | jantar (m) | [ʒãt'aɾ] |
| to have dinner | jantar (vi) | [ʒãt'aɾ] |

| appetite | apetite (m) | [ɐpət'itə] |
| Enjoy your meal! | Bom apetite! | [bõ ɐpət'itə] |

| to open (~ a bottle) | abrir (vt) | [ɐbr'iɾ] |
| to spill (liquid) | derramar (vt) | [dəʀɐm'aɾ] |
| to spill out (vi) | derramar-se (vp) | [dəʀɐm'arsə] |

| to boil (vi) | estar a ferver | [əʃt'ar ɐ fərv'eɾ] |
| to boil (vt) | ferver (vt) | [fərv'eɾ] |
| boiled (~ water) | fervido | [fərv'idu] |
| to chill, cool down (vt) | arrefecer (vt) | [ɐʀəfəs'eɾ] |
| to chill (vi) | arrefecer-se (vp) | [ɐʀəfəs'ersə] |

| taste, flavor | sabor, gosto (m) | [sɐb'oɾ], [g'oʃtu] |
| aftertaste | gostinho (m) | [guʃt'iɲu] |

| to be on a diet | fazer dieta | [fɐz'er dj'ɛtə] |
| diet | dieta (f) | [dj'ɛtə] |
| vitamin | vitamina (f) | [vitɐm'inɐ] |
| calorie | caloria (f) | [kɐlur'iɐ] |
| vegetarian (n) | vegetariano (m) | [vəʒətɐrj'ɐnu] |
| vegetarian (adj) | vegetariano | [vəʒətɐrj'ɐnu] |

| fats (nutrient) | gorduras (f pl) | [gurd'uɾɐʃ] |
| proteins | proteínas (f pl) | [prute'inɐʃ] |
| carbohydrates | hidratos (m pl) de carbono | [idr'atuʃ də kɐrb'ɔnu] |
| slice (of lemon, ham) | fatia (f) | [fɐt'iɐ] |
| piece (of cake, pie) | bocado, pedaço (m) | [buk'adu], [pəd'asu] |
| crumb (of bread) | migalha (f) | [mig'aʎɐ] |

## 52. Table setting

| spoon | colher (f) | [kuʎ'ɛɾ] |
| knife | faca (f) | [f'akɐ] |
| fork | garfo (m) | [g'aɾfu] |
| cup (of coffee) | chávena (f) | [ʃ'avənɐ] |
| plate (dinner ~) | prato (m) | [pr'atu] |
| saucer | pires (m) | [p'irəʃ] |
| napkin (on table) | guardanapo (m) | [guɐrdɐn'apu] |
| toothpick | palito (m) | [pɐl'itu] |

## 53. Restaurant

| restaurant | restaurante (m) | [ʀəʃtaur'ãtə] |
| coffee house | café (m) | [kɐf'ɛ] |

| , bar | **bar** (m) | [baɾ] |
| room | **salão** (m) **de chá** | [sɐlˈãu də ʃa] |
| | | |
| iter | **empregado** (m) **de mesa** | [ẽpɾɐgˈadu də mˈezɐ] |
| itress | **empregada** (f) **de mesa** | [ẽpɾɐgˈadɐ də mˈezɐ] |
| tender | **barman** (m) | [bˈarmɐn] |
| | | |
| nu | **ementa** (f) | [emˈẽtɐ] |
| e list | **lista** (f) **de vinhos** | [lˈiʃtɐ də vˈiɲuʃ] |
| ook a table | **reservar uma mesa** | [ʀɐzɐɾvˈaɾ ˈumɐ mˈezɐ] |
| | | |
| ırse, dish | **prato** (m) | [pɾˈatu] |
| order (meal) | **pedir** (vt) | [pədˈiɾ] |
| nake an order | **pedir** (vi) | [pədˈiɾ] |
| | | |
| eritif | **aperitivo** (m) | [epəɾitˈivu] |
| petizer | **entrada** (f) | [ẽtɾˈadɐ] |
| ssert | **sobremesa** (f) | [sobɾɐmˈezɐ] |
| | | |
| ck | **conta** (f) | [kˈõtɐ] |
| pay the check | **pagar a conta** | [pɐgˈaɾ ɐ kˈõtɐ] |
| give change | **dar o troco** | [daɾ u tɾˈoku] |
| | **gorjeta** (f) | [guɾʒˈetɐ] |

# Family, relatives and friends

## 54. Personal information. Forms

| | | |
|---|---|---|
| name, first name | **nome** (m) | [n'omə] |
| family name | **apelido** (m) | [ɐpəl'idu] |
| date of birth | **data** (f) **de nascimento** | [d'atɐ də nɐʃsim'ẽtu] |
| place of birth | **local** (m) **de nascimento** | [luk'al də nɐʃsim'ẽtu] |
| | | |
| nationality | **nacionalidade** (f) | [nɐsiunɐlid'adə] |
| place of residence | **lugar** (m) **de residência** | [lug'ar də ʀɐzid'ẽsiɐ] |
| country | **país** (m) | [pɐ'iʃ] |
| profession (occupation) | **profissão** (f) | [prufis'ãu] |
| | | |
| gender, sex | **sexo** (m) | [s'ɛksu] |
| height | **estatura** (f) | [əʃtɐt'urɐ] |
| weight | **peso** (m) | [p'ezu] |

## 55. Family members. Relatives

| | | |
|---|---|---|
| mother | **mãe** (f) | [mẽj] |
| father | **pai** (m) | [paj] |
| son | **filho** (m) | [f'iʎu] |
| daughter | **filha** (f) | [f'iʎɐ] |
| | | |
| younger daughter | **filha** (f) **mais nova** | [f'iʎɐ m'ajʃ n'ɔvɐ] |
| younger son | **filho** (m) **mais novo** | [f'iʎu m'ajʃ n'ovu] |
| eldest daughter | **filha** (f) **mais velha** | [f'iʎɐ m'ajʃ v'ɛʎɐ] |
| eldest son | **filho** (m) **mais velho** | [f'iʎu m'ajʃ v'ɛʎu] |
| | | |
| brother | **irmão** (m) | [irm'ãu] |
| elder brother | **irmão mais velho** | [irm'ãu m'ajʃ v'ɛʎu] |
| younger brother | **irmão mais novo** | [irm'ãu m'ajʃ n'ovu] |
| sister | **irmã** (f) | [irm'ã] |
| elder sister | **irmã mais velha** | [irm'ã m'ajʃ v'ɛʎɐ] |
| younger sister | **irmã mais nova** | [irm'ã m'ajʃ n'ɔvɐ] |
| | | |
| cousin (masc.) | **primo** (m) | [pr'imu] |
| cousin (fem.) | **prima** (f) | [pr'imɐ] |
| mom | **mamã** (f) | [mɐm'ã] |
| dad, daddy | **papá** (m) | [pɐp'a] |
| parents | **pais** (pl) | [p'ajʃ] |
| child | **criança** (f) | [krj'ãsɐ] |
| children | **crianças** (f pl) | [krj'ãsɐʃ] |

| ndmother | avó (f) | [ɐv'ɔ] |
| ndfather | avô (m) | [ɐv'o] |
| ndson | neto (m) | [n'ɛtu] |
| nddaughter | neta (f) | [n'ɛtɐ] |
| ndchildren | netos (pl) | [n'ɛtuʃ] |
| le | tio (m) | [t'iu] |
| t | tia (f) | [t'iɐ] |
| hew | sobrinho (m) | [subr'iɲu] |
| ce | sobrinha (f) | [subr'iɲɐ] |
| ther-in-law fe's mother) | sogra (f) | [s'ɔgrɐ] |
| er-in-law sband's father) | sogro (m) | [s'ogru] |
| -in-law ughter's husband) | genro (m) | [ʒ'ẽʀu] |
| omother | madrasta (f) | [mɐdr'aʃtɐ] |
| ofather | padrasto (m) | [pɐdr'aʃtu] |
| nt | criança (f) de colo | [krj'ãsɐ də k'ɔlu] |
| oy (infant) | bebé (m) | [bəb'ɛ] |
| e boy, kid | menino (m) | [mən'inu] |
| e | mulher (f) | [muʎ'ɛr] |
| sband | marido (m) | [mɐr'idu] |
| ouse (husband) | esposo (m) | [əʃp'ozu] |
| ouse (wife) | esposa (f) | [əʃp'ozɐ] |
| rried (masc.) | casado | [kɐz'adu] |
| rried (fem.) | casada | [kɐz'adɐ] |
| gle (unmarried) | solteiro | [sɔlt'ejru] |
| helor | solteirão (m) | [sɔltejr'ãu] |
| orced (masc.) | divorciado | [divursj'adu] |
| ow | viúva (f) | [vj'uvɐ] |
| ower | viúvo (m) | [vj'uvu] |
| ative | parente (m) | [pɐr'ẽtə] |
| se relative | parente (m) próximo | [pɐr'ẽtə pr'ɔsimu] |
| tant relative | parente (m) distante | [pɐr'ẽtə diʃt'ãtə] |
| atives | parentes (m pl) | [pɐr'ẽtəʃ] |
| han (boy) | órfão (m) | ['ɔrfãu] |
| han (girl) | órfã (f) | ['ɔrfã] |
| rdian (of minor) | tutor (m) | [tut'or] |
| adopt (a boy) | adotar (vt) | [ɐdɔt'ar] |
| adopt (a girl) | adotar (vt) | [ɐdɔt'ar] |

## 6. Friends. Coworkers

| nd (masc.) | amigo (m) | [ɐm'igu] |
| nd (fem.) | amiga (f) | [ɐm'igɐ] |

| friendship | amizade (f) | [ɐmiz'adə] |
| to be friends | ser amigos | [ser ɐm'iguʃ] |

| buddy (masc.) | amigo (m) | [ɐm'igu] |
| buddy (fem.) | amiga (f) | [ɐm'igɐ] |
| partner | parceiro (m) | [pɐrs'ɐjru] |

| chief (boss) | chefe (m) | [ʃ'ɛfə] |
| superior | superior (m) | [supɐrj'or] |
| owner, proprietor | proprietário (m) | [prupriɛt'ariu] |
| subordinate | subordinado (m) | [suburdin'adu] |
| colleague | colega (m) | [kul'ɛgɐ] |

| acquaintance (person) | conhecido (m) | [kuɲəs'idu] |
| fellow traveler | companheiro (m) de viagem | [kõpɐɲ'ɐjru də vj'aʒẽj] |
| classmate | colega (m) de classe | [kul'ɛgɐ də kl'asə] |

| neighbor (masc.) | vizinho (m) | [viz'iɲu] |
| neighbor (fem.) | vizinha (f) | [viz'iɲɐ] |
| neighbors | vizinhos (pl) | [viz'iɲuʃ] |

## 57. Man. Woman

| woman | mulher (f) | [muʎ'ɛɾ] |
| girl (young woman) | rapariga (f) | [ʀɐpɐr'igɐ] |
| bride | noiva (f) | [n'ojvɐ] |

| beautiful (adj) | bonita | [bun'itɐ] |
| tall (adj) | alta | ['altɐ] |
| slender (adj) | esbelta | [əʒb'ɛltɐ] |
| short (adj) | de estatura média | [də əʃtɐt'urɐ m'ɛdiɐ] |

| blonde (n) | loura (f) | [l'orɐ] |
| brunette (n) | morena (f) | [mur'enɐ] |

| ladies' (adj) | de senhora | [də səɲ'orɐ] |
| virgin (girl) | virgem (f) | [v'irʒẽj] |
| pregnant (adj) | grávida | [gr'avidɐ] |

| man (adult male) | homem (m) | ['ɔmẽj] |
| blond (n) | louro (m) | [l'oru] |
| brunet (n) | moreno (m) | [mur'enu] |
| tall (adj) | alto | ['altu] |
| short (adj) | de estatura média | [də əʃtɐt'urɐ m'ɛdiɐ] |

| rude (rough) | rude | [ʀ'udə] |
| stocky (adj) | atarracado | [ɐtɐʀɐk'adu] |
| robust (adj) | robusto | [ʀub'uʃtu] |
| strong (adj) | forte | [f'ɔrtə] |

| ength | força (f) | [f'ɔrsɐ] |
| ut, fat (adj) | gordo | [g'ordu] |
| arthy (adj) | moreno | [mur'enu] |
| ll-built (adj) | esbelto | [əʒb'ɛltu] |
| gant (adj) | elegante | [eləg'ãtə] |

## 8. Age

| e | idade (f) | [id'adə] |
| uth (young age) | juventude (f) | [ʒuvẽt'udə] |
| ung (adj) | jovem | [ʒ'ɔvẽj] |
| unger (adj) | mais novo | [m'ajʃ n'ovu] |
| er (adj) | mais velho | [m'ajʃ v'ɛʎu] |
| ung man | jovem (m) | [ʒ'ɔvẽj] |
| nager | adolescente (m) | [ɐduləʃs'ẽtə] |
| y, fellow | rapaz (m) | [ʀɐp'aʒ] |
| man | velhote (m) | [vɛʎ'ɔtə] |
| woman | velhota (f) | [vɛʎ'ɔtɐ] |
| ult | adulto | [ed'ultu] |
| ldle-aged (adj) | de meia-idade | [də mɐjɐ id'adə] |
| erly (adj) | de certa idade | [də s'ɛrtɐ id'adə] |
| (adj) | idoso | [id'ozu] |
| rement | reforma (f) | [ʀəf'ɔrmɐ] |
| etire (from job) | reformar-se (vp) | [ʀəfurm'arsə] |
| ree | reformado (m) | [ʀəfurm'adu] |

## 9. Children

| ld | criança (f) | [krj'ãsɐ] |
| ldren | crianças (f pl) | [krj'ãsɐʃ] |
| ns | gémeos (m pl) | [ʒ'ɛmiuʃ] |
| dle | berço (m) | [b'ersu] |
| le | guizo (m) | [g'izu] |
| per | fralda (f) | [fr'aldɐ] |
| cifier | chucha (f) | [ʃ'uʃɐ] |
| oy carriage | carrinho (m) de bebé | [kɐʀ'iɲu də bəb'ɛ] |
| dergarten | jardim (m) de infância | [ʒɐrd'ĩ də ĩf'ãsiɐ] |
| bysitter | babysitter (f) | [bɐbisit'er] |
| ldhood | infância (f) | [ĩf'ãsiɐ] |
| l | boneca (f) | [bun'ɛkɐ] |

| toy | brinquedo (m) | [brĩk'edu] |
| construction set | jogo (m) de armar | [ʒ'ogu də ɐrm'ar] |

| well-bred (adj) | bem-educado | [bẽj eduk'adu] |
| ill-bred (adj) | mal-educado | [mal eduk'adu] |
| spoiled (adj) | mimado | [mim'adu] |

| to be naughty | ser travesso | [ser trɐv'ɛsu] |
| mischievous (adj) | travesso, traquinas | [trɐv'ɛsu], [trɐk'ineʃ] |
| mischievousness | travessura (f) | [trɐvəs'urɐ] |
| mischievous child | criança (f) travessa | [krj'ãsɐ trɐv'ɛsɐ] |

| obedient (adj) | obediente | [ɔbədj'ẽtə] |
| disobedient (adj) | desobediente | [dəzɔbədj'ẽtə] |

| docile (adj) | dócil | [d'ɔsil] |
| clever (smart) | inteligente | [ĩtəliʒ'ẽtə] |
| child prodigy | menino (m) prodígio | [mən'inu prud'iʒiu] |

## 60. Married couples. Family life

| to kiss (vt) | beijar (vt) | [bɐjʒ'ar] |
| to kiss (vi) | beijar-se (vp) | [bɐjʒ'arsə] |
| family (n) | família (f) | [fɐm'iliɐ] |
| family (as adj) | familiar | [fɐmilj'ar] |
| couple | casal (m) | [kɐz'al] |
| marriage (state) | matrimónio (m) | [mɐtrim'ɔniu] |
| hearth (home) | lar (m) | [lar] |
| dynasty | dinastia (f) | [dinɐʃt'iɐ] |

| date | encontro (m) | [ẽk'õtru] |
| kiss | beijo (m) | [b'ɐjʒu] |

| love (for sb) | amor (m) | [ɐm'or] |
| to love (sb) | amar (vt) | [ɐm'ar] |
| beloved | amado, querido | [ɐm'adu], [kər'idu] |

| tenderness | ternura (f) | [tərn'urɐ] |
| tender (affectionate) | terno, afetuoso | [t'ɛrnu], [ɐfɛtu'ozu] |
| faithfulness | fidelidade (f) | [fidəlid'adə] |
| faithful (adj) | fiel | [fj'ɛl] |
| care (attention) | cuidado (m) | [kuid'adu] |
| caring (~ father) | carinhoso | [kɐriɲ'ozu] |

| newlyweds | recém-casados (m pl) | [ʀɐs'ẽj kɐz'aduʃ] |
| honeymoon | lua de mel (f) | [l'uɐ də mɛl] |
| to get married (ab. woman) | casar-se (vp) | [kɐz'arsə] |
| to get married (ab. man) | casar-se (vp) | [kɐz'arsə] |
| wedding | boda (f) | [b'odɐ] |

| | | |
|---|---|---|
| den wedding | **bodas** (f pl) **de ouro** | [b'odeʃ də 'oru] |
| iiversary | **aniversário** (m) | [ənivərs'ariu] |
| | | |
| er (masc.) | **amante** (m) | [ɐm'ãtə] |
| tress | **amante** (f) | [ɐm'ãtə] |
| | | |
| ıltery | **adultério** (m) | [ɐdult'ɛriu] |
| ːheat on ... | **cometer adultério** | [kumət'er ɐdult'ɛriu] |
| mmit adultery) | | |
| lous (adj) | **ciumento** | [sium'ẽtu] |
| ɔe jealous | **ser ciumento** | [ser sium'ẽtu] |
| ɔrce | **divórcio** (m) | [div'ɔrsiu] |
| livorce (vi) | **divorciar-se** (vp) | [divursj'arsə] |
| | | |
| ɟuarrel (vi) | **discutir, brigar** (vi) | [diʃkut'ir], [brig'ar] |
| ɔe reconciled | **fazer as pazes** | [fɐz'er ɐʃ p'azəʃ] |
| ether (adv) | **juntos** | [ʒ'ũtuʃ] |
| ( | **sexo** (m) | [s'ɛksu] |
| | | |
| ɔpiness | **felicidade** (f) | [fəlisid'adə] |
| ɔpy (adj) | **feliz** | [fəl'iʃ] |
| ifortune (accident) | **infelicidade** (f) | [ĩfəlisid'adə] |
| 1appy (adj) | **infeliz** | [ĩfəl'iʃ] |

# Character. Feelings. Emotions

## 61. Feelings. Emotions

| | | |
|---|---|---|
| feeling (emotion) | sentimento (m) | [sẽtim'ẽtu] |
| feelings | sentimentos (m pl) | [sẽtim'ẽtuʃ] |
| to feel (vt) | sentir (vt) | [sẽt'ir] |
| hunger | fome (f) | [f'ɔmə] |
| to be hungry | ter fome | [ter f'ɔmə] |
| thirst | sede (f) | [s'edə] |
| to be thirsty | ter sede | [ter s'edə] |
| sleepiness | sonolência (f) | [sunul'ẽsiɐ] |
| to feel sleepy | ter sono | [ter s'onu] |
| tiredness | cansaço (m) | [kãs'asu] |
| tired (adj) | cansado | [kãs'adu] |
| to get tired | estar cansado | [əʃt'ar kãs'adu] |
| mood (humor) | humor (m) | [um'or] |
| boredom | tédio (m) | [t'ɛdiu] |
| to be bored | aborrecer-se (vp) | [ɐburəs'ersə] |
| seclusion | isolamento (m) | [izulɐm'ẽtu] |
| to seclude oneself | isolar-se | [izul'arsə] |
| to worry (make anxious) | preocupar (vt) | [priɔkup'ar] |
| to be worried | preocupar-se (vp) | [priɔkup'arsə] |
| worrying (n) | preocupação (f) | [priɔkupɐs'ãu] |
| anxiety | ansiedade (f) | [ãsiɛd'adə] |
| preoccupied (adj) | preocupado | [priɔkup'adu] |
| to be nervous | estar nervoso | [əʃt'ar nɐrv'ozu] |
| to panic (vi) | entrar em pânico | [ẽtr'ar ẽ p'ɐniku] |
| hope | esperança (f) | [əʃpər'ãsɐ] |
| to hope (vi, vt) | esperar (vt) | [əʃpər'ar] |
| certainty | certeza (f) | [sərt'ezɐ] |
| certain, sure (adj) | certo | [s'ɛrtu] |
| uncertainty | indecisão (f) | [ĩdəsiz'ãu] |
| uncertain (adj) | indeciso | [ĩdəs'izu] |
| drunk (adj) | ébrio, bêbado | ['ɛbriu], [b'ebɐdu] |
| sober (adj) | sóbrio | [s'ɔbriu] |
| weak (adj) | fraco | [fr'aku] |
| happy (adj) | feliz | [fəl'iʃ] |
| to scare (vt) | assustar (vt) | [ɐsuʃt'ar] |

| / (madness) | fúria (f) | [fʼuriɐ] |
| ɪe (fury) | ira, raiva (f) | [irɐ], [ʀʼajvɐ] |

| ɔression | depressão (f) | [dəprəsʼãu] |
| comfort | desconforto (m) | [dəʃkõfʼortu] |
| nfort | conforto (m) | [kõfʼortu] |
| ʼegret (be sorry) | lamentar (vt) | [ləmẽtʼar] |
| ɪret | lamento (m) | [lɐmʼẽtu] |
| d luck | azar (m), má sorte (f) | [ɐzʼar], [ma sʼortə] |
| ɪness | tristeza (f) | [triʃtʼezɐ] |

| ɪme (remorse) | vergonha (f) | [vɐrgʼoɲɐ] |
| dness | alegria (f) | [ɐləgrʼiɐ] |
| husiasm, zeal | entusiasmo (m) | [ẽtuzjʼaʒmu] |
| husiast | entusiasta (m) | [ẽtuzjʼaʃtɐ] |
| ɪhow enthusiasm | mostrar entusiasmo | [muʃtrʼar ẽtuzjʼaʒmu] |

## 2. Character. Personality

| ɪracter | caráter (m) | [kɐrʼatɛr] |
| ɪracter flaw | falha (f) de caráter | [fʼaʎɐ də kɐrʼatɛr] |
| ɪd | mente (f) | [mʼẽtə] |
| ɪson | razão (f) | [ʀɐzʼãu] |

| ɪscience | consciência (f) | [kõʃsjʼẽsiɐ] |
| ɔit (custom) | hábito (m) | [ʼabitu] |
| ɪity | habilidade (f) | [ɐbilidʼadə] |
| ɪ (e.g., ~ swim) | saber | [sɐbʼer] |

| ɪent (adj) | paciente | [pɐsjʼẽtə] |
| ɔatient (adj) | impaciente | [ĩpɐsjʼẽtə] |
| ɪous (inquisitive) | curioso | [kurjʼozu] |
| ɪosity | curiosidade (f) | [kuriuzidʼadə] |

| desty | modéstia (f) | [mudʼɛʃtiɐ] |
| dest (adj) | modesto | [mudʼɛʃtu] |
| nodest (adj) | imodesto | [imudʼɛʃtu] |

| ɪness | preguiça (f) | [prəgʼisɐ] |
| y (adj) | preguiçoso | [prəgisʼozu] |
| y person (masc.) | preguiçoso (m) | [prəgisʼozu] |

| ɪning (n) | astúcia (f) | [ɐʃtʼusiɐ] |
| ɪning (as adj) | astuto | [ɐʃtʼutu] |
| trust | desconfiança (f) | [dəʃkõfjʼãsɐ] |
| trustful (adj) | desconfiado | [dəʃkõfjʼadu] |

| ɪerosity | generosidade (f) | [ʒənəruzidʼadə] |
| ɪerous (adj) | generoso | [ʒənərʼozu] |
| ɪnted (adj) | talentoso | [tɐlẽtʼozu] |

| talent | **talento** (m) | [tɐl'ẽtu] |
| courageous (adj) | **corajoso** | [kurɐʒ'ozu] |
| courage | **coragem** (f) | [kur'aʒẽj] |
| honest (adj) | **honesto** | [on'ɛʃtu] |
| honesty | **honestidade** (f) | [onɛʃtid'adə] |

| careful (cautious) | **prudente** | [prud'ẽtə] |
| brave (courageous) | **valente** | [vɐl'ẽtə] |
| serious (adj) | **sério** | [s'ɛriu] |
| strict (severe, stern) | **severo** | [sɐv'ɛru] |

| decisive (adj) | **decidido** | [dəsid'idu] |
| indecisive (adj) | **indeciso** | [ĩdəs'izu] |
| shy, timid (adj) | **tímido** | [t'imidu] |
| shyness, timidity | **timidez** (f) | [timid'eʃ] |

| confidence (trust) | **confiança** (f) | [kõfj'ãsɐ] |
| to believe (trust) | **confiar** (vt) | [kõfj'ar] |
| trusting (naïve) | **crédulo** | [kr'ɛdulu] |

| sincerely (adv) | **sinceramente** | [sĩsɛrem'ẽtə] |
| sincere (adj) | **sincero** | [sĩs'ɛru] |
| sincerity | **sinceridade** (f) | [sĩsərid'adə] |
| open (person) | **aberto** | [ɐb'ɛrtu] |

| calm (adj) | **calmo** | [k'almu] |
| frank (sincere) | **franco** | [fr'ãku] |
| naïve (adj) | **ingénuo** | [ĩʒ'ɛnuu] |
| absent-minded (adj) | **distraído** | [diʃtrɐ'idu] |
| funny (odd) | **engraçado** | [ẽgrɐs'adu] |

| greed | **ganância** (f) | [gɐn'ãsiɐ] |
| greedy (adj) | **ganacioso** | [genɐsj'ozu] |
| stingy (adj) | **avarento** | [ɐvɐr'ẽtu] |
| evil (adj) | **mau** | [m'au] |
| stubborn (adj) | **teimoso** | [tɐjm'ozu] |
| unpleasant (adj) | **desagradável** | [dəzɐgrɐd'avɛl] |

| selfish person (masc.) | **egoísta** (m) | [egu'iʃtɐ] |
| selfish (adj) | **egoísta** | [egu'iʃtɐ] |
| coward | **cobarde** (m) | [kub'ardə] |
| cowardly (adj) | **cobarde** | [kub'ardə] |

## 63. Sleep. Dreams

| to sleep (vi) | **dormir** (vi) | [durm'ir] |
| sleep, sleeping | **sono** (m) | [s'onu] |
| dream | **sonho** (m) | [s'oɲu] |
| to dream (in sleep) | **sonhar** (vi) | [suɲ'ar] |
| sleepy (adj) | **sonolento** | [sunul'ẽtu] |

| d | cama (f) | [k'eme] |
| ttress | colchão (m) | [kɔlʃ'ãu] |
| nket (comforter) | cobertor (m) | [kubərt'or] |
| ow | almofada (f) | [almuf'adə] |
| et | lençol (m) | [lẽs'ɔl] |
| | | |
| omnia | insónia (f) | [ĩs'ɔniɐ] |
| epless (adj) | insone | [ĩs'ɔnə] |
| eping pill | sonífero (m) | [sun'iferu] |
| ake a sleeping pill | tomar um sonífero | [tum'ar ũ sun'iferu] |
| | | |
| eel sleepy | estar sonolento | [əʃt'ar sunul'ẽtu] |
| awn (vi) | bocejar (vi) | [busəʒ'ar] |
| jo to bed | ir para a cama | [ir p'ɐrɐ ɐ k'eme] |
| nake up the bed | fazer a cama | [fɐz'er ɐ k'eme] |
| all asleep | adormecer (vi) | [ɐdurməs'er] |
| | | |
| htmare | pesadelo (m) | [pəzɐd'elu] |
| oring | ronco (m) | [ʀ'õku] |
| snore (vi) | ressonar (vi) | [ʀəsun'ar] |
| | | |
| rm clock | despertador (m) | [dəʃpərtɐd'or] |
| vake (vt) | acordar, despertar (vt) | [ɐkurd'ar], [dəʃpərt'ar] |
| vake up | acordar (vi) | [ɐkurd'ar] |
| jet up (vi) | levantar-se (vp) | [ləvɐt'arsə] |
| vash up (vi) | lavar-se (vp) | [lɐv'arsə] |

## 4.  Humour. Laughter. Gladness

| nor (wit, fun) | humor (m) | [um'or] |
| ise of humor | sentido (m) de humor | [sẽt'idu də um'or] |
| nave fun | divertir-se (vp) | [divərt'irsə] |
| eerful (adj) | alegre | [ɐl'ɛgrə] |
| rriment, fun | alegria (f) | [ɐləgr'iɐ] |
| | | |
| ile | sorriso (m) | [suʀ'izu] |
| smile (vi) | sorrir (vi) | [suʀ'ir] |
| start laughing | começar a rir | [kuməs'ar ɐ ʀir] |
| augh (vi) | rir (vi) | [ʀir] |
| gh, laughter | riso (m) | [ʀ'izu] |
| | | |
| ecdote | anedota (f) | [ɐnəd'ɔtə] |
| ny (anecdote, etc.) | engraçado | [ẽgrɐs'adu] |
| ny (odd) | ridículo | [ʀid'ikulu] |
| | | |
| oke (vi) | fazer piadas | [fɐz'er pj'adɐʃ] |
| e (verbal) | piada (f) | [pj'adə] |
| (emotion) | alegria (f) | [ɐləgr'iɐ] |
| ejoice (vi) | regozijar-se (vp) | [ʀəguziʒ'arsə] |
| d, cheerful (adj) | alegre | [ɐl'ɛgrə] |

## 65. Discussion, conversation. Part 1

| | | |
|---|---|---|
| communication | comunicação (f) | [kumunikɐs'ãu] |
| to communicate | comunicar-se (vp) | [kumunik'arsə] |
| | | |
| conversation | conversa (f) | [kõv'ɛrsɐ] |
| dialog | diálogo (m) | [dj'alugu] |
| discussion (discourse) | discussão (f) | [diʃkus'ãu] |
| debate | debate (m) | [dəb'atə] |
| to debate (vi) | debater (vt) | [dəbet'er] |
| | | |
| interlocutor | interlocutor (m) | [ĩtɛrlukut'or] |
| topic (theme) | tema (m) | [t'emɐ] |
| point of view | ponto (m) de vista | [p'õtu də v'iʃtɐ] |
| opinion (viewpoint) | opinião (f) | [ɔpinj'ãu] |
| speech (talk) | discurso (m) | [diʃk'ursu] |
| | | |
| discussion (of report, etc.) | discussão (f) | [diʃkus'ãu] |
| to discuss (vt) | discutir (vt) | [diʃkut'ir] |
| talk (conversation) | conversa (f) | [kõv'ɛrsɐ] |
| to talk (vi) | conversar (vi) | [kõvɐrs'ar] |
| meeting | encontro (m) | [ẽk'õtru] |
| to meet (vi, vt) | encontrar-se (vp) | [ẽkõtr'arsə] |
| | | |
| proverb | provérbio (m) | [pruv'ɛrbiu] |
| saying | ditado (m) | [dit'adu] |
| riddle (poser) | adivinha (f) | [ɐdiv'iɲɐ] |
| to ask a riddle | dizer uma adivinha | [diz'er 'umɐ ɐdiv'iɲɐ] |
| password | senha (f) | [s'eɲɐ] |
| secret | segredo (m) | [səgr'edu] |
| | | |
| oath (vow) | juramento (m) | [ʒurɐm'ẽtu] |
| to swear (an oath) | jurar (vi) | [ʒur'ar] |
| promise | promessa (f) | [prum'ɛsɐ] |
| to promise (vt) | prometer (vt) | [prumət'er] |
| | | |
| advice (counsel) | conselho (m) | [kõs'ɐʎu] |
| to advise (vt) | aconselhar (vt) | [ɐkõsəʎ'ar] |
| to follow one's advice | seguir o conselho | [səg'ir u kõs'ɐʎu] |
| to listen to ... (obey) | escutar (vt) | [əʃkut'ar] |
| | | |
| news | novidade (f) | [nuvid'adə] |
| sensation (news) | sensação (f) | [sẽsɐs'ãu] |
| information (data) | informação (f) | [ĩfurmɐs'ãu] |
| conclusion (decision) | conclusão (f) | [kõkluz'ãu] |
| voice | voz (f) | [vɔʒ] |
| compliment | elogio (m) | [eluʒ'iu] |
| kind (nice) | amável | [ɐm'avɛl] |
| | | |
| word | palavra (f) | [pɐl'avrɐ] |
| phrase | frase (f) | [fr'azə] |

| swer | resposta (f) | [Rəʃpˈɔʃtə] |
| th | verdade (f) | [vərdˈadə] |
| | mentira (f) | [mẽtˈirɐ] |

| ught | pensamento (m) | [pẽsɐmˈẽtu] |
| a (inspiration) | ideia (f) | [idˈɛjɐ] |
| tasy | fantasia (f) | [fãtɐzˈiɐ] |

## 6. Discussion, conversation. Part 2

| pected (adj) | estimado | [əʃtimˈadu] |
| espect (vt) | respeitar (vt) | [Rəʃpɐjtˈar] |
| pect | respeito (m) | [Rəʃpˈejtu] |
| ar ... (letter) | Estimado ... , Caro ... | [əʃtimˈadu], [kˈaru] |

| ntroduce (present) | apresentar (vt) | [ɛprəzẽtˈar] |
| make acquaintance | conhecer (vt) | [kuɲəsˈer] |
| ention | intenção (f) | [ĩtẽsˈãu] |
| ntend (have in mind) | tencionar (vt) | [tẽsiunˈar] |
| h | desejo (m) | [dəzˈeʒu] |
| vish (~ good luck) | desejar (vt) | [dəzəʒˈar] |

| prise (astonishment) | surpresa (f) | [surprˈezɐ] |
| surprise (amaze) | surpreender (vt) | [surpriẽdˈer] |
| be surprised | surpreender-se (vp) | [surpriẽdˈersə] |

| jive (vt) | dar (vt) | [dar] |
| ake (get hold of) | pegar (vt) | [pegˈar] |
| jive back | devolver (vt) | [dəvolvˈer] |
| return (give back) | devolver (vt) | [dəvolvˈer] |

| apologize (vi) | desculpar-se (vp) | [dəʃkulpˈarsə] |
| ology | desculpa (f) | [dəʃkˈulpɐ] |
| orgive (vt) | perdoar (vt) | [pərduˈar] |

| alk (speak) | falar (vi) | [fɐlˈar] |
| isten (vi) | escutar (vt) | [əʃkutˈar] |
| near out | ouvir até o fim | [ovˈir etˈɛ u fĩ] |
| understand (vt) | compreender (vt) | [kõpriẽdˈer] |

| show (display) | mostrar (vt) | [muʃtrˈar] |
| ook at ... | olhar para ... | [oʎˈar pˈɐrɐ] |
| call (with one's voice) | chamar (vt) | [ʃɐmˈar] |
| distract (disturb) | distrair (vt) | [diʃtrɐˈir] |
| disturb (vt) | perturbar (vt) | [pərturbˈar] |
| pass (to hand sth) | entregar (vt) | [ẽtrəgˈar] |

| mand (request) | pedido (m) | [pədˈidu] |
| equest (ask) | pedir (vt) | [pədˈir] |
| mand (firm request) | exigência (f) | [eziʒˈẽsiɐ] |

| to demand (request firmly) | exigir (vt) | [eziʒ'ir] |
| to tease (nickname) | chamar nomes (vt) | [ʃɐm'ar n'oməʃ] |
| to mock (make fun of) | zombar (vt) | [zõb'ar] |
| mockery, derision | zombaria (f) | [zõbɐr'iɐ] |
| nickname | apelido (m) | [ɐpəl'idu] |

| allusion | alusão (f) | [ɐluz'ãu] |
| to allude (vi) | aludir (vt) | [ɐlud'ir] |
| to imply (vt) | subentender (vt) | [subẽtẽd'er] |

| description | descrição (f) | [dəʃkris'ãu] |
| to describe (vt) | descrever (vt) | [dəʃkrɐv'er] |
| praise (compliments) | elogio (m) | [ɐluʒ'iu] |
| to praise (vt) | elogiar (vt) | [ɐluʒj'ar] |

| disappointment | desapontamento (m) | [dəzɐpõtɐm'ẽtu] |
| to disappoint (vt) | desapontar (vt) | [dəzɐpõt'ar] |
| to be disappointed | desapontar-se (vp) | [dəzɐpõt'arsə] |

| supposition | suposição (f) | [supuzis'ãu] |
| to suppose (assume) | supor (vt) | [sup'or] |
| warning (caution) | advertência (f) | [ɐdvɐrt'ẽsiɐ] |
| to warn (vt) | advertir (vt) | [ɐdvɐrt'ir] |

## 67. Discussion, conversation. Part 3

| to talk into (convince) | convencer (vt) | [kõvẽs'er] |
| to calm down (vt) | acalmar (vt) | [ɐkalm'ar] |

| silence (~ is golden) | silêncio (m) | [sil'ẽsiu] |
| to keep silent | ficar em silêncio | [fik'ar ẽ sil'ẽsiu] |
| to whisper (vi, vt) | sussurrar (vt) | [susuʀ'ar] |
| whisper | sussurro (m) | [sus'uʀu] |

| frankly, sincerely (adv) | francamente | [frãkɐm'ẽtə] |
| in my opinion ... | a meu ver ... | [ɐ m'eu ver] |

| detail (of the story) | detalhe (m) | [dət'aʎə] |
| detailed (adj) | detalhado | [dətɐʎ'adu] |
| in detail (adv) | detalhadamente | [dətɐʎadɐm'ẽtə] |

| hint, clue | dica (f) | [d'ikɐ] |
| to give a hint | dar uma dica | [dar 'umɐ d'ikɐ] |

| look (glance) | olhar (m) | [ɔʎ'ar] |
| to have a look | dar uma vista de olhos | [dar 'umɐ v'iʃtɐ də 'ɔʎuʃ] |
| fixed (look) | fixo | [f'iksu] |
| to blink (vi) | piscar (vi) | [piʃk'ar] |
| to wink (vi) | pestanejar (vt) | [pəʃtɐnəʒ'ar] |
| to nod (in assent) | acenar (vt) | [ɐsən'ar] |

| h | suspiro (m) | [suʃp'iru] |
| sigh (vi) | suspirar (vi) | [suʃpir'aɾ] |
| shudder (vi) | estremecer (vi) | [əʃtrəməs'eɾ] |
| sture | gesto (m) | [ʒ'ɛʃtu] |
| ouch (one's arm, etc.) | tocar (vt) | [tuk'aɾ] |
| seize (by the arm) | agarrar (vt) | [ɐgɐʀ'aɾ] |
| ap (on the shoulder) | bater de leve | [bɐt'eɾ də l'ɛvə] |

| ok out! | Cuidado! | [kuid'adu] |
| ally? | A sério? | [ɐ s'ɛriu] |
| you sure? | Tens a certeza? | [tẽjʃ ɐ sɐɾt'ezɐ] |
| od luck! | Boa sorte! | [b'oɐ s'ɔɾtə] |
| e! | Compreendi! | [kõpriẽd'i] |
| a pity! | Que pena! | [kə p'enɐ] |

<hr>

## 8. Agreement. Refusal

| isent (agreement) | consentimento (m) | [kõsẽtim'ẽtu] |
| agree (say yes) | consentir (vi) | [kõsẽt'ir] |
| oroval | aprovação (f) | [ɐpruvɐs'ãu] |
| approve (vt) | aprovar (vt) | [ɐpruv'aɾ] |

| usal | recusa (f) | [ʀək'uzɐ] |
| efuse (vi, vt) | negar-se (vt) | [nəg'arsə] |

| eat! | Está ótimo! | [əʃt'a 'ɔtimu] |
| right! | Muito bem! | [m'ũjtu bẽj] |
| ay! (I agree) | Está bem! | [əʃt'a bẽj] |

| bidden (adj) | proibido | [pruib'idu] |
| forbidden | é proibido | [ɛ pruib'idu] |
| impossible | é impossível | [ɛ ĩpus'ivɛl] |
| orrect (adj) | incorreto | [ĩkuʀ'ɛtu] |

| eject (~ a demand) | rejeitar (vt) | [ʀəʒejt'aɾ] |
| support (cause, idea) | apoiar (vt) | [ɐpoj'aɾ] |
| accept (~ an apology) | aceitar (vt) | [ɐsɐjt'aɾ] |

| confirm (vt) | confirmar (vt) | [kõfirm'aɾ] |
| ifirmation | confirmação (f) | [kõfirmɐs'ãu] |
| mission | permissão (f) | [pərmis'ãu] |
| oermit (vt) | permitir (vt) | [pərmit'ir] |

| cision | decisão (f) | [dəsiz'ãu] |
| say nothing | não dizer nada | [n'ãu diz'eɾ n'adə] |

| idition (term) | condição (f) | [kõdis'ãu] |
| cuse (pretext) | pretexto (m) | [prət'ɛʃtu] |
| ise (compliments) | elogio (m) | [eluʒ'iu] |
| oraise (vt) | elogiar (vt) | [eluʒj'aɾ] |

## 69. Success. Good luck. Failure

| | | |
|---|---|---|
| success | êxito, sucesso (m) | ['ɛzitu], [sus'ɛsu] |
| successfully (adv) | com êxito | [kõ 'ɛzitu] |
| successful (adj) | bem sucedido | [bẽj susəd'idu] |
| | | |
| good luck | sorte (f) | [s'ɔrtə] |
| Good luck! | Boa sorte! | [b'oɐ s'ɔrtə] |
| lucky (e.g., ~ day) | feliz | [fəl'iʃ] |
| lucky (fortunate) | sortudo, felizardo | [surt'udu], [fəliz'ardu] |
| | | |
| failure | fracasso (m) | [frɐk'asu] |
| misfortune | pouca sorte (f) | [p'okɐ s'ɔrtə] |
| bad luck | azar (m), má sorte (f) | [ɐz'ar], [ma s'ɔrtə] |
| unsuccessful (adj) | mal sucedido | [mal susəd'idu] |
| catastrophe | catástrofe (f) | [kɐt'aʃtrufə] |
| | | |
| pride | orgulho (m) | [ɔrg'uʎu] |
| proud (adj) | orgulhoso | [ɔrguʎ'ozu] |
| to be proud | estar orgulhoso | [əʃt'ar ɔrguʎ'ozu] |
| | | |
| winner | vencedor (m) | [vẽsəd'or] |
| to win (vi) | vencer (vi) | [vẽs'er] |
| to lose (not win) | perder (vt) | [pərd'er] |
| try | tentativa (f) | [tẽtɐt'ivɐ] |
| to try (vi) | tentar (vt) | [tẽt'ar] |
| chance (opportunity) | chance (m) | [ʃ'ãsə] |

## 70. Quarrels. Negative emotions

| | | |
|---|---|---|
| shout (scream) | grito (m) | [gr'itu] |
| to shout (vi) | gritar (vi) | [grit'ar] |
| to start to cry out | começar a gritar | [kuməs'ar ɐ grit'ar] |
| | | |
| quarrel | discussão (f) | [diʃkus'ãu] |
| to quarrel (vi) | discutir (vt) | [diʃkut'ir] |
| fight (scandal) | escândalo (m) | [əʃk'ãdəlu] |
| to have a fight | criar escândalo | [kri'ar əʃk'ãdɐlu] |
| conflict | conflito (m) | [kõfl'itu] |
| misunderstanding | mal-entendido (m) | [malẽtẽd'idu] |
| | | |
| insult | insulto (m) | [ĩs'ultu] |
| to insult (vt) | insultar (vt) | [ĩsult'ar] |
| insulted (adj) | insultado | [ĩsult'adu] |
| resentment | ofensa (f) | [ɔf'ẽsɐ] |
| to offend (vt) | ofender (vt) | [ɔfẽd'er] |
| to take offense | ofender-se (vp) | [ɔfẽd'ersə] |
| indignation | indignação (f) | [ĩdignɐs'ãu] |
| to be indignant | indignar-se (vp) | [ĩdign'arsə] |

| nplaint | queixa (f) | [kˈɐjʃɐ] |
| complain (vi, vt) | queixar-se (vp) | [kɐjʃˈarsə] |
| ology | desculpa (f) | [dəʃkˈulpɐ] |
| apologize (vi) | desculpar-se (vp) | [dəʃkulpˈarsə] |
| beg pardon | pedir perdão | [pədˈir pərdˈãu] |
| icism | crítica (f) | [krˈitikɐ] |
| criticize (vt) | criticar (vt) | [kritikˈar] |
| cusation | acusação (f) | [ɐkuzɐsˈãu] |
| accuse (vt) | acusar (vt) | [ɐkuzˈar] |
| enge | vingança (f) | [vĩgˈãsɐ] |
| revenge (vt) | vingar (vt) | [vĩgˈar] |
| pay back | pagar de volta | [pɐgˈar də vˈɔltɐ] |
| dain | desprezo (m) | [dəʃprˈezu] |
| despise (vt) | desprezar (vt) | [dəʃprəzˈar] |
| red, hate | ódio (m) | [ˈɔdiu] |
| hate (vt) | odiar (vt) | [odjˈar] |
| vous (adj) | nervoso | [nərvˈozu] |
| be nervous | estar nervoso | [əʃtˈar nərvˈozu] |
| gry (mad) | zangado | [zãgˈadu] |
| make angry | zangar (vt) | [zãgˈar] |
| miliation | humilhação (f) | [umiʎɐsˈãu] |
| humiliate (vt) | humilhar (vt) | [umiʎˈar] |
| humiliate oneself | humilhar-se (vp) | [umiʎˈarsə] |
| ock | choque (m) | [ʃˈɔkə] |
| shock (vt) | chocar (vt) | [ʃukˈar] |
| ble (annoyance) | aborrecimento (m) | [ɐbuʀəsimˈẽtu] |
| pleasant (adj) | desagradável | [dəzɐgrɐdˈavɛl] |
| r (dread) | medo (m) | [mˈedu] |
| ible (storm, heat) | terrível | [tərˈivɛl] |
| ary (e.g., ~ story) | assustador | [ɐsuʃtɐdˈor] |
| ror | horror (m) | [ɔʀˈor] |
| ful (crime, news) | horrível | [ɔʀˈivɛl] |
| begin to tremble | começar a tremer | [kuməsˈar ɐ trəmˈer] |
| cry (weep) | chorar (vi) | [ʃurˈar] |
| start crying | começar a chorar | [kuməsˈar ɐ ʃurˈar] |
| r | lágrima (f) | [lˈagrimɐ] |
| lt | falta (f) | [fˈaltɐ] |
| lt (feeling) | culpa (f) | [kˈulpɐ] |
| honor (disgrace) | desonra (f) | [dəzˈõʀɐ] |
| test | protesto (m) | [prutˈɛʃtu] |
| ess | stress (m) | [strˈɛs] |

| | | |
|---|---|---|
| to disturb (vt) | **perturbar** (vt) | [pərturb'ar] |
| to be furious | **zangar-se com ...** | [zãg'arsə kõ] |
| mad, angry (adj) | **zangado** | [zãg'adu] |
| to end (~ a relationship) | **terminar** (vt) | [tərmin'ar] |
| to swear (at sb) | **praguejar** | [prɐgəʒ'ar] |
| | | |
| to be scared | **assustar-se** | [ɐsuʃt'arsə] |
| to hit (strike with hand) | **golpear** (vt) | [gɔlpj'ar] |
| to fight (vi) | **bater-se** (vp) | [bet'ersə] |
| | | |
| to settle (a conflict) | **resolver** (vt) | [ʀəzolv'er] |
| discontented (adj) | **descontente** | [dəʃkõt'ẽtə] |
| furious (adj) | **furioso** | [furj'ozu] |
| | | |
| It's not good! | **Não está bem!** | [n'ãu əʃt'a bẽj] |
| It's bad! | **É mau!** | [ɛ m'au] |

# ledicine

## 1. Diseases

|  |  |  |
|---|---|---|
| kness | doença (f) | [du'ẽsɐ] |
| be sick | estar doente | [əʃt'ar du'ẽtɐ] |
| alth | saúde (f) | [sɐ'udə] |
| ny nose (coryza) | nariz (m) a escorrer | [nɐr'iʃ ɐ əʃkuʀ'er] |
| gina | amigdalite (f) | [ɐmigdɐl'itə] |
| d (illness) | constipação (f) | [kõʃtipɐs'ãu] |
| catch a cold | constipar-se (vp) | [kõʃtip'arsə] |
| nchitis | bronquite (f) | [brõk'itə] |
| eumonia | pneumonia (f) | [pneumun'iɐ] |
| influenza | gripe (f) | [gr'ipə] |
| ar-sighted (adj) | míope | [m'iupə] |
| -sighted (adj) | presbita | [prəʒb'itə] |
| abismus (crossed eyes) | estrabismo (m) | [əʃtrɐb'iʒmu] |
| ss-eyed (adj) | estrábico | [əʃtr'abiku] |
| aract | catarata (f) | [kɐtɐr'atɐ] |
| ucoma | glaucoma (m) | [glauk'omɐ] |
| oke | AVC (m), apoplexia (f) | [avɛs'ɛ], [ɐpɔplɛks'iɐ] |
| art attack | ataque (m) cardíaco | [ɐt'akə kɐrd'iɐku] |
| ocardial infarction | enfarte (m) do miocârdio | [ẽf'artə du miɔk'ardiu] |
| alysis | paralisia (f) | [pɐrəliz'iɐ] |
| paralyze (vt) | paralisar (vt) | [pɐrəliz'ar] |
| rgy | alergia (f) | [ɐlərʒ'iɐ] |
| hma | asma (f) | ['aʒmɐ] |
| betes | diabetes (f) | [diɐb'ɛtəʃ] |
| thache | dor (f) de dentes | [dor də d'ẽtəʃ] |
| ies | cârie (f) | [k'ariə] |
| rrhea | diarreia (f) | [diɐʀ'ɐjɐ] |
| istipation | prisão (f) de ventre | [priz'ãu də v'ẽtrə] |
| mach upset | desarranjo (m) intestinal | [dəzɐʀ'ãʒu ĩtəʃtin'al] |
| d poisoning | intoxicação (f) alimentar | [ĩtɔksikɐs'ãu ɐlimẽt'ar] |
| nave a food poisoning | intoxicar-se | [ĩtɔksik'arsə] |
| nritis | artrite (f) | [ɐrtr'itə] |
| ets | raquitismo (m) | [ʀɐkit'iʒmu] |
| umatism | reumatismo (m) | [ʀiumɐt'iʒmu] |

| | | |
|---|---|---|
| atherosclerosis | **arteriosclerose** (f) | [ɐrtɐrioʃklər'ozə] |
| gastritis | **gastrite** (f) | [geʃtr'itə] |
| appendicitis | **apendicite** (f) | [ɐpẽdis'itə] |
| cholecystitis | **colecistite** (f) | [kulɛsiʃt'itə] |
| ulcer | **úlcera** (f) | ['ulsərɐ] |
| | | |
| measles | **sarampo** (m) | [sɐr'ãpu] |
| German measles | **rubéola** (f) | [ʀub'ɛulɐ] |
| jaundice | **iterícia** (f) | [itɐr'isiɐ] |
| hepatitis | **hepatite** (f) | [ɛpɐt'itə] |
| | | |
| schizophrenia | **esquizofrenia** (f) | [əʃkizofrən'iɐ] |
| rabies (hydrophobia) | **raiva** (f) | [ʀ'ajvɐ] |
| neurosis | **neurose** (f) | [neur'ozə] |
| concussion | **comoção** (f) **cerebral** | [kumus'ãu sərəbr'al] |
| | | |
| cancer | **cancro** (m) | [k'ãkru] |
| sclerosis | **esclerose** (f) | [əʃklər'ozə] |
| multiple sclerosis | **esclerose** (f) **múltipla** | [əʃklər'ozə m'ultiplɐ] |
| | | |
| alcoholism | **alcoolismo** (m) | [alkuul'iʒmu] |
| alcoholic (n) | **alcoólico** (m) | [alku'ɔliku] |
| syphilis | **sífilis** (f) | [s'ifiliʃ] |
| AIDS | **SIDA** (f) | [s'idɐ] |
| | | |
| tumor | **tumor** (m) | [tum'or] |
| malignant (adj) | **maligno** | [mɐl'ignu] |
| benign (adj) | **benigno** | [bən'ignu] |
| | | |
| fever | **febre** (f) | [f'ɛbrə] |
| malaria | **malâria** (f) | [mɐl'ariɐ] |
| gangrene | **gangrena** (f) | [gãgr'enɐ] |
| seasickness | **enjoo** (m) | [ẽʒ'ou] |
| epilepsy | **epilepsia** (f) | [epilɛps'iɐ] |
| | | |
| epidemic | **epidemia** (f) | [epidəm'iɐ] |
| typhus | **tifo** (m) | [t'ifu] |
| tuberculosis | **tuberculose** (f) | [tubɛrkul'ozə] |
| cholera | **cólera** (f) | [k'ɔlərɐ] |
| plague (bubonic ~) | **peste** (f) | [p'ɛʃtɐ] |

## 72. Symptoms. Treatments. Part 1

| | | |
|---|---|---|
| symptom | **sintoma** (m) | [sĩt'omɐ] |
| temperature | **temperatura** (f) | [tẽpərɐt'urɐ] |
| high temperature | **febre** (f) | [f'ɛbrə] |
| pulse | **pulso** (m) | [p'ulsu] |
| | | |
| giddiness | **vertigem** (f) | [vərt'iʒẽj] |
| hot (adj) | **quente** | [k'ẽtɐ] |

| vering | calafrio (m) | [kelefr'iu] |
| e (e.g., ~ face) | pâlido | [p'alidu] |
| | | |
| ıgh | tosse (f) | [t'ɔsə] |
| cough (vi) | tossir (vi) | [tɔs'ir] |
| sneeze (vi) | espirrar (vi) | [əʃpiʀ'ar] |
| ıt | desmaio (m) | [dəʒm'aju] |
| aint (vi) | desmaiar (vi) | [dəʒmɐj'ar] |
| | | |
| ise (hématome) | nódoa (f) negra | [n'ɔduɐ n'egrɐ] |
| np (lump) | galo (m) | [g'alu] |
| oruise oneself | magoar-se (vp) | [mɐgu'arsə] |
| ise (contusion) | pisadura (f) | [pizɐd'urɐ] |
| jet bruised | aleijar-se (vp) | [ɐlɐjʒ'arsə] |
| | | |
| imp (vi) | coxear (vi) | [kɔksj'ar] |
| location | deslocação (f) | [dəʒlukɐs'ãu] |
| dislocate (vt) | deslocar (vt) | [dəʒluk'ar] |
| cture | fratura (f) | [frat'urɐ] |
| nave a fracture | fraturar (vt) | [frɐtur'ar] |
| | | |
| (e.g., paper ~) | corte (m) | [k'ɔrtə] |
| cut oneself | cortar-se (vp) | [kurt'arsə] |
| eding | hemorragia (f) | [emuʀɐʒ'iɐ] |
| | | |
| n (injury) | queimadura (f) | [kɐjmɐd'urɐ] |
| scald oneself | queimar-se (vp) | [kɐjm'arsə] |
| | | |
| orick (vt) | picar (vt) | [pik'ar] |
| orick oneself | picar-se (vp) | [pik'arsə] |
| njure (vt) | lesionar (vt) | [ləziun'ar] |
| ıry | lesão (m) | [ləz'ãu] |
| und | ferida (f), ferimento (m) | [fər'idɐ], [fərim'ẽtu] |
| ıma | trauma (m) | [tr'aumɐ] |
| | | |
| oe delirious | delirar (vi) | [dəlir'ar] |
| stutter (vi) | gaguejar (vi) | [gɐgəʒ'ar] |
| nstroke | insolação (f) | [ĩsulɐs'ãu] |

## 3. Symptoms. Treatments. Part 2

| n | dor (f) | [dor] |
| nter (in foot, etc.) | farpa (f) | [f'arpɐ] |
| | | |
| eat (perspiration) | suor (m) | [su'ɔr] |
| sweat (perspire) | suar (vi) | [su'ar] |
| niting | vómito (m) | [v'ɔmitu] |
| nvulsions | convulsões (f pl) | [kõvuls'ojʃ] |
| gnant (adj) | grávida | [gr'avidɐ] |
| oe born | nascer (vi) | [nɐʃs'er] |

| | | |
|---|---|---|
| delivery, labor | **parto** (m) | [p'artu] |
| to deliver (~ a baby) | **dar á luz** | [dar a luʃ] |
| abortion | **aborto** (m) | [ɐb'ortu] |
| | | |
| breathing, respiration | **respiração** (f) | [ʀɐʃpiʀes'ãu] |
| inhalation | **inspiração** (f) | [ĩʃpiʀes'ãu] |
| exhalation | **expiração** (f) | [əʃpiʀes'ãu] |
| to exhale (vi) | **expirar** (vi) | [əʃpir'ar] |
| to inhale (vi) | **inspirar** (vi) | [ĩʃpir'ar] |
| | | |
| disabled person | **inválido** (m) | [ĩv'alidu] |
| cripple | **aleijado** (m) | [ɐlɐjʒ'adu] |
| drug addict | **toxicodependente** (m) | [tɔksikɔdəpẽd'ẽtə] |
| | | |
| deaf (adj) | **surdo** | [s'urdu] |
| dumb, mute | **mudo** | [m'udu] |
| deaf-and-dumb (adj) | **surdo-mudo** | [s'urdu m'udu] |
| | | |
| mad, insane (adj) | **louco** | [l'oku] |
| madman | **louco** (m) | [l'oku] |
| madwoman | **louca** (f) | [l'okɐ] |
| to go insane | **ficar louco** | [fik'ar l'oku] |
| | | |
| gene | **gene** (m) | [ʒ'ɛnə] |
| immunity | **imunidade** (f) | [imunid'adə] |
| hereditary (adj) | **hereditârio** | [eɾədit'ariu] |
| congenital (adj) | **congénito** | [kõʒ'ɛnitu] |
| | | |
| virus | **vírus** (m) | [v'iruʃ] |
| microbe | **micróbio** (m) | [mikr'ɔbiu] |
| bacterium | **bactéria** (f) | [bakt'ɛriɐ] |
| infection | **infeção** (f) | [ĩfɛs'ãu] |

## 74. Symptoms. Treatments. Part 3

| | | |
|---|---|---|
| hospital | **hospital** (m) | [ɔʃpit'al] |
| patient | **paciente** (m) | [pɐsj'ẽtə] |
| | | |
| diagnosis | **diagnóstico** (m) | [diɐgn'ɔʃtiku] |
| cure | **cura** (f) | [k'urɐ] |
| medical treatment | **tratamento** (m) **médico** | [tɾɐtɐm'ẽtu m'ɛdiku] |
| to get treatment | **curar-se** (vp) | [kur'arsə] |
| to treat (vt) | **tratar** (vt) | [tɾɐt'ar] |
| to nurse (look after) | **cuidar** (vt) | [kuid'ar] |
| care (nursing ~) | **cuidados** (m pl) | [kuid'aduʃ] |
| | | |
| operation, surgery | **operação** (f) | [ɔpɐɾes'ãu] |
| to bandage (head, limb) | **pôr uma ligadura** | [por 'umɐ ligɐd'urɐ] |
| bandaging | **ligadura** (f) | [ligɐd'urɐ] |
| vaccination | **vacinação** (f) | [vɐsinɐs'ãu] |

| /accinate (vt) | vacinar (vt) | [vɐsin'ar] |
| :ction, shot | injeção (f) | [ĩʒɛs'ãu] |
| ɟive an injection | dar uma injeção | [dar 'umɐ ĩʒɛs'ãu] |
| ick | ataque (m) | [ɐt'akɐ] |
| putation | amputação (f) | [ãputɐs'ãu] |
| imputate (vt) | amputar (vt) | [ãput'ar] |
| ɲa | coma (m) | [k'omɐ] |
| ɔe in a coma | estar em coma | [əʃt'ar ẽ k'omɐ] |
| ɔnsive care | reanimação (f) | [ʀiɐnimɐs'ãu] |
| 'ecover (~ from flu) | recuperar-se (vp) | [ʀɐkupər'arsə] |
| :te (patient's ~) | estado (m) | [əʃt'adu] |
| ɲsciousness | consciência (f) | [kõʃsj'ẽsiɐ] |
| ʲmory (faculty) | memória (f) | [məm'ɔriɐ] |
| ɵxtract (tooth) | tirar (vt) | [tir'ar] |
| ʲg | chumbo (m), obturação (f) | [ʃ'ũbu], [ɔbturɐs'ãu] |
| ȷll (a tooth) | chumbar, obturar (vt) | [ʃũb'ar], [ɔbtur'ar] |
| ɔnosis | hipnose (f) | [ipn'ɔzə] |
| ʲypnotize (vt) | hipnotizar (vt) | [ipnutiz'ar] |

## 5. Doctors

| :tor | médico (m) | [m'ɛdiku] |
| 'se | enfermeira (f) | [ẽfɐrm'ejʀɐ] |
| /ate physician | médico (m) pessoal | [m'ɛdiku pəsu'al] |
| ɲtist | dentista (m) | [dẽt'iʃtɐ] |
| ɲthalmologist | oculista (m) | [ɔkul'iʃtɐ] |
| ɵrnist | terapeuta (m) | [tərɐp'eutɐ] |
| ɟeon | cirurgião (m) | [sirurʒj'ãu] |
| /chiatrist | psiquiatra (m) | [psiki'atrɐ] |
| ȷiatrician | pediatra (m) | [pədj'atrɐ] |
| /chologist | psicólogo (m) | [psik'ɔlugu] |
| ʲecologist | ginecologista (m) | [ʒinɛkuluʒ'iʃtɐ] |
| 'diologist | cardiologista (m) | [kɐrdiuluʒ'iʃtɐ] |

## 6. Medicine. Drugs. Accessories

| ʲdicine, drug | medicamento (m) | [mədikɐm'ẽtu] |
| ɲedy | remédio (m) | [ʀəm'ɛdiu] |
| ɔrescribe (vt) | receitar (vt) | [ʀəsɐjt'ar] |
| :scription | receita (f) | [ʀəs'ejtɐ] |
| ȷlet, pill | comprimido (m) | [kõprim'idu] |
| ɵtment | pomada (f) | [pum'adɐ] |

| | | |
|---|---|---|
| ampule | ampola (f) | [ãp'ɔlɐ] |
| mixture | preparado (m) | [prɐpɐr'adu] |
| syrup | xarope (m) | [ʃɐr'ɔpɐ] |
| pill | cápsula (f) | [k'apsulɐ] |
| powder | remédio (m) em pó | [ʀɐm'ɛdiu ẽ pɔ] |

| | | |
|---|---|---|
| bandage | ligadura (f) | [liged'urɐ] |
| cotton wool | algodão (m) | [algud'ãu] |
| iodine | iodo (m) | [j'odu] |

| | | |
|---|---|---|
| Band-Aid | penso (m) rápido | [p'ẽsu ʀ'apidu] |
| eyedropper | conta-gotas (f) | [k'õtɐ g'otɐʃ] |
| thermometer | termómetro (m) | [tɐrm'ɔmɐtru] |
| syringe | seringa (f) | [sɐr'ĩgɐ] |

| | | |
|---|---|---|
| wheelchair | cadeira (m) de rodas | [kɐd'ejrɐ dɐ ʀ'ɔdɐʃ] |
| crutches | muletas (f pl) | [mul'etɐʃ] |

| | | |
|---|---|---|
| painkiller | analgésico (m) | [ɐnalʒ'ɛziku] |
| laxative | laxante (m) | [laʃ'ãtɐ] |
| spirit (ethanol) | álcool (m) | ['alkuɔl] |
| medicinal herbs | ervas (f pl) medicinais | ['ɛrvɐʃ mɐdisin'ajʃ] |
| herbal (~ tea) | de ervas | [dɐ 'ɛrvɐʃ] |

## 77. Smoking. Tobacco products

| | | |
|---|---|---|
| tobacco | tabaco (m) | [tɐb'aku] |
| cigarette | cigarro (m) | [sig'aʀu] |
| cigar | charuto (m) | [ʃɐr'utu] |
| pipe | cachimbo (m) | [kɐʃ'ĩbu] |
| pack (of cigarettes) | maço (m) | [m'asu] |

| | | |
|---|---|---|
| matches | fósforos (m pl) | [f'ɔʃfuruʃ] |
| matchbox | caixa (f) de fósforos | [k'ajʃɐ dɐ f'ɔʃfuruʃ] |
| lighter | isqueiro (m) | [iʃk'ejru] |
| ashtray | cinzeiro (m) | [sĩz'ejru] |
| cigarette case | cigarreira (f) | [sigɐʀ'ejrɐ] |

| | | |
|---|---|---|
| cigarette holder | boquilha (f) | [buk'iʎɐ] |
| filter (cigarette tip) | filtro (m) | [f'iltru] |

| | | |
|---|---|---|
| to smoke (vi, vt) | fumar (vi, vt) | [fum'ar] |
| to light a cigarette | acender um cigarro | [ɐsẽd'er ũ sig'aʀu] |

| | | |
|---|---|---|
| smoking | tabagismo (m) | [tɐbɐʒ'iʒmu] |
| smoker | fumador (m) | [fumɐd'or] |

| | | |
|---|---|---|
| stub, butt (of cigarette) | beata (f) | [bj'atɐ] |
| smoke, fumes | fumo (m) | [f'umu] |
| ash | cinza (f) | [s'ĩzɐ] |

# UMAN HABITAT

## ity

| | | |
|---|---|---|
| , town | cidade (f) | [sid'adə] |
| ɔital city | capital (f) | [kɐpit'al] |
| ɑge | aldeia (f) | [ald'eje] |
| | | |
| / map | mapa (m) da cidade | [m'apɐ dɐ sid'adə] |
| ʌntown | centro (m) da cidade | [s'ẽtru dɐ sid'adə] |
| ɔurb | subúrbio (m) | [sub'urbiu] |
| ɔurban (adj) | suburbano | [suburb'ɐnu] |
| | | |
| skirts | periferia (f) | [pərifər'iɐ] |
| /irons (suburbs) | arredores (m pl) | [ɐrɐd'orəʃ] |
| / block | quarteirão (m) | [kuɐrtejr'ɐ̃u] |
| idential block | quarteirão (m) residencial | [kuɐrtejr'ɐ̃u ʀɐzidẽsj'al] |
| | | |
| ffic | tráfego (m) | [tr'afɐgu] |
| ffic lights | semáforo (m) | [səm'afuru] |
| ɔlic transportation | transporte (m) público | [trɐ̃ʃp'ɔrtə p'ubliku] |
| ərsection | cruzamento (m) | [kruzam'ẽtu] |
| | | |
| sswalk | passadeira (f) para peões | [pɐsɐd'ejrɐ p'ɐrɐ pi'ojʃ] |
| Jestrian underpass | passagem (f) subterrânea | [pɐs'aʒẽj subtər'ɐniɐ] |
| ɔross (vt) | cruzar, atravessar (vt) | [kruz'ar], [ɐtrɐvəs'ar] |
| Jestrian | peão (m) | [pj'ɐ̃u] |
| əwalk | passeio (m) | [pɐs'eju] |
| | | |
| Jge | ponte (f) | [p'õtə] |
| ηk (riverbank) | marginal (f) | [mɐrʒin'al] |
| ntain | fonte (f) | [f'õtə] |
| | | |
| ɔe | alameda (f) | [ɐlɐm'edɐ] |
| ˙k | parque (m) | [p'arkə] |
| Jlevard | bulevar (m) | [buləv'ar] |
| Jare | praça (f) | [pr'asɐ] |
| ˙nue (wide street) | avenida (f) | [ɐvən'idɐ] |
| ɔet | rua (f) | [ʀ'uɐ] |
| ɔ street | travessa (f) | [trɐv'ɛsɐ] |
| ɑd end | beco (m) sem saída | [b'eku sẽ sɐ'idɐ] |
| ɹse | casa (f) | [k'azɐ] |
| Iding | edifício, prédio (m) | [edif'isiu], [pr'ɛdiu] |

| skyscraper | arranha-céus (m) | [ɐʀ'ɐɲɐ s'ɛuʃ] |
| facade | fachada (f) | [feʃ'adɐ] |
| roof | telhado (m) | [təʎ'adu] |
| window | janela (f) | [ʒɐn'ɛlɐ] |
| arch | arco (m) | ['arku] |
| column | coluna (f) | [kul'unɐ] |
| corner | esquina (f) | [əʃk'inɐ] |

| store window | montra (f) | [m'õtrɐ] |
| store sign | letreiro (m) | [lətr'ejru] |
| poster | cartaz (m) | [kɐrt'aʃ] |
| advertising poster | cartaz (m) publicitário | [kɐrt'aʃ publisit'ariu] |
| billboard | painel (m) publicitário | [pajn'ɛl publisit'ariu] |

| garbage, trash | lixo (m) | [l'iʃu] |
| garbage can | cesta (f) do lixo | [s'eʃtɐ du l'iʃu] |
| to litter (vi) | jogar lixo na rua | [ʒug'ar l'iʃu nɐ ʀ'uɐ] |
| garbage dump | aterro (m) sanitário | [ɐt'eʀu sɐnit'ariu] |

| phone booth | cabine (f) telefónica | [kɐb'inɐ tələf'ɔnikɐ] |
| lamppost | candeeiro (m) de rua | [kãdj'ejru də ʀ'uɐ] |
| bench (park ~) | banco (m) | [b'ãku] |

| police officer | polícia (m) | [pul'isiɐ] |
| police | polícia (f) | [pul'isiɐ] |
| beggar | mendigo (m) | [mẽd'igu] |
| homeless, bum | sem-abrigo (m) | [sɛnɐbr'igu] |

## 79. Urban institutions

| store | loja (f) | [l'ɔʒɐ] |
| drugstore, pharmacy | farmácia (f) | [fɐrm'asiɐ] |
| optical store | ótica (f) | ['ɔtikɐ] |
| shopping mall | centro (m) comercial | [s'ẽtru kumərsj'al] |
| supermarket | supermercado (m) | [supɛrmərk'adu] |

| bakery | padaria (f) | [pɐdɐr'iɐ] |
| baker | padeiro (m) | [pad'ejru] |
| candy store | pastelaria (f) | [pɐʃtələr'iɐ] |
| grocery store | mercearia (f) | [mərsiɐr'iɐ] |
| butcher shop | talho (m) | [t'aʎu] |

| produce store | loja (f) de legumes | [l'ɔʒɐ də ləg'uməʃ] |
| market | mercado (m) | [mərk'adu] |

| coffee house | café (m) | [kɐf'ɛ] |
| restaurant | restaurante (m) | [ʀəʃtaur'ãtə] |
| pub | cervejaria (f) | [sərvəʒɐr'iɐ] |
| pizzeria | pizzaria (f) | [pitzɐr'iɐ] |
| hair salon | salão (m) de cabeleireiro | [sɐl'ãu də kɐbələjr'ejru] |

|  |  |  |
|---|---|---|
| st office | correios (m pl) | [kuʀ'ɐjuʃ] |
| cleaners | lavandaria (f) | [levãdɐɾ'iɐ] |
| oto studio | estúdio (m) fotográfico | [əʃt'udiu futugɾ'afiku] |
| e store | sapataria (f) | [sɐpɐtɐɾ'iɐ] |
| okstore | livraria (f) | [livɾɐɾ'iɐ] |
| orting goods store | loja (f) de artigos de desporto | [l'ɔʒɐ də ɐɾt'iguʃ də dəʃp'ortu] |
| thes repair | reparação (f) de roupa | [ʀɐpɐɾɐs'ãu də ʀ'opɐ] |
| nal wear rental | aluguer (m) de roupa | [ɐlug'ɛr də ʀ'opɐ] |
| vie rental store | aluguer (m) de filmes | [ɐlug'ɛr də f'ilməʃ] |
| us | circo (m) | [s'irku] |
| ) | jardim (m) zoológico | [ʒɐrd'ĩ zuul'ɔʒiku] |
| vie theater | cinema (m) | [sin'emɐ] |
| seum | museu (m) | [muz'eu] |
| ary | biblioteca (f) | [bibliut'ɛkɐ] |
| ater | teatro (m) | [tə'atru] |
| era | ópera (f) | ['ɔpɐɾɐ] |
| htclub | clube (m) noturno | [kl'ubə nɔt'urnu] |
| ino | casino (m) | [kɐz'inu] |
| sque | mesquita (f) | [məʃk'itɐ] |
| agogue | sinagoga (f) | [sinɐg'ɔgɐ] |
| hedral | catedral (f) | [kɐtɐdɾ'al] |
| ple | templo (m) | [t'ẽplu] |
| rch | igreja (f) | [igɾ'ɐʒɐ] |
| lege | instituto (m) | [ĩʃtit'utu] |
| versity | universidade (f) | [univɐrsid'adə] |
| ool | escola (f) | [əʃk'ɔlɐ] |
| fecture | prefeitura (f) | [pɾəfejt'urɐ] |
| hall | câmara (f) municipal | [k'emɐɾɐ munisip'al] |
| el | hotel (m) | [ɔt'ɛl] |
| k | banco (m) | [b'ãku] |
| bassy | embaixada (f) | [ẽbajʃ'adɐ] |
| el agency | agência (f) de viagens | [ɐʒ'ẽsiɐ də vj'aʒẽjʃ] |
| ormation office | agência (f) de informações | [ɐʒ'ẽsiɐ də ĩfurmɐs'ojʃ] |
| ney exchange | casa (f) de câmbio | [k'azɐ də k'ãbiu] |
| way | metro (m) | [m'ɛtru] |
| spital | hospital (m) | [ɔʃpit'al] |
| station | posto (m) de gasolina | [p'oʃtu də gɐzul'inɐ] |
| king lot | parque (m) de estacionamento | [p'arkə də əʃtɐsiunɐm'ẽtu] |

## 80. Signs

| store sign | letreiro (m) | [lətr'ejɾu] |
| notice (written text) | inscrição (f) | [ĩʃkris'ãu] |
| poster | cartaz, póster (m) | [kɐrt'aʃ], [p'ɔʃtɛr] |
| direction sign | sinal (m) informativo | [sin'al ĩfurmɐt'ivu] |
| arrow (sign) | seta (f) | [s'ɛtɐ] |

| caution | aviso (m), advertência (f) | [ɐv'izu], [ɐdvərt'ẽsiɐ] |
| warning sign | sinal (m) de aviso | [sin'al də ɐv'izu] |
| to warn (vt) | avisar, advertir (vt) | [ɐviz'ar], [ɐdvərt'ir] |

| day off | dia (m) de folga | [d'iɐ də f'ɔlgɐ] |
| timetable (schedule) | horário (m) | [ɔr'ariu] |
| opening hours | horário (m) de funcionamento | [ɔr'ariu də fũsiunɐm'ẽtu] |

| WELCOME! | BEM-VINDOS! | [bẽjv'ĩduʃ] |
| ENTRANCE | ENTRADA | [ẽtr'adɐ] |
| EXIT | SAÍDA | [sɐ'idɐ] |

| PUSH | EMPURRE | [ẽp'uʀə] |
| PULL | PUXE | [p'uʃə] |
| OPEN | ABERTO | [ɐb'ɛrtu] |
| CLOSED | FECHADO | [fəʃ'adu] |

| WOMEN | MULHER | [muʎ'ɛr] |
| MEN | HOMEM | ['ɔmẽj] |

| DISCOUNTS | DESCONTOS | [dəʃk'õtuʃ] |
| SALE | SALDOS | [s'alduʃ] |
| NEW! | NOVIDADE! | [nuvid'adə] |
| FREE | GRÁTIS | [gr'atiʃ] |

| ATTENTION! | ATENÇÃO! | [ɐtẽs'ãu] |
| NO VACANCIES | NÃO HÁ VAGAS | [n'ãu a v'agɐʃ] |
| RESERVED | RESERVADO | [ʀəzərv'adu] |

| ADMINISTRATION | ADMINISTRAÇÃO | [ɐdminiʃtrɐs'ãu] |
| STAFF ONLY | SOMENTE PESSOAL AUTORIZADO | [sɔm'ẽtə pəsu'al auturiz'adu] |

| BEWARE OF THE DOG! | CUIDADO CÃO FEROZ | [kuid'adu k'ãu fər'ɔʃ] |
| NO SMOKING | PROIBIDO FUMAR! | [pruib'idu fum'ar] |
| DO NOT TOUCH! | NÃO TOCAR | [n'ãu tuk'ar] |

| DANGEROUS | PERIGOSO | [pərig'ozu] |
| DANGER | PERIGO | [pər'igu] |
| HIGH TENSION | ALTA TENSÃO | ['altɐ tẽs'ãu] |
| NO SWIMMING! | PROIBIDO NADAR | [pruib'idu nəd'ar] |
| OUT OF ORDER | AVARIADO | [ɐvərj'adu] |

| AMMABLE | INFLAMÁVEL | [ĩflem'avɛl] |
| RBIDDEN | PROIBIDO | [pruib'idu] |
| TRESPASSING! | ENTRADA PROIBIDA | [ẽtr'adɐ pruib'idɐ] |
| ET PAINT | CUIDADO TINTA FRESCA | [kuid'adu t'ĩtɐ fr'eʃkɐ] |

## 1. Urban transportation

| s | autocarro (m) | [autɔk'aʀu] |
| eetcar | elétrico (m) | [el'ɛtriku] |
| ley | troleicarro (m) | [trulɛik'aʀu] |
| te (of bus) | itinerário (m) | [itinɐr'ariu] |
| nber (e.g., bus ~) | número (m) | [n'umɐru] |
| ɟo by ... | ir de ... | [ir dɐ] |
| ɟet on (~ the bus) | entrar em ... | [ẽtr'ar ẽj] |
| ɟet off ... | descer de ... | [dɐʃs'er dɐ] |
| p (e.g., bus ~) | paragem (f) | [pɐr'aʒẽj] |
| ɕt stop | próxima paragem (f) | [pr'ɔsimɐ pɐr'aʒẽj] |
| ninus | ponto (m) final | [p'õtu fin'al] |
| ɪedule | horário (m) | [ɔr'ariu] |
| ʋait (vt) | esperar (vt) | [ɐʃpɐr'ar] |
| et | bilhete (m) | [biʎ'etɐ] |
| ɘ | custo (m) do bilhete | [k'uʃtu du biʎ'etɐ] |
| ɕhier (ticket seller) | bilheteiro (m) | [biʎɐt'ejru] |
| et inspection | controlo (m) dos bilhetes | [kõtr'olu duʃ biʎ'etɐʃ] |
| ɪductor | revisor (m) | [ʀɐviz'or] |
| ɔe late (for ...) | atrasar-se (vp) | [etrez'arsɐ] |
| niss (~ the train, etc.) | perder (vt) | [pɐrd'er] |
| ɔe in a hurry | estar com pressa | [ɐʃt'ar kõ pr'ɛsɐ] |
| i, cab | táxi (m) | [t'aksi] |
| i driver | taxista (m) | [taks'iʃtɐ] |
| taxi | de táxi | [dɐ t'aksi] |
| i stand | praça (f) de táxis | [pr'asɐ dɐ t'aksiʃ] |
| ɕall a taxi | chamar um táxi | [ʃɐm'ar ũ t'aksi] |
| ake a taxi | apanhar um táxi | [ɐpɐɲ'ar ũ t'aksi] |
| fic | tráfego (m) | [tr'afɐgu] |
| ffic jam | engarrafamento (m) | [ẽgɐʀɐfɐm'ẽtu] |
| h hour | horas (f pl) de ponta | ['ɔrɐʃ dɐ p'õtɐ] |
| ɔark (vi) | estacionar (vi) | [ɐʃtɐsiun'ar] |
| ɔark (vt) | estacionar (vt) | [ɐʃtɐsiun'ar] |
| ɕking lot | parque (m) de estacionamento | [p'arkɐ dɐ ɐʃtɐsiunɐm'ẽtu] |
| ɔway | metro (m) | [m'ɛtru] |

| station | estação (f) | [əʃtes'ãu] |
| to take the subway | ir de metro | [ir də m'ɛtru] |
| train | comboio (m) | [kõb'ɔju] |
| train station | estação (f) | [əʃtes'ãu] |

## 82. Sightseeing

| monument | monumento (m) | [munum'ẽtu] |
| fortress | fortaleza (f) | [furtel'ezɐ] |
| palace | palácio (m) | [pel'asiu] |
| castle | castelo (m) | [keʃt'ɛlu] |
| tower | torre (f) | [t'oʀə] |
| mausoleum | mausoléu (m) | [mauzul'ɛu] |

| architecture | arquitetura (f) | [ɐrkitɛt'urɐ] |
| medieval (adj) | medieval | [mədiɛv'al] |
| ancient (adj) | antigo | [ãt'igu] |
| national (adj) | nacional | [nɐsiun'al] |
| well-known (adj) | conhecido | [kuɲəs'idu] |

| tourist | turista (m) | [tur'iʃtɐ] |
| guide (person) | guia (m) | [g'iɐ] |
| excursion, guided tour | excursão (f) | [əʃkurs'ãu] |
| to show (vt) | mostrar (vt) | [muʃtr'ar] |
| to tell (vt) | contar (vt) | [kõt'ar] |

| to find (vt) | encontrar (vt) | [ẽkõtr'ar] |
| to get lost (lose one's way) | perder-se (vp) | [pərd'ersə] |
| map (e.g., subway ~) | mapa (m) | [m'apɐ] |
| map (e.g., city ~) | mapa (m) | [m'apɐ] |

| souvenir, gift | lembrança (f), presente (m) | [lẽbr'ãsɐ], [prəz'ẽtə] |
| gift shop | loja (f) de presentes | [l'ɔʒɐ də prəz'ẽtəʃ] |
| to take pictures | fotografar (vt) | [futugrɐf'ar] |
| to be photographed | fotografar-se | [futugrɐf'arsə] |

## 83. Shopping

| to buy (purchase) | comprar (vt) | [kõpr'ar] |
| purchase | compra (f) | [k'õprɐ] |
| to go shopping | fazer compras | [fɐz'er k'õprɐʃ] |
| shopping | compras (f pl) | [k'õprɐʃ] |

| to be open (ab. store) | estar aberta | [əʃt'ar ɐb'ɛrtɐ] |
| to be closed | estar fechada | [əʃt'ar feʃ'adɐ] |

| footwear | calçado (m) | [kals'adu] |
| clothes, clothing | roupa (f) | [ʀ'opɐ] |

| smetics | cosméticos (m pl) | [kuʒm'ɛtikuʃ] |
| d products | alimentos (m pl) | [ɐlim'ẽtuʃ] |
| present | presente (m) | [prɐz'ẽtɐ] |
| | | |
| esman | vendedor (m) | [vẽdɐd'or] |
| eswoman | vendedora (f) | [vẽdɐd'orɐ] |
| | | |
| ck out, cash desk | caixa (f) | [k'ajʃɐ] |
| ror | espelho (m) | [ɐʃp'ɐʎu] |
| nter (in shop) | balcão (m) | [balk'ãu] |
| ng room | cabine (f) de provas | [kɐb'inɐ dɐ pr'ɔvɐʃ] |
| | | |
| ry on | provar (vt) | [pruv'ar] |
| it (ab. dress, etc.) | servir (vi) | [sɐrv'ir] |
| ike (I like ...) | gostar (vt) | [guʃt'ar] |
| | | |
| e | preço (m) | [pr'esu] |
| e tag | etiqueta (f) de preço | [etik'etɐ dɐ pr'esu] |
| ost (vt) | custar (vt) | [kuʃt'ar] |
| w much? | Quanto? | [ku'ãtu] |
| count | desconto (m) | [dɐʃk'õtu] |
| | | |
| xpensive (adj) | não caro | [n'ãu k'aru] |
| ap (adj) | barato | [bɐr'atu] |
| ensive (adj) | caro | [k'aru] |
| expensive | É caro | [ɛ k'aru] |
| | | |
| tal (n) | aluguer (m) | [ɐlug'ɛr] |
| ent (~ a tuxedo) | alugar (vt) | [ɐlug'ar] |
| dit | crédito (m) | [kr'ɛditu] |
| credit (adv) | a crédito | [ɐ kr'ɛditu] |

## 4. Money

| ney | dinheiro (m) | [diɲ'ejru] |
| rency exchange | câmbio (m) | [k'ãbiu] |
| change rate | taxa (f) de câmbio | [t'aʃɐ dɐ k'ãbiu] |
| M | Caixa Multibanco (m) | [k'ajʃɐ multib'ãku] |
| n | moeda (f) | [mu'ɛdɐ] |
| | | |
| lar | dólar (m) | [d'ɔlar] |
| o | euro (m) | ['euru] |
| | | |
| | lira (f) | [l'irɐ] |
| utschmark | marco (m) | [m'arku] |
| nc | franco (m) | [fr'ãku] |
| und sterling | libra (f) esterlina | [l'ibrɐ ɐʃtɐrl'inɐ] |
| n | iene (m) | [j'ɛnɐ] |
| ot | dívida (f) | [d'ividɐ] |
| otor | devedor (m) | [dɐvɐd'or] |

| to lend (money) | emprestar (vt) | [ẽpɾəʃt'aɾ] |
| to borrow (vi, vt) | pedir emprestado | [pəd'iɾ ẽpɾəʃt'adu] |

| bank | banco (m) | [b'ãku] |
| account | conta (f) | [k'õtɐ] |
| to deposit (vt) | depositar (vt) | [dəpuzit'aɾ] |
| to deposit into the account | depositar na conta | [dəpuzit'aɾ nɐ k'õtɐ] |
| to withdraw (vt) | levantar (vt) | [ləvãt'aɾ] |

| credit card | cartão (m) de crédito | [kɐɾt'ãu də kɾ'ɛditu] |
| cash | dinheiro (m) vivo | [diɲ'ejɾu v'ivu] |
| check | cheque (m) | [ʃ'ɛkə] |
| to write a check | passar um cheque | [pɐs'aɾ ũ ʃ'ɛkə] |
| checkbook | livro (m) de cheques | [l'ivɾu də ʃ'ɛkəʃ] |

| wallet | carteira (f) | [kɐɾt'ejɾɐ] |
| change purse | porta-moedas (m) | [p'ɔɾtɐ mu'ɛdeʃ] |
| billfold | carteira (f) | [kɐɾt'ejɾɐ] |
| safe | cofre (m) | [k'ɔfɾə] |

| heir | herdeiro (m) | [eɾd'ejɾu] |
| inheritance | herança (f) | [eɾ'ãsɐ] |
| fortune (wealth) | fortuna (f) | [fuɾt'unɐ] |

| lease, rent | arrendamento (m) | [ɐʀẽdɐm'ẽtu] |
| rent money | renda (f) de casa | [ʀ'ẽdɐ də k'azɐ] |
| to rent (sth from sb) | alugar (vt) | [ɐlug'aɾ] |

| price | preço (m) | [pɾ'esu] |
| cost | custo (m) | [k'uʃtu] |
| sum | soma (f) | [s'omɐ] |

| to spend (vt) | gastar (vt) | [gɐʃt'aɾ] |
| expenses | gastos (m pl) | [g'aʃtuʃ] |
| to economize (vi, vt) | economizar (vi) | [ekɔnumiz'aɾ] |
| economical | económico | [ekun'ɔmiku] |

| to pay (vi, vt) | pagar (vt) | [pɐg'aɾ] |
| payment | pagamento (m) | [pɐgɐm'ẽtu] |
| change (give the ~) | troco (m) | [tɾ'oku] |

| tax | imposto (m) | [ĩp'ɔʃtu] |
| fine | multa (f) | [m'ultɐ] |
| to fine (vt) | multar (vt) | [mult'aɾ] |

## 85. Post. Postal service

| post office | correios (m pl) | [kuʀ'ejuʃ] |
| mail (letters, etc.) | correio (m) | [kuʀ'eju] |
| mailman | carteiro (m) | [kɐɾt'ejɾu] |

| ening hours | **horário** (m) | [ɔr'ariu] |
| er | **carta** (f) | [k'artɐ] |
| istered letter | **carta** (f) **registada** | [k'artɐ ʀɐʒiʃt'adɐ] |
| stcard | **postal** (m) | [puʃt'al] |
| egram | **telegrama** (m) | [tɐlɐgr'ɐmɐ] |
| cel | **encomenda** (f) **postal** | [ẽkum'ẽdɐ puʃt'al] |
| ney transfer | **remessa** (f) **de dinheiro** | [ʀɐm'ɛsɐ dɐ diɲ'ɐjru] |
| eceive (vt) | **receber** (vt) | [ʀɐsɐb'er] |
| end (vt) | **enviar** (vt) | [ẽvj'ar] |
| ding | **envio** (m) | [ẽv'iu] |
| dress | **endereço** (m) | [ẽdɐr'esu] |
| code | **código** (m) **postal** | [k'ɔdigu puʃt'al] |
| der | **remetente** (m) | [ʀɐmɐt'ẽtɐ] |
| eiver, addressee | **destinatário** (m) | [dɐʃtinɐt'ariu] |
| ne | **nome** (m) | [n'omɐ] |
| ily name | **apelido** (m) | [ɐpɐl'idu] |
| e (of postage) | **tarifa** (f) | [tɐr'ifɐ] |
| ndard (adj) | **normal** | [nɔrm'al] |
| nomical (adj) | **económico** | [ekun'ɔmiku] |
| ght | **peso** (m) | [p'ezu] |
| weigh up (vt) | **pesar** (vt) | [pɐz'ar] |
| velope | **envelope** (m) | [ẽvɐl'ɔpɐ] |
| tage stamp | **selo** (m) | [s'elu] |
| stamp an envelope | **colar o selo** | [kul'ar u s'elu] |

# Dwelling. House. Home

## 86. House. Dwelling

| | | |
|---|---|---|
| house | casa (f) | [k'azɐ] |
| at home (adv) | em casa | [ẽ k'azɐ] |
| courtyard | pàtio (m) | [p'atiu] |
| fence | cerca (f) | [s'erkɐ] |
| | | |
| brick (n) | tijolo (m) | [tiʒ'olu] |
| brick (as adj) | de tijolos | [də tiʒ'oluʃ] |
| stone (n) | pedra (f) | [p'ɛdrɐ] |
| stone (as adj) | de pedra | [də p'ɛdrɐ] |
| concrete (n) | betão (m) | [bət'ãu] |
| concrete (as adj) | de betão | [də bət'ãu] |
| | | |
| new (new-built) | novo | [n'ovu] |
| old (adj) | velho | [v'ɛʎu] |
| decrepit (house) | decrépito | [dəkr'ɛpitu] |
| modern (adj) | moderno | [mud'ɛrnu] |
| multistory (adj) | de muitos andares | [də m'ujtuʃ ãd'arəʃ] |
| high (adj) | alto | ['altu] |
| | | |
| floor, story | andar (m) | [ãd'ar] |
| single-story (adj) | de um andar | [də ũ ãd'ar] |
| ground floor | andar (m) de baixo | [ãdar də b'ajʃu] |
| top floor | andar (m) de cima | [ãdar də s'imɐ] |
| | | |
| roof | telhado (m) | [təʎ'adu] |
| chimney (stack) | chaminé (f) | [ʃemin'ɛ] |
| roof tiles | telha (f) | [t'eʎɐ] |
| tiled (adj) | de telha | [də t'eʎɐ] |
| loft (attic) | sótão (m) | [s'ɔtãu] |
| | | |
| window | janela (f) | [ʒen'ɛlɐ] |
| glass | vidro (m) | [v'idru] |
| window ledge | parapeito (m) | [pɐrɐp'ejtu] |
| shutters | portadas (f pl) | [purt'adəʃ] |
| | | |
| wall | parede (f) | [pɐr'edɐ] |
| balcony | varanda (f) | [vɐr'ãdɐ] |
| downspout | tubo (m) de queda | [t'ubu də k'ɛdɐ] |
| upstairs (to be ~) | em cima | [ẽ s'imɐ] |
| to go upstairs | subir (vi) | [sub'ir] |
| to come down | descer (vi) | [dəʃs'er] |
| to move (to new premises) | mudar-se (vp) | [mud'arsə] |

## 7. House. Entrance. Lift

| rance | entrada (f) | [ẽtr'adə] |
|---|---|---|
| irs (stairway) | escada (f) | [əʃk'adə] |
| ps | degraus (m pl) | [dəgr'auʃ] |
| iisters | corrimão (m) | [kuʀim'ãu] |
| by (hotel ~) | hall (m) | [ɔl] |
| ilbox | caixa (f) de correio | [k'ajʃe də kuʀ'eju] |
| sh container | caixote (m) do lixo | [kajʃ'otə du l'iʃu] |
| sh chute | conduta (f) do lixo | [kõd'utə du l'iʃu] |
| vator | elevador (m) | [eləved'or] |
| ght elevator | elevador (m) de carga | [eləved'or də k'argə] |
| vator cage | cabine (f) | [kɐb'inə] |
| ake the elevator | pegar o elevador | [pəg'ar u eləved'or] |
| artment | apartamento (m) | [ɐpɐrtem'ẽtu] |
| idents, inhabitants | moradores (m pl) | [murɐd'orəʃ] |
| ghbor (masc.) | vizinho (m) | [viz'iɲu] |
| ghbor (fem.) | vizinha (f) | [viz'iɲɐ] |
| ghbors | vizinhos (pl) | [viz'iɲuʃ] |

## 8. House. Electricity

| ctricity | eletricidade (f) | [elɛtrisid'adə] |
|---|---|---|
| it bulb | lâmpada (f) | [l'ãpedə] |
| itch | interruptor (m) | [ĩtəʀupt'or] |
| e | fusível (m) | [fuz'ivɛl] |
| ɔle, wire (electric ~) | fio, cabo (m) | [f'iu], [k'abu] |
| ing | instalação (f) elétrica | [ĩʃteles'ãu el'ɛtrikə] |
| ctricity meter | contador (m) de eletricidade | [kõted'or də elɛtrisid'adə] |
| idings | leitura (f) | [lejt'urɐ] |

## 9. House. Doors. Locks

| ɔr | porta (f) | [p'ɔrtə] |
|---|---|---|
| iicle gate | portão (m) | [purt'ãu] |
| idle, doorknob | maçaneta (f) | [mɐsɐn'etɐ] |
| unlock (unbolt) | destrancar (vt) | [dəʃtrãk'ar] |
| ɔpen (vt) | abrir (vt) | [ɐbr'ir] |
| :lose (vt) | fechar (vt) | [fəʃ'ar] |
| / | chave (f) | [ʃ'avə] |
| ich (of keys) | molho (m) | [m'oʎu] |

| | | |
|---|---|---|
| to creak (door hinge) | ranger (vi) | [ʀãʒ'er] |
| creak | rangido (m) | [ʀãʒ'idu] |
| hinge (of door) | dobradiça (f) | [dubʀed'isɐ] |
| doormat | tapete (m) de entrada | [tɐp'etə də ẽtr'adɐ] |

| | | |
|---|---|---|
| door lock | fechadura (f) | [fəʃed'uʀɐ] |
| keyhole | buraco (m) da fechadura | [bur'aku də fəʃed'uʀɐ] |
| bolt (sliding bar) | ferrolho (m) | [fəʀ'ɔʎu] |
| door latch | ferrolho, fecho (m) | [fəʀ'ɔʎu], [f'eʃu] |
| padlock | cadeado (m) | [kɐdj'adu] |

| | | |
|---|---|---|
| to ring (~ the door bell) | tocar (vt) | [tuk'ar] |
| ringing (sound) | toque (m) | [t'ɔkə] |
| doorbell | campainha (f) | [kãpɐ'iɲɐ] |
| doorbell button | botão (m) | [but'ãu] |
| knock (at the door) | batida (f) | [bɐt'idɐ] |
| to knock (vi) | bater (vi) | [bɐt'er] |

| | | |
|---|---|---|
| code | código (m) | [k'ɔdigu] |
| code lock | fechadura (f) de código | [fəʃed'uʀɐ də k'ɔdigu] |
| door phone | telefone (m) de porta | [tələf'onə də p'ɔrtɐ] |
| number (on the door) | número (m) | [n'uməru] |
| doorplate | placa (f) de porta | [pl'akɐ də p'ɔrtɐ] |
| peephole | vigia (f), olho (m) mágico | [viʒ'iɐ], ['oʎu m'aʒiku] |

## 90. Country house

| | | |
|---|---|---|
| village | aldeia (f) | [ald'ejɐ] |
| vegetable garden | horta (f) | ['ɔrtɐ] |
| fence | cerca (f) | [s'erkɐ] |

| | | |
|---|---|---|
| picket fence | paliçada (f) | [pɐlis'adɐ] |
| wicket gate | cancela (f) | [kãs'ɛlɐ] |

| | | |
|---|---|---|
| granary | celeiro (m) | [səl'ejru] |
| cellar | adega (f) | [ɐd'ɛgɐ] |

| | | |
|---|---|---|
| shed (in garden) | galpão, barracão (m) | [galp'ãu], [bɐʀɐk'ãu] |
| well (water) | poço (m) | [p'osu] |

| | | |
|---|---|---|
| stove (wood-fired ~) | fogão (f) | [fug'ãu] |
| to stoke the stove | atiçar o fogo | [ɐtis'ar u f'ogu] |

| | | |
|---|---|---|
| firewood | lenha (f) | [l'eɲɐ] |
| log (firewood) | acha, lenha (f) | [aʃɐ], [l'eɲɐ] |

| | | |
|---|---|---|
| veranda, stoop | varanda (f) | [veʀ'ãdɐ] |
| terrace (patio) | alpendre (m) | [alp'ẽdrə] |
| front steps | degraus (m pl) de entrada | [dəgr'auʃ də ẽtr'adɐ] |
| swing (hanging seat) | balouço (m) | [bɐl'osu] |

## 1. Villa. Mansion

| | | |
|---|---|---|
| .ntry house | **casa** (f) **de campo** | [k'azɐ də k'ãpu] |
| a (by sea) | **vila** (f) | [v'ilɐ] |
| g (of building) | **ala** (f) | ['alɐ] |
| den | **jardim** (m) | [ʒɐrd'ĩ] |
| k | **parque** (m) | [p'arkə] |
| ɔical greenhouse | **estufa** (f) | [əʃt'ufɐ] |
| ook after (garden, etc.) | **cuidar de ...** | [kuidar də] |
| mming pool | **piscina** (f) | [piʃs'inɐ] |
| n | **ginàsio** (m) | [ʒin'aziu] |
| nis court | **campo** (m) **de ténis** | [k'ãpu də t'ɛniʃ] |
| ne theater room | **cinema** (m) | [sin'emɐ] |
| age | **garagem** (f) | [gɐr'aʒẽj] |
| ⁄ate property | **propriedade** (f) **privada** | [prupriɛd'adə priv'adɐ] |
| ⁄ate land | **terreno** (m) **privado** | [təʀ'enu priv'adu] |
| rning (caution) | **advertência** (f) | [ɐdvərt'ẽsiɐ] |
| rning sign | **sinal** (m) **de aviso** | [sin'al də ɐv'izu] |
| ;urity | **guarda** (f) | [gu'ardɐ] |
| ;urity guard | **guarda** (m) | [gu'ardɐ] |
| glar alarm | **alarme** (m) | [ɐl'armə] |

## 2. Castle. Palace

| | | |
|---|---|---|
| ;tle | **castelo** (m) | [kɐʃt'ɛlu] |
| ace | **palàcio** (m) | [pɐl'asiu] |
| ress | **fortaleza** (f) | [furtɐl'ezɐ] |
| ll (round castle) | **muralha** (f) | [mur'aʎɐ] |
| ⁄er | **torre** (f) | [t'oʀɐ] |
| ɐp, donjon | **torre** (f) **de menagem** | [t'oʀɐ də mɐn'aʒẽj] |
| tcullis | **grade** (f) | [gr'adə] |
| ierground passage | **passagem** (f) **subterránea** | [pɐs'aʒẽj subtər'ɐniɐ] |
| at | **fosso** (m) | [f'osu] |
| ain | **corrente, cadeia** (f) | [kuʀ'ẽtɐ], [kɐd'ɐjɐ] |
| ɔw loop | **seteira** (f) | [sɐt'ɐjrɐ] |
| gnificent (adj) | **magnífico** | [magn'ifiku] |
| jestic (adj) | **majestoso** | [mɐʒɐʃt'ozu] |
| ɔregnable (adj) | **inexpugnàvel** | [inəʃpugn'avɛl] |
| dieval (adj) | **medieval** | [mədiɛv'al] |

## 93. Apartment

| | | |
|---|---|---|
| apartment | apartamento (m) | [ɐpɐrtɐm'ẽtu] |
| room | quarto (m) | [ku'artu] |
| bedroom | quarto (m) de dormir | [ku'artu də durm'ir] |
| dining room | sala (f) de jantar | [s'alɐ də ʒãt'ar] |
| living room | sala (f) de estar | [s'alɐ də əʃt'ar] |
| study (home office) | escritório (m) | [əʃkrit'ɔriu] |
| | | |
| entry room | antessala (f) | [ãtəs'alɐ] |
| bathroom | quarto (m) de banho | [ku'artu də b'eɲu] |
| half bath | quarto (m) de banho | [ku'artu də b'eɲu] |
| | | |
| ceiling | teto (m) | [t'ɛtu] |
| floor | chão, soalho (m) | [ʃ'ãu], [su'aʎu] |
| corner | canto (m) | [k'ãtu] |

## 94. Apartment. Cleaning

| | | |
|---|---|---|
| to clean (vi, vt) | arrumar, limpar (vt) | [ɐʀum'ar], [lĩp'ar] |
| to put away (to stow) | arrumar, guardar (vt) | [ɐʀum'ar], [guɐrd'ar] |
| dust | pó (m) | [pɔ] |
| dusty (adj) | empoeirado | [ẽpɔejr'adu] |
| to dust (vt) | limpar o pó | [lĩp'ar u pɔ] |
| vacuum cleaner | aspirador (m) | [ɐʃpirɐd'or] |
| to vacuum (vt) | aspirar (vt) | [ɐʃpir'ar] |
| | | |
| to sweep (vi, vt) | varrer (vt) | [vɐʀ'er] |
| sweepings | varredura (f), cisco (m) | [vɐʀɐd'urɐ], [s'iʃku] |
| order | arrumação (f), ordem (f) | [ɐʀumɐs'ãu], ['ɔrdẽj] |
| disorder, mess | desordem (f) | [dəz'ɔrdẽj] |
| | | |
| mop | esfregona (f) | [əʃfrɐg'onɐ] |
| dust cloth | pano (m), trapo (m) | [p'ɐnu], [tr'apu] |
| broom | vassoura (f) | [vɐs'orɐ] |
| dustpan | pà (f) de lixo | [pa də l'iʃu] |

## 95. Furniture. Interior

| | | |
|---|---|---|
| furniture | mobiliàrio (m) | [mubilj'ariu] |
| table | mesa (f) | [m'ezɐ] |
| chair | cadeira (f) | [kɐd'ejrɐ] |
| bed | cama (f) | [k'ɐmɐ] |
| couch, sofa | divã (m) | [div'ã] |
| armchair | cadeirão (m) | [kɐdejr'ãu] |
| bookcase | biblioteca (f) | [bibliut'ɛkɐ] |
| shelf | prateleira (f) | [prɐtəl'ejrɐ] |

| of shelves | estante (f) | [əʃt'ãtə] |
| rdrobe | guarda-vestidos (m) | [gu'ardɐ vəʃt'iduʃ] |
| it rack | cabide (m) de parede | [kɐb'idə də pɐr'edə] |
| it stand | cabide (m) de pé | [kɐb'idə də pɛ] |
| sser | cómoda (f) | [k'ɔmudɐ] |
| fee table | mesinha (f) de centro | [məz'iɲɐ də s'ẽtru] |
| ror | espelho (m) | [əʃp'ɐʎu] |
| pet | tapete (m) | [tɐp'etə] |
| , small carpet | tapete (m) pequeno | [tɐp'etə pək'enu] |
| place | lareira (f) | [lɐr'ɐjrɐ] |
| idle | vela (f) | [v'ɛlɐ] |
| idlestick | castiçal (m) | [kɐʃtis'al] |
| pes | cortinas (f pl) | [kurt'inɐʃ] |
| lpaper | papel (m) de parede | [pɐp'ɛl də pɐr'edə] |
| ids (jalousie) | estores (f pl) | [əʃt'orəʃ] |
| ie lamp | candeeiro (m) de mesa | [kãdj'ejru də m'ezɐ] |
| il lamp (sconce) | candeeiro (m) de parede | [kãdj'ejru də pɐr'edə] |
| ir lamp | candeeiro (m) de pé | [kãdj'ejru də pɛ] |
| indelier | lustre (m) | [l'uʃtrə] |
| (of chair, table) | perna (f) | [p'ɛrnɐ] |
| irest | braço (m) | [br'asu] |
| ːk (backrest) | costas (f pl) | [k'ɔʃtɐʃ] |
| iwer | gaveta (f) | [gɐv'etɐ] |

## 6. Bedding

| iclothes | roupa (f) de cama | [ʀ'opɐ də k'ɐmɐ] |
| ɔw | almofada (f) | [almuf'adɐ] |
| ɔwcase | fronha (f) | [fr'oɲɐ] |
| nket (comforter) | cobertor (m) | [kubɐrt'or] |
| ɛet | lençol (m) | [lẽs'ɔl] |
| ɪspread | colcha (f) | [k'olʃɐ] |

## 7. Kitchen

| ːhen | cozinha (f) | [kuz'iɲɐ] |
| ː | gàs (m) | [g'aʃ] |
| ː cooker | fogão (m) a gàs | [fug'ãu ɐ g'aʃ] |
| ctric cooker | fogão (m) elétrico | [fug'ãu el'ɛtriku] |
| ɛn | forno (m) | [f'ornu] |
| ːrowave oven | forno (m) de micro-ondas | [f'ornu də mikrɔ'õdɐʃ] |
| igerator | frigorífico (m) | [frigur'ifiku] |

| freezer | congelador (m) | [kõʒɐlɐd'or] |
| dishwasher | màquina (f) de lavar louça | [m'akinɐ dɐ lɐv'ar l'osɐ] |

| meat grinder | moedor (m) de carne | [muɐd'or dɐ k'arnɐ] |
| juicer | espremedor (m) | [ɐʃprɐmɐd'or] |
| toaster | torradeira (f) | [tuʀɐd'ɐjʀɐ] |
| mixer | batedeira (f) | [bɐtɐd'ɐjʀɐ] |

| coffee maker | màquina (f) de café | [m'akinɐ dɐ kɐf'ɛ] |
| coffee pot | cafeteira (f) | [kɐfɐt'ɐjʀɐ] |
| coffee grinder | moinho (m) de café | [mu'iɲu dɐ kɐf'ɛ] |

| kettle | chaleira (f) | [ʃɐl'ɐjʀɐ] |
| teapot | bule (m) | [b'ulɐ] |
| lid | tampa (f) | [t'ãpɐ] |
| tea strainer | coador (f) de chà | [kuɐd'or dɐ ʃa] |

| spoon | colher (f) | [kuʎ'ɛr] |
| teaspoon | colher (f) de chà | [kuʎ'ɛr dɐ ʃa] |
| tablespoon | colher (f) de sopa | [kuʎ'ɛr dɐ s'opɐ] |
| fork | garfo (m) | [g'arfu] |
| knife | faca (f) | [f'akɐ] |

| tableware (dishes) | louça (f) | [l'osɐ] |
| plate (dinner ~) | prato (m) | [pr'atu] |
| saucer | pires (m) | [p'irɐʃ] |

| shot glass | càlice (m) | [k'alisɐ] |
| glass (~ of water) | copo (m) | [k'ɔpu] |
| cup | chàvena (f) | [ʃ'avɐnɐ] |

| sugar bowl | açucareiro (m) | [ɐsukɐr'ɐjru] |
| salt shaker | saleiro (m) | [sɐl'ɐjru] |
| pepper shaker | pimenteiro (m) | [pimẽt'ɐjru] |
| butter dish | manteigueira (f) | [mãtiig'ɐjʀɐ] |

| saucepan | panela (f) | [pɐn'ɛlɐ] |
| frying pan | frigideira (f) | [friʒid'ɐjʀɐ] |
| ladle | concha (f) | [k'õʃɐ] |
| colander | passador (m) | [pɐsɐd'or] |
| tray | bandeja (f) | [bãd'ɛʒɐ] |

| bottle | garrafa (f) | [gɐʀ'afɐ] |
| jar (glass) | boião (m) de vidro | [boj'ãu dɐ v'idru] |
| can | lata (f) | [l'atɐ] |

| bottle opener | abridor (m) de garrafas | [ɐbrid'or dɐ gɐʀ'afɐʃ] |
| can opener | abre-latas (m) | [abrɐ l'atɐʃ] |
| corkscrew | saca-rolhas (m) | [s'akɐ ʀ'oʎɐʃ] |
| filter | filtro (m) | [f'iltru] |
| to filter (vt) | filtrar (vt) | [filtr'ar] |

| sh | lixo (m) | [l'iʃu] |
| sh can | balde (m) do lixo | [b'aldə du l'iʃu] |

## 8. Bathroom

| hroom | quarto (m) de banho | [ku'artu də b'eɲu] |
| ter | àgua (f) | ['aguɐ] |
| , faucet | torneira (f) | [turn'ejrɐ] |
| water | àgua (f) quente | ['aguɐ k'ẽtə] |
| d water | àgua (f) fria | ['aguɐ fr'iɐ] |

| thpaste | pasta (f) de dentes | [p'aʃtɐ də d'ẽtəʃ] |
| orush one's teeth | escovar os dentes | [əʃkuv'ar uʃ d'ẽtəʃ] |
| thbrush | escova (f) de dentes | [əʃk'ovɐ də d'ẽtəʃ] |

| shave (vi) | barbear-se (vp) | [bɐrbj'arsə] |
| aving foam | espuma (f) de barbear | [əʃp'umɐ də bɐrbj'ar] |
| or | màquina (f) de barbear | [m'akinɐ də bɐrbi'ar] |

| vash (one's hands, etc.) | lavar (vt) | [lɐv'ar] |
| ake a bath | lavar-se (vp) | [lɐv'arsə] |
| ower | duche (m) | [d'uʃə] |
| ake a shower | tomar um duche | [tum'ar ũ d'uʃə] |

| htub | banheira (f) | [bɐɲ'ejrɐ] |
| et (toilet bowl) | sanita (f) | [sɐn'itɐ] |
| k (washbasin) | lavatório (m) | [lɐvɐt'ɔriu] |

| ip | sabonete (m) | [sɐbun'etə] |
| ip dish | saboneteira (f) | [sɐbunɐt'ejrɐ] |

| onge | esponja (f) | [əʃp'õʒɐ] |
| ampoo | champô (m) | [ʃãp'o] |
| vel | toalha (f) | [tu'aʎɐ] |
| hrobe | roupão (m) de banho | [ʀop'ãu də b'eɲu] |

| ndry (process) | lavagem (f) | [lɐv'aʒẽj] |
| shing machine | màquina (f) de lavar | [m'akinɐ də lɐv'ar] |
| io the laundry | lavar a roupa | [lɐv'ar ɐ ʀ'opɐ] |
| ndry detergent | detergente (m) | [dətərʒ'ẽtə] |

## 9. Household appliances

| set | televisor (m) | [tələviz'or] |
| e recorder | gravador (m) | [grɐvɐd'or] |
| eo, VCR | videogravador (m) | [vidiɔgrɐvɐd'or] |
| iio | ràdio (m) | [ʀ'adiu] |
| yer (CD, MP3, etc.) | leitor (m) | [lɐjt'or] |

| video projector | projetor (m) | [pruʒɛt'or] |
| home movie theater | cinema (m) em casa | [sin'emɐ ẽ k'azɐ] |
| DVD player | leitor (m) de DVD | [lɐjt'or dɐ dɛvɛd'e] |
| amplifier | amplificador (m) | [ãplifikɐd'or] |
| video game console | console (f) de jogos | [kõs'olɐ dɐ ʒ'ɔguʃ] |

| video camera | cámara (f) de vídeo | [k'emɐrɐ dɐ v'idiu] |
| camera (photo) | máquina (f) fotogràfica | [m'akinɐ futugr'afikɐ] |
| digital camera | cámara (f) digital | [k'emɐrɐ diʒit'al] |

| vacuum cleaner | aspirador (m) | [ɐʃpirɐd'or] |
| iron (e.g., steam ~) | ferro (m) de engomar | [f'ɛru dɐ ẽgum'ar] |
| ironing board | tàbua (f) de engomar | [t'abuɐ dɐ ẽgum'ar] |

| telephone | telefone (m) | [tɐlɐf'onɐ] |
| mobile phone | telemóvel (m) | [tɛlɛm'ɔvɛl] |
| typewriter | máquina (f) de escrever | [m'akinɐ dɐ ɐʃkrɐv'er] |
| sewing machine | máquina (f) de costura | [m'akinɐ dɐ kuʃt'urɐ] |

| microphone | microfone (m) | [mikrɔf'onɐ] |
| headphones | auscultadores (m pl) | [auʃkultɐd'orɐʃ] |
| remote control (TV) | controlo remoto (m) | [kõtr'olu ʀɐm'ɔtu] |

| CD, compact disc | CD (m) | [s'ɛdɛ] |
| cassette | cassete (f) | [kas'ɛtɐ] |
| vinyl record | disco (m) de vinil | [d'iʃku dɐ vin'il] |

## 100. Repairs. Renovation

| renovations | renovação (f) | [ʀɐnuvɐs'ãu] |
| to renovate (vt) | renovar (vt), fazer obras | [ʀɐnuv'ar], [fɐz'er 'ɔbrɐʃ] |
| to repair (vt) | reparar (vt) | [ʀɐpɐr'ar] |

| to put in order | arranjar (vt) | [ɐʀãʒ'ar] |
| to redo (do again) | refazer (vt) | [ʀɐfɐz'er] |

| paint | tinta (f) | [t'ĩtɐ] |
| to paint (~ a wall) | pintar (vt) | [pĩt'ar] |

| house painter | pintor (m) | [pĩt'or] |
| paintbrush | pincel (m) | [pĩs'ɛl] |

| whitewash | cal (f) | [kal] |
| to whitewash (vt) | caiar (vt) | [kaj'ar] |

| wallpaper | papel (m) de parede | [pɐp'ɛl dɐ pɐr'edɐ] |
| to wallpaper (vt) | colar o papel | [kul'ar u pɐp'ɛl] |

| varnish | verniz (m) | [vɐrn'iʒ] |
| to varnish (vt) | envernizar (vt) | [ẽvɐrniz'ar] |

## 01. Plumbing

| er | àgua (f) | ['aguɐ] |
|---|---|---|
| water | àgua (f) quente | ['aguɐ k'ẽtə] |
| d water | àgua (f) fria | ['aguɐ fr'iɐ] |
| , faucet | torneira (f) | [turn'ejrɐ] |
| | | |
| p (of water) | gota (f) | [g'otɐ] |
| drip (vi) | gotejar (vi) | [gɔtəʒ'ar] |
| eak (ab. pipe) | vazar (vt) | [vɐz'ar] |
| k (pipe ~) | vazamento (m) | [vɐzɐm'ẽtu] |
| ddle | poça (f) | [p'ɔsɐ] |
| | | |
| e | tubo (m) | [t'ubu] |
| p valve | vàlvula (f) | [v'alvulɐ] |
| be clogged up | entupir-se (vp) | [ẽtup'irsə] |
| | | |
| ls | ferramentas (f pl) | [fərɐm'ẽtɐʃ] |
| ustable wrench | chave (f) inglesa | [ʃ'avə ĩgl'ezɐ] |
| unscrew, untwist (vt) | desenroscar (vt) | [dəzẽruʃk'ar] |
| screw (tighten) | enroscar (vt) | [ẽruʃk'ar] |
| | | |
| unclog (vt) | desentupir (vt) | [dəzẽtup'ir] |
| mber | canalizador (m) | [kɐnɐlizɐd'or] |
| sement | cave (f) | [k'avə] |
| verage (system) | sistema (m) de esgotos | [siʃt'emɐ də əʒg'ɔtuʃ] |

## 02. Fire. Conflagration

| (to catch ~) | fogo (m) | [f'ogu] |
|---|---|---|
| ne | chama (f) | [ʃ'emɐ] |
| ark | faísca (f) | [fɐ'iʃkɐ] |
| oke (from fire) | fumo (m) | [f'umu] |
| ch (flaming stick) | tocha (f) | [t'ɔʃɐ] |
| npfire | fogueira (f) | [fug'ejrɐ] |
| | | |
| s, gasoline | gasolina (f) | [gɐzul'inɐ] |
| osene (for aircraft) | querosene (m) | [kəruz'ɛnə] |
| mmable (adj) | inflamàvel | [ĩflɐm'avɛl] |
| olosive (adj) | explosivo | [əʃpluz'ivu] |
| SMOKING | PROIBIDO FUMAR! | [pruib'idu fum'ar] |
| | | |
| ety | segurança (f) | [səgur'ãsɐ] |
| nger | perigo (m) | [pər'igu] |
| ngerous (adj) | perigoso | [pərig'ozu] |
| | | |
| catch fire | incendiar-se (vp) | [ĩsẽdj'arsə] |
| olosion | explosão (f) | [əʃpluz'ãu] |
| set fire | incendiar (vt) | [ĩsẽdj'ar] |

| incendiary (arsonist) | **incendiàrio** (m) | [ĩsẽdj'ariu] |
| arson | **incêndio** (m) **criminoso** | [ĩs'ẽdiu krimin'ozu] |

| to blaze (vi) | **arder** (vi) | [ɐrd'er] |
| to burn (be on fire) | **queimar** (vi) | [kɐjm'ar] |
| to burn down | **queimar tudo** (vi) | [kɐjm'ar t'udu] |

| to call the fire department | **chamar os bombeiros** | [ʃɐm'ar uʃ bõb'ɐjruʃ] |
| fireman | **bombeiro** (m) | [bõb'ɐjru] |
| fire truck | **carro** (m) **de bombeiros** | [k'ɐʀu də bõb'ɐjruʃ] |
| fire department | **corpo** (m) **de bombeiros** | [k'orpu də bõb'ɐjruʃ] |
| fire truck ladder | **escada** (f) **extensivel** | [əʃk'adɐ əʃtẽsiv'ɛl] |

| fire hose | **mangueira** (f) | [mãg'ɐjɾɐ] |
| fire extinguisher | **extintor** (m) | [əʃtĩt'or] |
| helmet | **capacete** (m) | [kɐpɐs'etə] |
| siren | **sirene** (f) | [sir'ɛnə] |

| to call out | **gritar** (vi) | [grit'ar] |
| to call for help | **chamar por socorro** | [ʃɐm'ar pur suk'oʀu] |
| rescuer | **salvador** (m) | [salvɐd'or] |
| to rescue (vt) | **salvar, resgatar** (vt) | [salv'ar], [ʀɐʒgɐt'ar] |

| to arrive (vi) | **chegar** (vi) | [ʃɐg'ar] |
| to extinguish (vt) | **apagar** (vt) | [ɐpɐg'ar] |
| water | **àgua** (f) | ['aguɐ] |
| sand | **areia** (f) | [ɐr'ɐjɐ] |

| ruins (destruction) | **ruínas** (f pl) | [ʀu'inɐʃ] |
| to collapse (building, etc.) | **ruir** (vi) | [ʀu'ir] |
| to fall down (vi) | **desmoronar** (vi), | [dəʒmurun'ar] |
| to cave in (ceiling, floor) | **ir abaixo** | [ir ɐb'ajʃu] |

| piece of wreckage | **fragmento** (m) | [fragm'ẽtu] |
| ash | **cinza** (f) | [s'ĩzɐ] |

| to suffocate (die) | **sufocar** (vi) | [sufuk'ar] |
| to be killed (perish) | **ser morto, morrer** (vi) | [ser m'ortu], [muʀ'er] |

# UMAN ACTIVITIES

## ob. Business. Part 1

### 03.  Office. Working in the office

| | | |
|---|---|---|
| ce (of firm) | escritório (m) | [əʃkritˈɔriu] |
| ce (of director, etc.) | escritório (m) | [əʃkritˈɔriu] |
| nt desk | receção (f) | [ʀəsɛsˈãu] |
| cretary | secretário (m) | [səkrətˈariu] |
| cretary (fem.) | secretária (f) | [səkrətˈariɐ] |
| | | |
| ctor | diretor (m) | [dirɛtˈor] |
| nager | gerente (m) | [ʒərˈẽtə] |
| countant | contabilista (m) | [kõtɐbilˈiʃtə] |
| ployee | empregado (m) | [ẽprəgˈadu] |
| | | |
| niture | mobiliário (m) | [mubiljˈariu] |
| k | mesa (f) | [mˈezɐ] |
| k chair | cadeira (f) | [kɐdˈejrɐ] |
| st of drawers | bloco (m) de gavetas | [blˈɔku də gɐvˈetɐʃ] |
| nt stand | cabide (m) de pé | [kɐbˈidə də pɛ] |
| | | |
| mputer | computador (m) | [kõputədˈor] |
| nter | impressora (f) | [ĩprəsˈorɐ] |
| machine | fax (m) | [faks] |
| otocopier | fotocopiadora (f) | [futukupiɐdˈorɐ] |
| | | |
| per | papel (m) | [pɐpˈɛl] |
| ce supplies | artigos (m pl) de escritório | [ɐrtˈiguʃ də əʃkritˈɔriu] |
| use pad | tapete (m) de rato | [tɐpˈetə də ʀˈatu] |
| eet (of paper) | folha (f) | [fˈoʎɐ] |
| der, binder | pasta (f) | [pˈaʃtə] |
| | | |
| alog | catálogo (m) | [kɐtˈalugu] |
| one book (directory) | diretório (f) telefónico | [dirɛtˈɔriu tələfˈɔniku] |
| cumentation | documentação (f) | [dukumẽtɐsˈãu] |
| chure | brochura (f) | [bruʃˈurɐ] |
| g., 12 pages ~) | | |
| flet | flyer (m) | [flˈejər] |
| mple | amostra (f) | [ɐmˈɔʃtrɐ] |
| | | |
| ning meeting | formação (f) | [furmɐsˈãu] |
| eting (of managers) | reunião (f) | [ʀiunjˈãu] |
| ch time | hora (f) de almoço | [ˈɔrɐ də almˈosu] |

| to make a copy | fazer uma cópia | [fez'er 'umɐ k'ɔpiɐ] |
| to make copies | tirar cópias | [tir'ar k'ɔpiɐʃ] |
| to receive a fax | receber um fax | [ʀɐsɐb'er ũ faks] |
| to send a fax | enviar um fax | [ẽvj'ar ũ faks] |

| to call (by phone) | fazer uma chamada | [fez'er 'umɐ ʃɐm'adɐ] |
| to answer (vt) | responder (vt) | [ʀɐʃpõd'er] |
| to put through | passar (vt) | [pɐs'ar] |

| to arrange, to set up | marcar (vt) | [mɐrk'ar] |
| to demonstrate (vt) | demonstrar (vt) | [dɐmõʃtr'ar] |
| to be absent | estar ausente | [əʃt'ar auz'ẽtɐ] |
| absence | ausência (f) | [auz'ẽsiɐ] |

## 104. Business processes. Part 1

| business | negócio (m) | [nɐg'ɔsiu] |
| occupation | ocupação (f) | [ɔkupɐs'ãu] |
| firm | firma, empresa (f) | [f'irmɐ], [ẽpr'ezɐ] |
| company | companhia (f) | [kõpɐɲ'iɐ] |
| corporation | corporação (f) | [kurpurɐs'ãu] |
| enterprise | empresa (f) | [ẽpr'ezɐ] |
| agency | agência (f) | [ɐʒ'ẽsiɐ] |

| agreement (contract) | acordo (m) | [ɐk'ordu] |
| contract | contrato (m) | [kõtr'atu] |
| deal | acordo (m) | [ɐk'ordu] |
| order (to place an ~) | encomenda (f) | [ẽkum'ẽdɐ] |
| term (of contract) | condição (f) | [kõdis'ãu] |

| wholesale (adv) | por grosso | [pur gr'osu] |
| wholesale (adj) | grossista | [grus'iʃtɐ] |
| wholesale (n) | venda (f) por grosso | [v'ẽdɐ pur gr'osu] |
| retail (adj) | a retalho | [ɐ ʀɐt'aʎu] |
| retail (n) | venda (f) a retalho | [v'ẽdɐ ɐ ʀɐt'aʎu] |

| competitor | concorrente (m) | [kõkuʀ'ẽtɐ] |
| competition | concorrência (f) | [kõkuʀ'ẽsiɐ] |
| to compete (vi) | competir (vi) | [kõpɐt'ir] |

| partner (associate) | sócio (m) | [s'ɔsiu] |
| partnership | parceria (f) | [pɐrsɐr'iɐ] |

| crisis | crise (f) | [kr'izɐ] |
| bankruptcy | bancarrota (f) | [bãkɐʀ'otɐ] |
| to go bankrupt | entrar em falência | [ẽtr'ar ẽ fɐl'ẽsiɐ] |
| difficulty | dificuldade (f) | [difikuld'adɐ] |
| problem | problema (m) | [prubl'emɐ] |
| catastrophe | catástrofe (f) | [kɐt'aʃtrufɐ] |
| economy | economia (f) | [ekɔnum'iɐ] |

| nomic (~ growth) | económico | [ekun'ɔmiku] |
| nomic recession | recessão (f) económica | [ʀəsəs'ãu ekun'ɔmikɐ] |
| il (aim) | objetivo (m) | [ɔbʒɛt'ivu] |
| k | tarefa (f) | [tɐɾ'ɛfɐ] |
| rade (vi) | comercializar (vi) | [kumɐɾsiɐliz'aɾ] |
| work (distribution ~) | rede (f), cadeia (f) | [ʀ'edə], [kɐd'ɐjɐ] |
| entory (stock) | estoque (m) | [əʃt'ɔkə] |
| sortment | sortido (m) | [suɾt'idu] |
| der (leading company) | líder (m) | [l'idɛɾ] |
| je (~ company) | grande | [gɾ'ãdə] |
| nopoly | monopólio (m) | [munup'ɔliu] |
| ory | teoria (f) | [tiuɾ'iɐ] |
| ctice | prática (f) | [pɾ'atikɐ] |
| perience (in my ~) | experiência (f) | [əʃpəɾj'ẽsiɐ] |
| nd (tendency) | tendência (f) | [tẽd'ẽsiɐ] |
| velopment | desenvolvimento (m) | [dəzẽvɔlvim'ẽtu] |

## 05. Business processes. Part 2

| nefit, profit | rentabilidade (f) | [ʀẽtɐbilid'adə] |
| ofitable (adj) | rentável | [ʀẽt'avɛl] |
| egation (group) | delegação (f) | [dələgɐs'ãu] |
| ary | salário, ordenado (m) | [sɐl'aɾiu], [ɔɾdɐn'adu] |
| correct (an error) | corrigir (vt) | [kuʀiʒ'iɾ] |
| iiness trip | viagem (f) de negócios | [vj'aʒɐ̃j də nəg'ɔsiuʃ] |
| nmission | comissão (f) | [kumis'ãu] |
| control (vt) | controlar (vt) | [kõtɾul'aɾ] |
| iference | conferência (f) | [kõfəɾ'ẽsiɐ] |
| nse | licença (f) | [lis'ẽsɐ] |
| able (~ partner) | fiável | [fj'avɛl] |
| iative (undertaking) | empreendimento (m) | [ẽpɾiẽdim'ẽtu] |
| m (standard) | norma (f) | [n'ɔɾmɐ] |
| cumstance | circunstância (f) | [sirkũʃt'ãsiɐ] |
| y (of employee) | dever (m) | [dəv'eɾ] |
| anization (company) | empresa (f) | [ẽpɾ'ezɐ] |
| anization (process) | organização (f) | [ɔɾgɐnizɐs'ãu] |
| anized (adj) | organizado | [ɔɾgɐniz'adu] |
| ncellation | anulação (f) | [ɐnulɐs'ãu] |
| cancel (call off) | anular, cancelar (vt) | [ɐnul'aɾ], [kãsəl'aɾ] |
| ort (official ~) | relatório (m) | [ʀəlɐt'ɔriu] |
| ent | patente (f) | [pɐt'ẽtə] |
| patent (obtain patent) | patentear (vt) | [pɐtẽtj'aɾ] |

| to plan (vt) | planear (vt) | [plɐnj'ar] |
| bonus (money) | prémio (m) | [pr'ɛmiu] |
| professional (adj) | profissional | [prufisiun'al] |
| procedure | procedimento (m) | [prusədim'ẽtu] |

| to examine (contract, etc.) | examinar (vt) | [ezɐmin'ar] |
| calculation | cálculo (m) | [k'alkulu] |
| reputation | reputação (f) | [ʀəputɐs'ãu] |
| risk | risco (m) | [ʀ'iʃku] |

| to manage, to run | dirigir (vt) | [diriʒ'ir] |
| information | informação (f) | [ĩfurmɐs'ãu] |
| property | propriedade (f) | [prupriɛd'adə] |
| union | união (f) | [unj'ãu] |

| life insurance | seguro (m) de vida | [səg'uru də v'idɐ] |
| to insure (vt) | fazer um seguro | [fɐz'er ũ səg'uru] |
| insurance | seguro (m) | [səg'uru] |

| auction (~ sale) | leilão (m) | [lɐjl'ãu] |
| to notify (inform) | notificar (vt) | [nutifik'ar] |
| management (process) | gestão (f) | [ʒəʃt'ãu] |
| service (~ industry) | serviço (m) | [sərv'isu] |

| forum | fórum (m) | [f'ɔrũ] |
| to function (vi) | funcionar (vi) | [fũsiun'ar] |
| stage (phase) | estágio (m) | [əʃt'aʒiu] |
| legal (~ services) | jurídico | [ʒur'idiku] |
| lawyer (legal expert) | jurista (m) | [ʒur'iʃtɐ] |

## 106. Production. Works

| plant | fábrica (f) | [f'abrikɐ] |
| factory | fábrica (f) | [f'abrikɐ] |
| workshop | oficina (f) | [ɔfis'inɐ] |
| works, production site | local (m) de produção | [luk'al də prudus'ãu] |

| industry | indústria (f) | [ĩd'uʃtriɐ] |
| industrial (adj) | industrial | [ĩduʃtrj'al] |
| heavy industry | indústria (f) pesada | [ĩd'uʃtriɐ pəz'adɐ] |
| light industry | indústria (f) ligeira | [ĩd'uʃtriɐ liʒ'ejrɐ] |

| products | produção (f) | [prudus'ãu] |
| to produce (vt) | produzir (vt) | [pruduz'ir] |
| raw materials | matérias (f pl) primas | [mɐt'ɛriɐʃ pr'imɐʃ] |

| foreman | chefe (m) de brigada | [ʃ'ɛfə də brig'adɐ] |
| workers team | brigada (f) | [brig'adɐ] |
| worker | operário (m) | [ɔpər'ariu] |
| working day | dia (m) de trabalho | [d'iɐ də trɐb'aʎu] |

| | | |
|---|---|---|
| se | **pausa** (f) | [p'auzɐ] |
| eting | **reunião** (f) | [ʀiunj'ãu] |
| discuss (vt) | **discutir** (vt) | [diʃkut'ir] |
| | | |
| n | **plano** (m) | [pl'ɐnu] |
| ulfill the plan | **cumprir o plano** | [kũpr'ir u pl'ɐnu] |
| e of output | **taxa** (f) **de produção** | [t'aʃɐ də prudus'ãu] |
| ality | **qualidade** (f) | [kuɐlid'adə] |
| ecking (control) | **controle** (m) | [kõtr'ɔlə] |
| ality control | **controle** (m) **da qualidade** | [kõtr'ɔlə də kuɐlid'adə] |
| | | |
| rk safety | **segurança** (f) **no trabalho** | [səgur'ãsɐ nu trɐb'aʎu] |
| cipline | **disciplina** (f) | [diʃsipl'inɐ] |
| ation | **infração** (f) | [ĩfras'ãu] |
| safety rules, etc.) | | |
| violate (rules) | **violar** (vt) | [viul'ar] |
| | | |
| ke | **greve** (f) | [gr'ɛvə] |
| ker | **grevista** (m) | [grɛv'iʃtɐ] |
| e on strike | **estar em greve** | [əʃt'ar ẽ gr'ɛvə] |
| or union | **sindicato** (m) | [sĩdik'atu] |
| | | |
| nvent (machine, etc.) | **inventar** (vt) | [ĩvẽt'ar] |
| ention | **invenção** (f) | [ĩvẽs'ãu] |
| earch | **pesquisa** (f) | [pəʃk'izɐ] |
| mprove (make better) | **melhorar** (vt) | [məʎur'ar] |
| nnology | **tecnologia** (f) | [tɛknuluʒ'iɐ] |
| hnical drawing | **desenho** (m) **técnico** | [dəz'eɲu t'ɛkniku] |
| | | |
| d, cargo | **carga** (f) | [k'argɐ] |
| der (person) | **carregador** (m) | [kɐʀəgɐd'or] |
| oad (vehicle, etc.) | **carregar** (vt) | [kɐʀəg'ar] |
| ding (process) | **carregamento** (m) | [kɐʀəgɐm'ẽtu] |
| | | |
| unload (vi, vt) | **descarregar** (vt) | [dəʃkɐʀəg'ar] |
| oading | **descarga** (f) | [dəʃk'argɐ] |
| | | |
| nsportation | **transporte** (m) | [trãʃp'ɔrtə] |
| nsportation company | **companhia** (f) **de transporte** | [kõpɐɲ'iɐ də trãʃp'ɔrtə] |
| ransport (vt) | **transportar** (vt) | [trãʃpurt'ar] |
| | | |
| ght car | **vagão** (m) **de carga** | [vɐg'ãu də k'argɐ] |
| tern | **cisterna** (f) | [siʃt'ɛrnɐ] |
| ck | **camião** (m) | [kamj'ãu] |
| | | |
| chine tool | **máquina-ferramenta** (f) | [m'akinɐ fɐʀɐm'ẽtɐ] |
| chanism | **mecanismo** (m) | [məkɐn'iʒmu] |
| | | |
| ustrial waste | **resíduos** (m pl) **industriais** | [ʀəz'iduuʃ ĩduʃtrj'ajʃ] |
| cking (process) | **embalagem** (f) | [ẽbɐl'aʒẽj] |
| oack (vt) | **embalar** (vt) | [ẽbɐl'ar] |

## 107. Contract. Agreement

| | | |
|---|---|---|
| contract | contrato (m) | [kõtrˈatu] |
| agreement | acordo (m) | [ɐkˈordu] |
| addendum | adenda (f), anexo (m) | [ɐdˈẽdɐ], [ɐnˈɛksu] |
| to sign a contract | assinar o contrato | [ɐsinˈar u kõtrˈatu] |
| signature | assinatura (f) | [ɐsinɐtˈurɐ] |
| to sign (vt) | assinar (vt) | [ɐsinˈar] |
| stamp (seal) | carimbo (m) | [kɐrˈĩbu] |
| subject of contract | objeto (m) do contrato | [ɔbʒˈɛtu du kõtrˈatu] |
| clause | cláusula (f) | [klˈauzulɐ] |
| parties (in contract) | partes (f pl) | [pˈartɐʃ] |
| legal address | morada (f) jurídica | [murˈadɐ ʒurˈidikɐ] |
| to break the contract | violar o contrato | [viulˈar u kõtrˈatu] |
| commitment | obrigação (f) | [ɔbrigɐsˈãu] |
| responsibility | responsabilidade (f) | [ʁɐʃpõsɐbilidˈadə] |
| force majeure | força (f) maior | [fˈorsɐ mɐjˈor] |
| dispute | litígio (m), disputa (f) | [litˈiʒiu], [diʃpˈute] |
| penalties | multas (f pl) | [mˈultɐʃ] |

## 108. Import & Export

| | | |
|---|---|---|
| import | importação (f) | [ĩpurtɐsˈãu] |
| importer | importador (m) | [ĩpurtɐdˈor] |
| to import (vt) | importar (vt) | [ĩpurtˈar] |
| import (e.g., ~ goods) | de importação | [də ĩpurtɐsˈãu] |
| export | exportação (f) | [əʃpurtɐsˈãu] |
| exporter | exportador (m) | [əʃpurtɐdˈor] |
| to export (vi, vt) | exportar (vt) | [əʃpurtˈar] |
| export (e.g., ~ goods) | de exportação | [də əʃpurtɐsˈãu] |
| goods | mercadoria (f) | [mɐrkɐdurˈiɐ] |
| consignment, lot | lote (m) | [lˈotə] |
| weight | peso (m) | [pˈezu] |
| volume | volume (m) | [vulˈumə] |
| cubic meter | metro (m) cúbico | [mˈɛtru kˈubiku] |
| manufacturer | produtor (m) | [prudutˈor] |
| transportation company | companhia (f) de transporte | [kõpɐɲˈiɐ də trãʃpˈortə] |
| container | contentor (m) | [kõtẽtˈor] |
| border | fronteira (f) | [frõtˈejɾɐ] |
| customs | alfândega (f) | [alfˈãdəgɐ] |

| stoms duty | taxa (f) alfandegária | [t'aʃe alfãdəg'ariə] |
| stoms officer | funcionário (m) da alfândega | [fũsiun'ariu də alf'ãdəgə] |
| uggling | contrabando (m) | [kõtrəb'ãdu] |
| straband (goods) | contrabando (m) | [kõtrəb'ãdu] |

## 09. Finances

| ck (share) | ação (f) | [as'ãu] |
| nd (certificate) | obrigação (f) | [ɔbrigəs'ãu] |
| of exchange | letra (f) de câmbio | [l'etrə də k'ãbiu] |

| ck exchange | bolsa (f) | [b'olsə] |
| ck price | cotação (m) das ações | [kutəs'ãu deʃ as'ojʃ] |

| go down | tornar-se mais barato | [turn'arsə m'ajʃ bər'atu] |
| go up | tornar-se mais caro | [turn'arsə m'ajʃ k'aru] |

| areholding | parte (f) | [p'artə] |
| ntrolling interest | participação (f) maioritária | [pertisipəs'ãu məjurit'ariə] |
| estment | investimento (m) | [ĩveʃtim'ẽtu] |
| nvest (vt) | investir (vt) | [ĩveʃt'ir] |
| cent | percentagem (f) | [pərsẽt'aʒẽj] |
| erest (on investment) | juros (m pl) | [ʒ'uruʃ] |
| fit | lucro (m) | [l'ukru] |
| fitable (adj) | lucrativo | [lukrət'ivu] |
| | imposto (m) | [ĩp'oʃtu] |

| rency (foreign ~) | divisa (f) | [div'izə] |
| ional (adj) | nacional | [nəsiun'al] |
| change (currency ~) | câmbio (m) | [k'ãbiu] |

| countant | contabilista (m) | [kõtəbil'iʃtə] |
| counting | contabilidade (f) | [kõtəbilid'adə] |

| nkruptcy | bancarrota (f) | [bãkɐʀ'otə] |
| lapse, crash | falência (f) | [fel'ẽsiə] |
| n | ruína (f) | [ʀu'inə] |
| be ruined | arruinar-se (vp) | [ɐʀuin'arsə] |
| ation | inflação (f) | [ĩflas'ãu] |
| /aluation | desvalorização (f) | [dəʒvelurizes'ãu] |

| vital | capital (m) | [kepit'al] |
| ome | rendimento (m) | [ʀẽdim'ẽtu] |
| nover | volume (m) de negócios | [vul'umə də nəg'ɔsiuʃ] |
| ources | recursos (m pl) | [ʀək'ursuʃ] |
| netary resources | recursos (m pl) financeiros | [ʀək'ursuʃ finãs'ejruʃ] |
| erhead | despesas (f pl) gerais | [dəʃp'ezeʃ ʒər'ajʃ] |
| educe (expenses) | reduzir (vt) | [ʀəduz'ir] |

## 110. Marketing

| | | |
|---|---|---|
| marketing | marketing (m) | [m'arkɐtĩg] |
| market | mercado (m) | [mɐrk'adu] |
| market segment | segmento (m) do mercado | [sɛgm'ẽtu du mɐrk'adu] |
| product | produto (m) | [prud'utu] |
| goods | mercadoria (f) | [mɐrkɐdur'iɐ] |
| | | |
| brand | marca (f) | [m'arkɐ] |
| trademark | marca (f) comercial | [m'arkɐ kumɐrsj'al] |
| logotype | logótipo (m) | [lɔg'ɔtipu] |
| logo | logótipo (m) | [lɔg'ɔtipu] |
| | | |
| demand | demanda (f) | [dɐm'ãdɐ] |
| supply | oferta (f) | [ɔf'ɛrtɐ] |
| need | necessidade (f) | [nɐsɐsid'adɐ] |
| consumer | consumidor (m) | [kõsumid'or] |
| | | |
| analysis | análise (f) | [ɐn'alizɐ] |
| to analyze (vt) | analisar (vt) | [ɐnɐliz'ar] |
| positioning | posicionamento (m) | [puzisiunɐm'ẽtu] |
| to position (vt) | posicionar (vt) | [puzisiun'ar] |
| | | |
| price | preço (m) | [pr'esu] |
| pricing policy | política (f) de preços | [pul'itikɐ dɐ pr'esuʃ] |
| formation of price | formação (f) de preços | [furmɐs'ãu dɐ pr'esuʃ] |

## 111. Advertising

| | | |
|---|---|---|
| advertising | publicidade (f) | [publisid'adɐ] |
| to advertise (vt) | publicitar (vt) | [publisit'ar] |
| budget | orçamento (m) | [ɔrsɐm'ẽtu] |
| | | |
| ad, advertisement | anúncio (m) publicitário | [ɐn'ũsiu publisit'ariu] |
| TV advertising | publicidade (f) televisiva | [publisid'adɐ tɐlɐviz'ivɐ] |
| radio advertising | publicidade (f) na rádio | [publisid'adɐ nɐ ʀ'adiu] |
| outdoor advertising | publicidade (f) exterior | [publisid'adɐ ɐʃtɐrj'or] |
| | | |
| mass media | meios (m pl) de comunicação social | [m'ejuʃ dɐ kumunikɐs'ãu susj'al] |
| periodical (n) | periódico (m) | [pɐrj'ɔdiku] |
| image (public appearance) | imagem (f) | [im'aʒẽj] |
| | | |
| slogan | slogan (m) | [sl'ogɐn] |
| motto (maxim) | mote (m), divisa (f) | [m'ɔtɐ], [div'izɐ] |
| | | |
| campaign | campanha (f) | [kãp'ɐɲɐ] |
| advertising campaign | campanha (f) publicitária | [kãp'ɐɲɐ publisit'ariɐ] |
| target group | grupo (m) alvo | [gr'upu 'alvu] |

| siness card | cartão (m) de visita | [kɐrt'ãu də viz'itɐ] |
| flet | flyer (m) | [fl'ɐjɘr] |
| chure | brochura (f) | [bruʃ'urɐ] |
| ., 12 pages ~) | | |
| nphlet | folheto (m) | [fuʎ'etu] |
| vsletter | boletim (m) | [bulɘt'ĩ] |
| | | |
| re sign | letreiro (m) | [lɘtr'ejru] |
| ster | cartaz, póster (m) | [kɐrt'aʃ], [p'ɔʃtɛr] |
| oard | painel (m) publicitário | [pajn'ɛl publisit'ariu] |

## 12. Banking

| ık | banco (m) | [b'ãku] |
| nch (of bank, etc.) | sucursal, balcão (f) | [sukurs'al], [balk'ãu] |
| | | |
| ık clerk, consultant | consultor (m) | [kõsult'or] |
| nager (director) | gerente (m) | [ʒɘr'ẽtɐ] |
| | | |
| ıking account | conta (f) | [k'õtɐ] |
| ount number | número (m) da conta | [n'umɘru dɐ k'õtɐ] |
| ecking account | conta (f) corrente | [k'õtɐ kuʀ'ẽtɐ] |
| /ings account | conta (f) poupança | [k'õtɐ pop'ãsɐ] |
| | | |
| open an account | abrir uma conta | [ɐbr'ir 'umɐ k'õtɐ] |
| close the account | fechar uma conta | [fɘʃ'ar 'umɐ k'õtɐ] |
| deposit into the account | depositar na conta | [dɘpuzit'ar nɐ k'õtɐ] |
| ʌithdraw (vt) | levantar (vt) | [lɘvãt'ar] |
| | | |
| osit | depósito (m) | [dɘp'ozitu] |
| nake a deposit | fazer um depósito | [fɐz'er ũ dɘp'ozitu] |
| e transfer | transferência (f) bancária | [trãʃfɘr'ẽsiɐ bãk'ariɐ] |
| | | |
| vire, to transfer | transferir (vt) | [trãʃfɘr'ir] |
| | | |
| n | soma (f) | [s'omɐ] |
| v much? | Quanto? | [ku'ãtu] |
| | | |
| nature | assinatura (f) | [ɐsinɐt'urɐ] |
| sign (vt) | assinar (vt) | [ɐsin'ar] |
| | | |
| dit card | cartão (m) de crédito | [kɐrt'ãu də kr'ɛditu] |
| le | código (m) | [k'ɔdigu] |
| dit card number | número (m) do cartão de crédito | [n'umɘru du kɐrt'ãu də kr'ɛditu] |
| M | Caixa Multibanco (m) | [k'ajʃɐ multib'ãku] |
| | | |
| ǝck | cheque (m) | [ʃ'ɛkə] |
| vrite a check | passar um cheque | [pɐs'ar ũ ʃ'ɛkə] |
| eckbook | livro (m) de cheques | [l'ivru də ʃ'ɛkəʃ] |

| loan (bank ~) | empréstimo (m) | [ẽpr'ɛʃtimu] |
| to apply for a loan | pedir um empréstimo | [pəd'ir un ẽpr'ɛʃtimu] |
| to get a loan | obter um empréstimo | [ɔbt'er un ẽpr'ɛʃtimu] |
| to give a loan | conceder | [kõsəd'er |
| | um empréstimo | un ẽpr'ɛʃtimu] |
| guarantee | garantia (f) | [gərãt'iɐ] |

## 113. Telephone. Phone conversation

| telephone | telefone (m) | [tələf'ɔnə] |
| mobile phone | telemóvel (m) | [tɛlɛm'ɔvɛl] |
| answering machine | atendedor (m) de chamadas | [etẽdəd'or də ʃem'adəʃ] |
| | | |
| to call (telephone) | fazer uma chamada | [fez'er 'umɐ ʃem'adɐ] |
| phone call | chamada (f) | [ʃem'adɐ] |
| | | |
| to dial a number | marcar um número | [mɐrk'ar ũ n'uməru] |
| Hello! | Alô! | [el'o] |
| to ask (vt) | perguntar (vt) | [pərgũt'ar] |
| to answer (vi, vt) | responder (vt) | [ʀəʃpõd'er] |
| | | |
| to hear (vt) | ouvir (vt) | [ov'ir] |
| well (adv) | bem | [bẽj] |
| not well (adv) | mal | [mal] |
| noises (interference) | ruído (m) | [ʀu'idu] |
| | | |
| receiver | auscultador (m) | [auʃkultəd'or] |
| to pick up (~ the phone) | pegar o telefone | [pəg'ar u tələf'ɔnə] |
| to hang up (~ the phone) | desligar (vi) | [dəʒlig'ar] |
| | | |
| busy (adj) | ocupado | [ɔkup'adu] |
| to ring (ab. phone) | tocar (vi) | [tuk'ar] |
| telephone book | lista (f) telefónica | [l'iʃtɐ tələf'ɔnikɐ] |
| | | |
| local (adj) | local | [luk'al] |
| local call | chamada (f) local | [ʃem'adɐ luk'al] |
| long distance (~ call) | para outra cidade | [p'ɛrɐ 'otrɐ sid'adɐ] |
| long-distance call | chamada (f) para outra cidade | [ʃem'adɐ p'ɛrɐ 'otrɐ sid'adɐ] |
| | | |
| international (adj) | internacional | [ĩtərnɐsiun'al] |
| international call | chamada (f) internacional | [ʃem'adɐ ĩtərnɐsiun'al] |

## 114. Mobile telephone

| mobile phone | telemóvel (m) | [tɛlɛm'ɔvɛl] |
| display | ecrã (m) | [ɛkr'ã] |
| button | botão (m) | [but'ãu] |

| /I card | cartão SIM (m) | [kɐrt'ãu sim] |
| tery | bateria (f) | [bɐtər'iɐ] |
| be dead (battery) | descarregar-se | [dəʃkɐʀəg'arsə] |
| rger | carregador (m) | [kɐʀəged'or] |
| nu | menu (m) | [mɛn'u] |
| tings | definições (f pl) | [dəfinis'ojʃ] |
| e (melody) | melodia (f) | [məlud'iɐ] |
| select (vt) | escolher (vt) | [əʃkuʎ'er] |
| culator | calculadora (f) | [kalkulɐd'oɾɐ] |
| ce mail | atendedor (m) de chamadas | [etẽdəd'or də ʃem'adəʃ] |
| rm clock | despertador (m) | [dəʃpərtɐd'or] |
| tacts | contatos (m pl) | [kõt'atuʃ] |
| S (text message) | mensagem (f) de texto | [mẽs'aʒẽj də t'ɛʃtu] |
| bscriber | assinante (m) | [ɐsin'ãtə] |

| point pen | caneta (f) | [kɐn'etɐ] |
| ntain pen | caneta (f) tinteiro | [kɐn'etɐ tĩt'ejru] |
| cil | lápis (m) | [l'apiʃ] |
| hlighter | marcador (m) | [mɐrkɐd'or] |
| -tip pen | caneta (f) de feltro | [kɐn'etɐ də f'eltru] |
| epad | bloco (m) de notas | [bl'ɔku də n'ɔtəʃ] |
| enda (diary) | agenda (f) | [ɐʒ'ẽdɐ] |
| er | régua (f) | [ʀ'ɛguɐ] |
| culator | calculadora (f) | [kalkulɐd'oɾɐ] |
| ser | borracha (f) | [buʀ'aʃɐ] |
| mbtack | pionés (m) | [piun'ɛʃ] |
| per clip | clipe (m) | [kl'ipə] |
| e | cola (f) | [k'ɔlɐ] |
| pler | agrafador (m) | [ɐgɾɐfɐd'or] |
| e punch | furador (m) | [fuɾɐd'or] |
| ncil sharpener | afia-lápis (m) | [ɐf'iɐ l'apiʃ] |

| count (report) | relatório (m) | [ʀəlɐt'ɔriu] |
| eement | acordo (m) | [ɐk'ordu] |
| plication form | ficha (f) de inscrição | [f'iʃɐ də ĩʃkris'ãu] |
| hentic (adj) | autêntico | [aut'ẽtiku] |

| badge (identity tag) | crachá (m) | [kreʃʼa] |
| business card | cartão (m) de visita | [kɐrtʼãu də vizʼitɐ] |

| certificate (~ of quality) | certificado (m) | [sərtifikʼadu] |
| check (e.g., draw a ~) | cheque (m) | [ʃʼɛkə] |
| check (in restaurant) | conta (f) | [kʼõtɐ] |
| constitution | constituição (f) | [kõʃtituisʼãu] |

| contract | contrato (m) | [kõtrʼatu] |
| copy | cópia (f) | [kʼɔpiɐ] |
| copy (of contract, etc.) | exemplar (m) | [ezẽplʼar] |

| customs declaration | declaração (f) alfandegária | [dəklɐrɐsʼãu alfãdəgʼariɐ] |
| document | documento (m) | [dukumʼẽtu] |
| driver's license | carta (f) de condução | [kʼartɐ də kõdusʼãu] |
| addendum | adenda (f), anexo (m) | [ɐdʼẽdɐ], [ɐnʼɛksu] |
| form | questionário (m) | [kəʃtiunʼariu] |
| identity card, ID | bilhete (m) de identidade | [biʎʼetə də idẽtidʼadə] |
| inquiry (request) | inquérito (m) | [ĩkʼɛritu] |
| invitation card | convite (m) | [kõvʼitə] |
| invoice | fatura (f) | [fatʼurɐ] |

| law | lei (f) | [lɐj] |
| letter (mail) | carta (f) | [kʼartɐ] |
| letterhead | papel (m) timbrado | [pɐpʼɛl tĩbrʼadu] |
| list (of names, etc.) | lista (f) | [lʼiʃtɐ] |
| manuscript | manuscrito (m) | [mɐnuʃkrʼitu] |
| newsletter | boletim (m) | [bulɐtʼĩ] |
| note (short message) | bilhete (m) | [biʎʼetə] |

| pass (for worker, visitor) | passe (m) | [pʼasə] |
| passport | passaporte (m) | [pasɐpʼɔrtə] |
| permit | permissão (f) | [pərmisʼãu] |
| résumé | CV, currículo (m) | [sɛvʼɛ], [kuʀʼikulu] |
| debt note, IOU | vale (f), nota (f) promissória | [vʼalə], [nʼɔtə prumisʼɔriɐ] |

| receipt (for purchase) | recibo (m) | [ʀəsʼibu] |
| sales slip, receipt | talão (f) | [tɐlʼãu] |
| report | informe (m) | [ĩfʼɔrmə] |

| to show (ID, etc.) | mostrar (vt) | [muʃtrʼar] |
| to sign (vt) | assinar (vt) | [ɐsinʼar] |
| signature | assinatura (f) | [ɐsinɐtʼurɐ] |
| stamp (seal) | carimbo (m) | [kɐrʼĩbu] |
| text | texto (m) | [tʼɛʃtu] |
| ticket (for entry) | bilhete (m) | [biʎʼetə] |

| to cross out | riscar (vt) | [ʀiʃkʼar] |
| to fill out (~ a form) | preencher (vt) | [priẽʃʼer] |
| waybill | guia (f) de remessa | [gʼiɐ də ʀəmʼɛsɐ] |
| will (testament) | testamento (m) | [təʃtɐmʼẽtu] |

## 7. Kinds of business

| | | |
|---|---|---|
| :ounting services | **serviços** (m pl) **de contabilidade** | [sɐrv'isuʃ də kõtɐbilid'adə] |
| /ertising | **publicidade** (f) | [publisid'adə] |
| /ertising agency | **agência** (f) **de publicidade** | [ɐʒ'ẽsiɐ də publisid'adə] |
| conditioners | **ar condicionado** (m) | [ar kõdisiun'adu] |
| ine | **companhia** (f) **aérea** | [kõpɐɲ'iɐ ɐ'ɛriɐ] |
| | | |
| oholic drinks | **bebidas** (f pl) **alcoólicas** | [bəb'idɐʃ alku'ɔlikɐʃ] |
| iquities | **comércio** (m) **de antiguidades** | [kum'ɛrsiu də ãtiguid'adəʃ] |
| gallery | **galeria** (f) **de arte** | [gɐlər'iɐ də 'artə] |
| dit services | **serviços** (m pl) **de auditoria** | [sɐrv'isuʃ də auditur'iɐ] |
| | | |
| ıks | **negócios** (m pl) **bancários** | [nɐg'ɔsiuʃ bãk'ariuʃ] |
| | **bar** (m) | [bar] |
| ıuty parlor | **salão** (m) **de beleza** | [sɐl'ãu də bəl'ezɐ] |
| ɔkstore | **livraria** (f) | [livrɐr'iɐ] |
| wery | **cervejaria** (f) | [sɐrvəʒɐr'iɐ] |
| ;iness center | **centro** (m) **de escritórios** | [s'ẽtru də əʃkrit'ɔriuʃ] |
| ;iness school | **escola** (f) **de negócios** | [əʃk'ɔlɐ də nɐg'ɔsiuʃ] |
| | | |
| ;ino | **casino** (m) | [kɐz'inu] |
| ıstruction | **construção** (f) | [kõʃtrus'ãu] |
| ısulting | **serviços** (m pl) **de consultoria** | [sɐrv'isuʃ də kõsultur'iɐ] |
| | | |
| ıtal clinic | **estomatologia** (f) | [əʃtumɐtuluʒ'iɐ] |
| ;ign | **design** (m) | [diz'ajn] |
| ·gstore, pharmacy | **farmácia** (f) | [fɐrm'asiɐ] |
| cleaners | **lavandaria** (f) | [lɐvãdɐr'iɐ] |
| ployment agency | **agência** (f) **de emprego** | [ɐʒ'ẽsiɐ də ẽpr'egu] |
| | | |
| ıncial services | **serviços** (m pl) **financeiros** | [sɐrv'isuʃ finãs'ɐjruʃ] |
| d products | **alimentos** (m pl) | [ɐlim'ẽtuʃ] |
| eral home | **agência** (f) **funerária** | [ɐʒ'ẽsiɐ funɐr'ariɐ] |
| ıiture (e.g., house ~) | **mobiliário** (m) | [mubilj'ariu] |
| ˉment | **roupa** (f) | [ʀ'opɐ] |
| el | **hotel** (m) | [ɔt'ɛl] |
| | | |
| -cream | **gelado** (m) | [ʒəl'adu] |
| ustry | **indústria** (f) | [ĩd'uʃtriɐ] |
| urance | **seguro** (m) | [səg'uru] |
| ɔrnet | **internet** (f) | [ĩtɛrn'ɛtə] |
| ɛstment | **investimento** (m) | [ĩvəʃtim'ẽtu] |
| | | |
| /eler | **joalheiro** (m) | [ʒuɐʎ'ɐjru] |
| /elry | **joias** (f pl) | [ʒ'ɔjɐʃ] |
| ndry (shop) | **lavandaria** (f) | [lɐvãdɐr'iɐ] |

| legal advisor | serviços (m pl) jurídicos | [sərv'isuʃ ʒur'idikuʃ] |
| light industry | indústria (f) ligeira | [ĩd'uʃtriɐ liʒ'ejrɐ] |
| | | |
| magazine | revista (f) | [ʀɐv'iʃtɐ] |
| mail-order selling | vendas (f pl) por catálogo | [v'ẽdɐʃ pur kɐt'alugu] |
| medicine | medicina (f) | [mɐdis'inɐ] |
| movie theater | cinema (m) | [sin'emɐ] |
| museum | museu (m) | [muz'eu] |
| | | |
| news agency | agência (f) de notícias | [ɐʒ'ẽsiɐ dɐ nut'isiɐʃ] |
| newspaper | jornal (m) | [ʒurn'al] |
| nightclub | clube (m) noturno | [kl'ubɐ nɔt'urnu] |
| | | |
| oil (petroleum) | petróleo (m) | [pɐtr'ɔliu] |
| parcels service | serviço (m) de encomendas | [sərv'isu dɐ ẽkum'ẽdɐʃ] |
| pharmaceuticals | indústria (f) farmacêutica | [ĩd'uʃtriɐ fɐrmɐs'eutikɐ] |
| printing (industry) | poligrafia (f) | [poligrɐf'iɐ] |
| publishing house | editora (f) | [edit'orɐ] |
| | | |
| radio (~ station) | rádio (m) | [ʀ'adiu] |
| real estate | imobiliário (m) | [imubilj'ariu] |
| restaurant | restaurante (m) | [ʀɐʃtaur'ãtɐ] |
| | | |
| security agency | empresa (f) de segurança | [ẽpr'ezɐ dɐ sɐgur'ãsɐ] |
| sports | desporto (m) | [dɐʃp'ortu] |
| stock exchange | bolsa (f) | [b'olsɐ] |
| store | loja (f) | [l'ɔʒɐ] |
| supermarket | supermercado (m) | [supɛrmɐrk'adu] |
| swimming pool | piscina (f) | [piʃs'inɐ] |
| | | |
| tailors | alfaiataria (f) | [alfɐjɐtɐr'iɐ] |
| television | televisão (f) | [tɐlɐviz'ãu] |
| theater | teatro (m) | [tɐ'atru] |
| trade | comércio (m) | [kum'ɛrsiu] |
| transportation | serviços (m pl) de transporte | [sərv'isuʃ dɐ trãʃp'ortɐ] |
| | | |
| travel | viagens (m pl) | [vj'aʒẽjʃ] |
| | | |
| veterinarian | veterinário (m) | [vɐtɐrin'ariu] |
| warehouse | armazém (m) | [ɐrmɐz'ẽj] |
| waste collection | recolha (f) do lixo | [ʀɐk'oʎɐ du l'iʃu] |

# ob. Business. Part 2

## 8. Show. Exhibition

| | | |
|---|---|---|
| ibition, show | **feira** (f) | [f'ejɾɐ] |
| de show | **exposição** (f) **comercial** | [əʃpuzis'ãu kuməɾsj'al] |
| | | |
| ticipation | **participação** (f) | [pɐɾtisipes'ãu] |
| ʃarticipate (vi) | **participar** (vi) | [pɐɾtisip'aɾ] |
| ticipant (exhibitor) | **participante** (m) | [pɐɾtisip'ãtə] |
| | | |
| ɔctor | **diretor** (m) | [diɾɛt'oɾ] |
| ɪanizer's office | **direção** (f) | [diɾɛs'ãu] |
| ɪanizer | **organizador** (m) | [ɔɾgɐnized'oɾ] |
| ɔrganize (vt) | **organizar** (vt) | [ɔɾgɐniz'aɾ] |
| | | |
| ticipation form | **ficha** (f) **de inscrição** | [f'iʃɐ də ĩʃkris'ãu] |
| ill out (vt) | **preencher** (vt) | [priẽʃ'eɾ] |
| ails | **detalhes** (m pl) | [dət'aʎəʃ] |
| ɔrmation | **informação** (f) | [ĩfuɾmes'ãu] |
| | | |
| ɔe | **preço** (m) | [pɾ'esu] |
| luding | **incluindo** | [ĩklu'ĩdu] |
| nclude (vt) | **incluir** (vt) | [ĩklu'iɾ] |
| ɔay (vi, vt) | **pagar** (vt) | [pɐg'aɾ] |
| istration fee | **taxa** (m) **de inscrição** | [t'aʃɐ də ĩʃkris'ãu] |
| | | |
| rance | **entrada** (f) | [ẽtɾ'adɐ] |
| /ilion, hall | **pavilhão** (m) | [pɐviʎ'ãu] |
| egister (vt) | **inscrever** (vt) | [ĩʃkɾɐv'eɾ] |
| ɟge (identity tag) | **crachá** (m) | [kɾɐʃ'a] |
| | | |
| ɔth, stand | **stand** (m) | [st'ãd] |
| eserve, to book | **reservar** (vt) | [ʀəzəɾv'aɾ] |
| | | |
| ɔlay case | **vitrina** (f) | [vitɾ'inɐ] |
| ɔtlight | **foco, spot** (m) | [f'ɔku], [sp'ɔtə] |
| iign | **design** (m) | [diz'ajn] |
| ɔlace (put, set) | **pôr, colocar** (vt) | [poɾ], [kuluk'aɾ] |
| | | |
| tributor | **distribuidor** (m) | [diʃtɾibuid'oɾ] |
| ɔplier | **fornecedor** (m) | [fuɾnəsəd'oɾ] |
| supply (vt) | **fornecer** (vt) | [fuɾnəs'eɾ] |
| | | |
| ⊔ntry | **país** (m) | [pɐ'iʃ] |
| ɜign (adj) | **estrangeiro** | [əʃtɾãʒ'ejɾu] |

| product | produto (m) | [prud'utu] |
| association | associação (f) | [esusies'ãu] |
| conference hall | sala (f) de conferências | [s'ale de kõfer'ẽsieʃ] |
| congress | congresso (m) | [kõgr'ɛsu] |
| contest (competition) | concurso (m) | [kõk'ursu] |

| visitor | visitante (m) | [vizit'ãte] |
| to visit (attend) | visitar (vt) | [vizit'ar] |
| customer | cliente (m) | [klj'ẽte] |

## 119. Mass Media

| newspaper | jornal (m) | [ʒurn'al] |
| magazine | revista (f) | [ʀev'iʃte] |
| press (printed media) | imprensa (f) | [ĩpr'ẽse] |
| radio | rádio (m) | [ʀ'adiu] |
| radio station | estação (f) de rádio | [eʃtes'ãu de ʀ'adiu] |
| television | televisão (f) | [televiz'ãu] |

| presenter, host | apresentador (m) | [eprezẽted'or] |
| newscaster | locutor (m) | [lukut'or] |
| commentator | comentador (m) | [kumẽted'or] |

| journalist | jornalista (m) | [ʒurnel'iʃte] |
| correspondent (reporter) | correspondente (m) | [kuʀeʃpõd'ẽte] |
| press photographer | repórter (m) fotográfico | [ʀep'ortɛr futugr'afiku] |
| reporter | repórter (m) | [ʀep'ortɛr] |

| editor | redator (m) | [ʀedat'or] |
| editor-in-chief | redator-chefe (m) | [ʀedat'or ʃ'ɛfe] |

| to subscribe (to ...) | assinar a ... | [esin'ar e] |
| subscription | assinatura (f) | [esinet'ure] |
| subscriber | assinante (m) | [esin'ãte] |
| to read (vi, vt) | ler (vt) | [ler] |
| reader | leitor (m) | [lejt'or] |

| circulation (of newspaper) | tiragem (f) | [tir'aʒẽj] |
| monthly (adj) | mensal | [mẽs'al] |
| weekly (adj) | semanal | [semen'al] |
| issue (edition) | número (m) | [n'umeru] |
| new (~ issue) | recente | [ʀes'ẽte] |

| headline | título (m) | [t'itulu] |
| short article | pequeno artigo (m) | [pek'enu ert'igu] |
| column (regular article) | rubrica (f) | [ʀubr'ike] |
| article | artigo (m) | [ert'igu] |
| page | página (f) | [p'aʒine] |
| reportage, report | reportagem (f) | [ʀepurt'aʒẽj] |
| event (happening) | evento (m) | [ev'ẽtu] |

| sation (news) | sensação (f) | [sẽses'ãu] |
| ndal | escândalo (m) | [əʃk'ãdelu] |
| ndalous (adj) | escandaloso | [əʃkãdel'ozu] |
| at (~ scandal) | grande | [gr'ãdə] |
| | | |
| gram | programa (m) de TV | [prugr'eme də tɛv'ɛ] |
| rview | entrevista (f) | [ẽtrəv'iʃtə] |
| broadcast | transmissão (f) em direto | [trãʒmis'ãu ẽ dir'ɛtu] |
| nnel | canal (m) | [ken'al] |

## 20. Agriculture

| iculture | agricultura (f) | [egrikult'ure] |
| sant (masc.) | camponês (m) | [kãpun'eʃ] |
| sant (fem.) | camponesa (f) | [kãpun'eze] |
| ner | agricultor (m) | [egrikult'or] |
| | | |
| tor | trator (m) | [trat'or] |
| nbine, harvester | ceifeira-debulhadora (f) | [sejfejre dəbuʎed'ore] |
| | | |
| w | arado (m) | [er'adu] |
| low (vi, vt) | arar (vt) | [er'ar] |
| wland | campo (m) lavrado | [k'ãpu levr'adu] |
| ow (in field) | rego (m) | [ʀ'egu] |
| | | |
| ow (vi, vt) | semear (vt) | [semj'ar] |
| der | semeadora (f) | [semied'ore] |
| ving (process) | semeação (f) | [semies'ãu] |
| | | |
| the | gadanha (m) | [ged'eɲe] |
| now, to scythe | gadanhar (vt) | [gedeɲ'ar] |
| | | |
| de (tool) | pá (f) | [pa] |
| lig (to till) | cavar (vt) | [kev'ar] |
| | | |
| e | enxada (f) | [ẽʃ'ade] |
| loe, to weed | carpir (vt) | [kerp'ir] |
| ed (plant) | erva (f) daninha | ['ɛrve den'iɲe] |
| | | |
| tering can | regador (m) | [ʀeged'or] |
| vater (plants) | regar (vt) | [ʀeg'ar] |
| tering (act) | rega (f) | [ʀ'ege] |
| | | |
| hfork | forquilha (f) | [fork'iʎe] |
| e | ancinho (m) | [ãs'iɲu] |
| | | |
| ilizer | fertilizante (m) | [fertiliz'ãte] |
| ertilize (vt) | fertilizar (vt) | [fertiliz'ar] |
| nure (fertilizer) | estrume (m) | [əʃtr'ume] |
| d | campo (m) | [k'ãpu] |

| meadow | prado (m) | [pr'adu] |
| vegetable garden | horta (f) | ['ɔrtɐ] |
| orchard (e.g., apple ~) | pomar (m) | [pum'ar] |

| to pasture (vt) | pastar (vt) | [pɐʃt'ar] |
| herdsman | pastor (m) | [pɐʃt'or] |
| pastureland | pastagem (f) | [pɐʃt'aʒẽj] |

| cattle breeding | pecuária (f) | [pɐku'ariɐ] |
| sheep farming | criação (f) de ovelhas | [kriɐs'ãu də ɔv'ɐʎɐʃ] |

| plantation | plantação (f) | [plãtɐs'ãu] |
| row (garden bed ~s) | canteiro (m) | [kãt'ejru] |
| hothouse | invernadouro (m) | [ĩvɐrnɐd'oru] |

| drought (lack of rain) | seca (f) | [s'ekɐ] |
| dry (~ summer) | seco | [s'eku] |

| grain | cereal (m) | [sɐrj'al] |
| cereal crops | cereais (m pl) | [sɐrj'ajʃ] |
| to harvest, to gather | colher (vt) | [kuʎ'ɛr] |

| miller (person) | moleiro (m) | [mul'ejru] |
| mill (e.g., gristmill) | moinho (m) | [mu'iɲu] |
| to grind (grain) | moer (vt) | [mu'ɛr] |
| flour | farinha (f) | [fɐr'iɲɐ] |
| straw | palha (f) | [p'aʎɐ] |

## 121. Building. Building process

| construction site | canteiro (m) de obras | [kãt'ejru də 'ɔbrɐʃ] |
| to build (vt) | construir (vt) | [kõʃtru'ir] |
| construction worker | construtor (m) | [kõʃtrut'or] |

| project | projeto (m) | [pruʒ'ɛtu] |
| architect | arquiteto (m) | [ɐrkit'ɛtu] |
| worker | operário (m) | [ɔpɐr'ariu] |

| foundation (of building) | fundação (f) | [fũdɐs'ãu] |
| roof | telhado (m) | [tɐʎ'adu] |
| foundation pile | estaca (f) | [ɐʃt'akɐ] |
| wall | parede (f) | [pɐr'edɐ] |

| reinforcing bars | varões (m pl) para betão | [vɐr'ojʃ p'ɐrɐ bɐt'ãu] |
| scaffolding | andaime (m) | [ãd'ajmɐ] |

| concrete | betão (m) | [bɐt'ãu] |
| granite | granito (m) | [grɐn'itu] |
| stone | pedra (f) | [p'ɛdrɐ] |
| brick | tijolo (m) | [tiʒ'olu] |

| | | |
|---|---|---|
| ıd | areia (f) | [ɐɾ'ɐjɐ] |
| nent | cimento (m) | [sim'ẽtu] |
| ster (for walls) | emboço (m) | [ẽb'ɔsu] |
| ɔlaster (vt) | emboçar (vt) | [ẽbus'aɾ] |
| nt | tinta (f) | [t'ĩtɐ] |
| ɔaint (~ a wall) | pintar (vt) | [pĩt'aɾ] |
| rel | barril (m) | [bɐʀ'il] |
| | | |
| ne | grua (f), guindaste (m) | [gɾ'uɐ], [gĩd'aʃtɐ] |
| ift (vt) | erguer (vt) | [eɾg'eɾ] |
| ower (vt) | baixar (vt) | [bajʃ'aɾ] |
| | | |
| ldozer | buldózer (m) | [buld'ɔzɐɾ] |
| cavator | escavadora (f) | [ɐʃkɐvɐd'oɾɐ] |
| ɔop, bucket | caçamba (f) | [kɐs'ãbɐ] |
| lig (excavate) | escavar (vt) | [ɐʃkɐv'aɾ] |
| d hat | capacete (m) de proteção | [kɐpɐs'etɐ dɐ pɾutɛs'ãu] |

## 22. Science. Research. Scientists

| | | |
|---|---|---|
| ɜnce | ciência (f) | [sj'ẽsiɐ] |
| ɜntific (adj) | científico | [siẽt'ifiku] |
| ɜntist | cientista (m) | [siẽt'iʃtɐ] |
| ory | teoria (f) | [tiuɾ'iɐ] |
| | | |
| ɔm | axioma (m) | [ɐksj'omɐ] |
| ɪlysis | análise (f) | [ɐn'alizɐ] |
| ɐnalyze (vt) | analisar (vt) | [ɐnɐliz'aɾ] |
| ument (strong ~) | argumento (m) | [ɐɾgum'ẽtu] |
| ɔstance (matter) | substância (f) | [subʃt'ãsiɐ] |
| | | |
| ɔothesis | hipótese (f) | [ip'ɔtɐzɐ] |
| ɪmma | dilema (m) | [dil'emɐ] |
| sertation | tese (f) | [t'ɛzɐ] |
| ɟma | dogma (m) | [d'ɔgmɐ] |
| | | |
| ɔtrine | doutrina (f) | [dotɾ'inɐ] |
| earch | investigação (f) | [ĩvɐʃtigɐs'ãu] |
| lo research | investigar (vt) | [ĩvɐʃtig'aɾ] |
| ting | teste (m) | [t'ɛʃtɐ] |
| oratory | laboratório (m) | [lɐbuɾɐt'ɔriu] |
| | | |
| thod | método (m) | [m'ɛtudu] |
| lecule | molécula (f) | [mul'ɛkulɐ] |
| nitoring | monitoramento (m) | [munituɾɐm'ẽtu] |
| covery (act, event) | descoberta (f) | [dɐʃkub'ɛɾtɐ] |
| | | |
| stulate | postulado (m) | [puʃtul'adu] |
| nciple | princípio (m) | [pɾĩs'ipiu] |
| ɜcast | prognóstico (m) | [pɾugn'ɔʃtiku] |

| | | |
|---|---|---|
| prognosticate (vt) | **prognosticar** (vt) | [prugnuʃtik'ar] |
| synthesis | **síntese** (f) | [s'ĩtəzə] |
| trend (tendency) | **tendência** (f) | [tẽd'ẽsiə] |
| theorem | **teorema** (m) | [tiur'emɐ] |
| | | |
| teachings | **ensinamentos** (m pl) | [ẽsinɐm'ẽtuʃ] |
| fact | **facto** (m) | [f'aktu] |
| expedition | **expedição** (f) | [əʃpədis'ãu] |
| experiment | **experiência** (f) | [əʃpərj'ẽsiɐ] |
| | | |
| academician | **académico** (m) | [ɐkɐd'ɛmiku] |
| bachelor (e.g., ~ of Arts) | **bacharel** (m) | [bɐʃɐr'ɛl] |
| doctor (PhD) | **doutor** (m) | [dot'or] |
| Associate Professor | **docente** (m) | [dus'ẽtə] |
| Master (e.g., ~ of Arts) | **mestre** (m) | [m'ɛʃtrə] |
| professor | **professor** (m) **catedrático** | [prufəs'or kɐtədr'atiku] |

# rofessions and occupations

## 23. Job search. Dismissal

| | | |
|---|---|---|
| ff (work force) | trabalho (m) | [trɐb'aʎu] |
| | equipa (f) | [ek'ipɐ] |
| sonnel | pessoal (m) | [pəsu'al] |
| | | |
| eer | carreira (f) | [kɐʀ'ɐjɾɐ] |
| spects | perspetivas (f pl) | [pərʃpɛt'iveʃ] |
| ls (mastery) | mestria (f) | [mɛʃtr'iɐ] |
| | | |
| ection (screening) | seleção (f) | [sələs'ãu] |
| ployment agency | agência (f) de emprego | [ɐʒ'ẽsiɐ də ẽpr'egu] |
| umé | CV, currículo (m) | [sɛv'ɛ], [kuʀ'ikulu] |
| erview (for job) | entrevista (f) | [ẽtrɐv'iʃtɐ] |
| cancy, opening | vaga (f) | [v'agɐ] |
| | | |
| ary, pay | salário (m) | [səl'aɾiu] |
| ed salary | salário (m) fixo | [səl'aɾiu f'iksu] |
| /, compensation | pagamento (m) | [pɐgɐm'ẽtu] |
| | | |
| sition (job) | posto (m) | [p'oʃtu] |
| y (of employee) | dever (m) | [dəv'er] |
| ge of duties | gama (f) de deveres | [g'ɐmɐ də dəv'erəʃ] |
| sy (I'm ~) | ocupado | [ɔkup'adu] |
| | | |
| ire (dismiss) | despedir, demitir (vt) | [dəʃpəd'iɾ], [dəmit'iɾ] |
| missal | demissão (f) | [dəmis'ãu] |
| | | |
| employment | desemprego (m) | [dəzẽpr'egu] |
| employed (n) | desempregado (m) | [dəzẽprəg'adu] |
| rement | reforma (f) | [ʀəf'ɔrmɐ] |
| etire (from job) | reformar-se | [ʀəfurm'arsə] |

## 24. Business people

| | | |
|---|---|---|
| ector | diretor (m) | [dirɛt'or] |
| nager (director) | gerente (m) | [ʒər'ẽtə] |
| ss | patrão, chefe (m) | [pɐtr'ãu], [ʃ'ɛfə] |
| | | |
| erior | superior (m) | [supərj'or] |
| eriors | superiores (m pl) | [supərj'orəʃ] |
| sident | presidente (m) | [prəzid'ẽtə] |

| chairman | presidente (m) de direção | [prəzid'ẽtə də dirɛs'ãu] |
| deputy (substitute) | substituto (m) | [subʃtit'utu] |
| assistant | assistente (m) | [ɐsiʃt'ẽtə] |
| secretary | secretário (m) | [səkrət'ariu] |
| personal assistant | secretário (m) pessoal | [səkrət'ariu pəsu'al] |

| businessman | homem (m) de negócios | ['ɔmẽj də nəg'ɔsiuʃ] |
| entrepreneur | empresário (m) | [ẽprəz'ariu] |
| founder | fundador (m) | [fũdɐd'or] |
| to found (vt) | fundar (vt) | [fũd'ar] |

| incorporator | fundador, sócio (m) | [fũdɐd'or], [s'ɔsiu] |
| partner | parceiro, sócio (m) | [pɐrs'ejru], [s'ɔsiu] |
| stockholder | acionista (m) | [ɐsiun'iʃtə] |

| millionaire | milionário (m) | [miliun'ariu] |
| billionaire | bilionário (m) | [biliun'ariu] |
| owner, proprietor | proprietário (m) | [prupriɛt'ariu] |
| landowner | proprietário (m) de terras | [prupriɛt'ariu də t'ɛʀəʃ] |

| client | cliente (m) | [klj'ẽtə] |
| regular client | cliente (m) habitual | [klj'ẽtə ɐbitu'al] |
| buyer (customer) | comprador (m) | [kõprɐd'or] |
| visitor | visitante (m) | [vizit'ãtə] |

| professional (n) | profissional (m) | [prufisiun'al] |
| expert | perito (m) | [pər'itu] |
| specialist | especialista (m) | [əʃpəsiel'iʃtə] |

| banker | banqueiro (m) | [bãk'ejru] |
| broker | corretor (m) | [kuʀɛt'or] |

| cashier, teller | caixa (m, f) | [k'ajʃə] |
| accountant | contabilista (m) | [kõtəbil'iʃtə] |
| security guard | guarda (m) | [gu'ardə] |

| investor | investidor (m) | [ĩvəʃtid'or] |
| debtor | devedor (m) | [dəvəd'or] |
| creditor | credor (m) | [krɛd'or] |
| borrower | mutuário (m) | [mutu'ariu] |

| importer | importador (m) | [ĩpurtɐd'or] |
| exporter | exportador (m) | [əʃpurtɐd'or] |

| manufacturer | produtor (m) | [prudut'or] |
| distributor | distribuidor (m) | [diʃtribuid'or] |
| middleman | intermediário (m) | [ĩtərmədj'ariu] |

| consultant | consultor (m) | [kõsult'or] |
| sales representative | representante (m) | [ʀəprəzẽt'ãtə] |
| agent | agente (m) | [ɐʒ'ẽtə] |
| insurance agent | agente (m) de seguros | [ɐʒ'ẽtə də səg'uruʃ] |

## 25. Service professions

| | | |
|---|---|---|
| ok | cozinheiro (m) | [kuziɲ'ejɾu] |
| ef (kitchen chef) | cozinheiro chefe (m) | [kuziɲ'ejɾu ʃ'ɛfə] |
| ker | padeiro (m) | [pad'ejɾu] |
| | | |
| tender | barman (m) | [b'armɐn] |
| iter | empregado (m) de mesa | [ẽpɾɐg'adu də m'eze] |
| tress | empregada (f) de mesa | [ẽpɾɐg'adɐ də m'eze] |
| | | |
| yer, attorney | advogado (m) | [ɐdvug'adu] |
| yer (legal expert) | jurista (m) | [ʒuɾ'iʃtɐ] |
| ary | notário (m) | [nut'aɾiu] |
| | | |
| ctrician | eletricista (m) | [elɛtɾis'iʃtɐ] |
| mber | canalizador (m) | [kɐnɐlizɐd'oɾ] |
| penter | carpinteiro (m) | [kɐɾpĩt'ejɾu] |
| | | |
| sseur | massagista (m) | [mɐsɐʒ'iʃtɐ] |
| sseuse | massagista (f) | [mɐsɐʒ'iʃtɐ] |
| ctor | médico (m) | [m'ɛdiku] |
| i driver | taxista (m) | [taks'iʃtɐ] |
| ver | condutor (m) | [kõdut'oɾ] |
| ivery man | entregador (m) | [ẽtɾɐgɐd'oɾ] |
| | | |
| ambermaid | camareira (f) | [kɐmɐɾ'ejɾɐ] |
| curity guard | guarda (m) | [gu'aɾdɐ] |
| ht attendant | hospedeira (f) de bordo | [ɔʃpəd'ejɾɐ də b'ɔɾdu] |
| | | |
| cher (in primary school) | professor (m) | [pɾufəs'oɾ] |
| arian | bibliotecário (m) | [bibliutɐk'aɾiu] |
| nslator | tradutor (m) | [tɾɐdut'oɾ] |
| erpreter | intérprete (m) | [ĩt'ɛɾpɾɐtə] |
| de | guia (m) | [g'iɐ] |
| | | |
| rdresser | cabeleireiro (m) | [kɐbələjɾ'ejɾu] |
| ilman | carteiro (m) | [kɐɾt'ejɾu] |
| esman (store staff) | vendedor (m) | [vẽdɐd'oɾ] |
| | | |
| dener | jardineiro (m) | [ʒɐɾdiɲ'ejɾu] |
| mestic servant | criado (m) | [kɾj'adu] |
| id | criada (f) | [kɾj'adɐ] |
| aner (cleaning lady) | empregada (f) de limpeza | [ẽpɾɐg'adɐ də l̃p'eze] |

## 26. Military professions and ranks

| | | |
|---|---|---|
| vate | soldado (m) raso | [sold'adu ʀ'azu] |
| geant | sargento (m) | [sɐɾʒ'ẽtu] |

| lieutenant | tenente (m) | [tən'ētə] |
| captain | capitão (m) | [kəpit'ãu] |

| major | major (m) | [mɐʒ'ɔr] |
| colonel | coronel (m) | [kurun'ɛl] |
| general | general (m) | [ʒənər'al] |
| marshal | marechal (m) | [mɐrəʃ'al] |
| admiral | almirante (m) | [almir'ãtə] |

| military man | militar (m) | [milit'ar] |
| soldier | soldado (m) | [sold'adu] |
| officer | oficial (m) | [ɔfisj'al] |
| commander | comandante (m) | [kumãd'ãtə] |

| border guard | guarda (m) fronteiriço | [gu'ardɐ frõtejr'isu] |
| radio operator | operador (m) de rádio | [ɔpɐred'or də ʀ'adiu] |
| scout (searcher) | explorador (m) | [əʃplurɐd'or] |
| pioneer (sapper) | sapador (m) | [sɐpɐd'or] |
| marksman | atirador (m) | [etirɐd'or] |
| navigator | navegador (m) | [nɐvɐgɐd'or] |

## 127. Officials. Priests

| king | rei (m) | [ʀej] |
| queen | rainha (f) | [ʀɐ'iɲɐ] |

| prince | príncipe (m) | [pr'ĩsipə] |
| princess | princesa (f) | [prĩs'ezɐ] |

| tsar, czar | czar (m) | [kz'ar] |
| czarina | czarina (f) | [kzɐr'inɐ] |

| president | presidente (m) | [prɐzid'ētə] |
| Secretary (~ of State) | ministro (m) | [min'iʃtru] |
| prime minister | primeiro-ministro (m) | [prim'ejru min'iʃtru] |
| senator | senador (m) | [sɐnɐd'or] |

| diplomat | diplomata (m) | [diplum'atɐ] |
| consul | cônsul (m) | [k'õsul] |
| ambassador | embaixador (m) | [ẽbajʃɐd'or] |
| advisor (military ~) | conselheiro (m) | [kõsɐʎ'ejru] |

| official (civil servant) | funcionário (m) | [fũsiun'ariu] |
| prefect | prefeito (m) | [prɐf'ejtu] |
| mayor | Presidente (m) da Câmara | [prɐzid'ētə dɐ k'emɐrɐ] |

| judge | juiz (m) | [ʒu'iʃ] |
| district attorney (prosecutor) | procurador (m) | [prɔkurɐd'or] |
| missionary | missionário (m) | [misiun'ariu] |

| nk | monge (m) | [mˈõʒə] |
| ɔt | abade (m) | [ɐbˈadə] |
| bi | rabino (m) | [ʀɐbˈinu] |
| er | vizir (m) | [vizˈir] |
| ɐh | xá (m) | [ʃa] |
| ɛikh | xeque (m) | [ʃˈɛkə] |

## 28. Agricultural professions

| ɛkeeper | apicultor (m) | [ɐpikultˈor] |
| ɾder, shepherd | pastor (m) | [pɐʃtˈor] |
| onomist | agrónomo (m) | [ɐgrˈɔnumu] |
| tle breeder | criador (m) de gado | [kriɐdˈor də gˈadu] |
| ɛrinarian | veterinário (m) | [vətərinˈariu] |
| ner | agricultor (m) | [ɐgrikultˈor] |
| ɪemaker | vinicultor (m) | [vinikultˈor] |
| ɔlogist | zoólogo (m) | [zuˈɔlugu] |
| vboy | cowboy (m) | [kɔbˈɔj] |

## 29. Art professions

| or | ator (m) | [atˈor] |
| ress | atriz (f) | [ɐtrˈiʃ] |
| ger (masc.) | cantor (m) | [kãtˈor] |
| ger (fem.) | cantora (f) | [kãtˈorɐ] |
| ɪcer (masc.) | bailarino (m) | [bajlɐrˈinu] |
| ɪcer (fem.) | bailarina (f) | [bajlɐrˈinɐ] |
| forming artist (masc.) | artista (m) | [ɐrtˈiʃtɐ] |
| forming artist (fem.) | artista (f) | [ɐrtˈiʃtɐ] |
| ɪsician | músico (m) | [mˈuziku] |
| nist | pianista (m) | [piɐnˈiʃtɐ] |
| tar player | guitarrista (m) | [gitɐʀˈiʃtɐ] |
| ɪductor (orchestra ~) | maestro (m) | [mɐˈɛʃtru] |
| nposer | compositor (m) | [kõpuzitˈor] |
| ɔresario | empresário (m) | [ẽprəzˈariu] |
| vie director | realizador (m) | [ʀiɐlizedˈor] |
| ducer | produtor (m) | [prudutˈor] |
| iptwriter | argumentista (m) | [ɐrgumẽtˈiʃtɐ] |
| ɪc | crítico (m) | [krˈitiku] |
| ter | escritor (m) | [əʃkritˈor] |

| poet | poeta (m) | [pu'ɛtɐ] |
| sculptor | escultor (m) | [əʃkult'or] |
| artist (painter) | pintor (m) | [pĩt'or] |

| juggler | malabarista (m) | [mɐlɐbɐɾ'iʃtɐ] |
| clown | palhaço (m) | [pɐʎ'asu] |
| acrobat | acrobata (m) | [ɐkrub'atɐ] |
| magician | mágico (m) | [m'aʒiku] |

## 130. Various professions

| doctor | médico (m) | [m'ɛdiku] |
| nurse | enfermeira (f) | [ẽfɐrm'ejrɐ] |
| psychiatrist | psiquiatra (m) | [psiki'atrɐ] |
| dentist | estomatologista (m) | [əʃtumɐtuluʒ'iʃtɐ] |
| surgeon | cirurgião (m) | [sirurʒj'ãu] |

| astronaut | astronauta (m) | [ɐʃtrɔn'autɐ] |
| astronomer | astrónomo (m) | [ɐʃtr'ɔnumu] |
| pilot | piloto (m) | [pil'otu] |

| driver (of taxi, etc.) | motorista (m) | [mutuɾ'iʃtɐ] |
| engineer (train driver) | maquinista (m) | [mɐkin'iʃtɐ] |
| mechanic | mecânico (m) | [mɐk'ɐniku] |

| miner | mineiro (m) | [min'ejru] |
| worker | operário (m) | [ɔpɐɾ'ariu] |
| metalworker | serralheiro (m) | [sɐʀɐʎ'ejru] |
| joiner (carpenter) | marceneiro (m) | [mɐrsɐn'ejru] |
| turner | torneiro (m) | [turn'ejru] |
| construction worker | construtor (m) | [kõʃtrut'or] |
| welder | soldador (m) | [soldɐd'or] |

| professor (title) | professor (m) catedrático | [prufɐs'or kɐtɐdr'atiku] |
| architect | arquiteto (m) | [ɐrkit'ɛtu] |
| historian | historiador (m) | [iʃturiɐd'or] |
| scientist | cientista (m) | [siẽt'iʃtɐ] |
| physicist | físico (m) | [f'iziku] |
| chemist (scientist) | químico (m) | [k'imiku] |

| archeologist | arqueólogo (m) | [ɐrkj'ɔlugu] |
| geologist | geólogo (m) | [ʒj'ɔlugu] |
| researcher | investigador (m) | [ĩvɐʃtigɐd'or] |

| babysitter | babysitter (f) | [bɐbisit'er] |
| teacher, educator | professor (m) | [prufɐs'or] |

| editor | redator (m) | [ʀɐdat'or] |
| editor-in-chief | redator-chefe (m) | [ʀɐdat'or ʃ'ɛfɐ] |
| correspondent | correspondente (m) | [kuʀɐʃpõd'ẽtɐ] |

| | | |
|---|---|---|
| ist (fem.) | datilógrafa (f) | [dɐtil'ɔgrɐfɐ] |
| signer | designer (m) | [diz'ajnɐr] |
| nputer expert | especialista (m) em informática | [ɐʃpɐsiel'iʃtɐ ɐn ĩfurm'atikɐ] |
| grammer | programador (m) | [prugrɐmɐd'or] |
| jineer (designer) | engenheiro (m) | [ẽʒɐɲ'ejru] |
| | | |
| or | marujo (m) | [mɐr'uʒu] |
| iman | marinheiro (m) | [mɐriɲ'ejru] |
| cuer | salvador (m) | [salvɐd'or] |
| | | |
| man | bombeiro (m) | [bõb'ejru] |
| iceman | polícia (m) | [pul'isiɐ] |
| tchman | guarda-noturno (m) | [gu'ardɐ nɔt'urnu] |
| ective | detetive (m) | [dɐtɛt'ivɐ] |
| | | |
| stoms officer | funcionário (m) da alfândega | [fũsiun'ariu dɐ alf'ãdɐgɐ] |
| dyguard | guarda-costas (m) | [gu'ardɐ k'ɔʃtɐʃ] |
| son guard | guarda (m) prisional | [gu'ardɐ priziun'al] |
| pector | inspetor (m) | [ĩʃpɛt'or] |
| | | |
| ortsman | desportista (m) | [dɐʃpurt'iʃtɐ] |
| ner, coach | treinador (m) | [trɐjnɐd'or] |
| cher | carniceiro (m) | [kɐrnis'ejru] |
| obler | sapateiro (m) | [sɐpɐt'ejru] |
| rchant | comerciante (m) | [kumɐrsj'ãtɐ] |
| der (person) | carregador (m) | [kɐʀɐgɐd'or] |
| | | |
| hion designer | estilista (m) | [ɐʃtil'iʃtɐ] |
| del (fem.) | modelo (f) | [mud'elu] |

## 81. Occupations. Social status

| | | |
|---|---|---|
| oolboy | escolar (m) | [ɐʃkul'ar] |
| dent (college ~) | estudante (m) | [ɐʃtud'ãtɐ] |
| | | |
| losopher | filósofo (m) | [fil'ɔzufu] |
| onomist | economista (m) | [ekɔnum'iʃtɐ] |
| entor | inventor (m) | [ĩvẽt'or] |
| | | |
| employed (n) | desempregado (m) | [dɐzẽprɐg'adu] |
| ree | reformado (m) | [ʀɐfurm'adu] |
| /, secret agent | espião (m) | [ɐʃpj'ãu] |
| | | |
| soner | preso (m) | [pr'ezu] |
| ker | grevista (m) | [grɛv'iʃtɐ] |
| eaucrat | burocrata (m) | [burukr'atɐ] |
| veler | viajante (m) | [viɐʒ'ãtɐ] |
| nosexual | homossexual (m) | [ɔmɔsɛksu'al] |

| hacker | hacker (m) | ['akɛɾ] |
| hippie | hippie | ['ipi] |
| | | |
| bandit | bandido (m) | [bãd'idu] |
| hit man, killer | assassino (m) a soldo | [ɐsɐs'inu ɐ s'oldu] |
| drug addict | toxicodependente (m) | [tɔksikɔdəpẽd'ẽtə] |
| drug dealer | traficante (m) | [trɐfik'ãtə] |
| prostitute (fem.) | prostituta (f) | [pruʃtit'utə] |
| pimp | chulo (m) | [ʃ'ulu] |
| | | |
| sorcerer | bruxo (m) | [br'uʃu] |
| sorceress | bruxa (f) | [br'uʃɐ] |
| pirate | pirata (m) | [pir'atɐ] |
| slave | escravo (m) | [əʃkr'avu] |
| samurai | samurai (m) | [sɐmur'aj] |
| savage (primitive) | selvagem (m) | [sɛlv'aʒẽj] |

# ports

## 32. Kinds of sports. Sportspersons

| | | |
|---|---|---|
| ortsman | desportista (m) | [dəʃpurt'iʃtɐ] |
| d of sports | tipo (m) de desporto | [t'ipu də dəʃp'ortu] |
| | | |
| sketball | basquetebol (m) | [bɐʃkɛtəb'ɔl] |
| sketball player | jogador (m) de basquetebol | [ʒugɐd'or də bɐʃkɛtəb'ɔl] |
| | | |
| seball | beisebol (m) | [b'ɛjzbɔl] |
| seball player | jogador (m) de beisebol | [ʒugɐd'or də b'ɛjzbɔl] |
| | | |
| ocer | futebol (m) | [futəb'ɔl] |
| ocer player | futebolista (m) | [futəbul'iʃtɐ] |
| alkeeper | guarda-redes (m) | [gu'ardɐ ʀ'edəʃ] |
| | | |
| okey | hóquei (m) | ['ɔkej] |
| okey player | jogador (m) de hóquei | [ʒugɐd'or də 'ɔkej] |
| | | |
| leyball | voleibol (m) | [vɔlɐjb'ɔl] |
| leyball player | jogador (m) de voleibol | [ʒugɐd'or də vɔlɐjb'ɔl] |
| | | |
| king | boxe (m) | [b'ɔksə] |
| ker | boxeador, pugilista (m) | [bɔʃiɐd'or], [puʒil'iʃtɐ] |
| | | |
| estling | luta (f) | [l'utɐ] |
| estler | lutador (m) | [lutɐd'or] |
| | | |
| ate | karaté (m) | [karat'ɛ] |
| ate fighter | karateca (m) | [kɐrɐt'ɛkɐ] |
| | | |
| o | judo (m) | [ʒ'udu] |
| o athlete | judoca (m) | [ʒud'ɔkɐ] |
| | | |
| nis | ténis (m) | [t'ɛniʃ] |
| nis player | tenista (m) | [tɛn'iʃtɐ] |
| | | |
| mming | natação (f) | [nɐtɐs'ãu] |
| mmer | nadador (m) | [nɐdɐd'or] |
| | | |
| cing | esgrima (f) | [əʒgr'imɐ] |
| cer | esgrimista (m) | [əʒgrim'iʃtɐ] |
| ess | xadrez (m) | [ʃɐdr'eʃ] |
| ess player | xadrezista (m) | [ʃɐdrəz'iʃtɐ] |

| alpinism | alpinismo (m) | [alpin'iʒmu] |
| alpinist | alpinista (m) | [alpin'iʃtɐ] |

| running | corrida (f) | [kuʀ'idɐ] |
| runner | corredor (m) | [kuʀɐd'or] |

| athletics | atletismo (m) | [ɐtlɛt'iʒmu] |
| athlete | atleta (m) | [ɐtl'ɛtɐ] |

| horseback riding | hipismo (m) | [ip'iʒmu] |
| horse rider | cavaleiro (m) | [kɐvɐl'ɐjɾu] |

| figure skating | patinagem (f) artística | [pɐtin'aʒɐj ɐɾt'iʃtikɐ] |
| figure skater (masc.) | patinador (m) | [pɐtinɐd'or] |
| figure skater (fem.) | patinadora (f) | [pɐtinɐd'oɾɐ] |

| weightlifting | halterofilismo (m) | [altɛɾɔfil'iʒmu] |
| weightlifter | halterofilista (m) | [altɛɾɔfil'iʃtɐ] |

| car racing | corrida (f) de carros | [kuʀ'idɐ dɐ k'aʀuʃ] |
| racing driver | piloto (m) | [pil'otu] |

| cycling | ciclismo (m) | [sikl'iʒmu] |
| cyclist | ciclista (m) | [sikl'iʃtɐ] |

| broad jump | salto (m) em comprimento | [s'altu ẽ kõprim'ẽtu] |
| pole vault | salto (m) à vara | [s'altu a v'aɾɐ] |
| jumper | atleta (m) de saltos | [ɐtl'ɛtɐ dɐ s'altuʃ] |

## 133. Kinds of sports. Miscellaneous

| football | futebol (m) americano | [futɐb'ɔl ɐmɐrik'ɐnu] |
| badminton | badminton (m) | [badm'ĩtɔn] |

| biathlon | biatlo (m) | [bj'atlu] |
| billiards | bilhar (m) | [biʎ'ar] |

| bobsled | bobsleigh (m) | [bɔbsl'ɐj] |
| bodybuilding | musculação (f) | [muʃkulɐs'ãu] |
| water polo | pólo (m) aquático | [p'ɔlu ɐku'atiku] |

| handball | handebol (m) | [ãdɐb'ɔl] |
| golf | golfe (m) | [g'olfɐ] |

| rowing | remo (m) | [ʀ'ɛmu] |
| scuba diving | mergulho (m) | [mɐrg'uʎu] |

| cross-country skiing | corrida (f) de esqui | [kuʀ'idɐ dɐ ɐʃk'i] |
| ping-pong | ténis (m) de mesa | [t'ɛniʃ dɐ m'ezɐ] |

| ling | vela (f) | [v'ɛlɐ] |
| y racing | rali (m) | [ʀɐl'i] |
| by | rugbi (m) | [ʀ'egbi] |
| wboarding | snowboard (m) | [snoub'ɔrd] |
| hery | tiro (m) com arco | [t'iru kõ 'arku] |

## 34. Gym

| bell | barra (f) | [b'aʀɐ] |
| nbbells | halteres (m pl) | [alt'ɛɾɐʃ] |
| ning machine | aparelho (m) de musculaçao | [ɐpɐɾ'ɐʎu də muʃkulɐs'ɐu] |
| ycle trainer | bicicleta (f) ergométrica | [bisikl'ɛtɐ ergum'ɛtrikɐ] |
| admill | passadeira (f) | [pɐsɐd'ɐjɾɐ] |
| izontal bar | barra (f) fixa | [b'aʀɐ f'iksɐ] |
| allel bars | barras (f) paralelas | [b'aʀɐʃ pɐɾɐl'ɛlɐʃ] |
| lting horse | cavalo (m) | [kɐv'alu] |
| t (in gym) | tapete (m) de ginástica | [tɐp'etɐ də ʒin'aʃtikɐ] |
| p rope | corda (f) de saltar | [k'ɔrdɐ də salt'ar] |
| obics | aeróbica (f) | [ɛɛɾ'ɔbikɐ] |
| ja | ioga (f) | [j'ɔgɐ] |

## 35. Hockey

| key | hóquei (m) | ['ɔkɐj] |
| key player | jogador (m) de hóquei | [ʒugɐd'or də 'ɔkɐj] |
| lay hockey | jogar hóquei | [ʒug'ar 'ɔkɐj] |
| | gelo (m) | [ʒ'elu] |
| k | disco (m) | [d'iʃku] |
| key stick | taco (m) de hóquei | [t'aku də 'ɔkɐj] |
| skates | patins (m pl) de gelo | [pɐt'ĩʃ də ʒ'elu] |
| ard | muro (m) | [m'uru] |
| t | tiro (m) | [t'iru] |
| altender | guarda-redes (m) | [gu'ardɐ ʀ'edɐʃ] |
| al (score) | golo (m) | [g'olu] |
| core a goal | marcar um golo | [mɐrk'ar ũ g'olu] |
| iod | tempo (m) | [t'ẽpu] |
| ond period | segundo tempo (m) | [sɐg'ũdu t'ẽpu] |
| stitutes bench | banco (m) de reservas | [b'ãku də ʀɐz'ɛrvɐʃ] |

## 136. Football

| | | |
|---|---|---|
| soccer | futebol (m) | [futəb'ɔl] |
| soccer player | futebolista (m) | [futəbul'iʃte] |
| to play soccer | jogar futebol | [ʒug'ar futəb'ɔl] |
| | | |
| major league | Liga Principal (f) | [l'igɐ prĩsip'al] |
| soccer club | clube (m) de futebol | [kl'ubə də futəb'ɔl] |
| coach | treinador (m) | [trɐjnɐd'or] |
| owner, proprietor | proprietário (m) | [prupriɛt'ariu] |
| | | |
| team | equipa (f) | [ek'ipɐ] |
| team captain | capitão (m) da equipa | [kɐpit'ãu dɐ ek'ipɐ] |
| player | jogador (m) | [ʒugɐd'or] |
| substitute | jogador (m) de reserva | [ʒugɐd'or də ʀəz'ɛrvɐ] |
| | | |
| forward | atacante (m) | [ɐtɐk'ãtɐ] |
| center forward | avançado (m) centro | [ɐvãs'adu s'ẽtru] |
| striker, scorer | marcador (m) | [mɐrkɐd'or] |
| defender, back | defesa (m) | [dəf'ezɐ] |
| halfback | médio (m) | [m'ɛdiu] |
| | | |
| match | jogo (m) | [ʒ'ogu] |
| to meet (vi, vt) | defrontar-se (vp) | [dəfrõt'arsə] |
| final | final (m) | [fin'al] |
| semi-final | meia-final (f) | [m'ɐjɐ fin'al] |
| championship | campeonato (m) | [kãpiun'atu] |
| | | |
| period, half | tempo (m) | [t'ẽpu] |
| first period | primeiro tempo (m) | [prim'ɐjru t'ẽpu] |
| half-time | intervalo (m) | [ĩtərv'alu] |
| | | |
| goal | baliza (f) | [bɐl'izɐ] |
| goalkeeper | guarda-redes (m) | [gu'ardɐ ʀ'edəʃ] |
| goalpost | poste (m) | [p'ɔʃtə] |
| crossbar | travessa (f) | [trɐv'ɛsɐ] |
| net | rede (f) | [ʀ'edə] |
| to concede a goal | sofrer um golo | [sufr'er ũ g'olu] |
| | | |
| ball | bola (f) | [b'ɔlɐ] |
| pass | passe (m) | [p'asə] |
| kick | chute (m) | [ʃ'utə] |
| to kick (~ the ball) | chutar (vt) | [ʃut'ar] |
| free kick | tiro (m) livre | [t'iru l'ivrə] |
| corner kick | canto (m) | [k'ãtu] |
| | | |
| attack | ataque (m) | [ɐt'akə] |
| counterattack | contra-ataque (m) | [k'õtrɐ ɐt'akə] |
| combination | combinação (f) | [kõbinɐs'ãu] |
| referee | árbitro (m) | ['arbitru] |
| to whistle (vi) | apitar (vi) | [ɐpit'ar] |

| stle (sound) | apito (m) | [ɐp'itu] |
| l, misconduct | falta (f) | [f'altɐ] |
| commit a foul | cometer a falta | [kumɐt'eɾ ɐ f'altɐ] |
| send off | expulsar (vt) | [ɐʃpuls'aɾ] |

| ow card | cartão (m) amarelo | [kɐɾt'ãu ɐmɐɾ'ɛlu] |
| card | cartão (m) vermelho | [kɐɾt'ãu vɐɾm'eʎu] |
| qualification | desqualificação (f) | [dɐʃkuɐlifikɐs'ãu] |
| disqualify (vt) | desqualificar (vt) | [dɐʃkuɐlifik'aɾ] |

| alty kick | penálti (m) | [pɐn'alti] |
| ll | barreira (f) | [bɐʀ'ejɾɐ] |
| score (vi, vt) | marcar (vt) | [mɐɾk'aɾ] |
| al (score) | golo (m) | [g'olu] |
| score a goal | marcar um golo | [mɐɾk'aɾ ũ g'olu] |

| stitution | substituto (m) | [subʃtit'utu] |
| eplace (vt) | substituir (vt) | [subʃtitu'iɾ] |
| es | regulamento (m) | [ʀɐgulɐm'ẽtu] |
| tics | tática (f) | [t'atikɐ] |

| dium | estádio (m) | [ɐʃt'adiu] |
| nd (bleachers) | bancadas (f pl) | [bãk'adɐʃ] |
| , supporter | fã, adepto (m) | [fã], [ɐd'ɛptu] |
| shout (vi) | gritar (vi) | [grit'aɾ] |

| reboard | marcador (m) | [mɐɾkɐd'or] |
| re | resultado (m) | [ʀɐzult'adu] |

| eat | derrota (f) | [dɐʀ'ɔtɐ] |
| ose (not win) | perder (vt) | [pɐɾd'eɾ] |
| w | empate (m) | [ẽp'atɐ] |
| draw (vi) | empatar (vi) | [ẽpɐt'aɾ] |

| tory | vitória (f) | [vit'ɔɾiɐ] |
| win (vi, vt) | ganhar, vencer (vi, vt) | [gɐɲ'aɾ], [vẽs'eɾ] |
| ampion | campeão (m) | [kãpj'ãu] |
| st (adj) | melhor | [mɐʎ'ɔr] |
| congratulate (vt) | felicitar (vt) | [fɐlisit'aɾ] |

| nmentator | comentador (m) | [kumẽtɐd'or] |
| commentate (vt) | comentar (vt) | [kumẽt'aɾ] |
| adcast | transmissão (f) | [trãʒmis'ãu] |

## 37. Alpine skiing

| s | esqui (m) | [ɐʃk'i] |
| ski (vi) | esquiar (vi) | [ɐʃki'aɾ] |
| untain-ski resort | estância (f) de esqui | [ɐʃt'ãsiɐ dɐ ɐʃk'i] |
| lift | teleférico (m) | [tɐlɐf'ɛriku] |

| ski poles | bastões (m pl) de esqui | [bɐʃ'ojʃ də əʃk'i] |
| slope | declive (m) | [dəkl'ivə] |
| slalom | slalom (m) | [sl'alom] |

## 138. Tennis. Golf

| golf | golfe (m) | [g'olfə] |
| golf club | clube (m) de golfe | [kl'ubə də g'olfə] |
| golfer | jogador (m) de golfe | [ʒugɐd'or də g'olfə] |

| hole | buraco (m) | [bur'aku] |
| club | taco (m) | [t'aku] |
| golf trolley | trolley (m) | [trul'ɐj] |

| tennis | ténis (m) | [t'ɛniʃ] |
| tennis court | quadra (f) de ténis | [ku'adrɐ də t'ɛniʃ] |
| serve | saque (m) | [s'akə] |
| to serve (vt) | sacar (vi) | [sɐk'ar] |
| racket | raquete (f) | [ʀɐk'ɛtə] |
| net | rede (f) | [ʀ'edə] |
| ball | bola (f) | [b'ɔlɐ] |

## 139. Chess

| chess | xadrez (m) | [ʃɐdr'eʃ] |
| chessmen | peças (f pl) de xadrez | [p'ɛsəʃ də ʃɐdr'eʃ] |
| chess player | xadrezista (m) | [ʃɐdrəz'iʃtə] |
| chessboard | tabuleiro (m) de xadrez | [tɐbul'ɐjru də ʃɐdr'eʃ] |
| chessman | peça (f) de xadrez | [p'ɛsɐ də ʃɐdr'eʃ] |

| White (white pieces) | brancas (f pl) | [br'ãkəʃ] |
| Black (black pieces) | pretas (f pl) | [pr'etəʃ] |

| pawn | peão (m) | [pj'ãu] |
| bishop | bispo (m) | [b'iʃpu] |
| knight | cavalo (m) | [kɐv'alu] |
| rook (castle) | torre (f), roque (m) | [t'oʀə], [ʀ'ɔkə] |
| queen | dama (f) | [d'ɐmɐ] |
| king | rei (m) | [ʀɐj] |

| move | vez (f) | [veʒ] |
| to move (vi, vt) | mover (vt) | [muv'er] |
| to sacrifice (vt) | sacrificar (vt) | [sɐkrifik'ar] |
| castling | roque (m) | [ʀ'ɔkə] |
| check | xeque (m) | [ʃ'ɛkə] |
| checkmate | xeque-mate (m) | [ʃ'ɛkə m'atə] |
| chess tournament | torneio (m) de xadrez | [turn'ɐju də ʃɐdr'eʃ] |
| Grand Master | grão-mestre (m) | [gr'ãu m'ɛʃtrə] |

| combination | combinação (f) | [kõbines'ãu] |
| game (in chess) | partida (f) | [pert'ide] |
| checkers | jogo (m) de damas | [ʒ'ogu de d'emeʃ] |

## 140. Boxing

| boxing | boxe (m) | [b'ɔkse] |
| fight (bout) | combate (m) | [kõb'ate] |
| boxing match | duelo (m) | [du'ɛlu] |
| round (in boxing) | round, assalto (m) | [ʀ'õd], [es'altu] |

| ring | ringue (m) | [ʀ'ĩge] |
| gong | gongo (m) | [g'õgu] |

| punch | murro, soco (m) | [m'uʀu], [s'oku] |
| knock-down | knockdown (m) | [kn'ɔkdoun] |
| knockout | nocaute (m) | [nɔk'aute] |
| to knock out | nocautear (vt) | [nɔkautj'ar] |

| boxing glove | luva (f) de boxe | [l'uve de b'ɔkse] |
| referee | árbitro (m) | ['arbitru] |

| lightweight | peso-leve (m) | [p'ezu l'ɛve] |
| middleweight | peso-médio (m) | [p'ezu m'ɛdiu] |
| heavyweight | peso-pesado (m) | [p'ezu pez'adu] |

## 141. Sports. Miscellaneous

| Olympic Games | Jogos (m pl) Olímpicos | [ʒ'ɔguʃ ɔl'ĩpikuʃ] |
| winner | vencedor (m) | [vẽsed'or] |
| to be winning | vencer (vi) | [vẽs'er] |
| to win (vi) | ganhar (vi) | [gaɲ'ar] |

| leader | líder (m) | [l'idɛr] |
| to lead (vi) | liderar (vt) | [lider'ar] |

| first place | primeiro lugar (m) | [prim'ejru lug'ar] |
| second place | segundo lugar (m) | [seg'ũdu lug'ar] |
| third place | terceiro lugar (m) | [ters'ejru lug'ar] |

| medal | medalha (f) | [med'aʎe] |
| trophy | troféu (m) | [truf'ɛu] |
| prize cup (trophy) | taça (f) | [t'ase] |
| prize (in game) | prémio (m) | [pr'ɛmiu] |
| main prize | prémio (m) principal | [pr'ɛmiu prĩsip'al] |

| record | recorde (m) | [ʀek'ɔrde] |
| to set a record | estabelecer um recorde | [eʃtebeles'er ũ ʀek'ɔrde] |

| final | **final** (m) | [fin'al] |
| final (adj) | **final** | [fin'al] |

| champion | **campeão** (m) | [kãpj'ãu] |
| championship | **campeonato** (m) | [kãpiun'atu] |

| stadium | **estádio** (m) | [əʃt'adiu] |
| stand (bleachers) | **bancadas** (f pl) | [bãk'adeʃ] |
| fan, supporter | **fã, adepto** (m) | [fã], [ɐd'ɛptu] |
| opponent, rival | **adversário** (m) | [ɐdvərs'aɾiu] |

| start | **partida** (f) | [pɐrt'idɐ] |
| finish line | **chegada, meta** (f) | [ʃəg'adɐ], [m'ɛtɐ] |

| defeat | **derrota** (f) | [dəʀ'ɔtɐ] |
| to lose (not win) | **perder** (vt) | [pərd'er] |

| referee | **árbitro** (m) | ['arbitru] |
| jury | **júri** (m) | [ʒ'uɾi] |
| score | **resultado** (m) | [ʀəzult'adu] |
| draw | **empate** (m) | [ẽp'atɐ] |
| to draw (vi) | **empatar** (vi) | [ẽpɐt'ar] |
| point | **ponto** (m) | [p'õtu] |
| result (final score) | **resultado** (m) **final** | [ʀəzult'adu fin'al] |

| period | **tempo, período** (m) | [t'ẽpu pər'iwdu] |
| half-time | **intervalo** (m) | [ĩtərv'alu] |
| doping | **doping** (m) | [d'ɔpĩg] |
| to penalize (vt) | **penalizar** (vt) | [pənɐliz'ar] |
| to disqualify (vt) | **desqualificar** (vt) | [dəʃkuɐlifik'ar] |

| apparatus | **aparelho** (m) | [ɐpɐr'ɐʎu] |
| javelin | **dardo** (m) | [d'ardu] |
| shot put ball | **peso** (m) | [p'ezu] |
| ball (snooker, etc.) | **bola** (f) | [b'ɔlɐ] |

| aim (target) | **alvo** (m) | ['alvu] |
| target | **alvo** (m) | ['alvu] |
| to shoot (vi) | **atirar, disparar** (vi) | [ɐtir'ar], [diʃpər'ar] |
| precise (~ shot) | **preciso** | [prəs'izu] |

| trainer, coach | **treinador** (m) | [trɐjnɐd'or] |
| to train (sb) | **treinar** (vt) | [trɐjn'ar] |
| to train (vi) | **treinar-se** (vp) | [trɐjn'arsə] |
| training | **treino** (m) | [tr'ɐjnu] |

| gym | **ginásio** (m) | [ʒin'aziu] |
| exercise (physical) | **exercício** (m) | [ezərs'isiu] |
| warm-up (of athlete) | **aquecimento** (m) | [ɐkɛsim'ẽtu] |

# Education

## 142. School

| | | |
|---|---|---|
| school | escola (f) | [əʃkˈɔlɐ] |
| headmaster | diretor (m) de escola | [dirɛtˈor də əʃkˈɔlɐ] |
| pupil (boy) | aluno (m) | [ɐlˈunu] |
| pupil (girl) | aluna (f) | [ɐlˈunɐ] |
| schoolboy | escolar (m) | [əʃkulˈar] |
| schoolgirl | escolar (f) | [əʃkulˈar] |
| to teach (sb) | ensinar (vt) | [ẽsinˈar] |
| to learn (language, etc.) | aprender (vt) | [ɐprẽdˈer] |
| to learn by heart | aprender de cor | [ɐprẽdˈer də kor] |
| to study (work to learn) | estudar (vi) | [əʃtudˈar] |
| to be in school | andar na escola | [ãdar nɐ əʃkˈɔlɐ] |
| to go to school | ir à escola | [ir a əʃkˈɔlɐ] |
| alphabet | alfabeto (m) | [alfɐbˈɛtu] |
| subject (at school) | disciplina (f) | [diʃsiplˈinɐ] |
| classroom | sala (f) de aula | [sˈalɐ də ˈaulɐ] |
| lesson | lição, aula (f) | [lisˈãu], [ˈaulɐ] |
| recess | recreio (m) | [ʀəkrˈeju] |
| school bell | toque (m) | [tˈɔkə] |
| school desk | carteira (f) | [kɐrtˈejrɐ] |
| chalkboard | quadro (m) negro | [kuˈadru nˈegru] |
| grade | nota (f) | [nˈɔtɐ] |
| good grade | boa nota (f) | [bˈɔɐ nˈɔtɐ] |
| bad grade | nota (f) baixa | [nˈɔtɐ bˈajʃɐ] |
| to give a grade | dar uma nota | [dar ˈumɐ nˈɔtɐ] |
| mistake, error | erro (m) | [ˈeʀu] |
| to make mistakes | fazer erros | [fɐzˈer ˈeʀuʃ] |
| to correct (an error) | corrigir (vt) | [kuʀiʒˈir] |
| cheat sheet | cábula (f) | [kˈabulɐ] |
| homework | trabalho (m) de casa | [trɐbˈaʎu də kˈazɐ] |
| exercise (in education) | exercício (m) | [ezɐrsˈisiu] |
| to be present | estar presente | [əʃtˈar prəzˈẽtə] |
| to be absent | estar ausente | [əʃtˈar auzˈẽtə] |
| to miss school | faltar às aulas | [faltˈar aʃ ˈaulɐʃ] |

| to punish (vt) | punir (vt) | [pun'ir] |
| punishment | punição (f) | [punis'ãu] |
| conduct (behavior) | comportamento (m) | [kõpurtem'ẽtu] |

| report card | boletim (m) escolar | [bulət'ĩ əʃkul'ar] |
| pencil | lápis (m) | [l'apiʃ] |
| eraser | borracha (f) | [buʀ'aʃe] |
| chalk | giz (m) | [ʒiʃ] |
| pencil case | estojo (m) | [əʃt'oʒu] |

| schoolbag | pasta (f) escolar | [p'aʃtɐ əʃkul'ar] |
| pen | caneta (f) | [kɐn'etɐ] |
| school notebook | caderno (m) | [kɐd'ɛrnu] |
| textbook | manual (m) escolar | [mɐnu'al əʃkul'ar] |
| compasses | compasso (m) | [kõp'asu] |

| to draw (a blueprint, etc.) | traçar (vt) | [tres'ar] |
| technical drawing | desenho (m) técnico | [dəz'eɲu t'ɛkniku] |

| poem | poesia (f) | [puez'iɐ] |
| by heart (adv) | de cor | [də kor] |
| to learn by heart | aprender de cor | [ɐprẽd'er də kor] |

| school vacation | férias (f pl) | [f'ɛrieʃ] |
| to be on vacation | estar de férias | [əʃt'ar də f'ɛrieʃ] |
| to spend one's vacation | passar as férias | [pes'ar ɐʃ f'ɛrieʃ] |

| test (written math ~) | teste (m) | [t'ɛʃtə] |
| essay (composition) | composição, redação (f) | [kõpuzis'ãu], [ʀɐdas'ãu] |
| dictation | ditado (m) | [dit'adu] |
| exam | exame (m) | [ez'eme] |
| to take an exam | fazer exame | [fez'er ez'eme] |
| experiment (chemical ~) | experiência (f) | [əʃpərj'ẽsiɐ] |

## 143. College. University

| academy | academia (f) | [ɐkɐdɐm'iɐ] |
| university | universidade (f) | [univərsid'adə] |
| faculty (section) | faculdade (f) | [fɐkuld'adə] |

| student (masc.) | estudante (m) | [əʃtud'ãtə] |
| student (fem.) | estudante (f) | [əʃtud'ãtə] |
| lecturer (teacher) | professor (m) | [prufəs'or] |

| lecture hall, room | sala (f) de palestras | [s'alɐ də pɐl'ɛʃtrɐʃ] |
| graduate | graduado (m) | [grɐdu'adu] |
| diploma | diploma (m) | [dipl'omɐ] |
| dissertation | tese (f) | [t'ɛzə] |
| study (report) | estudo (m) | [əʃt'udu] |
| laboratory | laboratório (m) | [lɐburɐt'ɔriu] |

| lecture | palestra (f) | [pɐlˈɛʃtrɐ] |
| course mate | colega (m) de curso | [kulˈɛgɐ də kˈursu] |
| scholarship | bolsa (f) de estudos | [bˈolsɐ də əʃtˈuduʃ] |
| academic degree | grau (m) académico | [grˈau ɐkɐdˈɛmiku] |

## 144. Sciences. Disciplines

| mathematics | matemática (f) | [mɐtəmˈatikɐ] |
| algebra | álgebra (f) | [ˈalʒɐbrɐ] |
| geometry | geometria (f) | [ʒiumətrˈiɐ] |

| astronomy | astronomia (f) | [əʃtrunumˈiɐ] |
| biology | biologia (f) | [biuluʒˈiɐ] |
| geography | geografia (f) | [ʒiugrɐfˈiɐ] |
| geology | geologia (f) | [ʒiuluʒˈiɐ] |
| history | história (f) | [iʃtˈɔriɐ] |

| medicine | medicina (f) | [mədisˈinɐ] |
| pedagogy | pedagogia (f) | [pədəguʒˈiɐ] |
| law | direito (m) | [dirˈejtu] |

| physics | física (f) | [fˈizikɐ] |
| chemistry | química (f) | [kˈimikɐ] |
| philosophy | filosofia (f) | [filuzufˈiɐ] |
| psychology | psicologia (f) | [psikuluʒˈiɐ] |

## 145. Writing system. Orthography

| grammar | gramática (f) | [grɐmˈatikɐ] |
| vocabulary | léxico (m) | [lˈɛksiku] |
| phonetics | fonética (f) | [fonˈɛtikɐ] |

| noun | substantivo (m) | [subʃtɐtˈivu] |
| adjective | adjetivo (m) | [ɐdʒɛtˈivu] |
| verb | verbo (m) | [vˈɛrbu] |
| adverb | advérbio (m) | [ɐdvˈɛrbiu] |

| pronoun | pronome (m) | [prunˈomə] |
| interjection | interjeição (f) | [ĩtɛrʒɐjsˈãu] |
| preposition | preposição (f) | [prəpuzisˈãu] |

| root | raiz (f) da palavra | [ʀɐˈiʃ dɐ pɐlˈavrɐ] |
| ending | terminação (f) | [tərminɐsˈãu] |
| prefix | prefixo (m) | [prəfˈiksu] |
| syllable | sílaba (f) | [sˈilɐbɐ] |
| suffix | sufixo (m) | [sufˈiksu] |
| stress mark | acento (m) | [ɐsˈẽtu] |
| apostrophe | apóstrofo (m) | [ɐpˈɔʃtrofu] |

| period, dot | ponto (m) | [p'õtu] |
| comma | vírgula (f) | [v'irgulə] |
| semicolon | ponto e vírgula (m) | [p'õtu ə v'irgulə] |
| colon | dois pontos (m pl) | [d'ojʃ p'õtuʃ] |
| ellipsis | reticências (f pl) | [ʀɐtis'ēsiɐʃ] |
| question mark | ponto (m) de interrogação | [p'õtu də ĩtɐʀuges'ãu] |
| exclamation point | ponto (m) de exclamação | [p'õtu də əʃklɐmɐs'ãu] |
| quotation marks | aspas (f pl) | ['aʃpɐʃ] |
| in quotation marks | entre aspas | [ētrə 'aʃpɐʃ] |
| parenthesis | parênteses (m pl) | [peʀ'ētəzəʃ] |
| in parenthesis | entre parênteses | [ētrə peʀ'ētəzəʃ] |
| hyphen | hífen (m) | ['ifɛn] |
| dash | travessão (m) | [trevəs'ãu] |
| space (between words) | espaço (m) | [əʃp'asu] |
| letter | letra (f) | [l'etrɐ] |
| capital letter | letra (f) maiúscula | [l'etrɐ mɐj'uʃkulɐ] |
| vowel (n) | vogal (f) | [vug'al] |
| consonant (n) | consoante (f) | [kõsu'ãtə] |
| sentence | frase (f) | [fr'azə] |
| subject | sujeito (m) | [suʒ'ejtu] |
| predicate | predicado (m) | [prədik'adu] |
| line | linha (f) | [l'iɲə] |
| on a new line | em uma nova linha | [ɛn 'umə n'ɔvɐ l'iɲɐ] |
| paragraph | parágrafo (m) | [peʀ'agrɐfu] |
| word | palavra (f) | [pɐl'avrɐ] |
| group of words | grupo (m) de palavras | [gr'upu də pɐl'avrɐʃ] |
| expression | expressão (f) | [əʃprɐs'ãu] |
| synonym | sinónimo (m) | [sin'ɔnimu] |
| antonym | antónimo (m) | [ãt'ɔnimu] |
| rule | regra (f) | [ʀ'ɛgrɐ] |
| exception | exceção (f) | [əʃsɛs'ãu] |
| correct (adj) | correto | [kuʀ'ɛtu] |
| conjugation | conjugação (f) | [kõʒuges'ãu] |
| declension | declinação (f) | [dəklinɐs'ãu] |
| nominal case | caso (m) | [k'azu] |
| question | pergunta (f) | [pɐrg'ũtɐ] |
| to underline (vt) | sublinhar (vt) | [subliɲ'ar] |
| dotted line | linha (f) pontilhada | [l'iɲɐ põtiʎ'adɐ] |

## 146. Foreign languages

| | | |
|---|---|---|
| language | **língua** (f) | [l'ĩguɐ] |
| foreign (adj) | **estrangeiro** | [əʃtrãʒ'ejru] |
| foreign language | **língua** (f) **estrangeira** | [l'ĩguɐ əʃtrãʒ'ejrɐ] |
| to study (vt) | **estudar** (vt) | [əʃtud'ar] |
| to learn (language, etc.) | **aprender** (vt) | [ɐprẽd'er] |

| | | |
|---|---|---|
| to read (vi, vt) | **ler** (vt) | [ler] |
| to speak (vi, vt) | **falar** (vi) | [fɐl'ar] |
| to understand (vt) | **compreender** (vt) | [kõpriẽd'er] |
| to write (vt) | **escrever** (vt) | [əʃkrɐv'er] |

| | | |
|---|---|---|
| fast (adv) | **rapidamente** | [ʀapidɐm'ẽtə] |
| slowly (adv) | **devagar** | [dəvɐg'ar] |
| fluently (adv) | **fluentemente** | [fluẽtəm'ẽtə] |

| | | |
|---|---|---|
| rules | **regras** (f pl) | [ʀ'ɛgrɐʃ] |
| grammar | **gramática** (f) | [grɐm'atikɐ] |
| vocabulary | **léxico** (m) | [l'ɛksiku] |
| phonetics | **fonética** (f) | [fɔn'ɛtikɐ] |

| | | |
|---|---|---|
| textbook | **manual** (m) **escolar** | [mɐnu'al əʃkul'ar] |
| dictionary | **dicionário** (m) | [disiun'ariu] |
| teach-yourself book | **manual** (m) **de autoaprendizagem** | [mɐnu'al də 'autɔɐprẽdiz'aʒẽj] |
| phrasebook | **guia** (m) **de conversação** | [g'iɐ də kõvərsɐs'ãu] |

| | | |
|---|---|---|
| cassette | **cassete** (f) | [kas'ɛtə] |
| videotape | **cassete** (f) **de vídeo** | [kas'ɛtə də v'idiu] |
| CD, compact disc | **CD, disco** (m) **compacto** | [s'ɛdɛ], [d'iʃku kõp'aktu] |
| DVD | **DVD** (m) | [dɛvɛd'ɛ] |

| | | |
|---|---|---|
| alphabet | **alfabeto** (m) | [alfɐb'ɛtu] |
| to spell (vt) | **soletrar** (vt) | [suletr'ar] |
| pronunciation | **pronúncia** (f) | [prun'ũsiɐ] |

| | | |
|---|---|---|
| accent | **sotaque** (m) | [sut'akə] |
| with an accent | **com sotaque** | [kõ sut'akə] |
| without an accent | **sem sotaque** | [sẽ sut'akə] |

| | | |
|---|---|---|
| word | **palavra** (f) | [pɐl'avrɐ] |
| meaning | **sentido** (m) | [sẽt'idu] |

| | | |
|---|---|---|
| course (e.g., a French ~) | **cursos** (m pl) | [k'ursuʃ] |
| to sign up | **inscrever-se** (vp) | [ĩʃkrɐv'ersə] |
| teacher | **professor** (m) | [prufəs'or] |

| | | |
|---|---|---|
| translation (process) | **tradução** (f) | [trɐdus'ãu] |
| translation (text, etc.) | **tradução** (f) | [trɐdus'ãu] |
| translator | **tradutor** (m) | [trɐdut'or] |

| interpreter | intérprete (m) | [ĩt'ɛrprətə] |
| polyglot | poliglota (m) | [poligl'ɔtə] |
| memory | memória (f) | [məm'ɔriə] |

## 147. Fairy tale characters

| Santa Claus | Pai (m) Natal | [paj net'al] |
| Cinderella | Cinderela (f) | [sĩdər'ɛlə] |
| mermaid | sereia (f) | [sər'ejə] |
| Neptune | Neptuno (m) | [nɛpt'unu] |

| magician, wizard | mago (m) | [m'agu] |
| fairy | fada (f) | [f'adə] |
| magic (adj) | mágico | [m'aʒiku] |
| magic wand | varinha (f) mágica | [vər'iɲə m'aʒikə] |
| fairy tale | conto (m) de fadas | [k'õtu də f'adəʃ] |
| miracle | milagre (m) | [mil'agrə] |
| dwarf | anão (m) | [ɐn'ãu] |
| to turn into ... | transformar-se em ... | [trãʃfurm'arsə ɛn] |

| ghost | espetro (m) | [əʃp'ɛtru] |
| phantom | fantasma (m) | [fãt'aʒmə] |
| monster | monstro (m) | [m'õʃtru] |
| dragon | dragão (m) | [drɐg'ãu] |
| giant | gigante (m) | [ʒig'ãtə] |

## 148. Zodiac Signs

| Aries | Carneiro | [kɐrn'ejru] |
| Taurus | Touro | [t'oru] |
| Gemini | Gémeos | [ʒ'ɛmiuʃ] |
| Cancer | Caranguejo | [kɐrãg'eʒu] |
| Leo | Leão | [lj'ãu] |
| Virgo | Virgem | [v'irʒẽj] |

| Libra | Balança | [bɐl'ãsə] |
| Scorpio | Escorpião | [əʃkurpj'ãu] |
| Sagittarius | Sagitário | [sɐʒit'ariu] |
| Capricorn | Capricórnio | [kɐprik'ɔrniu] |
| Aquarius | Aquário | [ɐku'ariu] |
| Pisces | Peixes | [p'ejʃəʃ] |

| character | caráter (m) | [kɐr'atɛr] |
| features of character | traços (m pl) do caráter | [tr'asuʃ du kɐr'atɛr] |
| behavior | comportamento (m) | [kõpurtɐm'ẽtu] |
| to tell fortunes | predizer (vt) | [prədiz'er] |
| fortune-teller | adivinha (f) | [ɐdiv'iɲə] |
| horoscope | horóscopo (m) | [or'ɔʃkupu] |

# Arts

## 149. Theater

| theater | teatro (m) | [tə'atru] |
|---|---|---|
| opera | ópera (f) | ['ɔpərɐ] |
| operetta | opereta (f) | [opər'etɐ] |
| ballet | balé (m) | [bɐl'ɛ] |

| theater poster | cartaz (m) | [kɐrt'aʃ] |
|---|---|---|
| theatrical company | companhia (f) teatral | [kõpɐɲ'iɐ tiɐtr'al] |
| tour | turné (f) | [turn'ɛ] |
| to be on tour | estar em turné | [əʃt'ar ẽ turn'ɛ] |
| to rehearse (vi, vt) | ensaiar (vt) | [ẽsaj'ar] |
| rehearsal | ensaio (m) | [ẽs'aju] |
| repertoire | repertório (m) | [ʀəpərt'ɔriu] |

| performance | apresentação (f) | [eprəzẽtes'ãu] |
|---|---|---|
| theatrical show | espetáculo (m) | [əʃpɛt'akulu] |
| play | peça (f) | [p'ɛsɐ] |

| ticket | bilhete (m) | [biʎ'etə] |
|---|---|---|
| Box office | bilheteira (f) | [biʎət'ejrɐ] |
| lobby, foyer | hall (m) | [ɔl] |
| coat check | guarda-roupa (m) | [guardɐ ʀ'opɐ] |
| coat check tag | senha (f) numerada | [s'eɲɐ numər'adɐ] |
| binoculars | binóculo (m) | [bin'ɔkulu] |
| usher | lanterninha (f) | [lãtərn'iɲɐ] |

| orchestra seats | plateia (f) | [plɐt'ejɐ] |
|---|---|---|
| balcony | balcão (m) | [balk'ãu] |
| dress circle | primeiro balcão (m) | [prim'ejru balk'ãu] |
| box | camarote (m) | [kɐmər'ɔtə] |
| row | fila (f) | [f'ilɐ] |
| seat | assento (m) | [ɐs'ẽtu] |

| audience | público (m) | [p'ubliku] |
|---|---|---|
| spectator | espetador (m) | [əʃpətɐd'or] |
| to clap (vi, vt) | aplaudir (vt) | [eplaud'ir] |
| applause | aplausos (m pl) | [ɐpl'auzuʃ] |
| ovation | ovação (f) | [ɔves'ãu] |

| stage | palco (m) | [p'alku] |
|---|---|---|
| curtain | pano (m) de boca | [p'ɐnu də b'okɐ] |
| scenery | cenário (m) | [sən'ariu] |
| backstage | bastidores (m pl) | [bɐʃtid'orəʃ] |

| scene (e.g., the last ~) | cena (f) | [s'enɐ] |
| act | ato (m) | ['atu] |
| intermission | entreato (m) | [ẽtrj'atu] |

## 150. Cinema

| actor | ator (m) | [at'or] |
| actress | atriz (f) | [ɐtr'iʃ] |

| movies (industry) | cinema (m) | [sin'emɐ] |
| movie | filme (m) | [f'ilmə] |
| episode | episódio (m) | [epiz'ɔdiu] |

| detective | filme (m) policial | [f'ilmə pulisj'al] |
| action movie | filme (m) de ação | [f'ilmə də as'ãu] |
| adventure movie | filme (m) de aventuras | [f'ilmə də ɐvẽt'urɐʃ] |
| science fiction movie | filme (m) de ficção científica | [f'ilmə də fiks'ãu siẽt'ifikɐ] |
| horror movie | filme (m) de terror | [f'ilmə də tɐʀ'or] |

| comedy movie | comédia (f) | [kum'ɛdiɐ] |
| melodrama | melodrama (m) | [mɛlɔdr'emɐ] |
| drama | drama (m) | [dr'emɐ] |

| fictional movie | filme (m) ficcional | [f'ilmə fiksiun'al] |
| documentary | documentário (m) | [dukumẽt'ariu] |
| cartoon | desenho (m) animado | [dəz'ɐɲu ɐnim'adu] |
| silent movies | cinema (m) mudo | [sin'emɐ m'udu] |

| role (part) | papel (m) | [pɐp'ɛl] |
| leading role | papel (m) principal | [pɐp'ɛl prĩsip'al] |
| to play (vi, vt) | representar (vt) | [ʀəprəzẽt'ar] |

| movie star | estrela (f) de cinema | [əʃtr'elɐ də sin'emɐ] |
| well-known (adj) | conhecido | [kuɲəs'idu] |
| famous (adj) | famoso | [fɐm'ozu] |
| popular (adj) | popular | [pupul'ar] |

| script (screenplay) | argumento (m) | [ɐrgum'ẽtu] |
| scriptwriter | argumentista (m) | [ɐrgumẽt'iʃtɐ] |
| movie director | realizador (m) | [ʀiɐlizɐd'or] |
| producer | produtor (m) | [prudut'or] |
| assistant | assistente (m) | [ɐsiʃt'ẽtə] |
| cameraman | diretor (m) de fotografia | [dirɛt'or də futugrɐf'iɐ] |
| stuntman | duplo (m) | [d'uplu] |
| double | duplo (m) | [d'uplu] |

| to shoot a movie | filmar (vt) | [film'ar] |
| audition, screen test | audição (f) | [audis'ãu] |
| shooting | filmagem (f) | [film'aʒẽj] |

| movie crew | equipe (f) de filmagem | [ek'ipə də film'aʒēj] |
| movie set | set (m) de filmagem | [s'ɛtə də film'aʒēj] |
| camera | câmara (f) | [k'ɐmɐɾɐ] |

| movie theater | cinema (m) | [sin'emɐ] |
| screen (e.g., big ~) | ecrã, tela (m) | [ɛkɾ'ã], [t'ɛlɐ] |
| to show a movie | exibir um filme | [ezib'iɾ ũ f'ilmə] |

| soundtrack | pista (f) sonora | [p'iʃtɐ sun'ɔɾɐ] |
| special effects | efeitos (m pl) especiais | [ef'ɐjtuʃ əʃpəsj'ajʃ] |
| subtitles | legendas (f pl) | [ləʒ'ēdəʃ] |
| credits | genérico (m) | [ʒən'ɛɾiku] |
| translation | tradução (f) | [tɾɐdus'ãu] |

## 151. Painting

| art | arte (f) | ['aɾtə] |
| fine arts | belas-artes (f pl) | [bɛlɐz'aɾtəʃ] |
| art gallery | galeria (f) de arte | [gɐləɾ'iɐ də 'aɾtə] |
| art exhibition | exposição (f) de arte | [əʃpuzis'ãu də 'aɾtə] |

| painting (art) | pintura (f) | [pĩt'uɾɐ] |
| graphic art | arte (f) gráfica | ['aɾtə gɾ'afikɐ] |
| abstract art | arte (f) abstrata | ['aɾtə ɐbʃtɾ'atɐ] |
| impressionism | impressionismo (m) | [ĩpɾəsiun'iʒmu] |

| picture (painting) | pintura (f), quadro (m) | [pĩt'uɾɐ], [ku'adɾu] |
| drawing | desenho (m) | [dəz'ɐɲu] |
| poster | cartaz, póster (m) | [kɐɾt'aʃ], [p'ɔʃtɛɾ] |

| illustration (picture) | ilustração (f) | [iluʃtɾɐs'ãu] |
| miniature | miniatura (f) | [miniɐt'uɾə] |
| copy (of painting, etc.) | cópia (f) | [k'ɔpiɐ] |
| reproduction | reprodução (f) | [ʀəpɾudus'ãu] |

| mosaic | mosaico (m) | [muz'ajku] |
| stained glass | vitral (m) | [vitɾ'al] |
| fresco | fresco (m) | [fɾ'eʃku] |
| engraving | gravura (f) | [gɾɐv'uɾɐ] |

| bust (sculpture) | busto (m) | [b'uʃtu] |
| sculpture | escultura (f) | [əʃkult'uɾɐ] |
| statue | estátua (f) | [əʃt'atuɐ] |
| plaster of Paris | gesso (m) | [ʒ'esu] |
| plaster (as adj) | em gesso | [ẽ ʒ'esu] |

| portrait | retrato (m) | [ʀətɾ'atu] |
| self-portrait | autorretrato (m) | [autoʀətɾ'atu] |
| landscape painting | paisagem (f) | [pajz'aʒēj] |
| still life | natureza (f) morta | [nɐtuɾ'ezɐ m'ɔɾtɐ] |

| caricature | caricatura (f) | [keriket'ure] |
| sketch | esboço (m) | [eʒb'osu] |

| paint | tinta (f) | [tĩte] |
| watercolor | aguarela (f) | [aguer'ɛle] |
| oil (paint) | óleo (m) | ['ɔliu] |
| pencil | lápis (m) | [l'apiʃ] |
| Indian ink | tinta da China (f) | [tĩte de ʃine] |
| charcoal | carvão (m) | [kerv'ãu] |

| to draw (vi, vt) | desenhar (vt) | [dezeɲ'ar] |
| to paint (vi, vt) | pintar (vt) | [pĩt'ar] |

| to pose (vi) | posar (vi) | [poz'ar] |
| artist's model (masc.) | modelo (m) | [mud'elu] |
| artist's model (fem.) | modelo (f) | [mud'elu] |

| artist (painter) | pintor (m) | [pĩt'or] |
| work of art | obra (f) | ['ɔbre] |
| masterpiece | obra-prima (f) | ['ɔbre pr'ime] |
| artist's workshop | estúdio (m) | [eʃt'udiu] |

| canvas (cloth) | tela (f) | [t'ɛle] |
| easel | cavalete (m) | [kevel'ete] |
| palette | paleta (f) | [pel'ete] |

| frame (of picture, etc.) | moldura (f) | [mold'ure] |
| restoration | restauração (f) | [Reʃtaures'ãu] |
| to restore (vt) | restaurar (vt) | [Reʃtaur'ar] |

## 152. Literature & Poetry

| literature | literatura (f) | [literet'ure] |
| author (writer) | autor (m) | [aut'or] |
| pseudonym | pseudónimo (m) | [pseud'ɔnimu] |

| book | livro (m) | [l'ivru] |
| volume | volume (m) | [vul'ume] |
| table of contents | índice (m) | [ĩdise] |
| page | página (f) | [p'aʒine] |
| main character | protagonista (m) | [prutegun'iʃte] |
| autograph | autógrafo (m) | [aut'ɔgrefu] |

| short story | conto (m) | [k'õtu] |
| story (novella) | novela (f) | [nuv'ɛle] |
| novel | romance (m) | [Rum'ãse] |
| work (writing) | obra (f) | ['ɔbre] |
| fable | fábula (m) | [f'abule] |
| detective novel | romance (m) policial | [Rum'ãse pulisj'al] |
| poem (verse) | poesia (f) | [puez'ie] |

| poetry | poesia (f) | [puez'ie] |
| poem (epic, ballad) | poema (m) | [pu'eme] |
| poet | poeta (m) | [pu'ɛte] |

| fiction | ficção (f) | [fiks'ãu] |
| science fiction | ficção (f) científica | [fiks'ãu siɛt'ifike] |
| adventures | aventuras (f pl) | [evɐt'ureʃ] |
| educational literature | literatura (f) didática | [literet'ure did'atike] |
| children's literature | literatura (f) infantil | [literet'ure ĩfãt'il] |

## 153. Circus

| circus | circo (m) | [s'irku] |
| chapiteau circus | circo (m) ambulante | [s'irku ãbul'ãte] |
| program | programa (m) | [prugr'eme] |
| performance | apresentação (f) | [eprezẽtes'ãu] |

| act (circus ~) | número (m) | [n'umeru] |
| circus ring | arena (f) | [ɐr'ene] |

| pantomime (act) | pantomima (f) | [pãtum'ime] |
| clown | palhaço (m) | [peʎ'asu] |

| acrobat | acrobata (m) | [ekrub'ate] |
| acrobatics | acrobacia (f) | [ekrubes'ie] |
| gymnast | ginasta (m) | [ʒin'aʃte] |
| gymnastics | ginástica (f) | [ʒin'aʃtike] |
| somersault | salto (m) mortal | [s'altu murt'al] |

| athlete (strongman) | homem forte (m) | [ɔmɛj f'ɔrte] |
| animal-tamer | domador (m) | [dumed'or] |
| equestrian | cavaleiro (m) equilibrista | [kevel'ejru ekilibr'iʃte] |
| assistant | assistente (m) | [esiʃt'ẽte] |

| stunt | truque (m) | [tr'uke] |
| magic trick | truque (m) de mágica | [tr'uke de m'aʒike] |
| conjurer, magician | mágico (m) | [m'aʒiku] |

| juggler | malabarista (m) | [meleber'iʃte] |
| to juggle (vi, vt) | fazer malabarismos | [fez'er meleber'iʒmuʃ] |
| animal trainer | domador (m) | [dumed'or] |
| animal training | adestramento (m) | [edeʃtrem'ẽtu] |
| to train (animals) | adestrar (vt) | [edeʃtr'ar] |

## 154. Music. Pop music

| music | música (f) | [m'uzike] |
| musician | músico (m) | [m'uziku] |

| | | |
|---|---|---|
| musical instrument | instrumento (m) musical | [ĩʃtrum'ẽtu muzik'al] |
| to play ... | tocar ... | [tuk'ar] |
| | | |
| guitar | guitarra (f) | [git'aʀɐ] |
| violin | violino (m) | [viul'inu] |
| cello | violoncelo (m) | [viulõs'ɛlu] |
| double bass | contrabaixo (m) | [kõtrɐb'ajʃu] |
| harp | harpa (f) | ['arpɐ] |
| | | |
| piano | piano (m) | [pj'ɛnu] |
| grand piano | piano (m) de cauda | [pj'ɛnu dɐ k'audɐ] |
| organ | órgão (m) | ['ɔrgãu] |
| | | |
| wind instruments | instrumentos (m pl) de sopro | [ĩʃtrum'ẽtuʃ dɐ s'opru] |
| oboe | oboé (m) | [ɔbu'ɛ] |
| saxophone | saxofone (m) | [saksɔf'ɔnɐ] |
| clarinet | clarinete (m) | [klɐrin'etɐ] |
| flute | flauta (f) | [fl'autɐ] |
| trumpet | trompete (m) | [trõp'ɛtɐ] |
| | | |
| accordion | acordeão (m) | [ɐkɔrdj'ãu] |
| drum | tambor (m) | [tãb'or] |
| | | |
| duo | duo, dueto (m) | [d'uu], [du'etu] |
| trio | trio (m) | [tr'iu] |
| quartet | quarteto (m) | [kuɐrt'etu] |
| choir | coro (m) | [k'oru] |
| orchestra | orquestra (f) | [ɔrk'ɛʃtrɐ] |
| | | |
| pop music | música (f) pop | [m'uzikɐ p'ɔpɐ] |
| rock music | música (f) rock | [m'uzikɐ ʀ'ɔk] |
| rock group | grupo (m) de rock | [gr'upu dɐ ʀ'ɔkɐ] |
| jazz | jazz (m) | [ʒaz] |
| | | |
| idol | ídolo (m) | ['idulu] |
| admirer, fan | fã, admirador (m) | [fã], [ɐdmirɐd'or] |
| | | |
| concert | concerto (m) | [kõs'ertu] |
| symphony | sinfonia (f) | [sĩfun'iɐ] |
| composition | composição (f) | [kõpuzis'ãu] |
| to compose (write) | compor (vt) | [kõp'or] |
| | | |
| singing | canto (m) | [k'ãtu] |
| song | canção (f) | [kãs'ãu] |
| tune (melody) | melodia (f) | [mɐlud'iɐ] |
| rhythm | ritmo (m) | [ʀ'itmu] |
| blues | blues (m) | [bl'uz] |
| | | |
| sheet music | notas (f pl) | [n'ɔteʃ] |
| baton | batuta (f) | [bɐt'utɐ] |
| bow | arco (m) | ['arku] |

| string | **corda** (f) | [kˈɔrdɐ] |
| case (e.g., guitar ~) | **estojo** (m) | [ɐʃtˈoʒu] |

# Rest. Entertainment. Travel

## 155. Trip. Travel

| | | |
|---|---|---|
| tourism | **turismo** (m) | [tur'iʒmu] |
| tourist | **turista** (m) | [tur'iʃtɐ] |
| trip, voyage | **viagem** (f) | [vj'aʒɐ̃j] |
| | | |
| adventure | **aventura** (f) | [ɐvɐ̃t'urɐ] |
| trip, journey | **viagem** (f) | [vj'aʒɐ̃j] |
| | | |
| vacation | **férias** (f pl) | [f'ɛriɐʃ] |
| to be on vacation | **estar de férias** | [əʃt'ar də f'ɛriɐʃ] |
| rest | **descanso** (m) | [dəʃk'ãsu] |
| | | |
| train | **comboio** (m) | [kõb'ɔju] |
| by train | **de comboio** | [də kõb'ɔju] |
| airplane | **avião** (m) | [ɐvj'ãu] |
| by airplane | **de avião** | [də ɐvj'ãu] |
| | | |
| by car | **de carro** | [də k'aʀu] |
| by ship | **de navio** | [də nɐv'iu] |
| | | |
| luggage | **bagagem** (f) | [bɐg'aʒɐ̃j] |
| suitcase, luggage | **mala** (f) | [m'alɐ] |
| luggage cart | **carrinho** (m) | [kɐʀ'iɲu] |
| | | |
| passport | **passaporte** (m) | [pasɐp'ɔrtə] |
| visa | **visto** (m) | [v'iʃtu] |
| | | |
| ticket | **bilhete** (m) | [biʎ'etə] |
| air ticket | **bilhete** (m) **de avião** | [biʎ'etə də ɐvj'ãu] |
| | | |
| guidebook | **guia** (m) **de viagem** | [g'iɐ də vi'aʒɐ̃j] |
| map | **mapa** (m) | [m'apɐ] |
| | | |
| area (rural ~) | **local** (m), **area** (f) | [luk'al], [ɐr'ɛɐ] |
| place, site | **lugar, sítio** (m) | [lug'ar], [s'itiu] |
| | | |
| exotic (n) | **exotismo** (m) | [ezut'iʒmu] |
| exotic (adj) | **exótico** | [ez'ɔtiku] |
| amazing (adj) | **surpreendente** | [surprië̃d'ẽtə] |
| | | |
| group | **grupo** (m) | [gr'upu] |
| excursion | **excursão** (f) | [əʃkurs'ãu] |
| guide (person) | **guia** (m) | [g'iɐ] |

## 156. Hotel

| | | |
|---|---|---|
| hotel | **hotel** (m) | [ɔt'ɛl] |
| motel | **motel** (m) | [mut'ɛl] |
| | | |
| three-star | **três estrelas** | [tr'eʃ əʃtr'eleʃ] |
| five-star | **cinco estrelas** | [s'iku əʃtr'eleʃ] |
| to stay (in hotel, etc.) | **ficar** (vi, vt) | [fik'ar] |
| | | |
| room | **quarto** (m) | [ku'artu] |
| single room | **quarto** (m) **individual** | [ku'artu ĩdividu'al] |
| double room | **quarto** (m) **duplo** | [ku'artu d'uplu] |
| to book a room | **reservar um quarto** | [Rezərv'ar ũ ku'artu] |
| | | |
| half board | **meia pensão** (f) | [m'eje pẽs'ãu] |
| full board | **pensão** (f) **completa** | [pẽs'ãu kõpl'ɛte] |
| | | |
| with bath | **com banheira** | [kõ beɲ'ejɾe] |
| with shower | **com duche** | [kõ d'uʃə] |
| satellite television | **televisão** (m) **satélite** | [təleviz'ãu set'ɛlite] |
| air-conditioner | **ar** (m) **condicionado** | [ar kõdisiun'adu] |
| towel | **toalha** (f) | [tu'aʎe] |
| key | **chave** (f) | [ʃ'ave] |
| | | |
| administrator | **administrador** (m) | [edminiʃtɾed'or] |
| chambermaid | **camareira** (f) | [kemeɾ'ejɾe] |
| porter, bellboy | **bagageiro** (m) | [beɡeʒ'ejru] |
| doorman | **porteiro** (m) | [purt'ejru] |
| | | |
| restaurant | **restaurante** (m) | [Reʃtaur'ãte] |
| pub, bar | **bar** (m) | [bar] |
| breakfast | **pequeno-almoço** (m) | [pək'enu alm'osu] |
| dinner | **jantar** (m) | [ʒãt'ar] |
| buffet | **buffet** (m) | [buf'e] |
| | | |
| lobby | **hall** (m) **de entrada** | [ɔl də ẽtr'ade] |
| elevator | **elevador** (m) | [eleved'or] |
| | | |
| DO NOT DISTURB | **NÃO PERTURBE** | [n'ãu pərt'urbə] |
| NO SMOKING | **PROIBIDO FUMAR!** | [pruib'idu fum'ar] |

## 157. Books. Reading

| | | |
|---|---|---|
| book | **livro** (m) | [l'ivru] |
| author | **autor** (m) | [aut'or] |
| writer | **escritor** (m) | [əʃkrit'or] |
| to write (~ a book) | **escrever** (vt) | [əʃkrəv'er] |
| reader | **leitor** (m) | [ləjt'or] |
| to read (vi, vt) | **ler** (vt) | [ler] |

| reading (activity) | leitura (f) | [lejt'ure] |
| silently (to oneself) | para si | [p'ere si] |
| aloud (adv) | em voz alta | [ẽ vɔʒ 'alte] |

| to publish (vt) | publicar (vt) | [publik'ar] |
| publishing (process) | publicação (f) | [publikes'ãu] |
| publisher | editor (m) | [edit'or] |
| publishing house | editora (f) | [edit'ore] |

| to come out (be released) | sair (vi) | [se'ir] |
| release (of a book) | lançamento (m) | [lãsem'ẽtu] |
| print run | tiragem (f) | [tir'aʒẽj] |

| bookstore | livraria (f) | [livrer'ie] |
| library | biblioteca (f) | [bibliut'ɛke] |

| story (novella) | novela (f) | [nuv'ɛle] |
| short story | conto (m) | [k'õtu] |
| novel | romance (m) | [ʀum'ãse] |
| detective novel | romance (m) policial | [ʀum'ãse pulisj'al] |

| memoirs | memórias (f pl) | [mem'ɔrieʃ] |
| legend | lenda (f) | [l'ẽde] |
| myth | mito (m) | [m'itu] |

| poetry, poems | poesia (f) | [puez'ie] |
| autobiography | autobiografia (f) | [autobiugref'ie] |
| selected works | obras (f pl) escolhidas | ['ɔbreʃ eʃkuʎ'ideʃ] |
| science fiction | ficção (f) científica | [fiks'ãu siẽt'ifike] |

| title | título (m) | [t'itulu] |
| introduction | introdução (f) | [ĩtrudus'ãu] |
| title page | folha (f) de rosto | [f'oʎe de ʀ'oʃtu] |

| chapter | capítulo (m) | [kep'itulu] |
| extract | excerto (m) | [eʃs'ertu] |
| episode | episódio (m) | [epiz'ɔdiu] |

| plot (storyline) | tema (m) | [t'eme] |
| contents | conteúdo (m) | [kõtj'udu] |
| table of contents | índice (m) | ['ĩdise] |
| main character | protagonista (m) | [prutegun'iʃte] |

| volume | tomo, volume (m) | [t'omu], [vul'ume] |
| cover | capa (f) | [k'ape] |
| binding | encadernação (f) | [ẽkedernes'ãu] |
| bookmark | marcador (m) | [merked'or] |

| page | página (f) | [p'aʒine] |
| to flick through | folhear (vt) | [fuʎe'ar] |
| margins | margem (f) | [m'arʒẽj] |
| annotation | anotação (f) | [enutes'ãu] |

| footnote | nota (f) de rodapé | [n'ɔte de ʀodep'ɛ] |
| text | texto (m) | [t'ɛʃtu] |
| type, font | fonte (f) | [f'õte] |
| misprint, typo | gralha (f) | [gr'aʎe] |

| translation | tradução (f) | [tredus'ãu] |
| to translate (vt) | traduzir (vt) | [treduz'ir] |
| original (n) | original (m) | [oriʒin'al] |

| famous (adj) | famoso | [fem'ozu] |
| unknown (adj) | desconhecido | [deʃkuɲes'idu] |
| interesting (adj) | interessante | [ĩteres'ãte] |
| bestseller | best-seller (m) | [bɛsts'ɛler] |

| dictionary | dicionário (m) | [disiun'ariu] |
| textbook | manual (m) escolar | [menu'al eʃkul'ar] |
| encyclopedia | enciclopédia (f) | [ẽsiklup'ɛdie] |

## 158. Hunting. Fishing

| hunting | caça (f) | [k'ase] |
| to hunt (vi, vt) | caçar (vi) | [kes'ar] |
| hunter | caçador (m) | [kesed'or] |

| to shoot (vi) | atirar (vi) | [etir'ar] |
| rifle | caçadeira (f) | [kesed'ejre] |
| bullet (shell) | cartucho (m) | [kert'uʃu] |
| shot (lead balls) | chumbo (m) de caça | [ʃ'ũbu de k'ase] |

| trap (e.g., bear ~) | armadilha (f) | [ermed'iʎe] |
| snare (for birds, etc.) | armadilha (f) | [ermed'iʎe] |
| to fall into the trap | cair na armadilha | [ke'ir ne ermed'iʎe] |
| to lay a trap | pôr a armadilha | [p'or e ermed'iʎe] |

| poacher | caçador (m) furtivo | [kesed'or furt'ivu] |
| game (in hunting) | caça (f) | [k'ase] |
| hound dog | cão (m) de caça | [k'ãu de k'ase] |
| safari | safári (m) | [saf'ari] |
| mounted animal | animal (m) empalhado | [enim'al ẽpeʎ'adu] |

| fisherman | pescador (m) | [peʃked'or] |
| fishing | pesca (f) | [p'ɛʃke] |
| to fish (vi) | pescar (vt) | [peʃk'ar] |

| fishing rod | cana (f) de pesca | [k'ene de p'ɛʃke] |
| fishing line | linha (f) de pesca | [l'iɲe de p'ɛʃke] |
| hook | anzol (m) | [ãz'ɔl] |
| float | boia (f), flutuador (m) | [b'ɔje], [flutued'or] |
| bait | isca (f) | ['iʃke] |
| to cast a line | lançar a linha | [lãs'ar e l'iɲe] |

| to bite (ab. fish) | morder (vt) | [murd'er] |
| catch (of fish) | pesca (f) | [p'ɛʃɐ] |
| ice-hole | buraco (m) no gelo | [bur'aku nu ʒ'elu] |

| fishing net | rede (f) | [ʀ'edə] |
| boat | barco (m) | [b'arku] |
| to net (catch with net) | pescar com rede | [pəʃk'ar kõ ʀ'edə] |
| to cast the net | lançar a rede | [lãs'ar ɐ ʀ'edə] |
| to haul in the net | puxar a rede | [puʃ'ar ɐ ʀ'edə] |
| to fall into the net | cair nas malhas | [kɐ'ir neʃ m'aʎɐʃ] |

| whaler (person) | baleeiro (m) | [bɐlj'ejru] |
| whaleboat | baleeira (f) | [bɐlj'ejrɐ] |
| harpoon | arpão (m) | [ɐrp'ãu] |

## 159. Games. Billiards

| billiards | bilhar (m) | [biʎ'ar] |
| billiard room, hall | sala (f) de bilhar | [s'alɐ də biʎ'ar] |
| ball | bola (f) de bilhar | [b'ɔlɐ də biʎ'ar] |

| to pocket a ball | embolsar uma bola | [ẽbɔls'ar 'umɐ b'ɔlɐ] |
| cue | taco (m) | [t'aku] |
| pocket | bolsa (f) | [b'olsɐ] |

## 160. Games. Playing cards

| diamonds | ouros (m pl) | ['oruʃ] |
| spades | espadas (f pl) | [əʃp'adɐʃ] |
| hearts | copas (f pl) | [k'ɔpɐʃ] |
| clubs | paus (m pl) | [p'auʃ] |

| ace | ás (m) | [aʃ] |
| king | rei (m) | [ʀɐj] |
| queen | dama (f) | [d'ɐmɐ] |
| jack, knave | valete (m) | [vɐl'etɐ] |

| playing card | carta (f) de jogar | [k'artɐ də ʒug'ar] |
| cards | cartas (f pl) | [k'artɐʃ] |

| trump | trunfo (m) | [tr'ũfu] |
| deck of cards | baralho (m) | [bɐr'aʎu] |

| point | ponto (m) | [p'õtu] |
| to deal (vi, vt) | dar, distribuir (vt) | [dar], [diʃtribu'ir] |
| to shuffle (cards) | embaralhar (vt) | [ẽbɐrɐʎ'ar] |
| lead, turn (n) | vez, jogada (f) | [veʒ], [ʒug'adɐ] |
| cardsharp | batoteiro (m) | [bɐtut'ejru] |

## 161. Casino. Roulette

| | | |
|---|---|---|
| casino | **casino** (m) | [kɐz'inu] |
| roulette (game) | **roleta** (f) | [ʀul'etɐ] |
| bet, stake | **aposta** (f) | [ɐp'ɔʃtɐ] |
| to place bets | **apostar** (vt) | [ɐpuʃt'ar] |
| | | |
| red | **vermelho** (m) | [vɘrm'eʎu] |
| black | **preto** (m) | [pr'etu] |
| to bet on red | **apostar no vermelho** | [ɐpuʃt'ar nu vɘrm'eʎu] |
| to bet on black | **apostar no preto** | [ɐpuʃt'ar nu pr'etu] |
| | | |
| croupier (dealer) | **crupiê** (m, f) | [krupj'e] |
| rules (of game) | **regras** (f pl) **do jogo** | [ʀ'ɛgrɐʃ du ʒ'ogu] |
| chip | **ficha** (f) | [f'iʃe] |
| | | |
| to win (vi, vt) | **ganhar** (vi, vt) | [gaɲ'ar] |
| winnings | **ganho** (m) | [g'aɲu] |
| | | |
| to lose (~ 100 dollars) | **perder** (vt) | [pɘrd'er] |
| loss | **perda** (f) | [p'erdɐ] |
| | | |
| player | **jogador** (m) | [ʒugɐd'or] |
| blackjack (card game) | **blackjack** (m) | [blɐkʒ'ɐk] |
| craps (dice game) | **jogo** (m) **de dados** | [ʒ'ogu dɐ d'aduʃ] |
| dice | **dados** (m pl) | [d'aduʃ] |
| slot machine | **máquina** (f) **de jogo** | [m'akinɐ dɐ ʒ'ogu] |

## 162. Rest. Games. Miscellaneous

| | | |
|---|---|---|
| to walk, to stroll (vi) | **passear** (vi) | [pɐsj'ar] |
| walk, stroll | **passeio** (m) | [pɐs'ɐju] |
| road trip | **viagem** (f) **de carro** | [vj'aʒɐ̃j dɐ k'aʀu] |
| adventure | **aventura** (f) | [ɐvẽt'urɐ] |
| picnic | **piquenique** (m) | [pikɘn'ikɐ] |
| | | |
| game (chess, etc.) | **jogo** (m) | [ʒ'ogu] |
| player | **jogador** (m) | [ʒugɐd'or] |
| game (one ~ of chess) | **partida** (f) | [pɐrt'idɐ] |
| | | |
| collector (e.g., philatelist) | **colecionador** (m) | [kulɛsiunɐd'or] |
| to collect (vt) | **colecionar** (vt) | [kulɛsiun'ar] |
| collection | **coleção** (f) | [kulɛs'ɐ̃u] |
| | | |
| crossword puzzle | **palavras** (f pl) **cruzadas** | [pɐl'avrɐʃ kruz'adɐʃ] |
| racetrack (hippodrome) | **hipódromo** (m) | [ip'ɔdrumu] |
| discotheque | **discoteca** (f) | [diʃkut'ɛkɐ] |
| sauna | **sauna** (f) | [s'ɐunɐ] |
| lottery | **lotaria** (f) | [lutɘr'iɐ] |

| camping trip | viagem (f) de acampamento | [vj'aʒẽj də ɐkãpɐm'ẽtu] |
| camp | acampamento (m) | [ɐkãpɐm'ẽtu] |
| tent (for camping) | tenda (f) | [t'ẽdɐ] |
| compass | bússola (f) | [b'usulɐ] |
| camper | campista (m) | [kãp'iʃtɐ] |

| to watch (movie, etc.) | ver (vt), assistir à ... | [ver], [ɐsiʃt'ir a] |
| viewer | telespetador (m) | [tɛlɛʃpɛtɐd'or] |
| TV show | programa (m) de TV | [prugr'emɐ də tɛv'ɛ] |

## 163. Photography

| camera (photo) | máquina (f) fotográfica | [m'akinɐ futugr'afikɐ] |
| photo, picture | foto, fotografia (f) | [f'ɔtu], [futugrɐf'iɐ] |

| photographer | fotógrafo (m) | [fut'ɔgrɐfu] |
| photo studio | estúdio (m) fotográfico | [əʃt'udiu futugr'afiku] |
| photo album | álbum (m) de fotografias | [albũ də futugrɐf'iɐʃ] |

| camera lens | objetiva (f) | [ɔbʒɛt'ivɐ] |
| telephoto lens | teleobjetiva (f) | [tɛlɛɔbʒɛt'ivɐ] |
| filter | filtro (m) | [f'iltru] |
| lens | lente (f) | [l'ẽtɐ] |

| optics (high-quality ~) | ótica (f) | ['ɔtikɐ] |
| diaphragm (aperture) | abertura (f) | [ɐbərt'urɐ] |
| exposure time | exposição (f) | [əʃpuzis'ãu] |
| viewfinder | visor (m) | [viz'or] |
| digital camera | câmara (f) digital | [k'emɐrɐ diʒit'al] |
| tripod | tripé (m) | [trip'ɛ] |
| flash | flash (m) | [flaʃ] |

| to photograph (vt) | fotografar (vt) | [futugrɐf'ar] |
| to take pictures | tirar fotos | [tir'ar f'ɔtuʃ] |
| to be photographed | fotografar-se | [futugrɐf'arsə] |

| focus | foco (m) | [f'ɔku] |
| to adjust the focus | focar (vt) | [fuk'ar] |
| sharp, in focus (adj) | nítido | [n'itidu] |
| sharpness | nitidez (f) | [nitid'eʃ] |

| contrast | contraste (m) | [kõtr'aʃtə] |
| contrasty (adj) | contrastante | [kõtrɐʃt'ãtə] |

| picture (photo) | retrato (m) | [ʀɐtr'atu] |
| negative (n) | negativo (m) | [nɐgɐt'ivu] |
| film (a roll of ~) | filme (m) | [f'ilmə] |
| frame (still) | fotograma (m) | [futugr'emɐ] |
| to print (photos) | imprimir (vt) | [ĩprim'ir] |

## 164. Beach. Swimming

| | | |
|---|---|---|
| beach | **praia** (f) | [pr'ajɐ] |
| sand | **areia** (f) | [ɐr'ɐjɐ] |
| deserted (beach) | **deserto** | [dɐz'ɛrtu] |
| | | |
| suntan | **bronzeado** (m) | [brõzj'adu] |
| to get a tan | **bronzear-se** (vp) | [brõzj'arsɐ] |
| tan (adj) | **bronzeado** | [brõzj'adu] |
| sunscreen | **protetor** (m) **solar** | [prutɛt'or sul'ar] |
| | | |
| bikini | **biquíni** (m) | [bik'ini] |
| bathing suit | **fato** (m) **de banho** | [f'atu dɐ b'ɐɲu] |
| swim briefs | **calção** (m) **de banho** | [kals'ãu dɐ b'ɐɲu] |
| | | |
| swimming pool | **piscina** (f) | [piʃs'inɐ] |
| to swim (vi) | **nadar** (vi) | [nɐd'ar] |
| shower | **duche** (m) | [d'uʃɐ] |
| to change (one's clothes) | **mudar de roupa** | [mudar dɐ ʀ'opɐ] |
| towel | **toalha** (f) | [tu'aʎɐ] |
| | | |
| boat | **barco** (m) | [b'arku] |
| motorboat | **lancha** (f) | [l'ãʃɐ] |
| | | |
| water ski | **esqui** (m) **aquático** | [ɐʃk'i ɐku'atiku] |
| paddle boat | **barco** (m) **de pedais** | [b'arku dɐ pɐd'ajʃ] |
| surfing | **surf, surfe** (m) | [s'urfɐ] |
| surfer | **surfista** (m) | [surf'iʃtɐ] |
| | | |
| scuba set | **scuba** (m) | [sk'ubɐ] |
| flippers (swimfins) | **barbatanas** (f pl) | [bɐrbɐt'enɐʃ] |
| mask | **máscara** (f) | [m'aʃkɐrɐ] |
| diver | **mergulhador** (m) | [mɐrguʎɐd'or] |
| to dive (vi) | **mergulhar** (vi) | [mɐrguʎ'ar] |
| underwater (adv) | **debaixo d'água** | [dɐb'ajʃu d'aguɐ] |
| | | |
| beach umbrella | **guarda-sol** (m) | [gu'ardɐ s'ɔl] |
| beach chair | **espreguiçadeira** (f) | [ɐʃprɐgisɐd'ɐjrɐ] |
| sunglasses | **óculos** (m pl) **de sol** | ['ɔkuluʃ dɐ s'ɔl] |
| air mattress | **colchão** (m) **de ar** | [kɔlʃ'ãu dɐ 'ar] |
| | | |
| to play (amuse oneself) | **brincar** (vi) | [brĩk'ar] |
| to go for a swim | **ir nadar** | [ir nɐd'ar] |
| | | |
| beach ball | **bola** (f) **de praia** | [b'ɔlɐ dɐ pr'ajɐ] |
| to inflate (vt) | **encher** (vt) | [ẽʃ'er] |
| inflatable, air- (adj) | **inflável, de ar** | [ĩfl'avɛl], [dɐ 'ar] |
| | | |
| wave | **onda** (f) | ['õdɐ] |
| buoy | **boia** (f) | [b'ɔjɐ] |
| to drown (ab. person) | **afogar-se** (vp) | [ɐfug'arsɐ] |

| | | |
|---|---|---|
| to save, to rescue | **salvar** (vt) | [salv'ar] |
| life vest | **colete** (m) **salva-vidas** | [kul'etə s'alvɐ v'ideʃ] |
| to observe, to watch | **observar** (vt) | [ɔbsərv'ar] |
| lifeguard | **nadador-salvador** (m) | [nɐdɐd'or salvɐd'or] |

# TECHNICAL EQUIPMENT. TRANSPORTATION

## Technical equipment

### 165. Computer

| | | |
|---|---|---|
| computer | computador (m) | [kõputɐd'or] |
| notebook, laptop | portátil (m) | [purt'atil] |
| | | |
| to turn on | ligar (vt) | [lig'ar] |
| to turn off | desligar (vt) | [dəʒlig'ar] |
| | | |
| keyboard | teclado (m) | [tɛkl'adu] |
| key | tecla (f) | [t'ɛklɐ] |
| mouse | rato (m) | [ʀ'atu] |
| mouse pad | tapete (m) de rato | [tɐp'etə də ʀ'atu] |
| | | |
| button | botão (m) | [but'ãu] |
| cursor | cursor (m) | [kurs'or] |
| | | |
| monitor | monitor (m) | [munit'or] |
| screen | ecrã (m) | [ɛkr'ã] |
| | | |
| hard disk | disco (m) rígido | [d'iʃku ʀ'iʒidu] |
| hard disk volume | capacidade (f) do disco rígido | [kɐpɐsid'adə du d'iʃku ʀ'iʒidu] |
| memory | memória (f) | [məm'ɔriɐ] |
| random access memory | memória (f) operativa | [məm'ɔriɐ ɔpɐræt'ivɐ] |
| | | |
| file | ficheiro (m) | [fiʃ'ejru] |
| folder | pasta (f) | [p'aʃtɐ] |
| to open (vt) | abrir (vt) | [ɐbr'ir] |
| to close (vt) | fechar (vt) | [fəʃ'ar] |
| | | |
| to save (vt) | guardar (vt) | [guɐrd'ar] |
| to delete (vt) | apagar, eliminar (vt) | [ɐpɐg'ar], [elimin'ar] |
| to copy (vt) | copiar (vt) | [kupj'ar] |
| to sort (vt) | ordenar (vt) | [ɔrdən'ar] |
| to transfer (copy) | copiar (vt) | [kupj'ar] |
| | | |
| program | programa (m) | [prugr'ɐmɐ] |
| software | software (m) | [s'ɔftuɛr] |
| programmer | programador (m) | [prugrɐmɐd'or] |
| to program (vt) | programar (vt) | [prugrɐm'ar] |
| hacker | hacker (m) | ['akɛr] |

| password | senha (f) | [s'ɐɲɐ] |
| virus | vírus (m) | [v'iruʃ] |
| to find, to detect | detetar (vt) | [dətɛt'ar] |

| byte | byte (m) | [b'ajtə] |
| megabyte | megabyte (m) | [mɛgeb'ajtə] |

| data | dados (m pl) | [d'aduʃ] |
| database | base (f) de dados | [b'azə də d'aduʃ] |

| cable (USB, etc.) | cabo (m) | [k'abu] |
| to disconnect (vt) | desconectar (vt) | [dəʃkunɛt'ar] |
| to connect (sth to sth) | conetar (vt) | [kunɛt'ar] |

## 166. Internet. E-mail

| Internet | internet (f) | [ĩtɛrn'ɛtə] |
| browser | browser (m) | [br'auzɐr] |
| search engine | motor (m) de busca | [mut'or də b'uʃkɐ] |
| provider | provedor (m) | [pruvəd'or] |

| web master | webmaster (m) | [wɛbm'astɛr] |
| website | website, sítio web (m) | [wɛbsitə], [s'itiu wɛb] |
| web page | página (f) web | [p'aʒinɐ wɛb] |

| address | endereço (m) | [ẽdər'esu] |
| address book | livro (m) de endereços | [l'ivru də ẽdər'esuʃ] |

| mailbox | caixa (f) de correio | [k'ajʃɐ də kuʀ'ɐju] |
| mail | correio (m) | [kuʀ'ɐju] |
| full (adj) | cheia | [ʃ'ɐjɐ] |

| message | mensagem (f) | [mẽs'aʒɐj] |
| incoming messages | mensagens recebidas | [mẽs'aʒɐjʃ ʀəsəb'idɐʃ] |
| outgoing messages | mensagens enviadas | [mẽs'aʒɐjʃ ẽvj'adɐʃ] |
| sender | remetente (m) | [ʀəmət'ẽtə] |
| to send (vt) | enviar (vt) | [ẽvj'ar] |
| sending (of mail) | envio (m) | [ẽv'iu] |

| receiver | destinatário (m) | [dəʃtinɛt'ariu] |
| to receive (vt) | receber (vt) | [ʀəsəb'er] |

| correspondence | correspondência (f) | [kuʀəʃpõd'ẽsiɐ] |
| to correspond (vi) | corresponder-se (vp) | [kuʀəʃpõd'ersə] |

| file | ficheiro (m) | [fiʃ'ɐjru] |
| to download (vt) | fazer download, baixar (vt) | [fez'er daunl'oɐd], [bajʃ'ar] |
| to create (vt) | criar (vt) | [kri'ar] |
| to delete (vt) | apagar, eliminar (vt) | [ɐpɐg'ar], [elimin'ar] |

| deleted (adj) | eliminado | [elimin'adu] |
| connection (ADSL, etc.) | ligação (f) | [ligɐs'ãu] |
| speed | velocidade (f) | [vəlusid'adə] |
| modem | modem (m) | [m'ɔdɛm] |
| access | acesso (m) | [ɐs'ɛsu] |
| port (e.g., input ~) | porta (f) | [p'ɔrtɐ] |

| connection (make a ~) | conexão (f) | [kunɛks'ãu] |
| to connect to … (vi) | conetar (vi) | [kunɛt'ar] |

| to select (vt) | escolher (vt) | [əʃkuʎ'er] |
| to search (for …) | buscar (vt) | [buʃk'ar] |

## 167. Electricity

| electricity | eletricidade (f) | [elɛtrisid'adə] |
| electrical (adj) | elétrico | [el'ɛtriku] |
| electric power station | central (f) elétrica | [sẽtr'al el'ɛtrikɐ] |
| energy | energia (f) | [enərʒ'iɐ] |
| electric power | energia (f) elétrica | [enərʒ'iɐ el'ɛtrikɐ] |

| light bulb | lâmpada (f) | [l'ãpɐdɐ] |
| flashlight | lanterna (f) | [lãt'ɛrnɐ] |
| street light | poste (m) de iluminação | [p'ɔʃtɐ də iluminɐs'ãu] |

| light | luz (f) | [luʃ] |
| to turn on | ligar (vt) | [lig'ar] |
| to turn off | desligar (vt) | [dəʒlig'ar] |
| to turn off the light | apagar a luz | [ɐpɐg'ar ɐ luʃ] |

| to burn out (vi) | fundir (vi) | [fũd'ir] |
| short circuit | curto-circuito (m) | [k'urtu sirk'uitu] |
| broken wire | rutura (f) | [ʀut'urɐ] |
| contact | contacto (m) | [kõt'aktu] |

| light switch | interruptor (m) | [ĩtəʀupt'or] |
| wall socket | tomada (f) | [tum'adɐ] |
| plug | ficha (f) | [f'iʃɐ] |
| extension cord | extensão (f) | [əʃtẽs'ãu] |

| fuse | fusível (m) | [fuz'ivɛl] |
| cable, wire | fio, cabo (m) | [f'iu], [k'abu] |
| wiring | instalação (f) elétrica | [ĩtɐlɐs'ãu el'ɛtrikɐ] |

| ampere | ampere (m) | [ãp'ɛrə] |
| amperage | amperagem (f) | [ãpər'aʒẽj] |
| volt | volt (m) | [v'ɔltə] |
| voltage | voltagem (f) | [vɔlt'aʒẽj] |
| electrical device | aparelho (m) elétrico | [ɐpɐr'eʎu el'ɛtriku] |
| indicator | indicador (m) | [ĩdikɐd'or] |

| electrician | **eletricista** (m) | [elɛtris'iʃtɐ] |
| to solder (vt) | **soldar** (vt) | [sold'ar] |
| soldering iron | **ferro** (m) **de soldar** | [f'ɛʀu dǝ sold'ar] |
| electric current | **corrente** (f) **elétrica** | [kuʀ'ẽtɐ el'ɛtrikɐ] |

## 168. Tools

| tool, instrument | **ferramenta** (f) | [fǝʀɐm'ẽtɐ] |
| tools | **ferramentas** (f pl) | [fǝʀɐm'ẽtɐʃ] |
| equipment (factory ~) | **equipamento** (m) | [ekipɐm'ẽtu] |
| | | |
| hammer | **martelo** (m) | [mɐrt'ɛlu] |
| screwdriver | **chave** (f) **de fendas** | [ʃ'avɐ dǝ f'ẽdɐʃ] |
| ax | **machado** (m) | [mɐʃ'adu] |
| | | |
| saw | **serra** (f) | [s'ɛʀɐ] |
| to saw (vt) | **serrar** (vt) | [sǝʀ'ar] |
| plane (tool) | **plaina** (f) | [pl'ajnɐ] |
| to plane (vt) | **aplainar** (vt) | [ɐplajn'ar] |
| soldering iron | **ferro** (m) **de soldar** | [f'ɛʀu dǝ sold'ar] |
| to solder (vt) | **soldar** (vt) | [sold'ar] |
| | | |
| file (for metal) | **lima** (f) | [l'imɐ] |
| carpenter pincers | **tenaz** (f) | [tǝn'aʃ] |
| lineman's pliers | **alicate** (m) | [ɐlik'atǝ] |
| chisel | **formão** (m) | [furm'ãu] |
| | | |
| drill bit | **broca** (f) | [br'ɔkɐ] |
| electric drill | **berbequim** (f) | [bǝrbǝk'ĩ] |
| to drill (vi, vt) | **furar** (vt) | [fur'ar] |
| | | |
| knife | **faca** (f) | [f'akɐ] |
| pocket knife | **canivete** (m) | [kɐniv'ɛtǝ] |
| folding (~ knife) | **articulado** | [ɐrtikul'adu] |
| blade | **lâmina** (f) | [l'eminɐ] |
| | | |
| sharp (blade, etc.) | **afiado** | [ɐfj'adu] |
| blunt (adj) | **cego** | [s'ɛgu] |
| to become blunt | **embotar-se** (vp) | [ẽbut'arsǝ] |
| to sharpen (vt) | **afiar, amolar** (vt) | [ɐfj'ar], [ɐmul'ar] |
| | | |
| bolt | **parafuso** (m) | [pɐrɐf'uzu] |
| nut | **porca** (f) | [p'ɔrkɐ] |
| thread (of a screw) | **rosca** (f) | [ʀ'oʃkɐ] |
| wood screw | **parafuso** (m) **para madeira** | [pɐrɐf'uzu p'ɐrɐ mɐd'ejrɐ] |
| | | |
| nail | **prego** (m) | [pr'egu] |
| nailhead | **cabeça** (f) **do prego** | [kɐb'esɐ du pr'egu] |
| ruler (for measuring) | **régua** (f) | [ʀ'ɛguɐ] |

| | | |
|---|---|---|
| tape measure | **fita** (f) **métrica** | [f'itɐ m'ɛtrikɐ] |
| spirit level | **nível** (m) | [n'ivɛl] |
| magnifying glass | **lupa** (f) | [l'upɐ] |
| | | |
| measuring instrument | **medidor** (m) | [mədid'or] |
| to measure (vt) | **medir** (vt) | [məd'ir] |
| scale | **escala** (f) | [əʃk'alɐ] |
| (of thermometer, etc.) | | |
| readings | **leitura** (f) | [lɐjt'urɐ] |
| | | |
| compressor | **compressor** (m) | [kõprəs'or] |
| microscope | **microscópio** (m) | [mikrɔʃk'ɔpiu] |
| | | |
| pump (e.g., water ~) | **bomba** (f) | [b'õbɐ] |
| robot | **robô** (m) | [ʀob'o] |
| laser | **laser** (m) | [l'ejzɐr] |
| | | |
| wrench | **chave** (f) **de boca** | [ʃ'avɐ də b'okɐ] |
| adhesive tape | **fita** (f) **adesiva** | [f'itɐ ɐdəz'ivɐ] |
| glue | **cola** (f) | [k'ɔlɐ] |
| | | |
| emery paper | **lixa** (f) | [l'iʃɐ] |
| spring | **mola** (f) | [m'ɔlɐ] |
| magnet | **íman** (m) | ['imɐn] |
| gloves | **luvas** (f pl) | [l'uvɐʃ] |
| | | |
| rope | **corda** (f) | [k'ɔrdɐ] |
| cord | **cordel** (m) | [kurd'ɛl] |
| wire (e.g., telephone ~) | **fio** (m) | [f'iu] |
| cable | **cabo** (m) | [k'abu] |
| | | |
| sledgehammer | **marreta** (f) | [mɐʀ'ɛtɐ] |
| crowbar | **pé de cabra** (f) | [pɛ də k'abrɐ] |
| ladder | **escada** (f) **de mão** | [əʃk'adɐ də m'ãu] |
| stepladder | **escadote** (m) | [əʃkɐd'ɔtə] |
| | | |
| to screw (tighten) | **enroscar** (vt) | [ẽʀuʃk'ar] |
| to unscrew, untwist (vt) | **desenroscar** (vt) | [dəzẽʀuʃk'ar] |
| to tighten (vt) | **apertar** (vt) | [epərt'ar] |
| to glue, to stick | **colar** (vt) | [kul'ar] |
| to cut (vt) | **cortar** (vt) | [kurt'ar] |
| | | |
| malfunction (fault) | **falha** (f) | [f'aʎɐ] |
| repair (mending) | **conserto** (m) | [kõs'ɛrtu] |
| to repair, to mend (vt) | **consertar, reparar** (vt) | [kõsərt'ar], [ʀəpər'ar] |
| to adjust (machine, etc.) | **regular, ajustar** (vt) | [ʀəgul'ar], [ɐʒuʃt'ar] |
| | | |
| to check (to examine) | **verificar** (vt) | [vərifik'ar] |
| checking | **verificação** (f) | [vərifikɐs'ãu] |
| readings | **leitura** (f) | [lɐjt'urɐ] |
| reliable (machine) | **seguro** | [səg'uru] |
| complicated (adj) | **complicado** | [kõplik'adu] |

| | | |
|---|---|---|
| to rust (get rusted) | **enferrujar** (vi) | [ẽfəʀuʒ'ar] |
| rusty, rusted (adj) | **enferrujado** | [ẽfəʀuʒ'adu] |
| rust | **ferrugem** (f) | [fəʀ'uʒẽj] |

# Transportation

## 169. Airplane

| | | |
|---|---|---|
| airplane | avião (m) | [ɐvjˈãu] |
| air ticket | bilhete (m) de avião | [biʎˈetɐ dɐ ɐvjˈãu] |
| airline | companhia (f) aérea | [kõpɐɲˈiɐ ɐˈɛriɐ] |
| airport | aeroporto (m) | [ɐɛrɔpˈortu] |
| supersonic (adj) | supersónico | [supɐrsˈɔniku] |
| | | |
| captain | comandante (m) do avião | [kumãdˈãtɐ du ɐvjˈãu] |
| crew | tripulação (f) | [tripulɐsˈãu] |
| pilot | piloto (m) | [pilˈotu] |
| flight attendant | hospedeira (f) de bordo | [ɔʃpɐdˈejrɐ dɐ bˈɔrdu] |
| navigator | copiloto (m) | [kopilˈotu] |
| | | |
| wings | asas (f pl) | [ˈazɐʃ] |
| tail | cauda (f) | [kˈaudɐ] |
| cockpit | cabine (f) | [kɐbˈinɐ] |
| engine | motor (m) | [mutˈor] |
| undercarriage | trem (m) de aterragem | [trˈẽj dɐ ɐtɐʀˈaʒɐj] |
| turbine | turbina (f) | [turbˈinɐ] |
| | | |
| propeller | hélice (f) | [ˈɛlisɐ] |
| black box | caixa (f) negra | [kˈajʃɐ nˈegrɐ] |
| control column | coluna (f) de controle | [kulˈunɐ dɐ kõtrˈɔlɐ] |
| fuel | combustível (m) | [kõbuʃtˈivɛl] |
| | | |
| safety card | instruções (f pl) de segurança | [ĩʃtrusˈojʃ dɐ sɐgurˈãsɐ] |
| oxygen mask | máscara (f) de oxigénio | [mˈaʃkɐrɐ dɐ ɔksiʒˈɛniu] |
| uniform | uniforme (m) | [unifˈɔrmɐ] |
| life vest | colete (m) salva-vidas | [kulˈetɐ sˈalvɐ vˈidɐʃ] |
| parachute | paraquedas (m) | [pɐrɐkˈɛdɐʃ] |
| | | |
| takeoff | descolagem (f) | [dɐʃkulˈaʒɐj] |
| to take off (vi) | descolar (vi) | [dɐʃkulˈar] |
| runway | pista (f) de descolagem | [pˈiʃtɐ dɐ dɐʃkulˈaʒɐj] |
| | | |
| visibility | visibilidade (f) | [vizibilidˈadɐ] |
| flight (act of flying) | voo (m) | [vˈou] |
| altitude | altura (f) | [altˈurɐ] |
| air pocket | poço (m) de ar | [pˈosu dɐ ˈar] |
| | | |
| seat | assento (m) | [ɐsˈẽtu] |
| headphones | auscultadores (m pl) | [auʃkultedˈorɐʃ] |

| | | |
|---|---|---|
| folding tray | **mesa** (f) **rebatível** | [m'ezɐ ʀɐbɐt'ivɛl] |
| airplane window | **vigia** (f) | [viʒ'iɐ] |
| aisle | **passagem** (f) | [pɐs'aʒẽj] |

## 170. Train

| | | |
|---|---|---|
| train | **comboio** (m) | [kõb'ɔju] |
| suburban train | **comboio** (m) **suburbano** | [kõb'ɔju suburb'ɐnu] |
| express train | **comboio** (m) **rápido** | [kõb'ɔju ʀ'apidu] |
| diesel locomotive | **locomotiva** (f) **diesel** | [lukumut'ivɐ d'izɛl] |
| steam engine | **comboio** (m) **a vapor** | [kõb'ɔju ɐ vɐp'or] |
| | | |
| passenger car | **carruagem** (f) | [kɐʀu'aʒẽj] |
| dining car | **carruagem restaurante** (f) | [kɐʀu'aʒẽj ʀɐʃtaur'ãtɐ] |
| | | |
| rails | **trilhos** (m pl) | [tr'iʎuʃ] |
| railroad | **caminho de ferro** (m) | [kɐm'iɲu dɐ f'ɛʀu] |
| railway tie | **travessa** (f) | [trɐv'ɛsɐ] |
| | | |
| platform (railway ~) | **plataforma** (f) | [plɐtɐf'ɔrmɐ] |
| track (~ 1, 2, etc.) | **linha** (f) | [l'iɲɐ] |
| semaphore | **semáforo** (m) | [sɐm'afuru] |
| station | **estação** (f) | [ɐʃtɐs'ãu] |
| | | |
| engineer | **maquinista** (m) | [mɐkin'iʃtɐ] |
| porter (of luggage) | **bagageiro** (m) | [bɐgɐʒ'ɐjru] |
| train steward | **condutor** (m) | [kõdut'or] |
| passenger | **passageiro** (m) | [pɐsɐʒ'ɐjru] |
| conductor | **revisor** (m) | [ʀɐviz'or] |
| | | |
| corridor (in train) | **corredor** (m) | [kuʀɐd'or] |
| emergency break | **freio** (m) **de emergência** | [fr'ɐju dɐ emɐrʒ'ẽsiɐ] |
| | | |
| compartment | **compartimento** (m) | [kõpɐrtim'ẽtu] |
| berth | **cama** (f) | [k'ɐmɐ] |
| upper berth | **cama** (f) **de cima** | [k'ɐmɐ dɐ s'imɐ] |
| lower berth | **cama** (f) **de baixo** | [k'ɐmɐ dɐ b'ajʃu] |
| bed linen | **roupa** (f) **de cama** | [ʀ'opɐ dɐ k'ɐmɐ] |
| | | |
| ticket | **bilhete** (m) | [biʎ'etɐ] |
| schedule | **horário** (m) | [ɔr'ariu] |
| information display | **painel** (m) **de informação** | [pajn'ɛl dɐ ĩfurmɐs'ãu] |
| | | |
| to leave, to depart | **partir** (vt) | [pɐrt'ir] |
| departure (of train) | **partida** (f) | [pɐrt'idɐ] |
| to arrive (ab. train) | **chegar** (vi) | [ʃɐg'ar] |
| arrival | **chegada** (f) | [ʃɐg'adɐ] |
| | | |
| to arrive by train | **chegar de comboio** | [ʃɐg'ar dɐ kõb'ɔju] |
| to get on the train | **apanhar o comboio** | [ɐpɐɲ'ar u kõb'ɔju] |

| | | |
|---|---|---|
| to get off the train | **sair do comboio** | [se'ir du kõb'ɔju] |
| train wreck | **acidente** (m) **ferroviário** | [esid'ẽte fɛʀɔvj'ariu] |
| to be derailed | **descarrilar** (vi) | [deʃkeʀil'ar] |
| steam engine | **comboio** (m) **a vapor** | [kõb'ɔju e vep'or] |
| stoker, fireman | **fogueiro** (m) | [fug'ejru] |
| firebox | **fornalha** (f) | [furn'aʎe] |
| coal | **carvão** (m) | [keʀv'ãu] |

# 171. Ship

| | | |
|---|---|---|
| ship | **navio** (m) | [nev'iu] |
| vessel | **embarcação** (f) | [ẽberkes'ãu] |
| | | |
| steamship | **vapor** (m) | [vep'or] |
| riverboat | **navio** (m) | [nev'iu] |
| ocean liner | **transatlântico** (m) | [trãzetl'ãtiku] |
| cruiser | **cruzador** (m) | [kruzed'or] |
| | | |
| yacht | **iate** (m) | [j'ate] |
| tugboat | **rebocador** (m) | [ʀebuked'or] |
| barge | **barcaça** (f) | [beʀk'ase] |
| ferry | **ferry** (m) | [f'ɛʀi] |
| | | |
| sailing ship | **veleiro** (m) | [vel'ejru] |
| brigantine | **bergantim** (m) | [bergãt'ĩ] |
| ice breaker | **quebra-gelo** (m) | [k'ɛbre ʒ'ɛlu] |
| submarine | **submarino** (m) | [submer'inu] |
| | | |
| boat (flat-bottomed ~) | **bote, barco** (m) | [b'ɔte], [b'arku] |
| dinghy | **bote, dingue** (m) | [b'ɔte], [d'ĩge] |
| lifeboat | **bote** (m) **salva-vidas** | [b'ɔte s'alve v'ideʃ] |
| motorboat | **lancha** (f) | [l'ãʃe] |
| | | |
| captain | **capitão** (m) | [kepit'ãu] |
| seaman | **marinheiro** (m) | [meriɲ'ejru] |
| sailor | **marujo** (m) | [mer'uʒu] |
| crew | **tripulação** (f) | [tripules'ãu] |
| | | |
| boatswain | **contramestre** (m) | [kõtrem'ɛʃtre] |
| ship's boy | **grumete** (m) | [grum'ɛte] |
| cook | **cozinheiro** (m) **de bordo** | [kuziɲ'ejru de b'ɔrdu] |
| ship's doctor | **médico** (m) **de bordo** | [m'ɛdiku de b'ɔrdu] |
| | | |
| deck | **convés** (m) | [kõv'ɛʃ] |
| mast | **mastro** (m) | [m'aʃtru] |
| sail | **vela** (f) | [v'ɛle] |
| | | |
| hold | **porão** (m) | [pur'ãu] |
| bow (prow) | **proa** (f) | [pr'oe] |
| stern | **popa** (f) | [p'ope] |

| oar | remo (m) | [ʀ'ɛmu] |
| screw propeller | hélice (f) | ['ɛlisə] |

| cabin | camarote (m) | [kɐmɐr'ɔtə] |
| wardroom | sala (f) dos oficiais | [s'alɐ duʃ ɔfisj'ajʃ] |
| engine room | sala (f) das máquinas | [s'alɐ deʃ m'akinɐʃ] |
| bridge | ponte (m) de comando | [p'õtə də kum'ãdu] |
| radio room | sala (f) de comunicações | [s'alɐ də kumunikɐs'ojʃ] |
| wave (radio) | onda (f) | ['õdɐ] |
| logbook | diário (m) de bordo | [dj'ariu də b'ɔrdu] |

| spyglass | luneta (f) | [lun'ɛtɐ] |
| bell | sino (m) | [s'inu] |
| flag | bandeira (f) | [bãd'ejrɐ] |

| rope (mooring ~) | cabo (m) | [k'abu] |
| knot (bowline, etc.) | nó (m) | [nɔ] |
| deckrail | corrimão (m) | [kuʀim'ãu] |
| gangway | prancha (f) de embarque | [pr'ãʃe də ẽb'arkə] |

| anchor | âncora (f) | ['ãkurɐ] |
| to weigh anchor | recolher a âncora | [ʀəkuʎ'er ɐ 'ãkurɐ] |
| to drop anchor | lançar a âncora | [lãs'ar ɐ 'ãkurɐ] |
| anchor chain | amarra (f) | [ɐm'aʀɐ] |

| port (harbor) | porto (m) | [p'ortu] |
| berth, wharf | cais, amarradouro (m) | [kajʃ], [ɐmɐʀɐd'oru] |
| to berth (moor) | atracar (vi) | [etrɐk'ar] |
| to cast off | desatracar (vi) | [dəzetrɐk'ar] |

| trip, voyage | viagem (f) | [vj'aʒẽj] |
| cruise (sea trip) | cruzeiro (m) | [kruz'ejru] |
| course (route) | rumo (m), rota (f) | [ʀ'umu], [ʀ'ɔtɐ] |
| route (itinerary) | itinerário (m) | [itinɐr'ariu] |

| fairway | canal (m) navegável | [kɐn'al nɐvɐg'avɛl] |
| shallows (shoal) | baixio (m) | [bajʃ'iu] |
| to run aground | encalhar (vt) | [ẽkɐʎ'ar] |

| storm | tempestade (f) | [tẽpəʃt'adə] |
| signal | sinal (m) | [sin'al] |
| to sink (vi) | afundar-se (vp) | [ɐfũd'arsə] |
| Man overboard! | Homem ao mar! | ['ɔmẽj 'au m'ar] |
| SOS | SOS | [ɛsəo 'ɛsə] |
| ring buoy | boia (f) salva-vidas | [b'ɔjɐ s'alvɐ v'idɐʃ] |

## 172. Airport

| airport | aeroporto (m) | [ɐɛrɔp'ortu] |
| airplane | avião (m) | [ɐvj'ãu] |

| airline | companhia (f) aérea | [kõpəɲ'ie e'ɛrie] |
| air-traffic controller | controlador (m) de tráfego aéreo | [kõtruled'or də tr'afəgu e'ɛriu] |

| departure | partida (f) | [pert'ide] |
| arrival | chegada (f) | [ʃəg'ade] |
| to arrive (by plane) | chegar (vi) | [ʃəg'ar] |

| departure time | hora (f) de partida | ['ɔrɐ də pert'ide] |
| arrival time | hora (f) de chegada | ['ɔrɐ də ʃəg'ade] |

| to be delayed | estar atrasado | [əʃt'ar etrez'adu] |
| flight delay | atraso (m) de voo | [etr'azu də v'ou] |

| information board | painel (m) de informação | [pajn'ɛl də ĩfurmes'ãu] |
| information | informação (f) | [ĩfurmes'ãu] |
| to announce (vt) | anunciar (vt) | [enũsj'ar] |
| flight (e.g., next ~) | voo (m) | [v'ou] |

| customs | alfândega (f) | [alf'ãdəge] |
| customs officer | funcionário (m) da alfândega | [fũsiun'ariu de alf'ãdəge] |

| customs declaration | declaração (f) alfandegária | [dəkleres'ãu alfãdəg'arie] |
| to fill out (vt) | preencher (vt) | [priẽʃ'er] |
| to fill out the declaration | preencher a declaração | [priẽʃ'er e dəkleres'ãu] |
| passport control | controlo (m) de passaportes | [kõtr'olu də pasep'ɔrtəʃ] |

| luggage | bagagem (f) | [beg'aʒēj] |
| hand luggage | bagagem (f) de mão | [beg'aʒēj də m'ãu] |
| Lost Luggage Desk | Perdidos e Achados | [pərd'iduʃ i eʃ'aduʃ] |
| luggage cart | carrinho (m) | [keʀ'iɲu] |

| landing | aterragem (f) | [etəʀ'aʒēj] |
| landing strip | pista (f) de aterragem | [p'iʃte də etəʀ'aʒēj] |
| to land (vi) | aterrar (vi) | [etəʀ'ar] |
| airstairs | escada (f) de avião | [əʃk'ade də evj'ãu] |

| check-in | check-in (m) | [ʃɛk'in] |
| check-in desk | balcão (m) do check-in | [balk'ãu du ʃɛk'in] |
| to check-in (vi) | fazer o check-in | [fez'er u ʃɛk'in] |

| boarding pass | cartão (m) de embarque | [kert'ãu də ēb'arkə] |
| departure gate | porta (f) de embarque | [p'ɔrtə də ēb'arkə] |

| transit | trânsito (m) | [tr'ãzitu] |
| to wait (vt) | esperar (vi, vt) | [əʃpər'ar] |
| departure lounge | sala (f) de espera | [s'ale də əʃp'ɛrɐ] |
| to see off | despedir-se de ... | [dəʃpəd'irsə də] |
| to say goodbye | dizer adeus | [diz'er ed'ewʃ] |

## 173. Bicycle. Motorcycle

| bicycle | bicicleta (f) | [bisiklˈɛtɐ] |
| scooter | scotter, lambreta (f) | [skutˈeɾ], [lãbrˈetɐ] |
| motorcycle, bike | mota (f) | [mˈɔtɐ] |

| to go by bicycle | ir de bicicleta | [ir də bisiklˈɛtɐ] |
| handlebars | guiador (m) | [giɐdˈoɾ] |
| pedal | pedal (m) | [pɐdˈal] |
| brakes | travões (m pl) | [trɐvˈojʃ] |
| bicycle seat | selim (m) | [səlˈĩ] |

| pump | bomba (f) de ar | [bˈõbɐ də ˈar] |
| luggage rack | porta-bagagens (m) | [pˈɔrtɐ bɐgˈaʒẽjʃ] |
| front lamp | lanterna (f) | [lãtˈɛrnɐ] |
| helmet | capacete (m) | [kɐpɐsˈetə] |

| wheel | roda (f) | [ʀˈɔdɐ] |
| fender | guarda-lamas (m) | [guardɐ lˈɐmɐʃ] |
| rim | aro (m) | [ˈaru] |
| spoke | raio (m) | [ʀˈaju] |

# Cars

## 174. Types of cars

| | | |
|---|---|---|
| automobile, car | **carro, automóvel** (m) | [k'aʀu], [autum'ɔvɛl] |
| sports car | **carro** (m) **desportivo** | [k'aʀu dəʃpurt'ivu] |
| | | |
| limousine | **limusine** (f) | [limuz'inə] |
| off-road vehicle | **todo o terreno** (m) | [t'odu u təʀ'enu] |
| convertible | **descapotável** (m) | [dəʃkəput'avɛl] |
| minibus | **minibus** (m) | [m'inibɛz] |
| | | |
| ambulance | **ambulância** (f) | [ãbul'ãsiə] |
| snowplow | **limpa-neve** (m) | [l'ĩpɐ n'ɛvə] |
| | | |
| truck | **camião** (m) | [kamj'ãu] |
| tank truck | **camião-cisterna** (m) | [kamj'ãu siʃt'ɛrnɐ] |
| van (small truck) | **carrinha** (f) | [keʀ'iɲɐ] |
| tractor (big rig) | **caminhão-trator** (m) | [kemiɲ'ãu tret'or] |
| trailer | **atrelado** (m) | [etrɐl'adu] |
| | | |
| comfortable (adj) | **confortável** | [kõfurt'avɛl] |
| second hand (adj) | **usado** | [uz'adu] |

## 175. Cars. Bodywork

| | | |
|---|---|---|
| hood | **capô** (m) | [kɐp'o] |
| fender | **guarda-lamas** (m) | [guardə l'ɐmɐʃ] |
| roof | **tejadilho** (m) | [təʒed'iʎu] |
| | | |
| windshield | **para-brisa** (m) | [parɐbr'izə] |
| rear-view mirror | **espelho** (m) **retrovisor** | [əʃp'eʎu ʀɛtrɔviz'or] |
| windshield washer | **lavador** (m) | [lɐved'or] |
| windshield wipers | **limpa-para-brisas** (m) | [l'ĩpɐ p'arɐ br'izɐʃ] |
| | | |
| side window | **vidro** (m) **lateral** | [v'idru letɐr'al] |
| window lift | **elevador** (m) **do vidro** | [eləved'or du v'idru] |
| antenna | **antena** (f) | [ãt'enɐ] |
| sun roof | **teto solar** (m) | [t'ɛtu sul'ar] |
| | | |
| bumper | **para-choques** (m pl) | [p'arɐ ʃ'ɔkəʃ] |
| trunk | **bagageira** (f) | [bɐgɐʒ'ejrɐ] |
| roof luggage rack | **bagageira** (f) **de tejadilho** | [bɐgɐʒ'ejrɐ də təʒed'iʎu] |
| door | **porta** (f) | [p'ɔrtɐ] |

| door handle | maçaneta (f) | [mɐsɐnˈetɐ] |
| door lock | fechadura (f) | [fɐʃɐdˈurɐ] |

| license plate | matrícula (f) | [mɐtrˈikulɐ] |
| muffler | silenciador (m) | [silẽsiɐdˈor] |
| gas tank | tanque (m) de gasolina | [tˈãkə də gɐzulˈinɐ] |
| tail pipe | tubo (m) de escape | [tˈubu də əʃkˈapə] |

| gas, accelerator | acelerador (m) | [ɐsɐlɐrɐdˈor] |
| pedal | pedal (m) | [pɐdˈal] |
| gas pedal | pedal (m) do acelerador | [pɐdˈal du ɐsɐlɐrɐdˈor] |

| brake | travão (m) | [trɐvˈãu] |
| brake pedal | pedal (m) do travão | [pɐdˈal du trɐvˈãu] |
| to slow down (to brake) | travar (vt) | [trɐvˈar] |
| parking brake | travão (m) de mão | [trɐvˈãu də mˈãu] |

| clutch | embraiagem (f) | [ẽbrɐjˈaʒɐj] |
| clutch pedal | pedal (m) da embraiagem | [pɐdˈal dɐ ẽbrɐjˈaʒɐj] |
| clutch plate | disco (m) de embraiagem | [dˈiʃku də ẽbrɐjˈaʒɐj] |
| shock absorber | amortecedor (m) | [ɐmurtɐsɐdˈor] |

| wheel | roda (f) | [ʁˈɔdɐ] |
| spare tire | pneu (m) sobresselente | [pnˈeu sobrɐsɐlˈẽtɐ] |
| tire | pneu (m) | [pnˈeu] |
| hubcap | tampão (m) de roda | [tãpˈãu də ʁˈɔdɐ] |

| driving wheels | rodas (f pl) motrizes | [ʁˈɔdɐʃ mutrˈizɐʃ] |
| front-wheel drive (as adj) | de tração dianteira | [də trasˈãu diãtˈejrɐ] |
| rear-wheel drive (as adj) | de tração traseira | [də trasˈãu trɐzˈejrɐ] |
| all-wheel drive (as adj) | de tração às 4 rodas | [də trasˈãu aʃ kuˈatru ʁˈɔdɐʃ] |

| gearbox | caixa (f) de mudanças | [kˈajʃɐ də mudˈãsɐʃ] |
| automatic (adj) | automático | [autumˈatiku] |
| mechanical (adj) | mecânico | [mɐkˈɐniku] |
| gear shift | alavanca (f) das mudanças | [ɐlɐvˈãkɐ dɐʃ mudˈãsɐʃ] |

| headlight | farol (m) | [fɐrˈɔl] |
| headlights | faróis (m pl), luzes (f pl) | [fɐrˈɔjʃ], [lˈuzɐʃ] |

| low beam | médios (m pl) | [mˈɛdiuʃ] |
| high beam | máximos (m pl) | [mˈasimuʃ] |
| brake light | luzes (f pl) de stop | [lˈuzɐʃ də stˈɔp] |

| parking lights | mínimos (m pl) | [mˈinimuʃ] |
| hazard lights | luzes (f pl) de emergência | [lˈuzɐʃ də emərʒˈẽsiɐ] |
| fog lights | faróis (m pl) antinevoeiro | [fɐrˈɔjʃ ãtinɐvuˈejru] |

| turn signal | pisca-pisca (m) | [pˈiʃkɐ pˈiʃkɐ] |
| back-up light | luz (f) de marcha atrás | [lˈuʃ də mˈarʃɐ ɐtrˈaʃ] |

## 176. Cars. Passenger compartment

| | | |
|---|---|---|
| car inside | interior (m) do carro | [ĩtərj'or du k'aʀu] |
| leather (as adj) | de couro, de pele | [də k'oru], [də p'ɛlə] |
| velour (as adj) | de veludo | [də vəl'udu] |
| upholstery | estofos (m pl) | [əʃt'ɔfuʃ] |
| | | |
| instrument (gage) | indicador (m) | [ĩdikɐd'or] |
| dashboard | painel (m) de instrumentos | [pajn'ɛl də ĩʃtrum'ẽtuʃ] |
| speedometer | velocímetro (m) | [vəlus'imətru] |
| needle (pointer) | ponteiro (m) | [põt'ejru] |
| | | |
| odometer | conta-quilómetros (m) | [k'õtɐ kil'ɔmətruʃ] |
| indicator (sensor) | sensor (m) | [sẽs'or] |
| level | nível (m) | [n'ivɛl] |
| warning light | luz (f) avisadora | [luʃ ɐvizɐd'orɐ] |
| | | |
| steering wheel | volante (m) | [vul'ãtə] |
| horn | buzina (f) | [buz'inɐ] |
| button | botão (m) | [but'ãu] |
| switch | interruptor (m) | [ĩtəʀupt'or] |
| | | |
| seat | assento (m) | [ɐs'ẽtu] |
| backrest | costas (f pl) do assento | [k'ɔʃtɐʃ du ɐs'ẽtu] |
| headrest | cabeceira (f) | [kɐbəs'ejrɐ] |
| seat belt | cinto (m) de segurança | [s'ĩtu də səgur'ãsɐ] |
| to fasten the belt | apertar o cinto | [ɐpərt'ar u s'ĩtu] |
| adjustment (of seats) | regulação (f) | [ʀəguləs'ãu] |
| | | |
| airbag | airbag (m) | [ɛrb'ɛg] |
| air-conditioner | ar (m) condicionado | [ar kõdisiun'adu] |
| | | |
| radio | rádio (m) | [ʀ'adiu] |
| CD player | leitor (m) de CD | [lɛjt'or də s'ɛdɛ] |
| to turn on | ligar (vt) | [lig'ar] |
| antenna | antena (f) | [ãt'enɐ] |
| glove box | porta-luvas (m) | [p'ɔrtɐ l'uvɐʃ] |
| ashtray | cinzeiro (m) | [sĩz'ejru] |

## 177. Cars. Engine

| | | |
|---|---|---|
| engine, motor | motor (m) | [mut'or] |
| diesel (as adj) | diesel | [d'izɛl] |
| gasoline (as adj) | a gasolina | [ɐ gəzul'inɐ] |
| | | |
| engine volume | cilindrada (f) | [silĩdr'adɐ] |
| power | potência (f) | [put'ẽsiɐ] |
| horsepower | cavalo-vapor (m) | [kɐv'alu vɐp'or] |

| piston | pistão (m) | [piʃt'ãu] |
| cylinder | cilindro (m) | [sil'ĩdru] |
| valve | válvula (f) | [v'alvulɐ] |

| injector | injetor (m) | [ĩʒɛt'or] |
| generator | gerador (m) | [ʒɐred'or] |
| carburetor | carburador (m) | [kɐrbured'or] |
| engine oil | óleo (m) para motor | ['ɔliu p'ɐrɐ mut'or] |

| radiator | radiador (m) | [ʀɐdied'or] |
| coolant | refrigerante (m) | [ʀɐfriʒɐr'ãtɐ] |
| cooling fan | ventilador (m) | [vẽtilɐd'or] |

| battery (accumulator) | bateria (f) | [bɐtɐr'iɐ] |
| starter | dispositivo (m) de arranque | [diʃpuzit'ivu dɐ ɐʀ'ãkɐ] |
| ignition | ignição (f) | [ignis'ãu] |
| spark plug | vela (f) de ignição | [v'ɛlɐ dɐ ignis'ãu] |

| terminal (of battery) | borne (m) | [b'ɔrnɐ] |
| positive terminal | borne (m) positivo | [b'ɔrnɐ puzit'ivu] |
| negative terminal | borne (m) negativo | [b'ɔrnɐ nɐgɐt'ivu] |
| fuse | fusível (m) | [fuz'ivɛl] |

| air filter | filtro (m) de ar | [f'iltru dɐ 'ar] |
| oil filter | filtro (m) de óleo | [f'iltru dɐ 'ɔliu] |
| fuel filter | filtro (m) de combustível | [f'iltru dɐ kõbuʃt'ivɛl] |

## 178. Cars. Crash. Repair

| car accident | acidente (m) de carro | [ɐsid'ẽtɐ dɐ k'aʀu] |
| road accident | acidente (m) rodoviário | [ɐsid'ẽtɐ ʀodɔvj'ariu] |
| to run into ... | ir contra ... | [ir k'õtrɐ] |
| to have an accident | sofrer um acidente | [sufr'er ũ ɐsid'ẽtɐ] |
| damage | danos (m pl) | [d'ɐnuʃ] |
| intact (adj) | intato | [ĩt'atu] |

| breakdown | avaria (f) | [ɐvɐr'iɐ] |
| to break down (vi) | avariar (vi) | [ɐvɐrj'ar] |
| towrope | cabo (m) de reboque | [k'abu dɐ ʀɐb'ɔkɐ] |

| puncture | furo (m) | [f'uru] |
| to be flat | estar furado | [ɐʃt'ar fur'adu] |
| to pump up | encher (vt) | [ẽʃ'er] |
| pressure | pressão (f) | [prɐs'ãu] |
| to check (to examine) | verificar (vt) | [vɐrifik'ar] |

| repair | reparação (f) | [ʀɐpɐrɐs'ãu] |
| auto repair shop | oficina (f) de reparação de carros | [ɔfis'inɐ dɐ ʀɐpɐrɐs'ãu dɐ k'aʀuʃ] |

| spare part | peça (f) sobresselente | [p'ɛsɐ sobrəsəl'ẽtə] |
| part | peça (f) | [p'ɛsɐ] |

| bolt (with nut) | parafuso (m) | [pɐɾəf'uzu] |
| screw bolt (without nut) | parafuso (m) autoroscante | [pɐɾəf'uzu 'autɔɾɔʃk'ãtə] |
| nut | porca (f) | [p'ɔrkɐ] |
| washer | anilha (f) | [ɐn'iʎɐ] |
| bearing | rolamento (m) | [ʀulɐm'ẽtu] |

| tube | tubo (m) | [t'ubu] |
| gasket (head ~) | junta (f) | [ʒ'ũtɐ] |
| cable, wire | fio (m), cabo (m) | [f'iu], [k'abu] |

| jack | macaco (m) | [mɐk'aku] |
| wrench | chave (f) de boca | [ʃ'avɐ də b'okɐ] |
| hammer | martelo (m) | [mɐɾt'ɛlu] |
| pump | bomba (f) | [b'õbɐ] |
| screwdriver | chave (f) de fendas | [ʃ'avɐ də f'ẽdɐʃ] |

| fire extinguisher | extintor (m) | [əʃtĩt'or] |
| warning triangle | triângulo (m) de emergência | [trj'ãgulu də emərʒ'ẽsiɐ] |

| to stall (vi) | parar (vi) | [pɐɾ'ar] |
| stalling | paragem (f) | [pɐɾ'aʒẽj] |
| to be broken | estar quebrado | [əʃt'ar kəbr'adu] |

| to overheat (vi) | superaquecer-se (vp) | [supɛɾɐkəs'ersə] |
| to be clogged up | entupir (vi) | [ẽtup'ir] |
| to freeze up (pipes, etc.) | congelar (vi) | [kõʒəl'ar] |
| to burst (vi, ab. tube) | rebentar (vi) | [ʀəbẽt'ar] |

| pressure | pressão (f) | [prəs'ãu] |
| level | nível (m) | [n'ivɛl] |
| slack (~ belt) | frouxo | [fr'oʃu] |

| dent | mossa (f) | [m'ɔsɐ] |
| abnormal noise (motor) | ruído (m) anormal | [ʀu'idu ɐnɔrm'al] |
| crack | fissura (f) | [fis'urɐ] |
| scratch | aranhão (m) | [ɐɾɐɲ'ãu] |

## 179. Cars. Road

| road | estrada (f) | [əʃtr'adɐ] |
| highway | autoestrada (f) | [autoəʃtr'adɐ] |
| freeway | rodovia (f) | [ʀodov'iɐ] |
| direction (way) | direção (f) | [dirɛs'ãu] |
| distance | distância (f) | [diʃt'ãsiɐ] |
| bridge | ponte (f) | [p'õtə] |

| | | |
|---|---|---|
| parking lot | parque (m) de estacionamento | [p'arkə də əʃtesiunɐm'ẽtu] |
| square | praça (f) | [pr'asɐ] |
| interchange | nó (m) rodoviário | [nɔ ʀodɔvj'ariu] |
| tunnel | túnel (m) | [t'unɛl] |
| | | |
| gas station | posto (m) de gasolina | [p'oʃtu də gɐzul'inɐ] |
| parking lot | parque (m) de estacionamento | [p'arkə də əʃtesiunɐm'ẽtu] |
| gas pump | bomba (f) de gasolina | [b'õbɐ də gɐzul'inɐ] |
| auto repair shop | oficina (f) de reparação de carros | [ɔfis'inɐ də ʀɐpɐres'ãu də k'aʀuʃ] |
| to get gas | abastecer (vi) | [ɐbɐʃtəs'er] |
| fuel | combustível (m) | [kõbuʃt'ivɛl] |
| jerrycan | bidão (m) de gasolina | [bid'ãu də gɐzul'inɐ] |
| | | |
| asphalt | asfalto (m) | [ɐʃf'altu] |
| road markings | marcação (f) de estradas | [mɐrkɐs'ãu də əʃtr'adəʃ] |
| curb | lancil (m) | [lãs'il] |
| guardrail | proteção (f) guard-rail | [prutɛs'ãu guardʀe'il] |
| ditch | valeta (f) | [vɐl'etɐ] |
| roadside (shoulder) | berma (f) da estrada | [b'ɛrmɐ də əʃtr'adɐ] |
| lamppost | poste (m) de luz | [p'ɔʃtə də l'uʃ] |
| to drive (a car) | conduzir, guiar (vt) | [kõduz'ir], [gi'ar] |
| to turn (~ to the left) | virar (vi) | [vir'ar] |
| to make a U-turn | fazer inversão de marcha | [fɐz'er ĩvɐrs'ãu də m'arʃɐ] |
| reverse (~ gear) | marcha-atrás (f) | [m'arʃɐ ɐtr'aʃ] |
| | | |
| to honk (vi) | buzinar (vi) | [buzin'ar] |
| honk (sound) | buzina (f) | [buz'inɐ] |
| to get stuck | atolar-se (vp) | [ɐtul'arsə] |
| to spin (in mud) | patinar (vi) | [pɐtin'ar] |
| to cut, to turn off | desligar (vt) | [dəʒlig'ar] |
| speed | velocidade (f) | [vəlusid'adə] |
| to exceed the speed limit | exceder a velocidade | [əʃsəd'er ɐ vəlusid'adə] |
| to give a ticket | multar (vt) | [mult'ar] |
| traffic lights | semáforo (m) | [səm'afuru] |
| driver's license | carta (f) de condução | [k'artɐ də kõdus'ãu] |
| | | |
| grade crossing | passagem (f) de nível | [pɐs'aʒɐ̃j də n'ivɛl] |
| intersection | cruzamento (m) | [kruzɐm'ẽtu] |
| crosswalk | passadeira (f) para peões | [pɐsɐd'ejrɐ p'erɐ pi'ojʃ] |
| bend, curve | curva (f) | [k'urvɐ] |
| pedestrian zone | zona (f) pedonal | [z'onɐ pədun'al] |

## 180. Traffic signs

| | | |
|---|---|---|
| rules of the road | código (m) da estrada | [k'ɔdigu dɐ əʃtr'adɐ] |
| traffic sign | sinal (m) de trânsito | [sin'al də tr'ãzitu] |

| | | |
|---|---|---|
| passing (overtaking) | **ultrapassagem** (f) | [ultrɐpɐs'aʒëj] |
| curve | **curva** (f) | [k'urvɐ] |
| U-turn | **inversão de marcha** | [ĩvɐrs'ãu dǝ m'arʃɐ] |
| traffic circle | **rotunda** (f) | [ʀut'ũdɐ] |
| | | |
| No entry | **sentido proibido** | [sẽt'idu pruib'idu] |
| No vehicles allowed | **trânsito proibido** | [tr'ãzitu pruib'idu] |
| No passing | **proibição de ultrapassar** | [pruibis'ãu dǝ ultrɐpɐs'ar] |
| No parking | **estacionamento proibido** | [ǝʃtɐsiunɐm'ẽtu pruib'idu] |
| No stopping | **paragem proibida** | [pɐr'aʒëj pruib'idɐ] |
| | | |
| dangerous turn | **curva** (f) **perigosa** | [k'urvɐ pɐrig'ɔzɐ] |
| steep descent | **descida** (f) **perigosa** | [dǝʃs'idɐ pɐrig'ɔzɐ] |
| one-way traffic | **trânsito de sentido único** | [tr'ãzitu dǝ sẽt'idu 'uniku] |
| crosswalk | **passagem** (f) **para peões** | [pɐs'aʒëj p'ɛrɐ pi'ojʃ] |
| slippery road | **pavimento** (m) **escorregadio** | [pɐvim'ẽtu ǝʃkuʀɐged'iu] |
| YIELD | **cedência de passagem** | [sɐd'ẽsiɐ dǝ pɐs'aʒëj] |

# PEOPLE. LIFE EVENTS

## Life events

### 181. Holidays. Event

| | | |
|---|---|---|
| celebration, holiday | **festa** (f) | [f'ɛʃtɐ] |
| national day | **festa** (f) **nacional** | [f'ɛʃtɐ nɐsiun'al] |
| public holiday | **feriado** (m) | [fɐrj'adu] |
| to commemorate (vt) | **festejar** (vt) | [fɐʃtɐʒ'ar] |
| event (happening) | **evento** (m) | [ev'ẽtu] |
| event (organized activity) | **evento** (m) | [ev'ẽtu] |
| banquet (party) | **banquete** (m) | [bãk'etɐ] |
| reception (formal party) | **receção** (f) | [ʀɐsɛs'ãu] |
| feast | **festim** (m) | [fɐʃt'ĩ] |
| anniversary | **aniversário** (m) | [ɐnivɐrs'ariu] |
| jubilee | **jubileu** (m) | [ʒubil'eu] |
| to celebrate (vt) | **celebrar** (vt) | [sɐlɐbr'ar] |
| New Year | **Ano** (m) **Novo** | ['ɐnu n'ovu] |
| Happy New Year! | **Feliz Ano Novo!** | [fɐl'iʃ 'ɐnu n'ovu] |
| Santa Claus | **Pai** (m) **Natal** | [paj nɐt'al] |
| Christmas | **Natal** (m) | [nɐt'al] |
| Merry Christmas! | **Feliz Natal!** | [fɐl'iʃ nɐt'al] |
| Christmas tree | **árvore** (f) **de Natal** | ['arvurɐ dɐ nɐt'al] |
| fireworks | **fogo** (m) **de artifício** | [f'ogu dɐ ɐrtif'isiu] |
| wedding | **boda** (f) | [b'odɐ] |
| groom | **noivo** (m) | [n'ojvu] |
| bride | **noiva** (f) | [n'ojvɐ] |
| to invite (vt) | **convidar** (vt) | [kõvid'ar] |
| invitation card | **convite** (m) | [kõv'itɐ] |
| guest | **convidado** (m) | [kõvid'adu] |
| to visit | **visitar** (vt) | [vizit'ar] |
| (~ your parents, etc.) | | |
| to greet the guests | **receber os hóspedes** | [ʀɐsɐb'er uʃ 'ɔʃpɐdɐʃ] |
| gift, present | **presente** (m) | [prɐz'ẽtɐ] |
| to give (sth as present) | **oferecer** (vt) | [ɔfɐrɐs'er] |
| to receive gifts | **receber presentes** | [ʀɐsɐb'er prɐz'ẽtɐʃ] |

| | | |
|---|---|---|
| bouquet (of flowers) | ramo (m) de flores | [ʀˈemu də flˈorəʃ] |
| congratulations | felicitações (f pl) | [fəlisitɐsˈojʃ] |
| to congratulate (vt) | felicitar (vt),<br>dar os parabéns | [fəlisitˈaɾ],<br>[dar uʃ pɐɾɐbˈɐ̃jʃ] |
| | | |
| greeting card | cartão (m) de parabéns | [kɐɾtˈãu də pɐɾɐbˈɐ̃jʃ] |
| to send a postcard | enviar um postal | [ẽvjˈaɾ ũ puʃtˈal] |
| to get a postcard | receber um postal | [ʀəsəbˈeɾ ũ puʃtˈal] |
| | | |
| toast | brinde (m) | [brˈĩdə] |
| to offer (a drink, etc.) | oferecer (vt) | [ɔfəɾəsˈeɾ] |
| champagne | champanhe (m) | [ʃɐ̃pˈɐɲə] |
| | | |
| to have fun | divertir-se (vp) | [divəɾtˈiɾsə] |
| fun, merriment | diversão (f) | [divəɾsˈãu] |
| joy (emotion) | alegria (f) | [ɐləgɾˈiɐ] |
| | | |
| dance | dança (f) | [dˈãsɐ] |
| to dance (vi, vt) | dançar (vi) | [dãsˈaɾ] |
| | | |
| waltz | valsa (f) | [vˈalsɐ] |
| tango | tango (m) | [tˈãgu] |

## 182. Funerals. Burial

| | | |
|---|---|---|
| cemetery | cemitério (m) | [səmitˈɛriu] |
| grave, tomb | sepultura (f), túmulo (m) | [səpultˈuɾɐ], [tˈumulu] |
| cross | cruz (f) | [kruʃ] |
| gravestone | lápide (f) | [lˈapidə] |
| fence | cerca (f) | [sˈerkɐ] |
| chapel | capela (f) | [kɐpˈɛlɐ] |
| | | |
| death | morte (f) | [mˈɔrtə] |
| to die (vi) | morrer (vi) | [muʀˈeɾ] |
| the deceased | defunto (m) | [dəfˈũtu] |
| mourning | luto (m) | [lˈutu] |
| | | |
| to bury (vt) | enterrar, sepultar (vt) | [ẽtəʀˈaɾ], [səpultˈaɾ] |
| funeral home | agência (f) funerária | [ɐʒˈẽsiɐ funəɾˈariɐ] |
| funeral | funeral (m) | [funəɾˈal] |
| | | |
| wreath | coroa (f) de flores | [kurˈoɐ də flˈorəʃ] |
| casket | caixão (m) | [kajʃˈãu] |
| hearse | carro (m) funerário | [kˈaʀu funəɾˈariu] |
| shroud | mortalha (f) | [murtˈaʎɐ] |
| funeral procession | procissão (f) funerária | [prusisˈãu funəɾˈariɐ] |
| cremation urn | urna (f) funerária | [ˈurnɐ funəɾˈariɐ] |
| crematory | crematório (m) | [krəmetˈɔriu] |
| obituary | obituário (m),<br>necrologia (f) | [ɔbituˈariu],<br>[nəkruluʒˈiɐ] |

| to cry (weep) | chorar (vi) | [ʃur'ar] |
| to sob (vi) | soluçar (vi) | [sulus'ar] |

## 183. War. Soldiers

| platoon | pelotão (m) | [pəlut'ãu] |
| company | companhia (f) | [kõpɐɲ'iɐ] |
| regiment | regimento (m) | [ʀəʒim'ẽtu] |
| army | exército (m) | [ez'ɛrsitu] |
| division | divisão (f) | [diviz'ãu] |

| section, squad | destacamento (m) | [dəʃtɐkɐm'ẽtu] |
| host (army) | hoste (f) | ['ɔʃtə] |

| soldier | soldado (m) | [sold'adu] |
| officer | oficial (m) | [ɔfisj'al] |

| private | soldado (m) raso | [sold'adu ʀ'azu] |
| sergeant | sargento (m) | [sɐrʒ'ẽtu] |
| lieutenant | tenente (m) | [tən'ẽtə] |
| captain | capitão (m) | [kɐpit'ãu] |
| major | major (m) | [mɐʒ'ɔr] |
| colonel | coronel (m) | [kurun'ɛl] |
| general | general (m) | [ʒənər'al] |

| sailor | marujo (m) | [mɐr'uʒu] |
| captain | capitão (m) | [kɐpit'ãu] |
| boatswain | contramestre (m) | [kõtrɐm'ɛʃtrə] |

| artilleryman | artilheiro (m) | [ɐrtiʎ'ejru] |
| paratrooper | soldado (m) paraquedista | [sold'adu pɐrɐkəd'iʃtə] |
| pilot | piloto (m) | [pil'otu] |
| navigator | navegador (m) | [nɐvəgɐd'or] |
| mechanic | mecânico (m) | [mək'ɐniku] |

| pioneer (sapper) | sapador (m) | [sɐpɐd'or] |
| parachutist | paraquedista (m) | [pɐrɐkəd'iʃtə] |
| reconnaissance scout | explorador (m) | [əʃplurɐd'or] |
| sniper | franco-atirador (m) | [fr'ãkɔ ɐtirɐd'or] |

| patrol (group) | patrulha (f) | [pɐtr'uʎɐ] |
| to patrol (vt) | patrulhar (vt) | [pɐtruʎ'ar] |
| sentry, guard | sentinela (f) | [sẽtin'ɛlɐ] |

| warrior | guerreiro (m) | [gəʀ'ejru] |
| hero | herói (m) | [er'ɔj] |
| heroine | heroína (f) | [eru'inɐ] |
| patriot | patriota (m) | [pɐtrj'ɔtɐ] |
| traitor | traidor (m) | [trajd'or] |
| to betray (vt) | trair (vt) | [trɐ'ir] |

| | | |
|---|---|---|
| deserter | desertor (m) | [dəzərt'or] |
| to desert (vi) | desertar (vt) | [dəzərt'ar] |
| mercenary | mercenário (m) | [mərsən'ariu] |
| recruit | recruta (m) | [ʀəkr'utə] |
| volunteer | voluntário (m) | [vulũt'ariu] |
| dead (n) | morto (m) | [m'ortu] |
| wounded (n) | ferido (m) | [fər'idu] |
| prisoner of war | prisioneiro (m) de guerra | [priziun'ejru də g'ɛʀə] |

## 184. War. Military actions. Part 1

| | | |
|---|---|---|
| war | guerra (f) | [g'ɛʀə] |
| to be at war | guerrear (vt) | [gɛʀə'ar] |
| civil war | guerra (f) civil | [g'ɛʀə siv'il] |
| treacherously (adv) | perfidamente | [pərfidəm'ẽtə] |
| declaration of war | declaração (f) de guerra | [dəklərəs'ãu də g'ɛʀə] |
| to declare (~ war) | declarar (vt) guerra | [dəklər'ar g'ɛʀə] |
| aggression | agressão (f) | [ɐgrəs'ãu] |
| to attack (invade) | atacar (vt) | [ɐtɐk'ar] |
| to invade (vt) | invadir (vt) | [ĩvad'ir] |
| invader | invasor (m) | [ĩvaz'or] |
| conqueror | conquistador (m) | [kõkiʃtəd'or] |
| defense | defesa (f) | [dəf'ezə] |
| to defend (a country, etc.) | defender (vt) | [dəfẽd'er] |
| to defend oneself | defender-se (vp) | [dəfẽd'ersə] |
| enemy | inimigo (m) | [inim'igu] |
| foe, adversary | adversário (m) | [ɐdvərs'ariu] |
| enemy (as adj) | inimigo | [inim'igu] |
| strategy | estratégia (f) | [əʃtrɛt'ɛʒiə] |
| tactics | tática (f) | [t'atikə] |
| order | ordem (f) | ['ɔrdẽj] |
| command (order) | comando (m) | [kum'ãdu] |
| to order (vt) | ordenar (vt) | [ɔrdən'ar] |
| mission | missão (f) | [mis'ãu] |
| secret (adj) | secreto | [səkr'ɛtu] |
| battle | batalha (f) | [bɐt'aʎə] |
| combat | combate (m) | [kõb'atə] |
| attack | ataque (m) | [ɐt'akə] |
| storming (assault) | assalto (m) | [ɐs'altu] |
| to storm (vt) | assaltar (vt) | [ɐsalt'ar] |

| siege (to be under ~) | assédio, sítio (m) | [es'ɛdiu], [s'itiu] |
| offensive (n) | ofensiva (f) | [ɔfẽs'ivɐ] |
| to go on the offensive | passar à ofensiva | [pɐs'ar a ɔfẽs'ivɐ] |

| retreat | retirada (f) | [ʀɐtir'adɐ] |
| to retreat (vi) | retirar-se (vp) | [ʀɐtir'arsɐ] |

| encirclement | cerco (m) | [s'erku] |
| to encircle (vt) | cercar (vt) | [sɐrk'ar] |

| bombing (by aircraft) | bombardeio (m) | [bõberd'eju] |
| to drop a bomb | lançar uma bomba | [lãs'ar 'umɐ b'õbɐ] |
| to bomb (vt) | bombardear (vt) | [bõberdj'ar] |
| explosion | explosão (f) | [ɐʃpluz'ãu] |

| shot | tiro (m) | [t'iru] |
| to fire a shot | disparar um tiro | [diʃpɐr'ar ũ t'iru] |
| firing (burst of ~) | tiroteio (m) | [tirut'eju] |

| to take aim (at ...) | apontar para ... | [ɐpõt'ar p'ɐrɐ] |
| to point (a gun) | apontar (vt) | [ɐpõt'ar] |
| to hit (the target) | acertar (vt) | [ɐsɐrt'ar] |

| to sink (~ a ship) | afundar (vt) | [ɐfũd'ar] |
| hole (in a ship) | brecha (f) | [br'ɛʃɐ] |
| to founder, to sink (vi) | afundar (vi) | [ɐfũd'ar] |

| front (war ~) | frente (m) | [fr'ẽtɐ] |
| rear (homefront) | retaguarda (f) | [ʀɛtɐgu'ardɐ] |
| evacuation | evacuação (f) | [evɐkuɐs'ãu] |
| to evacuate (vt) | evacuar (vt) | [evɐku'ar] |

| trench | trincheira (f) | [trĩʃ'ejrɐ] |
| barbwire | arame (m) farpado | [ɐr'emɐ fɐrp'adu] |
| barrier (anti tank ~) | obstáculo (m) anticarro | [ɔbʃt'akulu ãtik'aʀu] |
| watchtower | torre (f) de vigia | [t'oʀɐ dɐ viʒ'iɐ] |

| hospital | hospital (m) | [ɔʃpit'al] |
| to wound (vt) | ferir (vt) | [fɐr'ir] |
| wound | ferida (f) | [fɐr'idɐ] |
| wounded (n) | ferido (m) | [fɐr'idu] |
| to be wounded | ficar ferido | [fik'ar fɐr'idu] |
| serious (wound) | grave | [gr'avɐ] |

## 185. War. Military actions. Part 2

| captivity | cativeiro (m) | [kɐtiv'ejru] |
| to take captive | capturar (vt) | [kɐptur'ar] |
| to be in captivity | estar em cativeiro | [ɐʃt'ar ẽ kɐtiv'ejru] |
| to be taken prisoner | ser aprisionado | [ser ɐpriziun'adu] |

| | | |
|---|---|---|
| concentration camp | campo (m) de concentração | [k'ãpu də kõsẽtrɐs'ãu] |
| prisoner of war | prisioneiro (m) de guerra | [priziun'ejɾu də g'ɛʀɐ] |
| to escape (vi) | escapar (vi) | [əʃkɐp'ar] |
| | | |
| to betray (vt) | trair (vt) | [trɐ'ir] |
| betrayer | traidor (m) | [trajd'or] |
| betrayal | traição (f) | [trajs'ãu] |
| | | |
| to execute (shoot) | fuzilar, executar (vt) | [fuzil'ar], [ezəkut'ar] |
| execution (by firing squad) | fuzilamento (m) | [fuzilɐm'ẽtu] |
| | | |
| equipment (military gear) | equipamento (m) | [ekipɐm'ẽtu] |
| shoulder board | platina (f) | [plɐt'inɐ] |
| gas mask | máscara (f) antigás | [m'aʃkɐrɐ ãtig'aʃ] |
| | | |
| radio transmitter | rádio (m) | [ʀ'adiu] |
| cipher, code | cifra (f), código (m) | [s'ifɾɐ], [k'ɔdigu] |
| secrecy | conspiração (f) | [kõʃpirɐs'ãu] |
| password | senha (f) | [s'eɲɐ] |
| | | |
| land mine | mina (f) | [m'inɐ] |
| to mine (road, etc.) | minar (vt) | [min'ar] |
| minefield | campo (m) minado | [k'ãpu min'adu] |
| | | |
| air-raid warning | alarme (m) aéreo | [ɐl'armɐ ɐ'ɛriu] |
| alarm (warning) | alarme (m) | [ɐl'armɐ] |
| signal | sinal (m) | [sin'al] |
| signal flare | sinalizador (m) | [sinɐlizɐd'or] |
| | | |
| headquarters | estado-maior (m) | [əʃt'adu mɐj'ɔr] |
| reconnaissance | reconhecimento (m) | [ʀəkuɲəsim'ẽtu] |
| situation | situação (f) | [situɐs'ãu] |
| report | informe (m) | [ĩf'ɔrmə] |
| ambush | emboscada (f) | [ẽbuʃk'adɐ] |
| reinforcement (of army) | reforço (m) | [ʀəf'orsu] |
| | | |
| target | alvo (m) | ['alvu] |
| proving ground | campo (m) de tiro | [k'ãpu də t'iru] |
| military exercise | manobras (f pl) | [mɐn'ɔbrɐʃ] |
| | | |
| panic | pânico (m) | [p'ɐniku] |
| devastation | devastação (f) | [dɐvɐʃtɐs'ãu] |
| destruction, ruins | ruínas (f pl) | [ʀu'inɐʃ] |
| to destroy (vt) | destruir (vt) | [dəʃtru'ir] |
| | | |
| to survive (vi, vt) | sobreviver (vi) | [sobrɐviv'er] |
| to disarm (vt) | desarmar (vt) | [dəzɐrm'ar] |
| to handle (~ a gun) | manusear (vt) | [mɐnuzj'ar] |
| | | |
| Attention! | Firmes! | [f'irməʃ] |
| At ease! | Descansar! | [dəʃkãs'ar] |

| feat (of courage) | façanha (f) | [fɐs'ɐɲɐ] |
| oath (vow) | juramento (m) | [ʒurɐm'ẽtu] |
| to swear (an oath) | jurar (vi) | [ʒur'ar] |

| decoration (medal, etc.) | condecoração (f) | [kõdəkurɐs'ãu] |
| to award (give medal to) | condecorar (vt) | [kõdəkur'ar] |
| medal | medalha (f) | [məd'aʎɐ] |
| order (e.g., ~ of Merit) | ordem (f) | ['ɔrdẽj] |

| victory | vitória (f) | [vit'ɔriɐ] |
| defeat | derrota (f) | [dəʀ'ɔtɐ] |
| armistice | armistício (m) | [ɐrmiʃt'isiu] |

| banner (standard) | bandeira (f) | [bãd'ɐjrɐ] |
| glory (honor, fame) | glória (f) | [gl'ɔriɐ] |
| parade | desfile (m) militar | [dəʃf'ilə milit'ar] |
| to march (on parade) | marchar (vi) | [mɐrʃ'ar] |

## 186. Weapons

| weapons | arma (f) | ['armɐ] |
| firearm | arma (f) de fogo | ['armɐ də f'ogu] |
| cold weapons (knives, etc.) | arma (f) branca | ['armɐ br'ãkɐ] |

| chemical weapons | arma (f) química | ['armɐ k'imikɐ] |
| nuclear (adj) | nuclear | [nuklə'ar] |
| nuclear weapons | arma (f) nuclear | ['armɐ nuklə'ar] |

| bomb | bomba (f) | [b'õbɐ] |
| atomic bomb | bomba (f) atómica | [b'õbɐ ɐt'ɔmikɐ] |

| pistol (gun) | pistola (f) | [piʃt'ɔlɐ] |
| rifle | caçadeira (f) | [kɐsɐd'ɐjrɐ] |
| submachine gun | pistola-metralhadora (f) | [piʃt'ɔlɐ mətrɐʎɐd'orɐ] |
| machine gun | metralhadora (f) | [mətrɐʎɐd'orɐ] |

| muzzle | boca (f) | [b'okɐ] |
| barrel | cano (m) | [k'ɐnu] |
| caliber | calibre (m) | [kɐl'ibrɐ] |

| trigger | gatilho (m) | [gɐt'iʎu] |
| sight (aiming device) | mira (f) | [m'irɐ] |
| magazine | carregador (m) | [kɐʀəgɐd'or] |
| butt (of rifle) | coronha (f) | [kur'oɲɐ] |

| hand grenade | granada (f) de mão | [grɐn'adɐ də m'ãu] |
| explosive | explosivo (m) | [əʃpluz'ivu] |
| bullet | bala (f) | [b'alɐ] |
| cartridge | cartucho (m) | [kɐrt'uʃu] |

| charge | carga (f) | [k'argɐ] |
|---|---|---|
| ammunition | munições (f pl) | [munis'ojʃ] |

| bomber (aircraft) | bombardeiro (m) | [bõbɐrd'ejru] |
|---|---|---|
| fighter | avião (m) de caça | [ɐvj'ãu dɐ k'asɐ] |
| helicopter | helicóptero (m) | [elik'ɔptɐru] |

| anti-aircraft gun | canhão (m) antiaéreo | [kɐɲ'ãu ãtiɐ'ɛriu] |
|---|---|---|
| tank | tanque (m) | [t'ãkɐ] |
| tank gun | canhão (m), peça (f) | [kɐɲ'ãu], [p'ɛsɐ] |

| artillery | artilharia (f) | [ɐrtiʎɐr'iɐ] |
|---|---|---|
| cannon | canhão (m) | [kɐɲ'ãu] |
| to lay (a gun) | fazer a pontaria | [fɐz'er ɐ põtɐr'iɐ] |

| shell (projectile) | obus (m) | [ɔb'uʃ] |
|---|---|---|
| mortar bomb | granada (f) de morteiro | [gren'adɐ dɐ murt'ejru] |
| mortar | morteiro (m) | [murt'ejru] |
| splinter (shell fragment) | estilhaço (m) | [əʃtiʎ'asu] |

| submarine | submarino (m) | [submɐr'inu] |
|---|---|---|
| torpedo | torpedo (m) | [turp'ɛdu] |
| missile | míssil (m) | [m'isil] |

| to load (gun) | carregar (vt) | [kɐʀɐg'ar] |
|---|---|---|
| to shoot (vi) | atirar, disparar (vi) | [ɐtir'ar], [diʃpɐr'ar] |
| to point at (the cannon) | apontar para … | [ɐpõt'ar p'ɐrɐ] |
| bayonet | baioneta (f) | [bajun'etɐ] |

| epee | espada (f) | [əʃp'adɐ] |
|---|---|---|
| saber (e.g., cavalry ~) | sabre (m) | [s'abrɐ] |
| spear (weapon) | lança (f) | [l'ãsɐ] |
| bow | arco (m) | ['arku] |
| arrow | flecha (f) | [fl'ɛʃɐ] |
| musket | mosquete (m) | [muʃk'ɛtɐ] |
| crossbow | besta (f) | [b'eʃtɐ] |

## 187. Ancient people

| primitive (prehistoric) | primitivo | [primit'ivu] |
|---|---|---|
| prehistoric (adj) | pré-histórico | [prɛjʃt'ɔriku] |
| ancient (~ civilization) | antigo | [ãt'igu] |

| Stone Age | Idade (f) da Pedra | [id'adɐ dɐ p'ɛdrɐ] |
|---|---|---|
| Bronze Age | Idade (f) do Bronze | [id'adɐ du br'õzɐ] |
| Ice Age | período (m) glacial | [pɐr'iudu glɐsj'al] |

| tribe | tribo (f) | [tr'ibu] |
|---|---|---|
| cannibal | canibal (m) | [kɐnib'al] |
| hunter | caçador (m) | [kɐsɐd'or] |

| to hunt (vi, vt) | caçar (vi) | [kɐsˈar] |
| mammoth | mamute (m) | [mɐmˈutə] |

| cave | caverna (f) | [kɐvˈɛrnɐ] |
| fire | fogo (m) | [fˈogu] |
| campfire | fogueira (f) | [fugˈɐjrɐ] |
| rock painting | pintura (f) rupestre | [pĩtˈurɐ ʀupˈɛʃtrɐ] |

| tool (e.g., stone ax) | ferramenta (f) | [fɐʀɐmˈẽtɐ] |
| spear | lança (f) | [lˈãsɐ] |
| stone ax | machado (m) de pedra | [mɐʃˈadu də pˈɛdrɐ] |
| to be at war | guerrear (vt) | [gɛʀɐˈar] |
| to domesticate (vt) | domesticar (vt) | [dumɐʃtikˈar] |

| idol | ídolo (m) | [ˈidulu] |
| to worship (vt) | adorar, venerar (vt) | [ɐdurˈar], [vɐnɐrˈar] |
| superstition | superstição (f) | [supɐrʃtisˈãu] |
| rite | ritual (m) | [ʀituˈal] |

| evolution | evolução (f) | [evulusˈãu] |
| development | desenvolvimento (m) | [dɐzẽvolvimˈẽtu] |
| disappearance (extinction) | desaparecimento (m) | [dɐzɐpɐrɐsimˈẽtu] |
| to adapt oneself | adaptar-se (vp) | [ɐdɐptˈarsə] |

| archeology | arqueologia (f) | [ɐrkiulɐʒˈiɐ] |
| archeologist | arqueólogo (m) | [ɐrkjˈɔlugu] |
| archeological (adj) | arqueológico | [ɐrkiulˈɔʒiku] |

| excavation site | local (m) das escavações | [lukˈal dɐʃ əʃkɐvɐsˈojʃ] |
| excavations | escavações (f pl) | [əʃkɐvɐsˈojʃ] |
| find (object) | achado (m) | [ɐʃˈadu] |
| fragment | fragmento (m) | [fragmˈẽtu] |

## 188. Middle Ages

| people (ethnic group) | povo (m) | [pˈovu] |
| peoples | povos (m pl) | [pˈɔvuʃ] |
| tribe | tribo (f) | [trˈibu] |
| tribes | tribos (f pl) | [trˈibuʃ] |

| barbarians | bárbaros (m pl) | [bˈarbɐruʃ] |
| Gauls | gauleses (m pl) | [gaulˈezəʃ] |
| Goths | godos (m pl) | [gˈoduʃ] |
| Slavs | eslavos (m pl) | [əʒlˈavuʃ] |
| Vikings | vikings (m pl) | [vikˈĩgəʃ] |

| Romans | romanos (m pl) | [ʀumˈɐnuʃ] |
| Roman (adj) | romano | [ʀumˈɐnu] |
| Byzantines | bizantinos (m pl) | [bizɐ̃tˈinuʃ] |
| Byzantium | Bizâncio | [bizˈãsiu] |

| Byzantine (adj) | bizantino | [bizãt'inu] |
| emperor | imperador (m) | [ĩpəred'or] |
| leader, chief | líder (m) | [l'idɛr] |
| powerful (~ king) | poderoso | [pudər'ozu] |
| king | rei (m) | [ʀej] |
| ruler (sovereign) | governante (m) | [guvərn'ãtə] |

| knight | cavaleiro (m) | [kəvel'ejru] |
| feudal lord | senhor feudal (m) | [səɲ'or feud'al] |
| feudal (adj) | feudal | [feud'al] |
| vassal | vassalo (m) | [vəs'alu] |

| duke | duque (m) | [d'ukə] |
| earl | conde (m) | [k'õdə] |
| baron | barão (m) | [bər'ãu] |
| bishop | bispo (m) | [b'iʃpu] |

| armor | armadura (f) | [ermed'urə] |
| shield | escudo (m) | [ɛz'udu] |
| sword | espada (f) | [əʃp'adə] |
| visor | viseira (f) | [viz'ejrə] |
| chainmail | cota (f) de malha | [k'ɔtə də m'aʎe] |

| crusade | cruzada (f) | [kruz'adə] |
| crusader | cruzado (m) | [kruz'adu] |

| territory | território (m) | [tərit'ɔriu] |
| to attack (invade) | atacar (vt) | [etek'ar] |
| to conquer (vt) | conquistar (vt) | [kõkiʃt'ar] |
| to occupy (invade) | ocupar, invadir (vt) | [ɔkup'ar], [ĩvad'ir] |

| siege (to be under ~) | assédio, sítio (m) | [əs'ɛdiu], [s'itiu] |
| besieged (adj) | sitiado | [sitj'adu] |
| to besiege (vt) | assediar, sitiar (vt) | [esədj'ar], [sitj'ar] |

| inquisition | inquisição (f) | [ĩkizis'ãu] |
| inquisitor | inquisidor (m) | [ĩkizid'or] |
| torture | tortura (f) | [turt'urə] |
| cruel (adj) | cruel | [kru'ɛl] |
| heretic | herege (m) | [er'ɛʒə] |
| heresy | heresia (f) | [erəz'iə] |

| seafaring | navegação (f) maritima | [nevəges'ãu merit'imə] |
| pirate | pirata (m) | [pir'atə] |
| piracy | pirataria (f) | [pirətər'iə] |
| boarding (attack) | abordagem (f) | [eburd'aʒẽj] |
| loot, booty | saque, pulhagem (f) | [s'akə], [puʎ'aʒẽj] |
| treasures | tesouros (m pl) | [təz'oruʃ] |

| discovery | descobrimento (m) | [dəʃkubrim'ẽtu] |
| to discover (new land, etc.) | descobrir (vt) | [dəʃkubr'ir] |
| expedition | expedição (f) | [əʃpədis'ãu] |

| musketeer | mosqueteiro (m) | [muʃkət'ejru] |
| cardinal | cardeal (m) | [kɐrdj'al] |
| heraldry | heráldica (f) | [er'aldikɐ] |
| heraldic (adj) | heráldico | [er'aldiku] |

## 189. Leader. Chief. Authorities

| king | rei (m) | [ʀɐj] |
| queen | rainha (f) | [ʀɐ'iɲɐ] |
| royal (adj) | real | [ʀə'al] |
| kingdom | reino (m) | [ʀ'ejnu] |

| prince | príncipe (m) | [pr'isipə] |
| princess | princesa (f) | [pr'is'ezɐ] |

| president | presidente (m) | [prəzid'ẽtə] |
| vice-president | vice-presidente (m) | [v'isə prəzid'ẽtə] |
| senator | senador (m) | [sənɐd'or] |
| monarch | monarca (m) | [mun'arkɐ] |
| ruler (sovereign) | governante (m) | [guvərn'ãtə] |
| dictator | ditador (m) | [ditɐd'or] |
| tyrant | tirano (m) | [tir'ɐnu] |
| magnate | magnata (m) | [mɛgn'atɐ] |

| director | diretor (m) | [dirɛt'or] |
| chief | chefe (m) | [ʃ'ɛfə] |
| manager (director) | dirigente (m) | [diriʒ'ẽtə] |
| boss | patrão (m) | [pɐtr'ãu] |
| owner | dono (m) | [d'onu] |
| head (~ of delegation) | chefe (m) | [ʃ'ɛfə] |
| authorities | autoridades (f pl) | [auturid'adəʃ] |
| superiors | superiores (m pl) | [supərj'orəʃ] |

| governor | governador (m) | [guvərnɐd'or] |
| consul | cônsul (m) | [k'õsul] |
| diplomat | diplomata (m) | [diplum'atɐ] |
| mayor | prefeito (m) | [prəf'ejtu] |
| sheriff | xerife (m) | [ʃɛr'ifə] |

| emperor | imperador (m) | [ĩpərɐd'or] |
| tsar, czar | czar (m) | [kz'ar] |
| pharaoh | faraó (m) | [fɐrɐ'ɔ] |
| khan | cão (m) | [k'ãu] |

## 190. Road. Way. Directions

| road | estrada (f) | [əʃtr'adɐ] |
| way (direction) | caminho (m) | [kɐm'iɲu] |

| freeway | **rodovia** (f) | [ʀɔdɔv'ie] |
| highway | **autoestrada** (f) | [autoeʃtr'ade] |
| interstate | **estrada** (f) **nacional** | [eʃtr'ade nesiun'al] |

| main road | **estrada** (f) **principal** | [eʃtr'ade prĩsip'al] |
| dirt road | **caminho** (m) **de terra batida** | [kem'iɲu də t'ɛʀe bet'ide] |

| pathway | **trilha** (f) | [tr'iʎe] |
| footpath (troddenpath) | **vereda** (f) | [vər'ede] |

| Where? | **Onde?** | ['õdə] |
| Where (to)? | **Para onde?** | [p'eɾe 'õdə] |
| Where ... from? | **De onde?** | [də 'õdə] |

| direction (way) | **direção** (f) | [dirɛs'ãu] |
| to point (~ the way) | **indicar** (vt) | [ĩdik'ar] |

| to the left | **para esquerda** | [p'eɾe əʃk'erde] |
| to the right | **para direita** | [p'eɾe dir'ejte] |
| straight ahead (adv) | **em frente** | [ẽ fr'ẽte] |
| back (e.g., to turn ~) | **para trás** | [p'eɾe tr'aʃ] |

| bend, curve | **curva** (f) | [k'urve] |
| to turn (~ to the left) | **virar** (vi) | [vir'ar] |
| to make a U-turn | **fazer inversão de marcha** | [fez'er ĩvərs'ãu də m'arʃe] |

| to be visible | **estar visível** | [əʃt'ar viz'ivɛl] |
| to appear (come into view) | **aparecer** (vi) | [epeɾes'er] |

| stop, halt (in journey) | **paragem** (f) | [per'aʒẽj] |
| to rest, to halt (vi) | **descansar** (vi) | [dəʃkãs'ar] |
| rest (pause) | **descanso** (m) | [dəʃk'ãsu] |

| to lose one's way | **perder-se** (vp) | [pərd'erse] |
| to lead to ... (ab. road) | **levar para ...** | [ləv'ar p'eɾe] |
| to arrive at ... | **chegar a ...** | [ʃəg'ar e] |
| stretch (of road) | **trecho** (m) | [tr'eʃu] |

| asphalt | **asfalto** (m) | [eʃf'altu] |
| curb | **lancil** (m) | [lãs'il] |
| ditch | **valeta** (f) | [vɐl'ete] |
| manhole | **tampa** (f) **de esgoto** | [t'ãpe də eʒg'otu] |
| roadside (shoulder) | **berma** (f) **da estrada** | [b'ɛrme de eʃtr'ade] |
| pit, pothole | **buraco** (m) | [bur'aku] |

| to go (on foot) | **ir** (vi) | [ir] |
| to pass (overtake) | **ultrapassar** (vt) | [ultɾepes'ar] |

| step (footstep) | **passo** (m) | [p'asu] |
| on foot (adv) | **a pé** | [ɐ pɛ] |

| to block (road) | **bloquear** (vt) | [bluk'jar] |
| boom barrier | **cancela** (f) | [kãs'ɛlɐ] |
| dead end | **beco** (m) **sem saída** | [b'eku sẽ sɐ'idɐ] |

## 191. Breaking the law. Criminals. Part 1

| bandit | **bandido** (m) | [bãd'idu] |
| crime | **crime** (m) | [kr'imɐ] |
| criminal (person) | **criminoso** (m) | [krimin'ozu] |

| thief | **ladrão** (m) | [lɐdr'ãu] |
| to steal (vi, vt) | **roubar** (vt) | [ʀob'ar] |
| stealing (larceny) | **roubo** (m) | [ʀ'obu] |
| theft | **furto** (m) | [f'urtu] |

| to kidnap (vt) | **raptar** (vt) | [ʀɐpt'ar] |
| kidnapping | **rapto** (m) | [ʀ'aptu] |
| kidnapper | **raptor** (m) | [ʀɐpt'or] |

| ransom | **resgate** (m) | [ʀɐʒg'atɐ] |
| to demand ransom | **pedir resgate** | [pɐd'ir ʀɐʒg'atɐ] |

| to rob (vt) | **roubar** (vt) | [ʀob'ar] |
| robbery | **assalto, roubo** (m) | [ɐs'altu], [ʀ'obu] |
| robber | **assaltante** (m) | [ɐsalt'ãtɐ] |

| to extort (vt) | **extorquir** (vt) | [ɐʃturk'ir] |
| extortionist | **extorsionário** (m) | [ɐʃtursiun'ariu] |
| extortion | **extorsão** (f) | [ɐʃturs'ãu] |

| to murder, to kill | **matar, assassinar** (vt) | [mɐt'ar], [ɐsɐsin'ar] |
| murder | **homicídio** (m) | [ɔmis'idiu] |
| murderer | **homicida, assassino** (m) | [ɔmis'idɐ], [ɐsɐs'inu] |

| gunshot | **tiro** (m) | [t'iru] |
| to fire a shot | **dar um tiro** | [dar ũ t'iru] |
| to shoot to death | **matar a tiro** | [mɐt'ar ɐ t'iru] |
| to shoot (vi) | **atirar, disparar** (vi) | [ɐtir'ar], [diʃper'ar] |
| shooting | **tiroteio** (m) | [tirut'ɐju] |

| incident (fight, etc.) | **acontecimento** (m) | [ɐkõtɐsim'ẽtu] |
| fight, brawl | **porrada** (f) | [puʀ'adɐ] |
| Help! | **Socorro!** | [suk'oʀu] |
| victim | **vítima** (f) | [v'itimɐ] |

| to damage (vt) | **danificar** (vt) | [dɐnifik'ar] |
| damage | **dano** (m) | [d'ɐnu] |
| dead body | **cadáver** (m) | [kɐd'avɛr] |
| grave (~ crime) | **grave** | [gr'avɐ] |
| to attack (vt) | **atacar** (vt) | [ɐtɐk'ar] |

| | | |
|---|---|---|
| to beat (dog, person) | **bater** (vt) | [bɐt'eɾ] |
| to beat up | **espancar** (vt) | [əʃpãk'aɾ] |
| to take (rob of sth) | **tirar** (vt) | [tir'aɾ] |
| to stab to death | **esfaquear** (vt) | [əʃfɐkj'aɾ] |
| to maim (vt) | **mutilar** (vt) | [mutil'aɾ] |
| to wound (vt) | **ferir** (vt) | [fəɾ'iɾ] |
| | | |
| blackmail | **chantagem** (f) | [ʃãt'aʒɐj] |
| to blackmail (vt) | **chantagear** (vt) | [ʃãteʒj'aɾ] |
| blackmailer | **chantagista** (m) | [ʃãteʒ'iʃtə] |
| | | |
| protection racket | **extorsão** (f) | [əʃtuɾs'ãu] |
| racketeer | **extorsionário** (m) | [əʃtursiun'ariu] |
| gangster | **gângster** (m) | [g'ãgʃtɛɾ] |
| mafia, Mob | **máfia** (f) | [m'afiə] |
| | | |
| pickpocket | **carteirista** (m) | [kɐɾtejɾ'iʃtə] |
| burglar | **assaltante, ladrão** (m) | [ɐsalt'ãtə], [lɐdr'ãu] |
| smuggling | **contrabando** (m) | [kõtɾɐb'ãdu] |
| smuggler | **contrabandista** (m) | [kõtɾɐbãd'iʃtə] |
| | | |
| forgery | **falsificação** (f) | [falsifikɐs'ãu] |
| to forge (counterfeit) | **falsificar** (vt) | [falsifik'aɾ] |
| fake (forged) | **falsificado** | [falsifik'adu] |

## 192. Breaking the law. Criminals. Part 2

| | | |
|---|---|---|
| rape | **violação** (f) | [viulɐs'ãu] |
| to rape (vt) | **violar** (vt) | [viul'aɾ] |
| rapist | **violador** (m) | [viulɐd'oɾ] |
| maniac | **maníaco** (m) | [mɐn'iɐku] |
| | | |
| prostitute (fem.) | **prostituta** (f) | [pruʃtit'utə] |
| prostitution | **prostituição** (f) | [pruʃtituis'ãu] |
| pimp | **chulo** (m) | [ʃ'ulu] |
| | | |
| drug addict | **toxicodependente** (m) | [tɔksikɔdəpẽd'ẽtə] |
| drug dealer | **traficante** (m) | [trɐfik'ãtə] |
| | | |
| to blow up (bomb) | **explodir** (vt) | [əʃplud'iɾ] |
| explosion | **explosão** (f) | [əʃpluz'ãu] |
| to set fire | **incendiar** (vt) | [ĩsẽdj'aɾ] |
| incendiary (arsonist) | **incendiário** (m) | [ĩsẽdj'ariu] |
| | | |
| terrorism | **terrorismo** (m) | [təɾuɾ'iʒmu] |
| terrorist | **terrorista** (m) | [təɾuɾ'iʃtə] |
| hostage | **refém** (m) | [ʀəf'ẽj] |
| | | |
| to swindle (vt) | **enganar** (vt) | [ẽgɐn'aɾ] |
| swindle | **engano** (m) | [ẽg'ɐnu] |

| swindler | vigarista (m) | [vigɐrˈiʃtɐ] |
| to bribe (vt) | subornar (vt) | [subuɾnˈar] |
| bribery | suborno (m) | [subˈoɾnu] |
| bribe | suborno (m) | [subˈoɾnu] |

| poison | veneno (m) | [vɐnˈenu] |
| to poison (vt) | envenenar (vt) | [ẽvɐnɐnˈar] |
| to poison oneself | envenenar-se (vp) | [ẽvɐnɐnˈarsɐ] |

| suicide (act) | suicídio (m) | [suisˈidiu] |
| suicide (person) | suicida (m) | [suisˈidɐ] |

| to threaten (vt) | ameaçar (vt) | [ɐmiɐsˈar] |
| threat | ameaça (f) | [ɐmjˈasɐ] |
| to make an attempt | atentar contra a vida de ... | [ɐtẽtˈar kˈõtɾɐ ɐ vˈidɐ dɐ] |
| attempt (attack) | atentado (m) | [ɐtẽtˈadu] |

| to steal (a car) | roubar (vt) | [ʀobˈar] |
| to hijack (a plane) | desviar (vt) | [dɐʒvjˈar] |

| revenge | vingança (f) | [vĩgˈãsɐ] |
| to revenge (vt) | vingar-se (vp) | [vĩgˈarsɐ] |

| to torture (vt) | torturar (vt) | [tuɾtuɾˈar] |
| torture | tortura (f) | [tuɾtˈurɐ] |
| to torment (vt) | atormentar (vt) | [ɐtuɾmẽtˈar] |

| pirate | pirata (m) | [piɾˈatɐ] |
| hooligan | desordeiro (m) | [dɐzoɾdˈɐjɾu] |
| armed (adj) | armado | [ɐɾmˈadu] |
| violence | violência (f) | [viulˈẽsiɐ] |
| illegal (unlawful) | ilegal | [ilɐgˈal] |

| spying (n) | espionagem (f) | [ɘʃpiunˈaʒẽj] |
| to spy (vi) | espionar (vi) | [ɘʃpiunˈar] |

## 193. Police. Law. Part 1

| justice | justiça (f) | [ʒuʃtˈisɐ] |
| court (court room) | tribunal (m) | [tribunˈal] |

| judge | juiz (m) | [ʒuˈiʃ] |
| jurors | jurados (m pl) | [ʒuɾˈaduʃ] |
| jury trial | tribunal (m) do júri | [tribunˈal du ʒˈuri] |
| to judge (vt) | julgar (vt) | [ʒulgˈar] |

| lawyer, attorney | advogado (m) | [ɐdvugˈadu] |
| accused | réu (m) | [ʀˈɛu] |
| dock | banco (m) dos réus | [bˈãku duʃ ʀˈɛuʃ] |

| charge | acusação (f) | [ɐkuzɐs'ãu] |
| accused | acusado (m) | [ɐkuz'adu] |

| sentence | sentença (f) | [sẽt'ẽsɐ] |
| to sentence (vt) | sentenciar (vt) | [sẽtẽsj'ar] |

| guilty (culprit) | culpado (m) | [kulp'adu] |
| to punish (vt) | punir (vt) | [pun'ir] |
| punishment | punição (f) | [punis'ãu] |

| fine (penalty) | multa (f) | [m'ultɐ] |
| life imprisonment | prisão (f) perpétua | [priz'ãu pɐrp'ɛtuɐ] |
| death penalty | pena (f) de morte | [p'enɐ dɐ m'ɔrtɐ] |
| electric chair | cadeira (f) elétrica | [kɐd'ejrɐ el'ɛtrikɐ] |
| gallows | forca (f) | [f'orkɐ] |

| to execute (vt) | executar (vt) | [ezɐkut'ar] |
| execution | execução (f) | [ezɐkus'ãu] |

| prison, jail | prisão (f) | [priz'ãu] |
| cell | cela (f) de prisão | [s'ɛlɐ dɐ priz'ãu] |

| escort | escolta (f) | [ɐʃk'ɔltɐ] |
| prison guard | guarda (m) prisional | [gu'ardɐ priziun'al] |
| prisoner | preso (m) | [pr'ezu] |

| handcuffs | algemas (f pl) | [alʒ'emɐʃ] |
| to handcuff (vt) | algemar (vt) | [alʒɐm'ar] |

| prison break | fuga, evasão (f) | [f'ugɐ], [evɐz'ãu] |
| to break out (vi) | fugir (vi) | [fuʒ'ir] |
| to disappear (vi) | desaparecer (vi) | [dɐzɐpɐrɐs'er] |
| to release (from prison) | soltar, libertar (vt) | [solt'ar], [libɐrt'ar] |
| amnesty | amnistia (f) | [emniʃt'iɐ] |

| police | polícia (f) | [pul'isiɐ] |
| police officer | polícia (m) | [pul'isiɐ] |
| police station | esquadra (f) de polícia | [ɐʃku'adrɐ dɐ pul'isiɐ] |
| billy club | cassetete (m) | [kasɐt'etɐ] |
| bullhorn | megafone (m) | [mɛgɐf'ɔnɐ] |

| patrol car | carro (m) de patrulha | [k'aʀu dɐ pɐtr'uʎɐ] |
| siren | sirene (f) | [sir'ɛnɐ] |
| to turn on the siren | ligar a sirene | [lig'ar ɐ sir'ɛnɐ] |
| siren call | toque (m) da sirene | [t'ɔkɐ dɐ sir'ɛnɐ] |

| crime scene | cena (f) do crime | [s'enɐ du kr'imɐ] |
| witness | testemunha (f) | [tɐʃtɐm'uɲɐ] |
| freedom | liberdade (f) | [libɐrd'adɐ] |
| accomplice | cúmplice (m) | [k'ũplisɐ] |
| to flee (vi) | escapar (vi) | [ɐʃkɐp'ar] |
| trace (to leave a ~) | traço (m) | [tr'asu] |

# 194. Police. Law. Part 2

| | | |
|---|---|---|
| search (investigation) | **procura** (f) | [prɔk'urɐ] |
| to look for ... | **procurar** (vt) | [prɔkur'ar] |
| suspicion | **suspeita** (f) | [suʃp'ejtɐ] |
| suspicious (suspect) | **suspeito** | [suʃp'ejtu] |
| to stop (cause to halt) | **parar** (vt) | [pɐr'ar] |
| to detain (keep in custody) | **deter** (vt) | [dɐt'er] |
| | | |
| case (lawsuit) | **caso** (m) | [k'azu] |
| investigation | **investigação** (f) | [ĩvɐʃtigɐs'ãu] |
| detective | **detetive** (m) | [dɐtɐt'ivɐ] |
| investigator | **investigador** (m) | [ĩvɐʃtigɐd'or] |
| hypothesis | **versão** (f) | [vɐrs'ãu] |
| | | |
| motive | **motivo** (m) | [mut'ivu] |
| interrogation | **interrogatório** (m) | [ĩtɐrugɐt'ɔriu] |
| to interrogate (vt) | **interrogar** (vt) | [ĩtɐrug'ar] |
| to question (vt) | **questionar** (vt) | [kɐʃtiun'ar] |
| check (identity ~) | **verificação** (f) | [vɐrifikɐs'ãu] |
| | | |
| round-up | **rusga** (f) | [ʀ'uʒgɐ] |
| search (~ warrant) | **busca** (f) | [b'uʃkɐ] |
| chase (pursuit) | **perseguição** (f) | [pɐrsɐgis'ãu] |
| to pursue, to chase | **perseguir** (vt) | [pɐrsɐg'ir] |
| to track (a criminal) | **seguir** (vt) | [sɐg'ir] |
| | | |
| arrest | **prisão** (f) | [priz'ãu] |
| to arrest (sb) | **prender** (vt) | [prẽd'er] |
| to catch (thief, etc.) | **pegar, capturar** (vt) | [pɐg'ar], [kaptur'ar] |
| capture | **captura** (f) | [kapt'urɐ] |
| | | |
| document | **documento** (m) | [dukum'ẽtu] |
| proof (evidence) | **prova** (f) | [pr'ɔvɐ] |
| to prove (vt) | **provar** (vt) | [pruv'ar] |
| footprint | **pegada** (f) | [pɐg'adɐ] |
| fingerprints | **impressões** (f pl) **digitais** | [ĩprɐs'ojʃ diʒit'ajʃ] |
| piece of evidence | **prova** (f) | [pr'ɔvɐ] |
| | | |
| alibi | **álibi** (m) | ['alibi] |
| innocent (not guilty) | **inocente** | [inus'ẽtɐ] |
| injustice | **injustiça** (f) | [ĩʒuʃt'isɐ] |
| unjust, unfair (adj) | **injusto** | [ĩʒ'uʃtu] |
| | | |
| criminal (adj) | **criminal** | [krimin'al] |
| to confiscate (vt) | **confiscar** (vt) | [kõfiʃk'ar] |
| drug (illegal substance) | **droga** (f) | [dr'ɔgɐ] |
| weapon, gun | **arma** (f) | ['armɐ] |
| to disarm (vt) | **desarmar** (vt) | [dɐzɐrm'ar] |
| to order (command) | **ordenar** (vt) | [ɔrdɐn'ar] |
| to disappear (vi) | **desaparecer** (vi) | [dɐzɐpɐrɐs'er] |

| | | |
|---|---|---|
| law | **lei** (f) | [lɐj] |
| legal, lawful (adj) | **legal** | [ləg'al] |
| illegal, illicit (adj) | **ilegal** | [iləg'al] |
| responsibility (blame) | **responsabilidade** (f) | [ʀəʃpõsɐbilid'adə] |
| responsible (adj) | **responsável** | [ʀəʃpõs'avɛl] |

# NATURE

# The Earth. Part 1

## 195. Outer space

| cosmos | cosmos (m) | [k'ɔʒmuʃ] |
| space (as adj) | cósmico | [k'ɔʒmiku] |
| outer space | espaço (m) cósmico | [əʃp'asu k'ɔʒmiku] |
| world | mundo (m) | [m'ũdu] |
| universe | universo (m) | [univ'ɛrsu] |
| galaxy | galáxia (f) | [gɐl'aksiɐ] |

| star | estrela (f) | [əʃtr'elɐ] |
| constellation | constelação (f) | [kõʃtɐlɐs'ãu] |
| planet | planeta (m) | [plɐn'etɐ] |
| satellite | satélite (m) | [sɐt'ɛlitə] |

| meteorite | meteorito (m) | [mətiur'itu] |
| comet | cometa (m) | [kum'etɐ] |
| asteroid | asteroide (m) | [ɐʃtɐr'ɔjdə] |

| orbit | órbita (f) | ['ɔrbitɐ] |
| to revolve | girar (vi) | [ʒir'ar] |
| (~ around the Earth) | | |
| atmosphere | atmosfera (f) | [ɐtmuʃf'ɛrɐ] |

| the Sun | Sol (m) | [sɔl] |
| solar system | Sistema (m) Solar | [siʃt'emɐ sul'ar] |
| solar eclipse | eclipse (m) solar | [ekl'ipsə sul'ar] |

| the Earth | Terra (f) | [t'ɛʀɐ] |
| the Moon | Lua (f) | [l'uɐ] |

| Mars | Marte (m) | [m'artə] |
| Venus | Vénus (m) | [v'ɛnuʃ] |
| Jupiter | Júpiter (m) | [ʒ'upitɛr] |
| Saturn | Saturno (m) | [sɐt'urnu] |

| Mercury | Mercúrio (m) | [mərk'uriu] |
| Uranus | Urano (m) | [ur'ɐnu] |
| Neptune | Neptuno (m) | [nɛpt'unu] |
| Pluto | Plutão (m) | [plut'ãu] |
| Milky Way | Via Láctea (f) | [v'iɐ l'atiɐ] |
| Great Bear | Ursa Maior (f) | [ursɐ mɐj'ɔr] |

| North Star | **Estrela Polar** (f) | [əʃtr'elɐ pul'ar] |
| Martian | **marciano** (m) | [mɐrsj'ɐnu] |
| extraterrestrial (n) | **extraterrestre** (m) | [əʃtrɐtɐʀ'ɛʃtrɐ] |
| alien | **alienígena** (m) | [ɐlien'iʒɐnɐ] |
| flying saucer | **disco** (m) **voador** | [d'iʃku vuɐd'or] |

| spaceship | **nave** (f) **espacial** | [n'avɐ əʃpɐsj'al] |
| space station | **estação** (f) **orbital** | [əʃtɐs'ãu ɔrbit'al] |
| blast-off | **lançamento** (m) | [lãsɐm'ẽtu] |

| engine | **motor** (m) | [mut'or] |
| nozzle | **bocal** (m) | [buk'al] |
| fuel | **combustível** (m) | [kõbuʃt'ivɛl] |

| cockpit, flight deck | **cabine** (f) | [kɐb'inɐ] |
| antenna | **antena** (f) | [ãt'enɐ] |
| porthole | **vigia** (f) | [viʒ'iɐ] |
| solar battery | **bateria** (f) **solar** | [bɐtɐr'iɐ sul'ar] |
| spacesuit | **traje** (m) **espacial** | [tr'aʒɐ əʃpɐsj'al] |

| weightlessness | **imponderabilidade** (f) | [ĩpõdɐrɐbilid'adɐ] |
| oxygen | **oxigénio** (m) | [ɔksiʒ'ɛniu] |

| docking (in space) | **acoplagem** (f) | [ɐkupl'aʒɐj] |
| to dock (vi, vt) | **fazer uma acoplagem** | [fɐz'er 'umɐ ɐkupl'aʒɐj] |

| observatory | **observatório** (m) | [ɔbsɐrvɐt'ɔriu] |
| telescope | **telescópio** (m) | [tɐlɐʃk'ɔpiu] |
| to observe (vt) | **observar** (vt) | [ɔbsɐrv'ar] |
| to explore (vt) | **explorar** (vt) | [əʃplur'ar] |

## 196. The Earth

| the Earth | **Terra** (f) | [t'ɛʀɐ] |
| globe (the Earth) | **globo** (m) **terrestre** | [ɡl'obu tɐr'ɛʃtrɐ] |
| planet | **planeta** (m) | [plɐn'etɐ] |

| atmosphere | **atmosfera** (f) | [ɐtmuʃf'ɛrɐ] |
| geography | **geografia** (f) | [ʒiuɡrɐf'iɐ] |
| nature | **natureza** (f) | [nɐtur'ezɐ] |

| globe (table ~) | **globo** (m) | [ɡl'obu] |
| map | **mapa** (m) | [m'apɐ] |
| atlas | **atlas** (m) | ['atlɐʃ] |

| Europe | **Europa** (f) | [eur'ɔpɐ] |
| Asia | **Ásia** (f) | ['aziɐ] |
| Africa | **África** (f) | ['afrikɐ] |
| Australia | **Austrália** (f) | [auʃtr'aliɐ] |
| America | **América** (f) | [ɐm'ɛrikɐ] |

| North America | América (f) do Norte | [ɐm'ɛrikɐ du n'ɔrtə] |
| South America | América (f) do Sul | [ɐm'ɛrikɐ du sul] |

| Antarctica | Antártida (f) | [ãt'artidɐ] |
| the Arctic | Ártico (m) | ['artiku] |

## 197. Cardinal directions

| north | norte (m) | [n'ɔrtə] |
| to the north | para norte | [p'ɐrɐ n'ɔrtə] |
| in the north | no norte | [nu n'ɔrtə] |
| northern (adj) | do norte | [du n'ɔrtə] |

| south | sul (m) | [sul] |
| to the south | para sul | [p'ɐrɐ sul] |
| in the south | no sul | [nu sul] |
| southern (adj) | do sul | [du sul] |

| west | oeste, ocidente (m) | [ɔ'ɛʃtə], [ɔsid'ẽtə] |
| to the west | para oeste | [p'ɐrɐ ɔ'ɛʃtə] |
| in the west | no oeste | [nu ɔ'ɛʃtə] |
| western (adj) | ocidental | [ɔsidẽt'al] |

| east | leste, oriente (m) | [l'ɛʃtə], [ɔrj'ẽtə] |
| to the east | para leste | [p'ɐrɐ l'ɛʃtə] |
| in the east | no leste | [nu l'ɛʃtə] |
| eastern (adj) | oriental | [ɔriẽt'al] |

## 198. Sea. Ocean

| sea | mar (m) | [mar] |
| ocean | oceano (m) | [ɔsj'ɐnu] |
| gulf (bay) | golfo (m) | [g'olfu] |
| straits | estreito (m) | [əʃtr'ejtu] |

| solid ground | terra (f) firme | [t'ɛRɐ f'irmə] |
| continent (mainland) | continente (m) | [kõtin'ẽtə] |
| island | ilha (f) | ['iʎɐ] |
| peninsula | península (f) | [pən'isulɐ] |
| archipelago | arquipélago (m) | [ɐrkip'ɛlɐgu] |

| bay, cove | baía (f) | [bɐ'iɐ] |
| harbor | porto (m) | [p'ortu] |
| lagoon | lagoa (f) | [lɐg'oɐ] |
| cape | cabo (m) | [k'abu] |

| atoll | atol (m) | [ɐt'ɔl] |
| reef | recife (m) | [Rəs'ifə] |

| coral | coral (m) | [kur'al] |
| coral reef | recife (m) de coral | [ʀəs'ifə də kur'al] |

| deep (adj) | profundo | [pruf'ũdu] |
| depth (deep water) | profundidade (f) | [prufũdid'adə] |
| abyss | abismo (m) | [eb'iʒmu] |
| trench (e.g., Mariana ~) | fossa (f) oceânica | [f'ɔsə ɔsj'ɛnikə] |

| current, stream | corrente (f) | [kuʀ'ẽtə] |
| to surround (bathe) | banhar (vt) | [beɲ'ar] |

| shore | litoral (m) | [litur'al] |
| coast | costa (f) | [k'ɔʃtə] |

| high tide | maré (f) alta | [mɐɾ'ɛ 'altə] |
| low tide | maré (f) baixa | [mɐɾ'ɛ b'ajʃə] |
| sandbank | restinga (f) | [ʀəʃt'ĩgə] |
| bottom | fundo (m) | [f'ũdu] |

| wave | onda (f) | ['õdə] |
| crest (~ of a wave) | crista (f) da onda | [kr'iʃtə də 'õdə] |
| froth (foam) | espuma (f) | [əʃp'umə] |

| storm | tempestade (f) | [tẽpəʃt'adə] |
| hurricane | furacão (m) | [furɐk'ãu] |
| tsunami | tsunami (m) | [tsun'ɛmi] |
| calm (dead ~) | calmaria (f) | [kalmɐɾ'iɐ] |
| quiet, calm (adj) | calmo | [k'almu] |

| pole | polo (m) | [p'ɔlu] |
| polar (adj) | polar | [pul'ar] |

| latitude | latitude (f) | [lɐtit'udə] |
| longitude | longitude (f) | [lõʒit'udə] |
| parallel | paralela (f) | [pɐɾɐl'ɛlə] |
| equator | equador (m) | [ekwɐd'or] |

| sky | céu (m) | [s'ɛu] |
| horizon | horizonte (m) | [ɔriz'õtə] |
| air | ar (m) | [ar] |

| lighthouse | farol (m) | [fɐɾ'ɔl] |
| to dive (vi) | mergulhar (vi) | [mərguʎ'ar] |
| to sink (ab. boat) | afundar-se (vp) | [ɐfũd'arsə] |
| treasures | tesouros (m pl) | [təz'oruʃ] |

## 199. Seas' and Oceans' names

| Atlantic Ocean | Oceano (m) Atlântico | [ɔsj'enu etl'ãtiku] |
| Indian Ocean | Oceano (m) Índico | [ɔsj'enu 'ĩdiku] |

| Pacific Ocean | Oceano (m) Pacífico | [ɔsj'ɐnu pɐs'ifiku] |
| Arctic Ocean | Oceano (m) Ártico | [ɔsj'ɐnu 'artiku] |

| Black Sea | Mar (m) Negro | [mar n'egru] |
| Red Sea | Mar (m) Vermelho | [mar vɐrm'eʎu] |
| Yellow Sea | Mar (m) Amarelo | [mar ɐmɐr'ɛlu] |
| White Sea | Mar (m) Branco | [mar br'ãku] |

| Caspian Sea | Mar (m) Cáspio | [mar k'aʃpiu] |
| Dead Sea | Mar (m) Morto | [mar m'ortu] |
| Mediterranean Sea | Mar (m) Mediterrâneo | [mar mɐditɐr'ɐniu] |

| Aegean Sea | Mar (m) Egeu | [mar eʒ'eu] |
| Adriatic Sea | Mar (m) Adriático | [mar ɐdɾj'atiku] |

| Arabian Sea | Mar (m) Arábico | [mar ɐr'abiku] |
| Sea of Japan | Mar (m) do Japão | [mar du ʒɐp'ãu] |
| Bering Sea | Mar (m) de Bering | [mar də bɐɾ'ĩg] |
| South China Sea | Mar (m) da China Meridional | [mar də ʃ'inɐ mɐridiun'al] |

| Coral Sea | Mar (m) de Coral | [mar də kur'al] |
| Tasman Sea | Mar (m) de Tasman | [mar də taʒmɐn] |
| Caribbean Sea | Mar (m) do Caribe | [mar du kɐr'ibə] |

| Barents Sea | Mar (m) de Barents | [mar də bɐɾ'ɛtʃ] |
| Kara Sea | Mar (m) de Kara | [mar də k'arɐ] |

| North Sea | Mar (m) do Norte | [mar du n'ɔrtə] |
| Baltic Sea | Mar (m) Báltico | [mar b'altiku] |
| Norwegian Sea | Mar (m) da Noruega | [mar dɐ noru'ɛgɐ] |

## 200. Mountains

| mountain | montanha (f) | [mõt'ɐɲɐ] |
| mountain range | cordilheira (f) | [kurdiʎ'ɐjɾɐ] |
| mountain ridge | serra (f) | [s'ɛʀɐ] |

| summit, top | cume (m) | [k'umə] |
| peak | pico (m) | [p'iku] |
| foot (of mountain) | sopé (m) | [sup'ɛ] |
| slope (mountainside) | declive (m) | [dɐkl'ivə] |

| volcano | vulcão (m) | [vulk'ãu] |
| active volcano | vulcão (m) ativo | [vulk'ãu at'ivu] |
| dormant volcano | vulcão (m) extinto | [vulk'ãu əʃt'ĩtu] |

| eruption | erupção (f) | [erups'ãu] |
| crater | cratera (f) | [krɐt'ɛʀɐ] |
| magma | magma (m) | [m'agmɐ] |

| lava | lava (f) | [l'avɐ] |
| molten (~ lava) | fundido | [fũd'idu] |

| canyon | desfiladeiro (m) | [dəffilɐd'ɐjru] |
| gorge | garganta (f) | [gɐrg'ãtɐ] |
| crevice | fenda (f) | [f'ẽdɐ] |
| abyss (chasm) | precipício (m) | [prəsip'isiu] |

| pass, col | passo, colo (m) | [p'asu], [k'ɔlu] |
| plateau | planalto (m) | [plɐn'altu] |
| cliff | falésia (f) | [fɐl'ɛziɐ] |
| hill | colina (f) | [kul'inɐ] |

| glacier | glaciar (m) | [glɐsj'ar] |
| waterfall | queda (f) d'água | [k'ɛdɐ d'aguɐ] |

| geyser | géiser (m) | [ʒ'ɛjzɛr] |
| lake | lago (m) | [l'agu] |

| plain | planície (f) | [plɐn'isiɐ] |
| landscape | paisagem (f) | [pajz'aʒẽj] |
| echo | eco (m) | ['ɛku] |

| alpinist | alpinista (m) | [alpin'iʃtɐ] |
| rock climber | escalador (m) | [əʃkɐlɐd'or] |

| to conquer (in climbing) | conquistar (vt) | [kõkiʃt'ar] |
| climb (an easy ~) | subida, escalada (f) | [sub'idɐ], [əʃkɐl'adɐ] |

## 201. Mountains names

| Alps | Alpes (m pl) | ['alpəʃ] |
| Mont Blanc | monte Branco (m) | [m'õtə br'ãku] |
| Pyrenees | Pirineus (m pl) | [pirin'euʃ] |

| Carpathians | Cárpatos (m pl) | [k'arpɐtuʃ] |
| Ural Mountains | montes (m pl) Urais | [m'õtəʃ ur'ajʃ] |

| Caucasus | Cáucaso (m) | [k'aukɐzu] |
| Elbrus | Elbrus (m) | [elbr'uʃ] |

| Altai | Altai (m) | [ɐlt'aj] |
| Tien Shan | Tian Shan (m) | [tiɐn ʃen] |
| Pamir Mountains | Pamir (m) | [pɐm'ir] |

| Himalayas | Himalaias (m pl) | [imɐl'ajɐʃ] |
| Everest | monte (m) Everest | [m'õtə evɐr'eʃt] |

| Andes | Cordilheira (f) dos Andes | [kurdiʎ'ejrɐ duʃ 'ãdəʃ] |
| Kilimanjaro | Kilimanjaro (m) | [kilimãʒ'aru] |

## 202. Rivers

| | | |
|---|---|---|
| river | **rio** (m) | [ʀ'iu] |
| spring (natural source) | **fonte, nascente** (f) | [f'õtə], [nɐʃs'ẽtə] |
| riverbed | **leito** (m) **do rio** | [l'ɐjtu du ʀ'iu] |
| basin | **bacia** (f) | [bɐs'iɐ] |
| to flow into ... | **desaguar no ...** | [dəzagu'ar nu] |
| | | |
| tributary | **afluente** (m) | [ɐflu'ẽtə] |
| bank (of river) | **margem** (f) | [m'aɾʒẽj] |
| | | |
| current, stream | **corrente** (f) | [kuʀ'ẽtə] |
| downstream (adv) | **rio abaixo** | [ʀ'iu ɐb'ajʃu] |
| upstream (adv) | **rio acima** | [ʀ'iu ɐs'imɐ] |
| | | |
| inundation | **inundação** (f) | [inũdɐs'ãu] |
| flooding | **cheia** (f) | [ʃ'ɐjɐ] |
| to overflow (vi) | **transbordar** (vi) | [trãʒburd'ar] |
| to flood (vt) | **inundar** (vt) | [inũd'ar] |
| | | |
| shallows (shoal) | **baixio** (m) | [bajʃ'iu] |
| rapids | **rápidos** (m pl) | [ʀ'apiduʃ] |
| | | |
| dam | **barragem** (f) | [bɐʀ'aʒẽj] |
| canal | **canal** (m) | [kɐn'al] |
| artificial lake | **reservatório** (m) **de água** | [ʀəzɐɾvɐt'ɔriu də 'aguɐ] |
| sluice, lock | **esclusa** (f) | [əʃkl'uzɐ] |
| | | |
| water body (pond, etc.) | **corpo** (m) **de água** | [k'ɔrpu də 'aguɐ] |
| swamp, bog | **pântano** (m) | [p'ãtɐnu] |
| marsh | **tremedal** (m) | [trəməd'al] |
| whirlpool | **remoinho** (m) | [ʀəmu'iɲu] |
| | | |
| stream (brook) | **arroio, regato** (m) | [ɐʀ'oju], [ʀəg'atu] |
| drinking (ab. water) | **potável** | [put'avɛl] |
| fresh (~ water) | **doce** | [d'osə] |
| | | |
| ice | **gelo** (m) | [ʒ'elu] |
| to freeze (ab. river, etc.) | **congelar-se** (vp) | [kõʒəl'arsə] |

## 203. Rivers' names

| | | |
|---|---|---|
| Seine | **rio Sena** (m) | [ʀ'iu s'enɐ] |
| Loire | **rio Loire** (m) | [ʀ'iu lu'ar] |
| | | |
| Thames | **rio Tamisa** (m) | [ʀ'iu təm'izɐ] |
| Rhine | **rio Reno** (m) | [ʀ'iu ʀ'enu] |
| Danube | **rio Danúbio** (m) | [ʀ'iu dɐn'ubiu] |
| Volga | **rio Volga** (m) | [ʀ'iu v'ɔlgɐ] |

| | | |
|---|---|---|
| Don | rio Don (m) | [ʀ'iu dɔn] |
| Lena | rio Lena (m) | [ʀ'iu l'enɐ] |
| | | |
| Yellow River | rio Amarelo (m) | [ʀ'iu ɐmɐr'ɛlu] |
| Yangtze | rio Yangtzé (m) | [ʀ'iu iãgtz'ɛ] |
| Mekong | rio Mekong (m) | [ʀ'iu mik'õg] |
| Ganges | rio Ganges (m) | [ʀ'iu g'ãʒɐʃ] |
| | | |
| Nile River | rio Nilo (m) | [ʀ'iu n'ilu] |
| Congo | rio Congo (m) | [ʀ'iu k'õgu] |
| Okavango | rio Cubango (m) | [ʀ'iu kub'ãgu] |
| Zambezi | rio Zambeze (m) | [ʀ'iu zãb'ɛzə] |
| Limpopo | rio Limpopo (m) | [ʀ'iu l̃p'opu] |
| Mississippi River | rio Mississipi (m) | [ʀ'iu misisip'i] |

## 204. Forest

| | | |
|---|---|---|
| forest | floresta (f), bosque (m) | [flur'ɛʃtɐ], [b'ɔʃkə] |
| forest (as adj) | florestal | [flurəʃt'al] |
| | | |
| thick forest | mata (f) cerrada | [m'atɐ sɐr'adɐ] |
| grove | arvoredo (m) | [ɐrvur'edu] |
| forest clearing | clareira (f) | [klɐr'ejɾɐ] |
| | | |
| thicket | matagal (f) | [mɐtɐg'al] |
| scrubland | mato (m) | [m'atu] |
| | | |
| footpath (troddenpath) | vereda (f) | [vɐr'edɐ] |
| gully | ravina (f) | [ʀɐv'inɐ] |
| | | |
| tree | árvore (f) | ['arvurɐ] |
| leaf | folha (f) | [f'oʎɐ] |
| leaves | folhagem (f) | [fuʎ'aʒẽj] |
| | | |
| fall of leaves | queda (f) das folha | [k'ɛdɐ dɐʃ f'oʎɐ] |
| to fall (ab. leaves) | cair (vi) | [kɐ'ir] |
| top (of the tree) | topo (m) | [t'opu] |
| | | |
| branch | ramo (m) | [ʀ'emu] |
| bough | galho (m) | [g'aʎu] |
| bud (on shrub, tree) | botão, rebento (m) | [but'ãu], [ʀɐb'ẽtu] |
| needle (of pine tree) | agulha (f) | [ɐg'uʎɐ] |
| pine cone | pinha (f) | [p'iɲɐ] |
| | | |
| hollow (in a tree) | buraco (m) de árvore | [bur'aku də 'arvurɐ] |
| nest | ninho (m) | [n'iɲu] |
| burrow (animal hole) | toca (f) | [t'ɔkɐ] |
| | | |
| trunk | tronco (m) | [tr'õku] |
| root | raiz (f) | [ʀɐ'iʃ] |

| bark | casca (f) de árvore | [k'aʃkɐ də 'arvurə] |
| moss | musgo (m) | [m'uʒgu] |

| to uproot (vt) | arrancar pela raiz | [ɐrãk'ar p'elɐ ʀɐ'iʃ] |
| to chop down | cortar (vt) | [kurt'ar] |
| to deforest (vt) | desflorestar (vt) | [dəʃflurəʃt'ar] |
| tree stump | toco, cepo (m) | [t'ɔku], [s'epu] |

| campfire | fogueira (f) | [fug'ejrɐ] |
| forest fire | incêndio (m) florestal | [ĩs'ẽdiu flurəʃt'al] |
| to extinguish (vt) | apagar (vt) | [ɐpɐg'ar] |

| forest ranger | guarda-florestal (m) | [gu'ardɐ flurəʃt'al] |
| protection | proteção (f) | [prutɛs'ãu] |
| to protect (~ nature) | proteger (vt) | [prutəʒ'er] |
| poacher | caçador (m) furtivo | [kɐsɐd'or furt'ivu] |
| trap (e.g., bear ~) | armadilha (f) | [ɐrmɐd'iʎɐ] |

| to gather, to pick (vt) | colher (vt) | [kuʎ'ɛr] |
| to lose one's way | perder-se (vp) | [pərd'ersə] |

## 205. Natural resources

| natural resources | recursos (m pl) naturais | [ʀək'ursuʃ nɐtur'ajʃ] |
| minerals | minerais (m pl) | [minɐr'ajʃ] |
| deposits | depósitos (m pl) | [dəp'ɔzituʃ] |
| field (e.g., oilfield) | jazida (f) | [ʒɐz'idɐ] |

| to mine (extract) | extrair (vt) | [əʃtrɐ'ir] |
| mining (extraction) | extração (f) | [əʃtras'ãu] |
| ore | minério (m) | [min'ɛriu] |
| mine (e.g., for coal) | mina (f) | [m'inɐ] |
| mine shaft, pit | poço (m) de mina | [p'osu də m'inɐ] |
| miner | mineiro (m) | [min'ejru] |

| gas | gás (m) | [gaʃ] |
| gas pipeline | gasoduto (m) | [gazɔd'utu] |

| oil (petroleum) | petróleo (m) | [pətr'ɔliu] |
| oil pipeline | oleoduto (m) | [ɔliud'utu] |
| oil well | poço (m) de petróleo | [p'osu də pətr'ɔliu] |
| derrick | torre (f) petrolífera | [t'oʀə pətrul'ifərɐ] |
| tanker | petroleiro (m) | [pətrul'ejru] |

| sand | areia (f) | [ɐr'ejɐ] |
| limestone | calcário (m) | [kalk'ariu] |
| gravel | cascalho (m) | [kɐʃk'aʎu] |
| peat | turfa (f) | [t'urfɐ] |
| clay | argila (f) | [ɐrʒ'ilɐ] |
| coal | carvão (m) | [kɐrv'ãu] |

| iron | ferro (m) | [f'ɛʀu] |
| gold | ouro (m) | ['oru] |
| silver | prata (f) | [pr'atɐ] |
| nickel | níquel (m) | [n'ikɛl] |
| copper | cobre (m) | [k'ɔbrə] |

| zinc | zinco (m) | [z'ĩku] |
| manganese | manganês (m) | [mãgɐn'eʃ] |
| mercury | mercúrio (m) | [mərk'uriu] |
| lead | chumbo (m) | [ʃ'ũbu] |

| mineral | mineral (m) | [minər'al] |
| crystal | cristal (m) | [kriʃt'al] |
| marble | mármore (m) | [m'armurə] |
| uranium | urânio (m) | [ur'ɐniu] |

# The Earth. Part 2

## 206. Weather

| | | |
|---|---|---|
| weather | **tempo** (m) | [t'ẽpu] |
| weather forecast | **previsão** (f) **do tempo** | [prəviz'ău du t'ẽpu] |
| temperature | **temperatura** (f) | [tẽpərɐt'urɐ] |
| thermometer | **termómetro** (m) | [tɐrm'ɔmɐtru] |
| barometer | **barómetro** (m) | [bɐr'ɔmɐtru] |
| | | |
| humid (adj) | **húmido** | ['umidu] |
| humidity | **humidade** (f) | [umid'adə] |
| heat (extreme ~) | **calor** (m) | [kɐl'or] |
| hot (torrid) | **cálido** | [k'alidu] |
| it's hot | **está muito calor** | [əʃt'a m'ũjtu kɐl'or] |
| | | |
| it's warm | **está calor** | [əʃt'a kɐl'or] |
| warm (moderately hot) | **quente** | [k'ẽtə] |
| | | |
| it's cold | **está frio** | [əʃt'a fr'iu] |
| cold (adj) | **frio** | [fr'iu] |
| | | |
| sun | **sol** (m) | [sɔl] |
| to shine (vi) | **brilhar** (vi) | [briʎ'ar] |
| sunny (day) | **de sol, ensolarado** | [də sɔl], [ẽsulɐr'adu] |
| to come up (vi) | **nascer** (vi) | [nɐʃs'er] |
| to set (vi) | **pôr-se** (vp) | [p'orsə] |
| | | |
| cloud | **nuvem** (f) | [n'uvẽj] |
| cloudy (adj) | **nublado** | [nubl'adu] |
| rain cloud | **nuvem** (f) **negra** | [n'uvẽj n'egrɐ] |
| somber (gloomy) | **escuro, cinzento** | [əʃk'uru], [sĩz'ẽtu] |
| | | |
| rain | **chuva** (f) | [ʃ'uvɐ] |
| it's raining | **está a chover** | [əʃt'a ɐ ʃuv'er] |
| rainy (day) | **chuvoso** | [ʃuv'ozu] |
| to drizzle (vi) | **chuviscar** (vi) | [ʃuviʃk'ar] |
| | | |
| pouring rain | **chuva** (f) **torrencial** | [ʃ'uvɐ turẽsj'al] |
| downpour | **chuvada** (f) | [ʃuv'adə] |
| heavy (e.g., ~ rain) | **forte** | [f'ortə] |
| puddle | **poça** (f) | [p'ɔsɐ] |
| to get wet (in rain) | **molhar-se** (vp) | [muʎ'arsə] |
| | | |
| fog (mist) | **nevoeiro** (m) | [nəvu'ɐjru] |
| foggy | **de nevoeiro** | [də nəvu'ɐjru] |

| snow | neve (f) | [n'ɛvə] |
| it's snowing | está a nevar | [əʃt'a ɐ nɛv'ar] |

## 207. Severe weather. Natural disasters

| thunderstorm | trovoada (f) | [truvu'adɐ] |
| lightning (~ strike) | relâmpago (m) | [ʀəl'ãpɐgu] |
| to flash (vi) | relampejar (vi) | [ʀəlãpeʒ'ar] |

| thunder | trovão (m) | [truv'ãu] |
| to thunder (vi) | trovejar (vi) | [truveʒ'ar] |
| it's thundering | está a trovejar | [əʃt'a ɐ truveʒ'ar] |

| hail | granizo (m) | [grɐn'izu] |
| it's hailing | está a cair granizo | [əʃt'a ɐ kɐ'ir grɐn'izu] |

| to flood (vt) | inundar (vt) | [inũd'ar] |
| flood, inundation | inundação (f) | [inũdɐs'ãu] |

| earthquake | terremoto (m) | [tɐʀɐm'ɔtu] |
| tremor, quake | abalo, tremor (m) | [ɐb'alu], [trɐm'or] |
| epicenter | epicentro (m) | [epis'ẽtru] |
| eruption | erupção (f) | [ɐrups'ãu] |
| lava | lava (f) | [l'avɐ] |

| twister | turbilhão (m) | [turbiʎ'ãu] |
| tornado | tornado (m) | [turn'adu] |
| typhoon | tufão (m) | [tuf'ãu] |

| hurricane | furacão (m) | [furɐk'ãu] |
| storm | tempestade (f) | [tẽpɐʃt'adə] |
| tsunami | tsunami (m) | [tsun'ɐmi] |

| cyclone | ciclone (m) | [sikl'ɔnə] |
| bad weather | mau tempo (m) | [m'au t'ẽpu] |
| fire (accident) | incêndio (m) | [ĩs'ẽdiu] |
| disaster | catástrofe (f) | [kɐt'aʃtrufə] |
| meteorite | meteorito (m) | [mɐtiur'itu] |

| avalanche | avalanche (f) | [ɐvɐl'ãʃə] |
| snowslide | deslizamento (f) de neve | [dɐʒlizɐm'ẽtu də n'ɛvə] |
| blizzard | nevasca (f) | [nɐv'aʃkɐ] |
| snowstorm | tempestade (f) de neve | [tẽpɐʃt'adə də n'ɛvə] |

## 208. Noises. Sounds

| silence (quiet) | silêncio (m) | [sil'ẽsiu] |
| sound | som (m) | [sõ] |

| noise | ruído, barulho (m) | [ʀu'idu], [bɐɾu'ʎu] |
| to make noise | fazer barulho | [fɐz'eɾ bɐɾu'ʎu] |
| noisy (adj) | ruidoso, barulhento | [ʀuid'ozu], [bɐɾuʎ'ẽtu] |
| | | |
| loudly (to speak, etc.) | alto | ['altu] |
| loud (voice, etc.) | alto | ['altu] |
| constant (continuous) | constante | [kõʃt'ãtə] |
| | | |
| shout (n) | grito (m) | [gɾ'itu] |
| to shout (vi) | gritar (vi) | [gɾit'aɾ] |
| whisper | sussurro (m) | [sus'uʀu] |
| to whisper (vi, vt) | sussurrar (vt) | [susuʀ'aɾ] |
| | | |
| barking (of dog) | latido (m) | [lɐt'idu] |
| to bark (vi) | ladrar, latir (vi) | [lɐdɾ'aɾ], [lɐt'iɾ] |
| | | |
| groan (of pain) | gemido (m) | [ʒɐm'idu] |
| to groan (vi) | gemer (vi) | [ʒɐm'eɾ] |
| cough | tosse (f) | [t'ɔsə] |
| to cough (vi) | tossir (vi) | [tos'iɾ] |
| | | |
| whistle | assobio (m) | [ɐsub'iu] |
| to whistle (vi) | assobiar (vi) | [ɐsubj'aɾ] |
| knock (at the door) | batida (f) | [bɐt'idɐ] |
| to knock (at the door) | bater (vi) | [bɐt'eɾ] |
| | | |
| to crack (vi) | estalar (vi) | [əʃtɐl'aɾ] |
| crack (plank, etc.) | estalido (m) | [əʃtɐl'idu] |
| | | |
| siren | sirene (f) | [sir'ɛnə] |
| whistle (factory ~) | apito (m) | [ɐp'itu] |
| to whistle (ship, train) | apitar (vi) | [ɐpit'aɾ] |
| honk (signal) | buzina (f) | [buz'inɐ] |
| to honk (vi) | buzinar (vi) | [buzin'aɾ] |

## 209. Winter

| winter (n) | inverno (m) | [ĩv'ɛɾnu] |
| winter (as adj) | de inverno | [də ĩv'ɛɾnu] |
| in winter | no inverno | [nu ĩv'ɛɾnu] |
| | | |
| snow | neve (f) | [n'ɛvə] |
| it's snowing | está a nevar | [əʃt'a ɐ nɛv'aɾ] |
| snowfall | queda (f) de neve | [k'ɛdɐ də n'ɛvə] |
| snowdrift | amontoado (m) de neve | [ɐmõtu'adu də n'ɛvə] |
| | | |
| snowflake | floco (m) de neve | [fl'ɔku də n'ɛvə] |
| snowball | bola (f) de neve | [b'ɔlɐ də n'ɛvə] |
| snowman | boneco (m) de neve | [bun'ɛku də n'ɛvə] |
| icicle | sincelo (m) | [sĩs'ɛlu] |

| December | dezembro (m) | [dəz'ẽbru] |
| January | janeiro (m) | [ʒen'ejru] |
| February | fevereiro (m) | [fəvər'ejru] |

| severe frost | gelo (m) | [ʒ'elu] |
| frosty (weather, air) | gelado, glacial | [ʒəl'adu], [glɐsj'al] |

| below zero (adv) | abaixo de zero | [ɐb'ajʃu də z'ɛru] |
| first frost | geada (f) | [ʒj'adɐ] |
| hoarfrost | geada (f) branca | [ʒj'adɐ br'ãkɐ] |

| cold (cold weather) | frio (m) | [fr'iu] |
| it's cold | está frio | [əʃt'a fr'iu] |

| fur coat | casaco (m) de peles | [kɐz'aku də p'ɛləʃ] |
| mittens | mitenes (f pl) | [mit'ɛnəʃ] |

| to get sick | adoecer (vi) | [ɐduɐs'er] |
| cold (illness) | constipação (m) | [kõʃtipɐs'ãu] |
| to catch a cold | constipar-se (vp) | [kõʃtip'arsə] |

| ice | gelo (m) | [ʒ'elu] |
| black ice | gelo (m) na estrada | [ʒ'elu nɐ əʃtr'adɐ] |
| to freeze (ab. river, etc.) | congelar-se (vp) | [kõʒəl'arsə] |
| ice floe | bloco (m) de gelo | [bl'ɔku də ʒ'elu] |

| skis | esqui (m) | [əʃk'i] |
| skier | esquiador (m) | [əʃkiɐd'or] |
| to ski (vi) | esquiar (vi) | [əʃki'ar] |
| to skate (vi) | patinar (vi) | [pɐtin'ar] |

# Fauna

## 210. Mammals. Predators

| | | |
|---|---|---|
| predator | **predador** (m) | [prɐdɐd'or] |
| tiger | **tigre** (m) | [t'igrɐ] |
| lion | **leão** (m) | [lj'ãu] |
| wolf | **lobo** (m) | [l'obu] |
| fox | **raposa** (f) | [ʀɐp'ozɐ] |
| | | |
| jaguar | **jaguar** (m) | [ʒɐgu'ar] |
| leopard | **leopardo** (m) | [liup'ardu] |
| cheetah | **chita** (f) | [ʃ'itɐ] |
| | | |
| black panther | **pantera** (f) | [pãt'erɐ] |
| puma | **puma** (m) | [p'umɐ] |
| snow leopard | **leopardo-das-neves** (m) | [liup'ardu dɐʒ n'ɛvɐʃ] |
| lynx | **lince** (m) | [l'ĩsɐ] |
| | | |
| coyote | **coiote** (m) | [koj'ɔtɐ] |
| jackal | **chacal** (m) | [ʃɐk'al] |
| hyena | **hiena** (f) | [j'enɐ] |

## 211. Wild animals

| | | |
|---|---|---|
| animal | **animal** (m) | [ɐnim'al] |
| beast (animal) | **besta** (f) | [b'eʃtɐ] |
| | | |
| squirrel | **esquilo** (m) | [ɐʃk'ilu] |
| hedgehog | **ouriço** (m) | [or'isu] |
| hare | **lebre** (f) | [l'ɛbrɐ] |
| rabbit | **coelho** (m) | [ku'eʎu] |
| | | |
| badger | **texugo** (m) | [tɛks'ugu] |
| raccoon | **guaxinim** (m) | [guaksin'ĩ] |
| hamster | **hamster** (m) | ['ɐmstɐr] |
| marmot | **marmota** (f) | [mɐrm'ɔtɐ] |
| | | |
| mole | **toupeira** (f) | [top'ɐjrɐ] |
| mouse | **rato** (m) | [ʀ'atu] |
| rat | **ratazana** (f) | [ʀɐtɐz'ɐnɐ] |
| bat | **morcego** (m) | [murs'egu] |
| ermine | **arminho** (m) | [ɐrm'iɲu] |
| sable | **zibelina** (f) | [zibɐl'inɐ] |

| marten | marta (f) | [m'artɐ] |
| weasel | doninha (f) | [dun'iɲɐ] |
| mink | vison (m) | [viz'õ] |

| beaver | castor (m) | [keʃt'or] |
| otter | lontra (f) | [l'õtrɐ] |

| horse | cavalo (m) | [kɐv'alu] |
| moose | alce (m) americano | ['alsɐ ɐmɐrik'ɐnu] |
| deer | veado (m) | [vj'adu] |
| camel | camelo (m) | [kɐm'elu] |

| bison | bisão (m) | [biz'ãu] |
| aurochs | auroque (m) | [aur'ɔkɐ] |
| buffalo | búfalo (m) | [b'ufɐlu] |

| zebra | zebra (f) | [z'ɛbrɐ] |
| antelope | antílope (m) | [ãt'ilupɐ] |
| roe deer | corça (f) | [k'ɔrsɐ] |
| fallow deer | gamo (m) | [g'ɐmu] |
| chamois | camurça (f) | [kɐm'ursɐ] |
| wild boar | javali (m) | [ʒɐvɐl'i] |

| whale | baleia (f) | [bɐl'ɐjɐ] |
| seal | foca (f) | [f'ɔkɐ] |
| walrus | morsa (f) | [m'ɔrsɐ] |
| fur seal | urso-marinho (m) | ['ursu mɐr'iɲu] |
| dolphin | golfinho (m) | [golf'iɲu] |

| bear | urso (m) | ['ursu] |
| polar bear | urso (m) branco | ['ursu br'ãku] |
| panda | panda (m) | [p'ãdɐ] |

| monkey | macaco (m) | [mɐk'aku] |
| chimpanzee | chimpanzé (m) | [ʃĩpãz'ɛ] |
| orangutan | orangotango (m) | [ɔrãgut'ãgu] |
| gorilla | gorila (m) | [gur'ilɐ] |
| macaque | macaco (m) | [mɐk'aku] |
| gibbon | gibão (m) | [ʒib'ãu] |

| elephant | elefante (m) | [elɐf'ãtɐ] |
| rhinoceros | rinoceronte (m) | [ʀinɔsɐr'õtɐ] |
| giraffe | girafa (f) | [ʒir'afɐ] |
| hippopotamus | hipopótamo (m) | [ipɔp'ɔtɐmu] |

| kangaroo | canguru (m) | [kãgur'u] |
| koala (bear) | coala (m) | [ku'alɐ] |

| mongoose | mangusto (m) | [mãg'uʃtu] |
| chinchilla | chinchila (f) | [ʃĩʃ'ilɐ] |
| skunk | doninha-fedorenta (f) | [duniɲɐ fɐdur'ẽtɐ] |
| porcupine | porco-espinho (m) | [p'ɔrkɔ ɐʃp'iɲu] |

## 212. Domestic animals

| | | |
|---|---|---|
| cat | gata (f) | [g'atɐ] |
| tomcat | gato (m) macho | [g'atu m'aʃu] |
| dog | cão (m) | [kʹɐ̃u] |
| | | |
| horse | cavalo (m) | [kɐv'alu] |
| stallion | garanhão (m) | [gɐrɐɲ'ɐ̃u] |
| mare | égua (f) | ['ɛguɐ] |
| | | |
| cow | vaca (f) | [v'akɐ] |
| bull | touro (m) | [t'oru] |
| ox | boi (m) | [boj] |
| | | |
| sheep | ovelha (f) | [ɔv'eʎɐ] |
| ram | carneiro (m) | [kɐrn'ejru] |
| goat | cabra (f) | [kʹabrɐ] |
| billy goat, he-goat | bode (m) | [b'ɔdə] |
| | | |
| donkey | burro (m) | [b'uʀu] |
| mule | mula (f) | [m'ulɐ] |
| | | |
| pig | porco (m) | [p'orku] |
| piglet | porquinho (m) | [purk'iɲu] |
| rabbit | coelho (m) | [ku'eʎu] |
| | | |
| hen (chicken) | galinha (f) | [gɐl'iɲɐ] |
| rooster | galo (m) | [g'alu] |
| | | |
| duck | pato (m), pata (f) | [p'atu], [p'atɐ] |
| drake | pato (m) | [p'atu] |
| goose | ganso (m) | [g'ɐ̃su] |
| | | |
| tom turkey | peru (m) | [pər'u] |
| turkey (hen) | perua (f) | [pər'uɐ] |
| | | |
| domestic animals | animais (m pl) domésticos | [ɐnim'ajʃ dum'ɛʃtikuʃ] |
| tame (e.g., ~ hamster) | domesticado | [dumɐʃtik'adu] |
| to tame (vt) | domesticar (vt) | [dumɐʃtik'ar] |
| to breed (vt) | criar (vt) | [kri'ar] |
| | | |
| farm | quinta (f) | [kʹĩtɐ] |
| poultry | aves (f pl) domésticas | ['avəʃ dum'ɛʃtikɐʃ] |
| cattle | gado (m) | [g'adu] |
| herd (cattle) | rebanho (m), manada (f) | [ʀəb'ɐɲu], [mɐn'adɐ] |
| | | |
| stable | estábulo (m) | [əʃt'abulu] |
| pigsty | pocilga (f) | [pus'ilgɐ] |
| cowshed | vacaria (m) | [vɐkɐr'iɐ] |
| rabbit hutch | coelheira (f) | [kuɛʎ'ejrɐ] |
| hen house | galinheiro (m) | [gɐliɲ'ejru] |

## 213. Dogs. Dog breeds

| | | |
|---|---|---|
| dog | cão (m) | [k'ãu] |
| sheepdog | cão pastor (m) | [k'ãu peʃt'or] |
| German shepherd dog | pastor-alemão (m) | [peʃt'or elem'ãu] |
| poodle | caniche (m) | [kan'iʃe] |
| dachshund | teckel (m) | [tɛkk'ɛl] |
| | | |
| bulldog | buldogue (m) | [buld'ɔge] |
| boxer | boxer (m) | [b'ɔksɐr] |
| mastiff | mastim (m) | [meʃt'ĩ] |
| rottweiler | rottweiler (m) | [ʀɔtv'ajlɐr] |
| Doberman | dobermann (m) | [dɔb'ɛrmɐn] |
| | | |
| basset | basset (m) | [bas'ɛt] |
| bobtail | pastor inglês (m) | [peʃt'or ĩgl'eʃ] |
| Dalmatian | dálmata (m) | [d'almɐte] |
| cocker spaniel | cocker spaniel (m) | [k'ɔkɐr spenj'ɛl] |
| | | |
| Newfoundland | terra-nova (m) | [tɛʀɐn'ɔve] |
| Saint Bernard | são-bernardo (m) | [sãubɐrn'ardu] |
| | | |
| husky | husky (m) | ['eski] |
| Chow Chow | Chow-chow (m) | [ʃɔuʃ'ɔu] |
| spitz | spitz alemão (m) | [ʃp'itz elem'ãu] |
| pug | carlindogue (m) | [kɐrlĩd'ɔge] |

## 214. Sounds made by animals

| | | |
|---|---|---|
| barking (n) | latido (m) | [lɐt'idu] |
| to bark (vi) | ladrar, latir (vi) | [lɐdr'ar], [lɐt'ir] |
| to meow (vi) | miar (vi) | [mj'ar] |
| to purr (vi) | ronronar (vi) | [ʀõʀun'ar] |
| | | |
| to moo (vi) | mugir (vi) | [muʒ'ir] |
| to bellow (bull) | bramir (vi) | [brɐm'ir] |
| to growl (vi) | rosnar (vi) | [ʀuʒn'ar] |
| | | |
| howl (n) | uivo (m) | ['ujvu] |
| to howl (vi) | uivar (vi) | [ujv'ar] |
| to whine (vi) | ganir (vi) | [gen'ir] |
| | | |
| to bleat (sheep) | balir (vi) | [bɐl'ir] |
| to oink, to grunt (pig) | grunhir (vi) | [gruɲ'ir] |
| to squeal (vi) | guinchar (vi) | [gĩʃ'ar] |
| | | |
| to croak (vi) | coaxar (vi) | [kuaʃ'ar] |
| to buzz (insect) | zumbir (vi) | [zũb'ir] |
| to stridulate (vi) | estridular, ziziar (vi) | [eʃtridul'ar], [zizj'ar] |

## 215. Young animals

| cub | cria (f), filhote (m) | [kr'ie], [fiʎ'ɔtə] |
| kitten | gatinho (m) | [gɐt'iɲu] |
| baby mouse | ratinho (m) | [ʀɐt'iɲu] |
| pup, puppy | cãozinho (m) | [kɐ̃uziɲu] |

| leveret | filhote (m) de lebra | [fiʎ'ɔtə də l'ɛbrɐ] |
| baby rabbit | coelhinho (m) | [kuɛʎ'iɲu] |
| wolf cub | filhote (m) de lobo | [fiʎ'ɔtə də l'obu] |
| fox cub | raposinho (m) | [ʀɐpuz'iɲu] |
| bear cub | ursinho (m) | [urs'iɲu] |

| lion cub | leãozinho (m) | [lj'ɐ̃uziɲu] |
| tiger cub | filhote (m) de tigre | [fiʎ'ɔtə də t'igrɐ] |
| elephant calf | filhote (m) de elefante | [fiʎ'ɔtə də eləf'ɐ̃tə] |

| piglet | porquinho (m) | [purk'iɲu] |
| calf (young cow, bull) | bezerro (m) | [bəz'eʀu] |
| kid (young goat) | cabrito (m) | [kɐbr'itu] |
| lamb | cordeiro (m) | [kurd'ejru] |
| fawn (young deer) | cria (f) de veado | [kr'ie də vj'adu] |
| young camel | cria (f) de camelo | [kr'ie də kɐm'elu] |

| baby snake | filhote (m) de serpente | [fiʎ'ɔtə də sərp'ẽtə] |
| baby frog | cria (f) de rã | [kr'ie də ʀɐ̃] |

| nestling | cria (f) de ave | [kr'ie də 'avə] |
| chick (of chicken) | pinto (m) | [p'ĩtu] |
| duckling | patinho (m) | [pɐt'iɲu] |

## 216. Birds

| bird | pássaro, ave (m) | [p'aseru], ['avə] |
| pigeon | pombo (m) | [p'õbu] |
| sparrow | pardal (m) | [perd'al] |
| tit | chapim-real (m) | [ʃɐp'ĩ ʀi'al] |
| magpie | pega-rabuda (f) | [p'ɛgɐ ʀɐb'udɐ] |

| raven | corvo (m) | [k'orvu] |
| crow | gralha (f) cinzenta | [gr'aʎɐ sĩz'ẽtɐ] |
| jackdaw | gralha-de-nuca cinzenta (f) | [gr'aʎɐ də n'ukɐ sĩz'ẽtɐ] |
| rook | gralha-calva (f) | [gr'aʎɐ k'alvɐ] |

| duck | pato (m) | [p'atu] |
| goose | ganso (m) | [g'ɐ̃su] |
| pheasant | faisão (m) | [fajz'ɐ̃u] |
| eagle | águia (f) | ['agiɐ] |

| hawk | açor (m) | [ɐsˈor] |
| falcon | falcão (m) | [falkˈãu] |
| vulture | abutre (m) | [ɐbˈutrə] |
| condor (Andean ~) | condor (m) | [kõdˈor] |

| swan | cisne (m) | [sˈiʒnə] |
| crane | grou (m) | [gro] |
| stork | cegonha (f) | [səgˈoɲɐ] |

| parrot | papagaio (m) | [pɐpɐgˈaju] |
| hummingbird | beija-flor (m) | [bˈɐjʒə flˈor] |
| peacock | pavão (m) | [pɐvˈãu] |

| ostrich | avestruz (f) | [ɐvəʃtrˈuʃ] |
| heron | garça (f) | [gˈarsə] |
| flamingo | flamingo (m) | [flɐmˈĩgu] |
| pelican | pelicano (m) | [pəlikˈɐnu] |
| nightingale | rouxinol (m) | [ʀoʃinˈɔl] |
| swallow | andorinha (f) | [ãdurˈiɲɐ] |

| thrush | tordo-zornal (m) | [tˈɔrdu zurnˈal] |
| song thrush | tordo-músico (m) | [tˈɔrdu mˈuziku] |
| blackbird | melro-preto (m) | [mˈɛlʀu prˈetu] |

| swift | andorinhão (m) | [ãduriɲˈãu] |
| lark | cotovia (f) | [kutuvˈiɐ] |
| quail | codorna (f) | [kɔdˈɔrnɐ] |

| woodpecker | pica-pau (m) | [pˈikɐ pˈau] |
| cuckoo | cuco (m) | [kˈuku] |
| owl | coruja (f) | [kurˈuʒɐ] |
| eagle owl | corujão, bufo (m) | [kɔruʒˈãu], [bˈufu] |
| wood grouse | tetraz-grande (m) | [tɛtrˈaʒ grˈãdə] |
| black grouse | tetraz-lira (m) | [tɛtrˈaʒ lˈirɐ] |
| partridge | perdiz-cinzenta (f) | [pərdiʃ sĩzˈẽtɐ] |

| starling | estorninho (m) | [əʃturnˈiɲu] |
| canary | canário (m) | [kɐnˈariu] |
| hazel grouse | galinha-do-mato (f) | [gɐlˈiɲɐ du mˈatu] |
| chaffinch | tentilhão (m) | [tẽtiʎˈãu] |
| bullfinch | dom-fafe (m) | [dõfˈafə] |

| seagull | gaivota (f) | [gajvˈɔtɐ] |
| albatross | albatroz (m) | [albɐtrˈɔʃ] |
| penguin | pinguim (m) | [pĩguˈĩ] |

## 217. Birds. Singing and sounds

| to sing (vi) | cantar (vi) | [kãtˈar] |
| to call (animal, bird) | gritar (vi) | [gritˈar] |

| to crow (rooster) | cantar (o galo) | [kãt'ar u g'alu] |
| cock-a-doodle-doo | cocorocó (m) | [kɔkuruk'ɔ] |

| to cluck (hen) | cacarejar (vi) | [kɐkɐreʒ'ar] |
| to caw (vi) | crocitar (vi) | [krɔsit'ar] |
| to quack (duck) | grasnar (vi) | [grɐʒn'ar] |
| to cheep (vi) | piar (vi) | [pj'ar] |
| to chirp, to twitter | chilrear, gorjear (vi) | [ʃilʀe'ar], [gurʒj'ar] |

## 218. Fish. Marine animals

| bream | brema (f) | [br'emɐ] |
| carp | carpa (f) | [k'arpɐ] |
| perch | perca (f) | [p'ɛrkɐ] |
| catfish | siluro (m) | [sil'uru] |
| pike | lúcio (m) | [l'usiu] |

| salmon | salmão (m) | [salm'ãu] |
| sturgeon | esturjão (m) | [əʃturʒ'ãu] |

| herring | arenque (m) | [ɐr'ẽkə] |
| Atlantic salmon | salmão (m) | [salm'ãu] |
| mackerel | cavala (m), sarda (f) | [kɐv'alɐ], [s'ardɐ] |
| flatfish | solha (f) | [s'oʎɐ] |

| zander, pike perch | zander (m) | [zãd'er] |
| cod | bacalhau (m) | [bɐkɐʎ'au] |
| tuna | atum (m) | [ɐt'ũ] |
| trout | truta (f) | [tr'utɐ] |
| eel | enguia (f) | [ẽg'iɐ] |
| electric ray | raia elétrica (f) | [ʀ'ajɐ el'ɛtrikɐ] |
| moray eel | moreia (f) | [mur'ɐjɐ] |
| piranha | piranha (f) | [pir'ɐɲɐ] |

| shark | tubarão (m) | [tubɐr'ãu] |
| dolphin | golfinho (m) | [golf'iɲu] |
| whale | baleia (f) | [bɐl'ɐjɐ] |

| crab | caranguejo (m) | [kɐrãg'eʒu] |
| jellyfish | medusa, alforreca (f) | [məd'uzɐ], [alfuʀ'ɛkɐ] |
| octopus | polvo (m) | [p'olvu] |

| starfish | estrela-do-mar (f) | [əʃtr'elɐ du m'ar] |
| sea urchin | ouriço-do-mar (m) | [or'isu du m'ar] |
| seahorse | cavalo-marinho (m) | [kɐv'alu mɐr'iɲu] |

| oyster | ostra (f) | ['ɔʃtrɐ] |
| shrimp | camarão (m) | [kɐmɐr'ãu] |
| lobster | lavagante (m) | [lɐveg'ãtə] |
| spiny lobster | lagosta (f) | [lɐg'oʃtɐ] |

## 219. Amphibians. Reptiles

| | | |
|---|---|---|
| snake | serpente, cobra (f) | [sərp'ētə], [k'ɔbrɐ] |
| venomous (snake) | venenoso | [vənən'ozu] |
| | | |
| viper | víbora (f) | [v'iburɐ] |
| cobra | cobra-capelo, naja (f) | [kɔbrɐkɐp'ɛlu], [n'aʒɐ] |
| python | piton (m) | [p'itɔn] |
| boa | jiboia (f) | [ʒib'ɔjɐ] |
| | | |
| grass snake | cobra-de-água (f) | [kɔbrɐdɐ'aguɐ] |
| rattle snake | cascavel (f) | [kɐʃkɐv'ɛl] |
| anaconda | anaconda (f) | [ɐnɐk'ōdɐ] |
| | | |
| lizard | lagarto (m) | [lɐg'artu] |
| iguana | iguana (f) | [igu'ɐnɐ] |
| monitor lizard | varano (m) | [vɐr'ɐnu] |
| salamander | salamandra (f) | [sɐlɐm'ãdrɐ] |
| chameleon | camaleão (m) | [kɐmɐlj'ãu] |
| scorpion | escorpião (m) | [əʃkurpj'ãu] |
| | | |
| turtle | tartaruga (f) | [tɐrtɐr'ugɐ] |
| frog | rã (f) | [ʀã] |
| toad | sapo (m) | [s'apu] |
| crocodile | crocodilo (m) | [krukud'ilu] |

## 220. Insects

| | | |
|---|---|---|
| insect, bug | inseto (m) | [ĩs'ɛtu] |
| butterfly | borboleta (f) | [burbul'etɐ] |
| ant | formiga (f) | [furm'igɐ] |
| fly | mosca (f) | [m'oʃkɐ] |
| mosquito | mosquito (m) | [muʃk'itu] |
| beetle | escaravelho (m) | [əʃkɐrɐv'ɛʎu] |
| | | |
| wasp | vespa (f) | [v'ɛʃpɐ] |
| bee | abelha (f) | [ɐb'eʎɐ] |
| bumblebee | zangão (m) | [zãg'ãu] |
| gadfly | moscardo (m) | [muʃk'ardu] |
| | | |
| spider | aranha (f) | [ɐr'ɐɲɐ] |
| spider's web | teia (f) de aranha | [t'ɐjɐ də ɐr'ɐɲɐ] |
| | | |
| dragonfly | libélula (f) | [lib'ɛlulɐ] |
| grasshopper | gafanhoto-do-campo (m) | [gɐfɐɲ'otu du k'ãpu] |
| moth (night butterfly) | traça (f) | [tr'asɐ] |
| | | |
| cockroach | barata (f) | [bɐr'atɐ] |
| tick | carraça (f) | [kɐʀ'asɐ] |

| flea | pulga (f) | [pʼulgɐ] |
| midge | borrachudo (m) | [buʀɐʃʼudu] |

| locust | gafanhoto (m) | [gɐfɐɲʼotu] |
| snail | caracol (m) | [kɐɾɐkʼɔl] |
| cricket | grilo (m) | [gɾʼilu] |
| lightning bug | pirilampo (m) | [piɾilʼãpu] |
| ladybug | joaninha (f) | [ʒuɐnʼiɲɐ] |
| cockchafer | besouro (m) | [bɐzʼoɾu] |

| leech | sanguessuga (f) | [sãgɐsʼugɐ] |
| caterpillar | lagarta (f) | [lɐgʼaɾtɐ] |
| earthworm | minhoca (f) | [miɲʼɔkɐ] |
| larva | larva (f) | [lʼaɾvɐ] |

## 221. Animals. Body parts

| beak | bico (m) | [bʼiku] |
| wings | asas (f pl) | [ʼazɐʃ] |
| foot (of bird) | pata (f) | [pʼatɐ] |

| feathering | plumagem (f) | [plumʼaʒɐ̃j] |
| feather | pena, pluma (f) | [pʼenɐ], [plʼumɐ] |
| crest | crista (f) | [kɾʼiʃtɐ] |

| gill | brânquias, guelras (f pl) | [bɾʼãkiɐʃ], [gʼɛlʀɐʃ] |
| spawn | ovas (f pl) | [ʼɔvɐʃ] |
| larva | larva (f) | [lʼaɾvɐ] |

| fin | barbatana (f) | [bɐɾbɐtʼɐnɐ] |
| scales (of fish, reptile) | escama (f) | [ɐʃkʼɐmɐ] |

| fang (canine) | canino (m) | [kɐnʼinu] |
| paw (e.g., cat's ~) | pata (f) | [pʼatɐ] |
| muzzle (snout) | focinho (m) | [fusʼiɲu] |
| mouth (of cat, dog) | boca (f) | [bʼokɐ] |

| tail | cauda (f), rabo (m) | [kʼaudɐ], [ʀʼabu] |
| whiskers | bigodes (m pl) | [bigʼɔdɐʃ] |

| hoof | casco (m) | [kʼaʃku] |
| horn | corno (m) | [kʼoɾnu] |

| carapace | carapaça (f) | [kɐɾɐpʼasɐ] |
| shell (of mollusk) | concha (f) | [kʼõʃɐ] |
| eggshell | casca (f) de ovo | [kʼaʃkɐ dɐ ʼovu] |

| animal's hair (pelage) | pelo (m) | [pʼelu] |

| pelt (hide) | pele (f), couro (m) | [pʼɛlɐ], [kʼoɾu] |

## 222. Actions of animals

| to fly (vi) | voar (vi) | [vu'ar] |
| to make circles | dar voltas | [dar v'ɔlteʃ] |
| to fly away | voar (vi) | [vu'ar] |
| to flap (~ the wings) | bater as asas | [bɐt'er ɐʃ 'azeʃ] |

| to peck (vi) | bicar (vi) | [bik'ar] |
| to sit on eggs | incubar (vt) | [ĩkub'ar] |
| to hatch out (vi) | sair do ovo | [sɐ'ir du 'ovu] |
| to build the nest | fazer o ninho | [fɐz'er u n'iɲu] |

| to slither, to crawl | rastejar (vi) | [ʀɐʃtɐʒ'ar] |
| to sting, to bite (insect) | picar (vt) | [pik'ar] |
| to bite (ab. animal) | morder (vt) | [murd'er] |

| to sniff (vt) | cheirar (vt) | [ʃejr'ar] |
| to bark (vi) | ladrar (vi) | [lɐdr'ar] |
| to hiss (snake) | silvar (vi) | [silv'ar] |
| to scare (vt) | assustar (vt) | [ɐsuʃt'ar] |
| to attack (vt) | atacar (vt) | [ɐtɐk'ar] |

| to gnaw (bone, etc.) | roer (vt) | [ʀu'er] |
| to scratch (with claws) | arranhar (vt) | [ɐʀɐɲ'ar] |
| to hide (vi) | esconder-se (vp) | [əʃkõd'erse] |

| to play (kittens, etc.) | brincar (vi) | [bɾĩk'ar] |
| to hunt (vi, vt) | caçar (vi) | [kɐs'ar] |
| to hibernate (vi) | hibernar (vi) | [ibɐrn'ar] |
| to become extinct | extinguir-se (vp) | [əʃtĩg'irse] |

## 223. Animals. Habitats

| habitat | habitat (m) | [abit'atə] |
| migration | migração (f) | [migrɐs'ãu] |

| mountain | montanha (f) | [mõt'ɐɲɐ] |
| reef | recife (m) | [ʀəs'ifə] |
| cliff | falésia (f) | [fɐl'ɛziɐ] |

| forest | floresta (f) | [flur'ɛʃtɐ] |
| jungle | selva (f) | [s'ɛlvɐ] |
| savanna | savana (f) | [sɐv'ɐnɐ] |
| tundra | tundra (f) | [t'ũdrɐ] |

| steppe | estepe (f) | [əʃt'ɛpə] |
| desert | deserto (m) | [dəz'ɛrtu] |
| oasis | oásis (m) | [o'aziʃ] |
| sea | mar (m) | [mar] |

| lake | lago (m) | [l'agu] |
| ocean | oceano (m) | [ɔsj'ɐnu] |

| swamp | pântano (m) | [p'ãtɐnu] |
| freshwater (adj) | de água doce | [də 'aguɐ d'osə] |
| pond | lagoa (f) | [lɐg'oɐ] |
| river | rio (m) | [ʀ'iu] |

| den | toca (f) do urso | [t'ɔkɐ du 'ursu] |
| nest | ninho (m) | [n'iɲu] |
| hollow (in a tree) | buraco (m) de árvore | [bur'aku də 'arvurɐ] |
| burrow (animal hole) | toca (f) | [t'ɔkɐ] |
| anthill | formigueiro (m) | [furmig'ejru] |

## 224. Animal care

| zoo | jardim (m) zoológico | [ʒɐrd'ĩ zuul'ɔʒiku] |
| nature preserve | reserva (f) natural | [ʀɐz'ɛrvɐ netur'al] |

| breeder, breed club | viveiro (m) | [viv'ejru] |
| open-air cage | jaula (f) de ar livre | [ʒ'aulɐ də ar l'ivrə] |
| cage | jaula, gaiola (f) | [ʒ'aulɐ], [gɐj'ɔlɐ] |
| kennel | casinha (f) de cão | [kɐz'iɲɐ də k'ãu] |

| dovecot | pombal (m) | [põb'al] |
| aquarium | aquário (m) | [ɐku'ariu] |
| dolphinarium | delfinário (m) | [dɛlfin'ariu] |

| to breed (animals) | criar (vt) | [kri'ar] |
| brood, litter | ninhada (f) | [niɲ'adɐ] |
| to tame (vt) | domesticar (vt) | [dumɐʃtik'ar] |
| feed (fodder, etc.) | ração (f) | [ʀɐs'ãu] |
| to feed (vt) | alimentar (vt) | [ɐlimẽt'ar] |
| to train (animals) | adestrar (vt) | [ɐdɐʃtr'ar] |

| pet store | loja (f) de animais | [l'ɔʒɐ də ɐnim'ajʃ] |
| muzzle (for dog) | açaime (m) | [ɐs'ajmə] |
| collar | coleira (f) | [kul'ejrɐ] |
| name (of animal) | nome (f) | [n'omə] |
| pedigree (of dog) | pedigree (m) | [pɛdigr'i] |

## 225. Animals. Miscellaneous

| pack (wolves) | alcateia (f) | [alkɐt'ejɐ] |
| flock (birds) | bando (m) | [b'ãdu] |
| shoal (fish) | cardume (m) | [kɐrd'umə] |
| herd of horses | manada (f) | [mɐn'adɐ] |
| male (n) | macho (m) | [m'aʃu] |

| female | fêmea (f) | [f'emiɐ] |
| hungry (adj) | faminto | [fɐm'ĩtu] |
| wild (adj) | selvagem | [sɛlv'aʒɐ̃j] |
| dangerous (adj) | perigoso | [pərig'ozu] |

## 226. Horses

| horse | cavalo (m) | [kɐv'alu] |
| breed (race) | raça (f) | [ʀ'asɐ] |

| foal, colt | potro (m) | [p'ɔtru] |
| mare | égua (f) | ['ɛguɐ] |

| mustang | mustangue (m) | [muʃt'ãgə] |
| pony | pónei (m) | [p'ɔnɐj] |
| draft horse | cavalo (m) de tiro | [kɐv'alu də t'iru] |

| mane | crina (f) | [kr'inɐ] |
| tail | cauda (f) | [k'audɐ] |

| hoof | casco (m) | [k'aʃku] |
| horseshoe | ferradura (f) | [fəʀɐd'urɐ] |
| to shoe (vt) | ferrar (vt) | [fəʀ'ar] |
| blacksmith | ferreiro (m) | [fəʀ'ɐjru] |

| saddle | sela (f) | [s'ɛlɐ] |
| stirrup | estribo (m) | [əʃtr'ibu] |
| bridle | brida (f) | [br'idɐ] |
| reins | rédeas (f pl) | [ʀ'ɛdiɐʃ] |
| whip (for riding) | chicote (m) | [ʃik'ɔtə] |

| rider | cavaleiro (m) | [kɐvɐl'ɐjru] |
| to break in (horse) | amansar (vt) | [ɐmãs'ar] |
| to saddle (vt) | colocar sela | [kuluk'ar s'ɛlɐ] |
| to mount a horse | montar no cavalo | [mõt'ar nu kɐv'alu] |

| gallop | galope (m) | [gɐl'ɔpə] |
| to gallop (vi) | galopar (vi) | [gɐlup'ar] |
| trot (n) | trote (m) | [tr'ɔtə] |
| at a trot (adv) | a trote | [ɐ tr'ɔtə] |
| to go at a trot | ir a trote | [ir ɐ tr'ɔtə] |

| racehorse | cavalo (m) de corrida | [kɐv'alu də kuʀ'idɐ] |
| horse racing | corridas (f pl) | [kuʀ'idɐʃ] |

| stable | estábulo (m) | [əʃt'abulu] |
| to feed (vt) | alimentar (vt) | [ɐlimẽt'ar] |
| hay | feno (m) | [f'enu] |
| to water (animals) | dar água | [dar 'aguɐ] |
| to wash (horse) | limpar (vt) | [lĩp'ar] |

| | | |
|---|---|---|
| to hobble (tether) | **pear, prender as patas** | [pi′ar], [prɛd′er ɐʃ p′ateʃ] |
| horse-drawn cart | **carroça** (f) | [kɐʁ′ɔsɐ] |
| to graze (vi) | **pastar** (vi) | [pɐʃt′ar] |
| to neigh (vi) | **relinchar** (vi) | [ʁɐlĩʃ′ar] |
| to kick (horse) | **dar um coice** | [dar ũ k′ojsɐ] |

# Flora

## 227. Trees

| tree | árvore (f) | ['arvurə] |
|---|---|---|
| deciduous (adj) | decídua | [dəs'iduə] |
| coniferous (adj) | conífera | [kun'ifərə] |
| evergreen (adj) | perene | [pər'ɛnə] |

| apple tree | macieira (f) | [məsj'ejrə] |
|---|---|---|
| pear tree | pereira (f) | [pər'ejrə] |
| sweet cherry tree | cerejeira (f) | [sərəʒ'ejrə] |
| sour cherry tree | ginjeira (f) | [ʒĩʒ'ejrə] |
| plum tree | ameixeira (f) | [əmejʃ'ejrə] |

| birch | bétula (f) | [b'ɛtulə] |
|---|---|---|
| oak | carvalho (m) | [kɐrv'aʎu] |
| linden tree | tília (f) | [t'iliə] |
| aspen | choupo-tremedor (m) | [ʃ'opu trəməd'or] |
| maple | bordo (m) | [b'ɔrdu] |

| spruce | espruce-europeu (m) | [əʃpr'usə eurup'eu] |
|---|---|---|
| pine | pinheiro (m) | [piɲ'ejru] |
| larch | alerce, lariço (m) | [əl'ɛrsə], [lɐr'isu] |
| fir tree | abeto (m) | [ɐb'ɛtu] |
| cedar | cedro (m) | [s'ɛdru] |

| poplar | choupo, álamo (m) | [ʃ'opu], ['aləmu] |
|---|---|---|
| rowan | tramazeira (f) | [trɐməz'ejrə] |
| willow | salgueiro (m) | [salg'ejru] |
| alder | amieiro (m) | [əmj'ejru] |

| beech | faia (f) | [f'ajə] |
|---|---|---|
| elm | ulmeiro (m) | [ulm'ejru] |

| ash (tree) | freixo (m) | [fr'ejʃu] |
|---|---|---|
| chestnut | castanheiro (m) | [kəʃtəɲ'ejru] |

| magnolia | magnólia (f) | [məgn'ɔliə] |
|---|---|---|
| palm tree | palmeira (f) | [palm'ejrə] |
| cypress | cipreste (m) | [sipr'ɛʃtə] |

| mangrove | mangue (m) | [m'ãgə] |
|---|---|---|
| baobab | embondeiro, baobá (m) | [ẽbõd'ejru], [baub'a] |
| eucalyptus | eucalipto (m) | [eukəl'iptu] |
| sequoia | sequoia (f) | [səku'ɔjə] |

## 228. Shrubs

| | | |
|---|---|---|
| bush | **arbusto** (m) | [ɐrb'uʃtu] |
| shrub | **arbusto** (m), **moita** (f) | [ɐrb'uʃtu], [m'ojtɐ] |
| grapevine | **videira** (f) | [vid'ejrɐ] |
| vineyard | **vinhedo** (m) | [viɲ'edu] |
| raspberry bush | **framboeseira** (f) | [frãbuez'ejrɐ] |
| blackcurrant bush | **groselheira-preta** (f) | [gruzɐʎejrɐ pr'etɐ] |
| redcurrant bush | **groselheira-vermelha** (f) | [gruzɐʎ'ejrɐ vɐrm'eʎɐ] |
| gooseberry bush | **groselheira** (f) **espinhosa** | [gruzɐʎ'ejrɐ ɐʃpiɲ'ɔzɐ] |
| acacia | **acácia** (f) | [ɐk'asiɐ] |
| barberry | **bérberis** (f) | [b'ɛrbɐriʃ] |
| jasmine | **jasmim** (m) | [ʒɐʒm'ĩ] |
| juniper | **junípero** (m) | [ʒun'ipɐru] |
| rosebush | **roseira** (f) | [ʀuz'ejrɐ] |
| dog rose | **roseira** (f) **brava** | [ʀuz'ejrɐ br'avɐ] |

## 229. Mushrooms

| | | |
|---|---|---|
| mushroom | **cogumelo** (m) | [kugum'ɛlu] |
| edible mushroom | **cogumelo** (m) **comestível** | [kugum'ɛlu kumɐʃt'ivɛl] |
| toadstool | **cogumelo** (m) **venenoso** | [kugum'ɛlu vɐnɐn'ozu] |
| cap (of mushroom) | **chapéu** (m) | [ʃɐp'ɛu] |
| stipe (of mushroom) | **pé, caule** (m) | [pɛ], [k'aulɐ] |
| cep (Boletus edulis) | **cepe-de-bordéus** (m) | [s'ɛpɐ dɐ burd'ɛuʃ] |
| orange-cap boletus | **boleto** (m) **áspero** | [bul'etu 'aʃpɐru] |
| birch bolete | **boleto** (m) **castanho** | [bul'etu kɐʃt'ɐɲu] |
| chanterelle | **cantarelo** (m) | [kãtɐr'ɛlu] |
| russula | **rússula** (f) | [ʀ'usulɐ] |
| morel | **morchela** (f) | [murʃ'ɛlɐ] |
| fly agaric | **agário-das-moscas** (m) | [ɐg'ariu dɐʒ m'oʃkɐʃ] |
| death cap | **cicuta** (f) **verde** | [sik'utɐ v'erdɐ] |

## 230. Fruits. Berries

| | | |
|---|---|---|
| fruit | **fruta** (f) | [fr'utɐ] |
| fruits | **frutas** (f pl) | [fr'utɐʃ] |
| apple | **maçã** (f) | [mɐs'ã] |
| pear | **pera** (f) | [p'erɐ] |
| plum | **ameixa** (f) | [ɐm'ejʃɐ] |
| strawberry | **morango** (m) | [mur'ãgu] |

| sour cherry | ginja (f) | [ʒĩʒɐ] |
| sweet cherry | cereja (f) | [sər'ɐʒɐ] |
| grape | uva (f) | ['uvɐ] |

| raspberry | framboesa (f) | [frãbu'ezɐ] |
| blackcurrant | groselha (f) preta | [gruz'ɐʎɐ pr'etɐ] |
| redcurrant | groselha (f) vermelha | [gruz'ɐʎɐ vərm'ɐʎɐ] |
| gooseberry | groselha (f) espinhosa | [gruz'ɐʎɐ əʃpiɲ'ɔzɐ] |
| cranberry | oxicoco (m) | [ɔksik'oku] |

| orange | laranja (f) | [lɐr'ãʒɐ] |
| mandarin | tangerina (f) | [tãʒər'inɐ] |
| pineapple | ananás (m) | [ɐnɐn'aʃ] |
| banana | banana (f) | [bɐn'ɐnɐ] |
| date | tâmara (f) | [t'ɐmɐrɐ] |

| lemon | limão (m) | [lim'ãu] |
| apricot | damasco (m) | [dɐm'aʃku] |
| peach | pêssego (m) | [p'esəgu] |
| kiwi | kiwi (m) | [kiv'i] |
| grapefruit | toranja (f) | [tur'ãʒɐ] |

| berry | baga (f) | [b'agɐ] |
| berries | bagas (f pl) | [b'agɐʃ] |
| cowberry | arando (m) vermelho | [ɐr'ãdu vərm'ɐʎu] |
| field strawberry | morango-silvestre (m) | [mur'ãgu silv'ɛʃtrə] |
| bilberry | mirtilo (m) | [mirt'ilu] |

## 231. Flowers. Plants

| flower | flor (f) | [flor] |
| bouquet (of flowers) | ramo (m) de flores | [ʀ'emu də fl'orəʃ] |

| rose (flower) | rosa (f) | [ʀ'ɔzɐ] |
| tulip | tulipa (f) | [tul'ipɐ] |
| carnation | cravo (m) | [kr'avu] |
| gladiolus | gladíolo (m) | [glɐd'iulu] |

| cornflower | centáurea (f) | [sẽt'auriɐ] |
| bluebell | campânula (f) | [kãp'ɐnulɐ] |
| dandelion | dente-de-leão (m) | [d'ẽtə də li'ãu] |
| camomile | camomila (f) | [kamum'ilɐ] |

| aloe | aloé (m) | [ɐlu'ɛ] |
| cactus | cato (m) | [k'atu] |
| rubber plant, ficus | fícus (m) | [f'ikuʃ] |

| lily | lírio (m) | [l'iriu] |
| geranium | gerânio (m) | [ʒər'ɐniu] |
| hyacinth | jacinto (m) | [ʒɐsĩtu] |

| mimosa | mimosa (f) | [mim'ɔzɐ] |
| narcissus | narciso (m) | [nars'izu] |
| nasturtium | capuchinha (f) | [kɐpuʃ'iɲɐ] |

| orchid | orquídea (f) | [ɔrk'idiɐ] |
| peony | peónia (f) | [pj'ɔniɐ] |
| violet | violeta (f) | [viul'etɐ] |

| pansy | amor-perfeito (m) | [ɐm'or pɐrf'ejtu] |
| forget-me-not | não-me-esqueças (m) | [n'ãu mɐ ɐʃk'esɐʃ] |
| daisy | margarida (f) | [mɐrgɐr'idɐ] |

| poppy | papoula (f) | [pɐp'olɐ] |
| hemp | cânhamo (m) | [k'ɐɲɐmu] |
| mint | hortelã (f) | [ɔrtɐl'ã] |
| lily of the valley | lírio-do-vale (m) | [l'iriu du v'alɐ] |
| snowdrop | campânula-branca (f) | [kãpɐnulɐ br'ãkɐ] |

| nettle | urtiga (f) | [urt'igɐ] |
| sorrel | azeda (f) | [ɐz'edɐ] |
| water lily | nenúfar (m) | [nɐn'ufar] |
| fern | feto (m), samambaia (f) | [f'ɛtu], [sɐmãb'ajɐ] |
| lichen | líquen (m) | [l'ikɛn] |

| tropical greenhouse | estufa (f) | [ɐʃt'ufɐ] |
| grass lawn | relvado (m) | [ʀɛlv'adu] |
| flowerbed | canteiro (m) de flores | [kãt'ejru dɐ fl'orɐʃ] |

| plant | planta (f) | [pl'ãtɐ] |
| grass, herb | erva (f) | ['ɛrvɐ] |
| blade of grass | folha (f) de erva | [f'oʎɐ dɐ 'ɛrvɐ] |

| leaf | folha (f) | [f'oʎɐ] |
| petal | pétala (f) | [p'ɛtɐlɐ] |
| stem | talo (m) | [t'alu] |
| tuber | tubérculo (m) | [tub'ɛrkulu] |

| young plant (shoot) | broto, rebento (m) | [br'out], [ʀɐb'ẽtu] |
| thorn | espinho (m) | [ɐʃp'iɲu] |

| to blossom (vi) | florescer (vi) | [flurɐʃs'er] |
| to fade, to wither | murchar (vi) | [murʃ'ar] |
| smell (odor) | cheiro (m) | [ʃ'ejru] |
| to cut (flowers) | cortar (vt) | [kurt'ar] |
| to pick (a flower) | colher (vt) | [kuʎ'ɛr] |

## 232. Cereals, grains

| grain | grão (m) | [gr'ãu] |
| cereal crops | cereais (m pl) | [sɐrj'ajʃ] |

| ear (of barley, etc.) | espiga (f) | [əʃp'igɐ] |
| wheat | trigo (m) | [tr'igu] |
| rye | centeio (m) | [sẽt'eju] |
| oats | aveia (f) | [ɐv'ejɐ] |
| millet | milho-miúdo (m) | [m'iʎu mi'udu] |
| barley | cevada (f) | [sɐv'adɐ] |

| corn | milho (m) | [m'iʎu] |
| rice | arroz (m) | [ɐʀ'ɔʒ] |
| buckwheat | trigo-sarraceno (m) | [tr'igu saʀɐs'enu] |

| pea plant | ervilha (f) | [erv'iʎɐ] |
| kidney bean | feijão (m) | [fɐjʒ'ãu] |
| soy | soja (f) | [s'ɔʒɐ] |
| lentil | lentilha (f) | [lẽt'iʎɐ] |
| beans (pulse crops) | fava (f) | [f'avɐ] |

## 233. Vegetables. Greens

| vegetables | legumes (m pl) | [lɐg'uməʃ] |
| greens | verduras (f pl) | [vərd'urɐʃ] |

| tomato | tomate (m) | [tum'atə] |
| cucumber | pepino (m) | [pəp'inu] |
| carrot | cenoura (f) | [sɐn'orɐ] |
| potato | batata (f) | [bɐt'atɐ] |
| onion | cebola (f) | [sɐb'olɐ] |
| garlic | alho (m) | ['aʎu] |

| cabbage | couve (f) | [k'ovə] |
| cauliflower | couve-flor (f) | [k'ovə fl'or] |
| Brussels sprouts | couve-de-bruxelas (f) | [k'ovə də bruʃ'ɛləʃ] |
| broccoli | brócolos (m pl) | [br'ɔkuluʃ] |

| beetroot | beterraba (f) | [bətəʀ'abɐ] |
| eggplant | beringela (f) | [bərĩʒ'ɛlɐ] |
| zucchini | curgete (f) | [kurʒ'ɛtə] |
| pumpkin | abóbora (f) | [ɐb'ɔburɐ] |
| turnip | nabo (m) | [n'abu] |

| parsley | salsa (f) | [s'alsɐ] |
| dill | funcho, endro (m) | [f'ũʃu], ['ẽdru] |
| lettuce | alface (f) | [alf'asə] |
| celery | aipo (m) | ['ajpu] |
| asparagus | espargo (m) | [əʃp'argu] |
| spinach | espinafre (m) | [əʃpin'afrə] |

| pea | ervilha (f) | [erv'iʎɐ] |
| beans | fava (f) | [f'avɐ] |
| corn (maize) | milho (m) | [m'iʎu] |

| kidney bean | feijão (m) | [fejʒ'ãu] |
| pepper | pimentão (m) | [pimẽt'ãu] |
| radish | rabanete (m) | [ʀɐbɐn'etə] |
| artichoke | alcachofra (f) | [alkɐʃ'ofɾɐ] |

# REGIONAL GEOGRAPHY

## Countries. Nationalities

### 234. Western Europe

| | | |
|---|---|---|
| Europe | Europa (f) | [eur'ɔpɐ] |
| European Union | União (f) Europeia | [unj'ãu eurup'ɐjɐ] |
| European (n) | europeu (m) | [eurup'eu] |
| European (adj) | europeu | [eurup'eu] |
| | | |
| Austria | Áustria (f) | ['auʃtriɐ] |
| Austrian (masc.) | austríaco (m) | [auʃtr'iɐku] |
| Austrian (fem.) | austríaca (f) | [auʃtr'iɐkɐ] |
| Austrian (adj) | austríaco | [auʃtr'iɐku] |
| | | |
| Great Britain | Grã-Bretanha (f) | [grãbrɐt'ɐɲɐ] |
| England | Inglaterra (f) | [ĩglet'ɛrɐ] |
| British (masc.) | inglês (m) | [ĩgl'eʃ] |
| British (fem.) | inglesa (f) | [ĩgl'ezɐ] |
| English, British (adj) | inglês | [ĩgl'eʃ] |
| | | |
| Belgium | Bélgica (f) | [b'ɛlʒikɐ] |
| Belgian (masc.) | belga (m) | [b'ɛlgɐ] |
| Belgian (fem.) | belga (f) | [b'ɛlgɐ] |
| Belgian (adj) | belga | [b'ɛlgɐ] |
| | | |
| Germany | Alemanha (f) | [ɐlɐm'ɐɲɐ] |
| German (masc.) | alemão (m) | [ɐlɐm'ãu] |
| German (fem.) | alemã (f) | [ɐlɐm'ã] |
| German (adj) | alemão | [ɐlɐm'ãu] |
| | | |
| Netherlands | Países (m pl) Baixos | [pɐ'izɐʃ b'ajʃuʃ] |
| Holland | Holanda (f) | [ɔl'ãdɐ] |
| Dutchman | holandês (m) | [ɔlãd'eʃ] |
| Dutchwoman | holandesa (f) | [ɔlãd'ezɐ] |
| Dutch (adj) | holandês | [ɔlãd'eʃ] |
| | | |
| Greece | Grécia (f) | [gr'ɛsiɐ] |
| Greek (masc.) | grego (m) | [gr'egu] |
| Greek (fem.) | grega (f) | [gr'egɐ] |
| Greek (adj) | grego | [gr'egu] |
| | | |
| Denmark | Dinamarca (f) | [dinɐm'arkɐ] |
| Dane (masc.) | dinamarquês (m) | [dinɐmɐrk'eʃ] |

| Dane (fem.) | dinamarquesa (f) | [dinɐmɐrk'eze] |
| Danish (adj) | dinamarquês | [dinɐmɐrk'eʃ] |

| Ireland | Irlanda (f) | [irl'ãdɐ] |
| Irishman | irlandês (m) | [irlãd'eʃ] |
| Irishwoman | irlandesa (f) | [irlãd'eze] |
| Irish (adj) | irlandês | [irlãd'eʃ] |

| Iceland | Islândia (f) | [iʒl'ãdiɐ] |
| Icelander (masc.) | islandês (m) | [iʒlãd'eʃ] |
| Icelander (fem.) | islandesa (f) | [iʒlãd'eze] |
| Icelandic (adj) | islandês | [iʒlãd'eʃ] |

| Spain | Espanha (f) | [ɐʃp'aɲɐ] |
| Spaniard (masc.) | espanhol (m) | [ɐʃpɐɲ'ɔl] |
| Spaniard (fem.) | espanhola (f) | [ɐʃpɐɲ'ɔlɐ] |
| Spanish (adj) | espanhol | [ɐʃpɐɲ'ɔl] |

| Italy | Itália (f) | [it'aliɐ] |
| Italian (masc.) | italiano (m) | [itɐlj'enu] |
| Italian (fem.) | italiana (f) | [itɐlj'enɐ] |
| Italian (adj) | italiano | [itɐlj'enu] |

| Cyprus | Chipre (m) | [ʃ'iprɐ] |
| Cypriot (masc.) | cipriota (m) | [siprj'ɔtɐ] |
| Cypriot (fem.) | cipriota (f) | [siprj'ɔtɐ] |
| Cypriot (adj) | cipriota | [siprj'ɔtɐ] |

| Malta | Malta (f) | [m'altɐ] |
| Maltese (masc.) | maltês (m) | [malt'eʃ] |
| Maltese (fem.) | maltesa (f) | [malt'eze] |
| Maltese (adj) | maltês | [malt'eʃ] |

| Norway | Noruega (f) | [nɔru'ɛgɐ] |
| Norwegian (masc.) | norueguês (m) | [nɔruɛg'eʃ] |
| Norwegian (fem.) | norueguesa (f) | [nɔruɛg'eze] |
| Norwegian (adj) | norueguês | [nɔruɛg'eʃ] |

| Portugal | Portugal (m) | [purtug'al] |
| Portuguese (masc.) | português (m) | [purtug'eʃ] |
| Portuguese (fem.) | portuguesa (f) | [purtug'eze] |
| Portuguese (adj) | português | [purtug'eʃ] |

| Finland | Finlândia (f) | [fĩl'ãdiɐ] |
| Finn (masc.) | finlandês (m) | [fĩlãd'eʃ] |
| Finn (fem.) | finlandesa (f) | [fĩlãd'eze] |
| Finnish (adj) | finlandês | [fĩlãd'eʃ] |

| France | França (f) | [fr'ãsɐ] |
| Frenchman | francês (m) | [frãs'eʃ] |
| Frenchwoman | francesa (f) | [frãs'eze] |
| French (adj) | francês | [frãs'eʃ] |

| Sweden | Suécia (f) | [su'ɛsiɐ] |
| Swede (masc.) | sueco (m) | [su'ɛku] |
| Swede (fem.) | sueca (f) | [su'ɛkɐ] |
| Swedish (adj) | sueco | [su'ɛku] |

| Switzerland | Suíça (f) | [su'isɐ] |
| Swiss (masc.) | suíço (m) | [su'isu] |
| Swiss (fem.) | suíça (f) | [su'isɐ] |
| Swiss (adj) | suíço | [su'isu] |

| Scotland | Escócia (f) | [əʃk'ɔsiɐ] |
| Scottish (masc.) | escocês (m) | [əʃkus'eʃ] |
| Scottish (fem.) | escocesa (f) | [əʃkus'ezɐ] |
| Scottish (adj) | escocês | [əʃkus'eʃ] |

| Vatican | Vaticano (m) | [vɐtik'ɐnu] |
| Liechtenstein | Liechtenstein (m) | [lieʃtẽʃtɐ'jn] |
| Luxembourg | Luxemburgo (m) | [luʃẽb'urgu] |
| Monaco | Mónaco (m) | [m'ɔnɐku] |

## 235. Central and Eastern Europe

| Albania | Albânia (f) | [alb'ɐniɐ] |
| Albanian (masc.) | albanês (m) | [albɐn'eʃ] |
| Albanian (fem.) | albanesa (f) | [albɐn'ezɐ] |
| Albanian (adj) | albanês | [albɐn'eʃ] |

| Bulgaria | Bulgária (f) | [bulg'ariɐ] |
| Bulgarian (masc.) | búlgaro (m) | [b'ulgɐru] |
| Bulgarian (fem.) | búlgara (f) | [b'ulgɐrɐ] |
| Bulgarian (adj) | búlgaro | [b'ulgɐru] |

| Hungary | Hungria (f) | [ũgr'iɐ] |
| Hungarian (masc.) | húngaro (m) | ['ũgɐru] |
| Hungarian (fem.) | húngara (f) | ['ũgɐrɐ] |
| Hungarian (adj) | húngaro | ['ũgɐru] |

| Latvia | Letónia (f) | [lɐt'ɔniɐ] |
| Latvian (masc.) | letão (m) | [lɐt'ãu] |
| Latvian (fem.) | letã (f) | [lɐt'ã] |
| Latvian (adj) | letão | [lɐt'ãu] |

| Lithuania | Lituânia (f) | [litu'ɐniɐ] |
| Lithuanian (masc.) | lituano (m) | [litu'ɐnu] |
| Lithuanian (fem.) | lituana (f) | [litu'ɐnɐ] |
| Lithuanian (adj) | lituano | [litu'ɐnu] |

| Poland | Polónia (f) | [pul'ɔniɐ] |
| Pole (masc.) | polaco (m) | [pul'aku] |
| Pole (fem.) | polaca (f) | [pul'akɐ] |

| Polish (adj) | polaco | [pul'aku] |
|---|---|---|
| Romania | Roménia (f) | [ʀum'ɛniɐ] |
| Romanian (masc.) | romeno (m) | [ʀum'enu] |
| Romanian (fem.) | romena (f) | [ʀum'enɐ] |
| Romanian (adj) | romeno | [ʀum'enu] |

| Serbia | Sérvia (f) | [s'ɛrviɐ] |
|---|---|---|
| Serbian (masc.) | sérvio (m) | [s'ɛrviu] |
| Serbian (fem.) | sérvia (f) | [s'ɛrviɐ] |
| Serbian (adj) | sérvio | [s'ɛrviu] |

| Slovakia | Eslováquia (f) | [əʒlɔv'akiɐ] |
|---|---|---|
| Slovak (masc.) | eslovaco (m) | [əʒlɔv'aku] |
| Slovak (fem.) | eslovaca (f) | [əʒlɔv'akɐ] |
| Slovak (adj) | eslovaco | [əʒlɔv'aku] |

| Croatia | Croácia (f) | [kru'asiɐ] |
|---|---|---|
| Croatian (masc.) | croata (m) | [kru'atɐ] |
| Croatian (fem.) | croata (f) | [kru'atɐ] |
| Croatian (adj) | croata | [kru'atɐ] |

| Czech Republic | República (f) Checa | [ʀɛp'ublikɐ ʃ'ɛkɐ] |
|---|---|---|
| Czech (masc.) | checo (m) | [ʃ'ɛku] |
| Czech (fem.) | checa (f) | [ʃ'ɛkɐ] |
| Czech (adj) | checo | [ʃ'ɛku] |

| Estonia | Estónia (f) | [əʃt'ɔniɐ] |
|---|---|---|
| Estonian (masc.) | estónio (m) | [əʃt'ɔniu] |
| Estonian (fem.) | estónia (f) | [əʃt'ɔniɐ] |
| Estonian (adj) | estónio (m) | [əʃt'ɔniu] |

| Bosnia-Herzegovina | Bósnia e Herzegovina (f) | [b'ɔʒniɐ i ɛrzɛgɔv'inɐ] |
|---|---|---|
| Macedonia | Macedónia (f) | [mɐsəd'ɔniɐ] |
| Slovenia | Eslovénia (f) | [əʒlɔv'ɛniɐ] |
| Montenegro | Montenegro (m) | [mõtən'egru] |

## 236. Former USSR countries

| Azerbaijan | Azerbaijão (m) | [ɐzərbajʒ'ãu] |
|---|---|---|
| Azerbaijani (masc.) | azeri (m) | [ɐzər'i] |
| Azerbaijani (fem.) | azeri (f) | [ɐzər'i] |
| Azerbaijani (adj) | azeri, azerbaijano | [ɐzər'i], [ɐzərbajʒ'enu] |

| Armenia | Arménia (f) | [ɐrm'ɛniɐ] |
|---|---|---|
| Armenian (masc.) | arménio (m) | [ɐrm'ɛniu] |
| Armenian (fem.) | arménia (f) | [ɐrm'ɛniɐ] |
| Armenian (adj) | arménio | [ɐrm'ɛniu] |

| Belarus | Bielorrússia (f) | [biɛlɔʀ'usiɐ] |
|---|---|---|
| Belarusian (masc.) | bielorrusso (m) | [biɛlɔʀ'usu] |

| | | |
|---|---|---|
| Belarusian (fem.) | bielorrussa (f) | [biɛlɔʀ'usɐ] |
| Belarusian (adj) | bielorrusso | [biɛlɔʀ'usu] |
| | | |
| Georgia | Geórgia (f) | [ʒj'ɔrʒiɐ] |
| Georgian (masc.) | georgiano (m) | [ʒiɔrʒj'enu] |
| Georgian (fem.) | georgiana (f) | [ʒiɔrʒj'enɐ] |
| Georgian (adj) | georgiano | [ʒiɔrʒj'enu] |
| Kazakhstan | Cazaquistão (m) | [kɐzɐkiʃt'ãu] |
| Kazakh (masc.) | cazaque (m) | [kɐz'akə] |
| Kazakh (fem.) | cazaque (f) | [kɐz'akə] |
| Kazakh (adj) | cazaque | [kɐz'akə] |
| | | |
| Kirghizia | Quirguizistão (m) | [kirgiziʃt'ãu] |
| Kirghiz (masc.) | quirguiz (m) | [kirgu'iʃ] |
| Kirghiz (fem.) | quirguiza (f) | [kirg'izɐ] |
| Kirghiz (adj) | quirguiz | [kirgu'iʃ] |
| | | |
| Moldavia | Moldávia (f) | [mold'aviɐ] |
| Moldavian (masc.) | moldavo (m) | [mɔld'avu] |
| Moldavian (fem.) | moldava (f) | [mɔld'avɐ] |
| Moldavian (adj) | moldavo | [mɔld'avu] |
| Russia | Rússia (f) | [ʀ'usiɐ] |
| Russian (masc.) | russo (m) | [ʀ'usu] |
| Russian (fem.) | russa (f) | [ʀ'usɐ] |
| Russian (adj) | russo | [ʀ'usu] |
| | | |
| Tajikistan | Tajiquistão (m) | [tɐʒikiʃt'ãu] |
| Tajik (masc.) | tajique (m) | [tɐʒ'ikə] |
| Tajik (fem.) | tajique (f) | [tɐʒ'ikə] |
| Tajik (adj) | tajique | [tɐʒ'ikə] |
| | | |
| Turkmenistan | Turquemenistão (m) | [turkəməniʃt'ãu] |
| Turkmen (masc.) | turcomeno (m) | [turkum'enu] |
| Turkmen (fem.) | turcomena (f) | [turkum'enɐ] |
| Turkmenian (adj) | turcomeno | [turkum'enu] |
| | | |
| Uzbekistan | Uzbequistão (f) | [uʒbəkiʃt'ãu] |
| Uzbek (masc.) | uzbeque (m) | [uʒb'ɛkə] |
| Uzbek (fem.) | uzbeque (f) | [uʒb'ɛkə] |
| Uzbek (adj) | uzbeque | [uʒb'ɛkə] |
| | | |
| Ukraine | Ucrânia (f) | [ukr'eniɐ] |
| Ukrainian (masc.) | ucraniano (m) | [ukrɐnj'enu] |
| Ukrainian (fem.) | ucraniana (f) | [ukrɐnj'enɐ] |
| Ukrainian (adj) | ucraniano | [ukrɐnj'enu] |

## 237. Asia

| | | |
|---|---|---|
| Asia | Ásia (f) | ['aziɐ] |
| Asian (adj) | asiático | [ɐzj'atiku] |

| Vietnam | Vietname (m) | [viɛtn'ɛmə] |
| Vietnamese (masc.) | vietnamita (m) | [viɛtnɐm'itɐ] |
| Vietnamese (fem.) | vietnamita (f) | [viɛtnɐm'itɐ] |
| Vietnamese (adj) | vietnamita | [viɛtnɐm'itɐ] |

| India | Índia (f) | ['ĩdiɐ] |
| Indian (masc.) | indiano (m) | [ĩdj'ɐnu] |
| Indian (fem.) | indiana (f) | [ĩdj'ɐnɐ] |
| Indian (adj) | indiano, hindu | [ĩdj'ɐnu], [ĩd'u] |

| Israel | Israel (m) | [iʒʀɐ'ɛl] |
| Israeli (masc.) | israelita (m) | [iʒʀɐɛl'itɐ] |
| Israeli (fem.) | israelita (f) | [iʒʀɐɛl'itɐ] |
| Israeli (adj) | israelita | [iʒʀɐɛl'itɐ] |

| Jew (n) | judeu (m) | [ʒud'eu] |
| Jewess (n) | judia (f) | [ʒud'iɐ] |
| Jewish (adj) | judeu | [ʒud'eu] |

| China | China (f) | [ʃ'inɐ] |
| Chinese (masc.) | chinês (m) | [ʃin'eʃ] |
| Chinese (fem.) | chinesa (f) | [ʃin'ezɐ] |
| Chinese (adj) | chinês | [ʃin'eʃ] |

| Korean (masc.) | coreano (m) | [kurj'ɐnu] |
| Korean (fem.) | coreana (f) | [kurj'ɐnɐ] |
| Korean (adj) | coreano | [kurj'ɐnu] |

| Lebanon | Líbano (m) | [l'ibɐnu] |
| Lebanese (masc.) | libanês (m) | [libɐn'eʃ] |
| Lebanese (fem.) | libanesa (f) | [libɐn'ezɐ] |
| Lebanese (adj) | libanês | [libɐn'eʃ] |

| Mongolia | Mongólia (f) | [mõg'ɔliɐ] |
| Mongolian (masc.) | mongol (m) | [mõg'ɔl] |
| Mongolian (fem.) | mongol (f) | [mõg'ɔl] |
| Mongolian (adj) | mongol | [mõg'ɔl] |

| Malaysia | Malásia (f) | [mɐl'aziɐ] |
| Malaysian (masc.) | malaio (m) | [mɐl'aju] |
| Malaysian (fem.) | malaia (f) | [mɐl'ajɐ] |
| Malaysian (adj) | malaio | [mɐl'aju] |

| Pakistan | Paquistão (m) | [pɐkiʃt'ãu] |
| Pakistani (masc.) | paquistanês (m) | [pɐkiʃtɐn'eʃ] |
| Pakistani (fem.) | paquistanesa (f) | [pɐkiʃtɐn'ezɐ] |
| Pakistani (adj) | paquistanês | [pɐkiʃtɐn'eʃ] |

| Saudi Arabia | Arábia (f) Saudita | [ɐr'abiɐ saud'itɐ] |
| Arab (masc.) | árabe (m) | ['arɐbɐ] |
| Arab (fem.) | árabe (f) | ['arɐbɐ] |
| Arabian (adj) | árabe | ['arɐbɐ] |

239

| Thailand | Tailândia (f) | [tajlˈãdiɐ] |
| Thai (masc.) | tailandês (m) | [tajlãdˈeʃ] |
| Thai (fem.) | tailandesa (f) | [tajlãdˈezɐ] |
| Thai (adj) | tailandês | [tajlãdˈeʃ] |

| Taiwan | Taiwan (m) | [tajwˈɐn] |
| Taiwanese (masc.) | taiwanês (m) | [tajwɐnˈeʃ] |
| Taiwanese (fem.) | taiwanesa (f) | [tajwɐnˈezɐ] |
| Taiwanese (adj) | taiwanês | [tajwɐnˈeʃ] |

| Turkey | Turquia (f) | [turkˈiɐ] |
| Turk (masc.) | turco (m) | [tˈurku] |
| Turk (fem.) | turca (f) | [tˈurkɐ] |
| Turkish (adj) | turco | [tˈurku] |

| Japan | Japão (m) | [ʒɐpˈãu] |
| Japanese (masc.) | japonês (m) | [ʒɐpunˈeʃ] |
| Japanese (fem.) | japonesa (f) | [ʒɐpunˈezɐ] |
| Japanese (adj) | japonês | [ʒɐpunˈeʃ] |

| Afghanistan | Afeganistão (m) | [ɐfɐɡɐniʃtˈãu] |
| Bangladesh | Bangladesh (m) | [bãɡlɐdˈɛʃ] |
| Indonesia | Indonésia (f) | [ĩdɔnˈɛziɐ] |
| Jordan | Jordânia (f) | [ʒurdˈɐniɐ] |

| Iraq | Iraque (m) | [irˈakɐ] |
| Iran | Irão (m) | [irˈãu] |
| Cambodia | Camboja (f) | [kãbˈɔdʒɐ] |
| Kuwait | Kuwait (m) | [kuwˈajt] |

| Laos | Laos (m) | [lɐuʃ] |
| Myanmar | Mianmar (m), Birmânia (f) | [miãmˈar], [birmˈɐniɐ] |
| Nepal | Nepal (m) | [nɐpˈal] |
| United Arab Emirates | Emirados Árabes Unidos (m pl) | [emirˈaduʃ ˈarɐbɐʃ unˈiduʃ] |

| Syria | Síria (f) | [sˈiriɐ] |
| Palestine | Palestina (f) | [pɐlɐʃtˈinɐ] |
| South Korea | Coreia do Sul (f) | [kurˈɐjɐ du sul] |
| North Korea | Coreia do Norte (f) | [kurˈɐjɐ du nˈɔrtɐ] |

## 238. North America

| United States of America | Estados Unidos da América (m pl) | [ɐʃtˈaduʃ unˈiduʃ dɐ ɐmˈɛrikɐ] |
| American (masc.) | americano (m) | [ɐmɐrikˈɐnu] |
| American (fem.) | americana (f) | [ɐmɐrikˈɐnɐ] |
| American (adj) | americano | [ɐmɐrikˈɐnu] |
| Canada | Canadá (m) | [kɐnɐdˈa] |
| Canadian (masc.) | canadiano (m) | [kɐnɐdjˈɐnu] |

| Canadian (fem.) | canadiana (f) | [kɐnɐdjˈɐnɐ] |
| Canadian (adj) | canadiano | [kɐnɐdjˈɐnu] |

| Mexico | México (m) | [mˈɛʃiku] |
| Mexican (masc.) | mexicano (m) | [mɐʃikˈɐnu] |
| Mexican (fem.) | mexicana (f) | [mɐʃikˈɐnɐ] |
| Mexican (adj) | mexicano | [mɐʃikˈɐnu] |

## 239. Central and South America

| Argentina | Argentina (f) | [ɐɾʒẽtˈinɐ] |
| Argentinian (masc.) | argentino (m) | [ɐɾʒẽtˈinu] |
| Argentinian (fem.) | argentina (f) | [ɐɾʒẽtˈinɐ] |
| Argentinian (adj) | argentino | [ɐɾʒẽtˈinu] |

| Brazil | Brasil (m) | [brɐzˈil] |
| Brazilian (masc.) | brasileiro (m) | [brɐzilˈejɾu] |
| Brazilian (fem.) | brasileira (f) | [brɐzilˈejɾɐ] |
| Brazilian (adj) | brasileiro | [brɐzilˈejɾu] |

| Colombia | Colômbia (f) | [kulˈõbiɐ] |
| Colombian (masc.) | colombiano (m) | [kulõbjˈɐnu] |
| Colombian (fem.) | colombiana (f) | [kulõbjˈɐnɐ] |
| Colombian (adj) | colombiano | [kulõbjˈɐnu] |

| Cuba | Cuba (f) | [kˈubɐ] |
| Cuban (masc.) | cubano (m) | [kubˈɐnu] |
| Cuban (fem.) | cubana (f) | [kubˈɐnɐ] |
| Cuban (adj) | cubano | [kubˈɐnu] |

| Chile | Chile (m) | [ʃˈilɐ] |
| Chilean (masc.) | chileno (m) | [ʃilˈenu] |
| Chilean (fem.) | chilena (f) | [ʃilˈenɐ] |
| Chilean (adj) | chileno | [ʃilˈenu] |

| Bolivia | Bolívia (f) | [bulˈiviɐ] |
| Venezuela | Venezuela (f) | [vɐnɐzuˈɛlɐ] |

| Paraguay | Paraguai (m) | [pɐɾɐguˈaj] |
| Peru | Peru (m) | [pɐɾˈu] |

| Suriname | Suriname (m) | [surinˈemɐ] |
| Uruguay | Uruguai (m) | [urugwˈaj] |
| Ecuador | Equador (m) | [ekwɐdˈoɾ] |

| The Bahamas | Bahamas, Baamas (f pl) | [baˈemɐʃ] |
| Haiti | Haiti (m) | [ajtˈi] |
| Dominican Republic | República (f) Dominicana | [ʀɛpˈublikɐ duminikˈɐnɐ] |
| Panama | Panamá (m) | [pɐnɐmˈa] |
| Jamaica | Jamaica (f) | [ʒɐmˈajkɐ] |

## 240. Africa

| Egypt | Egito (m) | [eʒ'itu] |
| Egyptian (masc.) | egípcio (m) | [eʒ'ipsiu] |
| Egyptian (fem.) | egípcia (f) | [eʒ'ipsiɐ] |
| Egyptian (adj) | egípcio | [eʒ'ipsiu] |

| Morocco | Marrocos | [mɐʀ'ɔkuʃ] |
| Moroccan (masc.) | marroquino (m) | [mɐʀuk'inu] |
| Moroccan (fem.) | marroquina (f) | [mɐʀuk'inɐ] |
| Moroccan (adj) | marroquino | [mɐʀuk'inu] |

| Tunisia | Tunísia (f) | [tun'iziɐ] |
| Tunisian (masc.) | tunisino (m) | [tuniz'inu] |
| Tunisian (fem.) | tunisina (f) | [tuniz'inɐ] |
| Tunisian (adj) | tunisino | [tuniz'inu] |

| Ghana | Gana (f) | [g'ɐnɐ] |
| Zanzibar | Zanzibar (m) | [zãzib'aɾ] |
| Kenya | Quénia (f) | [k'ɛniɐ] |
| Libya | Líbia (f) | [l'ibiɐ] |
| Madagascar | Madagáscar (m) | [mɐdɐg'aʃkaɾ] |

| Namibia | Namíbia (f) | [nɐm'ibiɐ] |
| Senegal | Senegal (m) | [sɐnɐg'al] |
| Tanzania | Tanzânia (f) | [tãz'eniɐ] |
| South Africa | África do Sul (f) | ['afrikɐ du sul] |

| African (masc.) | africano (m) | [ɐfrik'ɐnu] |
| African (fem.) | africana (f) | [ɐfrik'ɐnɐ] |
| African (adj) | africano | [ɐfrik'ɐnu] |

## 241. Australia. Oceania

| Australia | Austrália (f) | [auʃtr'aliɐ] |
| Australian (masc.) | australiano (m) | [auʃtrelj'ɐnu] |

| Australian (fem.) | australiana (f) | [auʃtrelj'ɐnɐ] |
| Australian (adj) | australiano | [auʃtrelj'ɐnu] |

| New Zealand | Nova Zelândia (f) | [n'ɔve zel'ãdiɐ] |
| New Zealander (masc.) | neozelandês (m) | [nɛɔzelãd'eʃ] |

| New Zealander (fem.) | neozelandesa (f) | [nɛɔzelãd'ezɐ] |
| New Zealand (as adj) | neozelandês | [nɛɔzelãd'eʃ] |

| Tasmania | Tasmânia (f) | [teʒm'eniɐ] |
| French Polynesia | Polinésia Francesa (f) | [pulin'ɛziɐ frãs'ezɐ] |

## 242. Cities

| Amsterdam | Amesterdão | [eməʃtɛrd'ãu] |
| Ankara | Ancara | [ăk'arɐ] |
| Athens | Atenas | [ɐt'enɐʃ] |
| Baghdad | Bagdade | [bɐgd'adə] |
| Bangkok | Banguecoque | [băgɐk'ɔkə] |
| Barcelona | Barcelona | [bɐrsəl'onɐ] |

| Beijing | Pequim | [pək'ĩ] |
| Beirut | Beirute | [bɐjr'utə] |
| Berlin | Berlim | [bɐrl'ĩ] |
| Bombay, Mumbai | Bombaim | [bõbɐ'ĩ] |
| Bonn | Bona | [b'ɔnɐ] |

| Bordeaux | Bordéus | [burd'ɛuʃ] |
| Bratislava | Bratislava | [bratiʒl'avɐ] |
| Brussels | Bruxelas | [bruʃ'ɛlɐʃ] |
| Bucharest | Bucareste | [bukɐr'ɛʃtə] |
| Budapest | Budapeste | [budɐp'ɛʃtə] |

| Cairo | Cairo | [k'ajru] |
| Calcutta | Calcutá | [kalkut'a] |
| Chicago | Chicago | [ʃik'agu] |
| Copenhagen | Copenhaga | [kɔpəɲ'agɐ] |

| Dar-es-Salaam | Dar es Salaam | [dar əʃ sɐl'aăm] |
| Delhi | Deli | [d'ɛli] |
| Dubai | Dubai | [dub'aj] |
| Dublin | Dublin, Dublim | [dubl'in], [dubl'ĩ] |
| Düsseldorf | Düsseldorf | [dusɛldɔrf] |

| Florence | Florença | [flor'ẽsɐ] |
| Frankfurt | Frankfurt | [fr'ăkfurt] |
| Geneva | Genebra | [ʒən'ɛbrɐ] |

| The Hague | Haia | ['ajɐ] |
| Hamburg | Hamburgo | [ăb'urgu] |
| Hanoi | Hanói | [ɐn'ɔj] |
| Havana | Havana | [ɐv'ɐnɐ] |
| Helsinki | Helsínquia | [ɛls'ĩkiɐ] |
| Hiroshima | Hiroshima | [iroʃ'imɐ] |
| Hong Kong | Hong Kong | [õg k'õg] |

| Istanbul | Istambul | [iʃtăb'ul] |
| Jerusalem | Jerusalém | [ʒəruzal'ẽj] |
| Kiev | Kiev | [kj'ɛv] |
| Kuala Lumpur | Kuala Lumpur | [ku'alɐ lũp'ur] |
| Lisbon | Lisboa | [liʒb'oɐ] |
| London | Londres | [l'õdrəʃ] |
| Los Angeles | Los Angeles | [luʃ ãʒ'eləʃ] |

| Lyons | Lyon | [li'ɔn] |
| Madrid | Madrid | [medr'id] |
| Marseille | Marselha | [mɐrs'ɐʎɐ] |
| Mexico City | Cidade do México | [sid'adə du m'ɛʃiku] |
| Miami | Miami | [mɐj'ami] |
| Montreal | Montreal | [mõtri'al] |
| Moscow | Moscovo | [muʃk'ovu] |
| Munich | Munique | [mun'ikə] |

| Nairobi | Nairóbi | [najr'ɔbi] |
| Naples | Nápoles | [n'apuləʃ] |
| New York | Nova York | [n'ɔvɐ j'ɔrk] |
| Nice | Nisa | [n'izɐ] |
| Oslo | Oslo | ['ɔʒlou] |
| Ottawa | Ottawa | [ɔt'auɐ] |

| Paris | Paris | [pɐr'iʃ] |
| Prague | Praga | [pr'agɐ] |
| Rio de Janeiro | Rio de Janeiro | [ʀ'iu də ʒɐn'ejru] |
| Rome | Roma | [ʀ'omɐ] |

| Saint Petersburg | São Petersburgo | [s'ãu pətɛrʒb'urgu] |
| Seoul | Seul | [sɛ'ul] |
| Shanghai | Xangai | [ʃãg'aj] |
| Singapore | Singapura | [sĩgɐp'urɐ] |
| Stockholm | Estocolmo | [əʃtuk'olmu] |
| Sydney | Sydney | [s'idnej] |

| Taipei | Taipé | [tajp'ɛ] |
| Tokyo | Tóquio | [t'ɔkiu] |
| Toronto | Toronto | [tur'õtu] |

| Venice | Veneza | [vɐn'ezɐ] |
| Vienna | Viena | [vj'enɐ] |
| Warsaw | Varsóvia | [vɐrs'ɔviɐ] |
| Washington | Washington | [w'ɐʃĩgtɔn] |

## 243. Politics. Government. Part 1

| politics | política (f) | [pul'itikɐ] |
| political (adj) | político | [pul'itiku] |
| politician | político (m) | [pul'itiku] |

| state (country) | estado (m) | [əʃt'adu] |
| citizen | cidadão (m) | [sided'ãu] |
| citizenship | cidadania (f) | [sidədɐn'iɐ] |

| national emblem | brasão (m) de armas | [brɐz'ãu də 'armɐʃ] |
| national anthem | hino (m) nacional | ['inu nɐsjun'al] |
| government | governo (m) | [guv'ernu] |

| head of state | Chefe (m) de Estado | [ʃˈɛfə də əʃtˈadu] |
| parliament | parlamento (m) | [pərlɐmˈẽtu] |
| party | partido (m) | [pərtˈidu] |

| capitalism | capitalismo (m) | [kɐpitɐlˈiʒmu] |
| capitalist (adj) | capitalista | [kɐpitɐlˈiʃtɐ] |

| socialism | socialismo (m) | [susiɐlˈiʒmu] |
| socialist (adj) | socialista | [susiɐlˈiʃtɐ] |

| communism | comunismo (m) | [kumunˈiʒmu] |
| communist (adj) | comunista | [kumunˈiʃtɐ] |
| communist (n) | comunista (m) | [kumunˈiʃtɐ] |

| democracy | democracia (f) | [dəmukrɐsˈiɐ] |
| democrat | democrata (m) | [dəmukrˈatɐ] |
| democratic (adj) | democrático | [dəmukrˈatiku] |
| Democratic party | Partido (m) Democrático | [pərtˈidu dəmukrˈatiku] |

| liberal (n) | liberal (m) | [libərˈal] |
| liberal (adj) | liberal | [libərˈal] |

| conservative (n) | conservador (m) | [kõsərvɐdˈor] |
| conservative (adj) | conservador | [kõsərvɐdˈor] |

| republic (n) | república (f) | [ʀɛpˈublikɐ] |
| republican (n) | republicano (m) | [ʀɛpublikˈɐnu] |
| Republican party | Partido (m) Republicano | [pərtˈidu ʀɛpublikˈɐnu] |

| poll, elections | eleições (f pl) | [ɐlɐjsˈõjʃ] |
| to elect (vt) | eleger (vt) | [ɐləʒˈer] |

| elector, voter | eleitor (m) | [ɐlɐjtˈor] |
| election campaign | campanha (f) eleitoral | [kãpˈɐɲɐ ɐlɐjturˈal] |

| voting (n) | votação (f) | [vutɐsˈãu] |
| to vote (vi) | votar (vi) | [vutˈar] |
| suffrage, right to vote | direito (m) de voto | [dirˈɐjtu də vˈɔtu] |

| candidate | candidato (m) | [kãdidˈatu] |
| to be a candidate | candidatar-se (vi) | [kãdidɐtˈarsə] |
| campaign | campanha (f) | [kãpˈɐɲɐ] |

| opposition (as adj) | da oposição | [də ɔpuzisˈãu] |
| opposition (n) | oposição (f) | [ɔpuzisˈãu] |

| visit | visita (f) | [vizˈitɐ] |
| official visit | visita (f) oficial | [vizˈitɐ ɔfisjˈal] |
| international (adj) | internacional | [ĩtərnɐsiunˈal] |

| negotiations | negociações (f pl) | [nəgusiɐsˈõjʃ] |
| to negotiate (vi) | negociar (vi) | [nəgusjˈar] |

## 244. Politics. Government. Part 2

| | | |
|---|---|---|
| society | sociedade (f) | [susiɛd'adə] |
| constitution | constituição (f) | [kõʃtituis'ãu] |
| power (political control) | poder (m) | [pud'er] |
| corruption | corrupção (f) | [kuʀups'ãu] |

| | | |
|---|---|---|
| law (justice) | lei (f) | [lɐj] |
| legal (legitimate) | legal | [ləg'al] |

| | | |
|---|---|---|
| justice (fairness) | justiça (f) | [ʒuʃt'isə] |
| just (fair) | justo | [ʒ'uʃtu] |

| | | |
|---|---|---|
| committee | comité (m) | [kumit'ɛ] |
| bill (draft law) | projeto-lei (m) | [pruʒ'ɛtu l'ɐj] |
| budget | orçamento (m) | [ɔrsɐm'ẽtu] |
| policy | política (f) | [pul'itikə] |
| reform | reforma (f) | [ʀəf'ɔrmə] |
| radical (adj) | radical | [ʀɐdik'al] |

| | | |
|---|---|---|
| power (strength, force) | força (f) | [f'ɔrsə] |
| powerful (adj) | poderoso | [pudər'ozu] |
| supporter | partidário (m) | [pɐrtid'ariu] |
| influence | influência (f) | [ĩflu'ẽsiə] |

| | | |
|---|---|---|
| regime (e.g., military ~) | regime (m) | [ʀəʒ'imə] |
| conflict | conflito (m) | [kõfl'itu] |
| conspiracy (plot) | conspiração (f) | [kõʃpiʀəs'ãu] |
| provocation | provocação (f) | [pruvukəs'ãu] |

| | | |
|---|---|---|
| to overthrow (regime, etc.) | derrubar (vt) | [dəʀub'ar] |
| overthrow (of government) | derrube (m), queda (f) | [dəʀ'ubə], [k'ɛdə] |
| revolution | revolução (f) | [ʀəvulus'ãu] |

| | | |
|---|---|---|
| coup d'état | golpe (m) de Estado | [g'ɔlpə də əʃt'adu] |
| military coup | golpe (m) militar | [g'ɔlpə milit'ar] |

| | | |
|---|---|---|
| crisis | crise (f) | [kr'izə] |
| economic recession | recessão (f) económica | [ʀəsəs'ãu ekun'ɔmikə] |
| demonstrator (protester) | manifestante (m) | [mɐnifəʃt'ãtə] |
| demonstration | manifestação (f) | [mɐnifəʃtəs'ãu] |
| martial law | lei (f) marcial | [lɐj mɐrsj'al] |
| military base | base (f) militar | [b'azə milit'ar] |

| | | |
|---|---|---|
| stability | estabilidade (f) | [əʃtəbilid'adə] |
| stable (adj) | estável | [əʃt'avɛl] |

| | | |
|---|---|---|
| exploitation | exploração (f) | [əʃpluʀəs'ãu] |
| to exploit (workers) | explorar (vt) | [əʃplur'ar] |
| racism | racismo (m) | [ʀas'iʒmu] |
| racist | racista (m) | [ʀas'iʃtə] |

| fascism | fascismo (m) | [feʃsˈiʒmu] |
| fascist | fascista (m) | [feʃsˈiʃtɐ] |

## 245. Countries. Miscellaneous

| foreigner | estrangeiro (m) | [əʃtrãʒˈejru] |
| foreign (adj) | estrangeiro | [əʃtrãʒˈejru] |
| abroad (adv) | no estrangeiro | [nu əʃtrãʒˈejru] |

| emigrant | emigrante (m) | [emigrˈãtə] |
| emigration | emigração (f) | [emigrɐsˈãu] |
| to emigrate (vi) | emigrar (vi) | [emigrˈar] |

| the West | Ocidente (m) | [ɔsidˈẽtə] |
| the East | Oriente (m) | [ɔrjˈẽtə] |
| the Far East | Extremo Oriente (m) | [əʃtrˈemu ɔrjˈẽtə] |

| civilization | civilização (f) | [sivilizɐsˈãu] |
| humanity (mankind) | humanidade (f) | [umɐnidˈadə] |

| world (earth) | mundo (m) | [mˈũdu] |
| peace | paz (f) | [paʒ] |
| worldwide (adj) | mundial | [mũdjˈal] |

| homeland | pátria (f) | [pˈatriɐ] |
| people (population) | povo (m) | [pˈovu] |
| population | população (f) | [pupulɐsˈãu] |
| people (a lot of ~) | gente (f) | [ʒˈẽtə] |

| nation (people) | nação (f) | [nɐsˈãu] |
| generation | geração (f) | [ʒɛrɐsˈãu] |

| territory (area) | território (m) | [tərritˈɔriu] |
| region | região (f) | [ʀəʒjˈãu] |
| state (part of a country) | estado (m) | [əʃtˈadu] |

| tradition | tradição (f) | [trɐdisˈãu] |
| custom (tradition) | costume (m) | [kuʃtˈumə] |
| ecology | ecologia (f) | [ɛkuluʒˈiɐ] |

| Indian (Native American) | índio (m) | [ˈĩdiu] |
| Gipsy (masc.) | cigano (m) | [sigˈɐnu] |
| Gipsy (fem.) | cigana (f) | [sigˈɐnɐ] |
| Gipsy (adj) | cigano | [sigˈɐnu] |

| empire | império (m) | [ĩpˈɛriu] |
| colony | colónia (f) | [kulˈɔniɐ] |
| slavery | escravidão (f) | [əʃkrɐvidˈãu] |
| invasion | invasão (f) | [ĩvazˈãu] |
| famine | fome (f) | [fˈomə] |

## 246. Major religious groups. Confessions

| | | |
|---|---|---|
| religion | religião (f) | [Rəliʒj'ãu] |
| religious (adj) | religioso | [Rəliʒj'ozu] |
| | | |
| faith, belief | crença (f) | [kr'ẽsɐ] |
| to believe (in God) | crer (vt) | [krer] |
| believer | crente (m) | [kr'ẽtə] |
| | | |
| atheism | ateísmo (m) | [ɐte'iʒmu] |
| atheist | ateu (m) | [ɐt'eu] |
| | | |
| Christianity | cristianismo (m) | [kriʃtiɐn'iʒmu] |
| Christian (n) | cristão (m) | [kriʃt'ãu] |
| Christian (adj) | cristão | [kriʃt'ãu] |
| | | |
| Catholicism | catolicismo (m) | [kɐtulis'iʒmu] |
| Catholic (n) | católico (m) | [kɐt'ɔliku] |
| Catholic (adj) | católico | [kɐt'ɔliku] |
| | | |
| Protestantism | protestantismo (m) | [prutəʃtãt'iʒmu] |
| Protestant Church | Igreja (f) Protestante | [igr'eʒɐ prutəʃt'ãtə] |
| Protestant | protestante (m) | [prutəʃt'ãtə] |
| | | |
| Orthodoxy | ortodoxia (f) | [ɔrtɔdɔks'iɐ] |
| Orthodox Church | Igreja (f) Ortodoxa | [igr'eʒɐ ɔrtɔd'ɔksɐ] |
| Orthodox | ortodoxo (m) | [ɔrtɔd'ɔksu] |
| | | |
| Presbyterianism | presbiterianismo (m) | [prəʒbitəriɐn'iʒmu] |
| Presbyterian Church | Igreja (f) Presbiteriana | [igr'eʒɐ prəʒbitərj'enɐ] |
| Presbyterian (n) | presbiteriano (m) | [prəʒbitərj'enu] |
| | | |
| Lutheranism | Igreja (f) Luterana | [igr'eʒɐ lutər'enɐ] |
| Lutheran (n) | luterano (m) | [lutər'enu] |
| | | |
| Baptist Church | Igreja (f) Batista | [igr'eʒɐ bat'iʃtə] |
| Baptist (n) | batista (m) | [bat'iʃtə] |
| | | |
| Anglican Church | Igreja (f) Anglicana | [igr'eʒɐ ãglik'enɐ] |
| Anglican (n) | anglicano (m) | [ãglik'enu] |
| Mormonism | mormonismo (m) | [murmun'iʒmu] |
| Mormon (n) | mórmon (m) | [m'ɔrmɔn] |
| | | |
| Judaism | Judaísmo (m) | [ʒudɐ'iʒmu] |
| Jew (n) | judeu (m) | [ʒud'eu] |
| | | |
| Buddhism | budismo (m) | [bud'iʒmu] |
| Buddhist (n) | budista (m) | [bud'iʃtə] |
| | | |
| Hinduism | hinduísmo (m) | [ĩdu'iʒmu] |
| Hindu (n) | hindu (m) | [ĩd'u] |

| Islam | Islão (m) | [iʒl'ãu] |
| Muslim (n) | muçulmano (m) | [musulm'enu] |
| Muslim (adj) | muçulmano | [musulm'enu] |

| Shiah Islam | Xiismo (m) | [ʃi'iʒmu] |
| Shiite (n) | xiita (m) | [ʃi'ite] |
| Sunni Islam | sunismo (m) | [sun'iʒmu] |
| Sunnite (n) | sunita (m) | [sun'ite] |

## 247. Religions. Priests

| priest | padre (m) | [p'adre] |
| the Pope | Papa (m) | [p'ape] |

| monk, friar | monge (m) | [m'õʒe] |
| nun | freira (f) | [fr'ejre] |
| pastor | pastor (m) | [peʃt'or] |

| abbot | abade (m) | [eb'ade] |
| vicar (parish priest) | vigário (m) | [vig'ariu] |
| bishop | bispo (m) | [b'iʃpu] |
| cardinal | cardeal (m) | [kerdj'al] |

| preacher | pregador (m) | [preged'or] |
| preaching | sermão (m) | [serm'ãu] |
| parishioners | paroquianos (pl) | [perukj'enuʃ] |

| believer | crente (m) | [kr'ẽte] |
| atheist | ateu (m) | [et'eu] |

## 248. Faith. Christianity. Islam

| Adam | Adão | [ed'ãu] |
| Eve | Eva | ['eve] |

| God | Deus (m) | [d'euʃ] |
| the Lord | Senhor (m) | [seɲ'or] |
| the Almighty | Todo Poderoso (m) | [t'odu puder'ozu] |

| sin | pecado (m) | [pek'adu] |
| to sin (vi) | pecar (vi) | [pek'ar] |
| sinner (masc.) | pecador (m) | [peked'or] |
| sinner (fem.) | pecadora (f) | [peked'ore] |

| hell | inferno (m) | [ĩf'ɛrnu] |
| paradise | paraíso (m) | [pere'izu] |
| Jesus | Jesus | [ʒez'uʃ] |
| Jesus Christ | Jesus Cristo | [ʒez'uʃ kr'iʃtu] |

| the Holy Spirit | Espírito (m) Santo | [əʃp'iritu s'ãtu] |
| the Savior | Salvador (m) | [salvɐd'or] |
| the Virgin Mary | Virgem Maria (f) | [v'irʒẽj mɐr'iɐ] |

| the Devil | Diabo (m) | [dj'abu] |
| devil's (adj) | diabólico | [diɐb'ɔliku] |
| Satan | Satanás (m) | [sɐtɐn'aʃ] |
| satanic (adj) | satânico | [sɐt'ɐniku] |

| angel | anjo (m) | ['ãʒu] |
| guardian angel | anjo (m) da guarda | ['ãʒu dɐ gu'ardɐ] |
| angelic (adj) | angélico | [ãʒ'ɛliku] |

| apostle | apóstolo (m) | [ɐp'ɔʃtulu] |
| archangel | arcanjo (m) | [ɐrk'ãʒu] |
| the Antichrist | anticristo (m) | [ãtikr'iʃtu] |

| Church | Igreja (f) | [igr'eʒɐ] |
| Bible | Bíblia (f) | [b'ibliɐ] |
| biblical (adj) | bíblico | [b'ibliku] |

| Old Testament | Velho Testamento (m) | [v'ɛʎu tɐʃtem'ẽtu] |
| New Testament | Novo Testamento (m) | [n'ovu tɐʃtem'ẽtu] |
| Gospel | Evangelho (m) | [evãʒ'ɛʎu] |
| Holy Scripture | Sagradas Escrituras (f pl) | [sɐgr'adɐʃ əʃkrit'urɐʃ] |
| heaven | Céu (m) | [s'ɛu] |

| Commandment | mandamento (m) | [mãdɐm'ẽtu] |
| prophet | profeta (m) | [pruf'ɛtɐ] |
| prophecy | profecia (f) | [prufɐs'iɐ] |

| Allah | Alá | [al'a] |
| Mohammed | Maomé | [maum'ɛ] |
| the Koran | Corão, Alcorão (m) | [kur'ãu], [alkur'ãu] |

| mosque | mesquita (f) | [məʃk'itɐ] |
| mullah | mulá (m) | [mul'a] |
| prayer | oração (f) | [ɔrɐs'ãu] |
| to pray (vi, vt) | rezar, orar (vi) | [ʀɐz'ar], [ɔr'ar] |

| pilgrimage | peregrinação (f) | [pərəgrinɐs'ãu] |
| pilgrim | peregrino (m) | [pərəgr'inu] |
| Mecca | Meca (f) | [m'ɛkɐ] |

| church | igreja (f) | [igr'eʒɐ] |
| temple | templo (m) | [t'ẽplu] |
| cathedral | catedral (f) | [kɐtɐdr'al] |
| Gothic (adj) | gótico | [g'ɔtiku] |
| synagogue | sinagoga (f) | [sinɐg'ɔgɐ] |
| mosque | mesquita (f) | [məʃk'itɐ] |
| chapel | capela (f) | [kɐp'ɛlɐ] |
| abbey | abadia (f) | [ɐbɐd'iɐ] |

| convent | convento (m) | [kõv'ẽtu] |
| monastery | mosteiro (m) | [muʃt'ejɾu] |

| bell (in church) | sino (m) | [s'inu] |
| bell tower | campanário (m) | [kãpɐn'aɾiu] |
| to ring (ab. bells) | repicar (vi) | [ʀəpik'aɾ] |

| cross | cruz (f) | [kɾuʃ] |
| cupola (roof) | cúpula (f) | [k'upulɐ] |
| icon | ícone (m) | ['ikɔnə] |

| soul | alma (f) | ['almɐ] |
| fate (destiny) | destino (m) | [dəʃt'inu] |
| evil (n) | mal (m) | [mal] |
| good (n) | bem (m) | [bẽj] |

| vampire | vampiro (m) | [vãp'iɾu] |
| witch (sorceress) | bruxa (f) | [bɾ'uʃɐ] |
| demon | demónio (m) | [dəm'ɔniu] |
| devil | diabo (m) | [dj'abu] |
| spirit | espírito (m) | [əʃp'iɾitu] |

| redemption (giving us ~) | redenção (f) | [ʀədẽs'ãu] |
| to redeem (vt) | redimir (vt) | [ʀədim'iɾ] |

| church service, mass | missa (f) | [m'isɐ] |
| to say mass | celebrar a missa | [sələbɾ'aɾ ɐ m'isɐ] |
| confession | confissão (f) | [kõfis'ãu] |
| to confess (vi) | confessar-se (vp) | [kõfəs'arsə] |

| saint (n) | santo (m) | [s'ãtu] |
| sacred (holy) | sagrado | [səgɾ'adu] |
| holy water | água (f) benta | ['aguɐ b'ẽtɐ] |

| ritual (n) | ritual (m) | [ʀitu'al] |
| ritual (adj) | ritual | [ʀitu'al] |
| sacrifice | sacrifício (m) | [səkɾif'isiu] |

| superstition | superstição (f) | [supəɾʃtis'ãu] |
| superstitious (adj) | supersticioso | [supəɾʃtisj'ozu] |
| afterlife | vida (f) depois da morte | [v'idɐ dəp'ojʃ dɐ m'ɔrtɐ] |
| eternal life | vida (f) eterna | [v'idɐ et'ɛrnɐ] |

# MISCELLANEOUS

## 249. Various useful words

|  |  |  |
|---|---|---|
| background (green ~) | fundo (m) | [f'ũdu] |
| balance (of situation) | equilíbrio (m) | [ekil'ibriu] |
| barrier (obstacle) | barreira (f) | [bɐr'ejrɐ] |
| base (basis) | base (f) | [b'azə] |
| beginning | começo (m) | [kum'esu] |
| category | categoria (f) | [kɐtəgur'iɐ] |
| cause (reason) | causa (f) | [k'auzɐ] |
| choice | variedade (f) | [vɐriɛd'adə] |
| coincidence | coincidência (f) | [kuĩsid'ẽsiɐ] |
| comfortable (~ chair) | cómodo | [k'ɔmudu] |
| comparison | comparação (f) | [kõpɐrɐs'ãu] |
| compensation | compensação (f) | [kõpẽsɐs'ãu] |
| degree (extent, amount) | grau (m) | [gr'au] |
| development | desenvolvimento (m) | [dəzẽvolvim'ẽtu] |
| difference | diferença (f) | [difər'ẽsɐ] |
| effect (e.g., of drugs) | efeito (m) | [ef'ejtu] |
| effort (exertion) | esforço (m) | [əʃf'orsu] |
| element | elemento (m) | [eləm'ẽtu] |
| end (finish) | fim (m) | [fĩ] |
| example (illustration) | exemplo (m) | [ez'ẽplu] |
| fact | facto (m) | [f'aktu] |
| frequent (adj) | frequente | [frəku'ẽtə] |
| growth (development) | crescimento (m) | [krəʃsim'ẽtu] |
| help | ajuda (f) | [ɐʒ'udə] |
| ideal | ideal | [idj'al] |
| kind (sort, type) | tipo (m) | [t'ipu] |
| labyrinth | labirinto (m) | [lɐbir'ĩtu] |
| mistake, error | erro (m) | ['eʀu] |
| moment | momento (m) | [mum'ẽtu] |
| object (thing) | objeto (m) | [ɔbʒ'ɛtu] |
| obstacle | obstáculo (m) | [ɔbʃt'akulu] |
| original (original copy) | original (m) | [ɔriʒin'al] |
| part (~ of sth) | parte (f) | [p'artə] |
| particle, small part | partícula (f) | [pɐrt'ikulə] |
| pause (break) | pausa (f) | [p'auzɐ] |

| position | posição (f) | [puzis'ãu] |
| principle | princípio (m) | [prĩs'ipiu] |
| problem | problema (m) | [prubl'emɐ] |

| process | processo (m) | [prus'ɛsu] |
| progress | progresso (m) | [prugr'ɛsu] |
| property (quality) | propriedade (f) | [prupriɛd'adǝ] |
| reaction | reação (f) | [ʀias'ãu] |
| risk | risco (m) | [ʀ'iʃku] |

| secret | mistério (m) | [miʃt'ɛriu] |
| section (sector) | secção (f) | [sɛks'ãu] |
| series | série (f) | [s'ɛriǝ] |
| shape (outer form) | forma (f) | [f'ɔrmɐ] |
| situation | situação (f) | [situɐs'ãu] |

| solution | solução (f) | [sulus'ãu] |
| standard (adj) | padrão | [pɐdr'ãu] |
| standard (level of quality) | padrão (m) | [pɐdr'ãu] |
| stop (pause) | paragem (f) | [pɐr'aʒẽj] |
| style | estilo (m) | [ǝʃt'ilu] |
| system | sistema (m) | [siʃt'emɐ] |

| table (chart) | tabela (f) | [tɐb'ɛlɐ] |
| tempo, rate | ritmo (m) | [ʀ'itmu] |
| term (word, expression) | termo (m) | [t'ermu] |
| thing (object, item) | coisa (f) | [k'ojzɐ] |
| truth | verdade (f) | [vǝrd'adǝ] |
| turn (please wait your ~) | vez (f) | [veʒ] |
| type (sort, kind) | tipo (m) | [t'ipu] |

| urgent (adj) | urgente | [urʒ'ẽtǝ] |
| urgently (adv) | urgentemente | [urʒẽtǝm'ẽtǝ] |
| utility (usefulness) | utilidade (f) | [utilid'adǝ] |

| variant (alternative) | variante (f) | [vɐrj'ãtǝ] |
| way (means, method) | modo (m) | [m'ɔdu] |
| zone | zona (f) | [z'onɐ] |

## 250. Modifiers. Adjectives. Part 1

| additional (adj) | suplementar | [suplǝmẽt'ar] |
| ancient (~ civilization) | antigo | [ãt'igu] |
| artificial (adj) | artificial | [ɐrtifisj'al] |
| back, rear (adj) | de trás | [dǝ traʃ] |
| bad (adj) | mau | [m'au] |

| beautiful (~ palace) | belo | [b'ɛlu] |
| beautiful (person) | bonito | [bun'itu] |
| big (in size) | grande | [gr'ãdǝ] |

| bitter (taste) | amargo | [em'argu] |
| blind (sightless) | cego | [s'ɛgu] |
| calm, quiet (adj) | calmo | [k'almu] |
| careless (negligent) | descuidado | [dəʃkuid'adu] |
| caring (~ father) | carinhoso | [kɐriɲ'ozu] |
| central (adj) | central | [sẽtr'al] |

| cheap (adj) | barato | [bɐr'atu] |
| cheerful (adj) | alegre | [ɐl'ɛgrɐ] |
| children's (adj) | infantil | [ĩfɐ̃t'il] |
| civil (~ law) | civil | [siv'il] |

| clandestine (secret) | clandestino | [klãdəʃt'inu] |
| clean (free from dirt) | limpo | [l'ĩpu] |
| clear (explanation, etc.) | claro | [kl'aru] |
| clever (smart) | inteligente | [ĩtəliʒ'ẽtə] |
| close (near in space) | próximo | [pr'ɔsimu] |

| closed (adj) | fechado | [fəʃ'adu] |
| cloudless (sky) | desanuviado | [dəzɐnuvj'adu] |
| cold (drink, weather) | frio | [fr'iu] |
| compatible (adj) | compatível | [kõpɐt'ivɛl] |

| contented (adj) | contente | [kõt'ẽtə] |
| continuous (adj) | contínuo | [kõt'inuu] |
| continuous (incessant) | ininterrupto | [inĩtəʀ'uptu] |
| convenient (adj) | útil | ['util] |
| cool (weather) | fresco | [fr'eʃku] |

| dangerous (adj) | perigoso | [pɐrig'ozu] |
| dark (room) | escuro | [əʃk'uru] |
| dead (not alive) | morto | [m'ortu] |
| dense (fog, smoke) | denso | [d'ẽsu] |

| different (adj) | diferente | [difər'ẽtə] |
| difficult (decision) | difícil | [dif'isil] |
| difficult (problem, task) | difícil, complexo | [dif'isil], [kõpl'ɛksu |
| dim, faint (light) | fraco | [fr'aku] |
| dirty (not clean) | sujo | [s'uʒu] |

| distant (faraway) | remoto, longínquo | [ʀəm'ɔtu], [lõʒ'ĩkuu] |
| distant (in space) | distante | [diʃt'ãtə] |
| dry (clothes, etc.) | seco | [s'eku] |
| easy (not difficult) | fácil | [f'asil] |

| empty (glass, room) | vazio | [vɐz'iu] |
| exact (amount) | exato | [ez'atu] |
| excellent (adj) | excelente | [əksəl'ẽtə] |
| excessive (adj) | excessivo | [əʃsəs'ivu] |
| expensive (adj) | caro | [k'aru] |
| exterior (adj) | externo | [əʃt'ɛrnu] |
| fast (quick) | rápido | [ʀ'apidu] |

| fatty (food) | gordo | [g'ordu] |
| fertile (land, soil) | fértil | [f'ɛrtil] |

| flat (~ panel display) | plano | [pl'ɐnu] |
| even (e.g., ~ surface) | liso | [l'izu] |
| foreign (adj) | estrangeiro | [əʃtrãʒ'ejru] |
| fragile (china, glass) | frágil | [fr'aʒil] |
| free (at no cost) | gratuito, grátis | [grɐt'uitu], [gr'atiʃ] |

| free (unrestricted) | livre | [l'ivrə] |
| fresh (~ water) | doce | [d'osə] |
| fresh (e.g., ~ bread) | fresco | [fr'eʃku] |
| frozen (food) | congelado | [kõʒəl'adu] |
| full (completely filled) | cheio | [ʃ'eju] |

| good (book, etc.) | bom | [bõ] |
| good (kindhearted) | bondoso | [bõd'ozu] |
| grateful (adj) | agradecido | [ɐgredəs'idu] |
| happy (adj) | feliz | [fəl'iʃ] |
| hard (not soft) | duro | [d'uru] |
| heavy (in weight) | pesado | [pəz'adu] |
| hostile (adj) | hostil | [oʃt'il] |
| hot (adj) | quente | [k'ẽtə] |

| huge (adj) | enorme | [en'ɔrmə] |
| humid (adj) | húmido | ['umidu] |
| hungry (adj) | faminto | [fem'ĩtu] |
| ill (sick, unwell) | doente | [du'ẽtə] |
| immobile (adj) | imóvel | [im'ɔvɛl] |

| important (adj) | importante | [ĩpurt'ãtə] |
| impossible (adj) | impossível | [ĩpus'ivɛl] |
| incomprehensible | incompreensível | [ĩkõpriẽs'ivɛl] |
| indispensable (adj) | indispensável | [ĩdiʃpẽs'avɛl] |

| inexperienced (adj) | inexperiente | [inəʃpərj'ẽtə] |
| insignificant (adj) | insignificante | [ĩsignifik'ãtə] |
| interior (adj) | interno | [ĩt'ɛrnu] |
| joint (~ decision) | conjunto | [kõʒ'ũtu] |
| last (e.g., ~ week) | passado | [pɐs'adu] |

| last (final) | último | ['ultimu] |
| left (e.g., ~ side) | esquerdo | [əʃk'erdu] |
| legal (legitimate) | legal | [ləg'al] |
| light (in weight) | leve | [l'ɛvə] |
| light (pale color) | claro | [kl'aru] |

| limited (adj) | limitado | [limit'adu] |
| liquid (fluid) | líquido | [l'ikidu] |
| long (e.g., ~ way) | longo | [l'õgu] |
| loud (voice, etc.) | alto | ['altu] |
| low (voice) | baixo | [b'ajʃu] |

## 251. Modifiers. Adjectives. Part 2

| | | |
|---|---|---|
| main (principal) | principal | [prĩsip'al] |
| matt (paint) | mate, baço | [m'atə], [b'asu] |
| meticulous (job) | meticuloso | [mətikul'ozu] |
| mysterious (adj) | enigmático | [enigm'atiku] |
| narrow (street, etc.) | estreito | [əʃtr'ejtu] |

| | | |
|---|---|---|
| native (of country) | natal | [nɐt'al] |
| nearby (adj) | perto | [p'ɛrtu] |
| near-sighted (adj) | míope | [m'iupə] |
| necessary (adj) | necessário | [nəsəs'ariu] |

| | | |
|---|---|---|
| negative (~ response) | negativo | [nəget'ivu] |
| neighboring (adj) | vizinho | [viz'iɲu] |
| nervous (adj) | nervoso | [nərv'ozu] |
| new (adj) | novo | [n'ovu] |
| next (e.g., ~ week) | seguinte | [səg'ĩtə] |

| | | |
|---|---|---|
| nice (kind) | encantador | [ẽkãted'or] |
| nice (voice) | agradável | [egrɐd'avɛl] |
| normal (adj) | normal | [nɔrm'al] |
| not big (adj) | não muito grande | [n'ãu m'ujtu gr'ãdə] |

| | | |
|---|---|---|
| unclear (adj) | não é clara | [n'ãu ɛ kl'arɐ] |
| not difficult (adj) | não difícil | [n'ãu dif'isil] |
| obligatory (adj) | obrigatório | [ɔbriget'ɔriu] |
| old (house) | velho | [v'ɛʎu] |
| open (adj) | aberto | [ɐb'ɛrtu] |

| | | |
|---|---|---|
| opposite (adj) | contrário | [kõtr'ariu] |
| ordinary (usual) | comum, normal | [kum'ũ], [nɔrm'al] |
| original (unusual) | original | [ɔriʒin'al] |
| past (recent) | mais recente | [m'ajʃ ʀəs'ẽtə] |

| | | |
|---|---|---|
| permanent (adj) | permanente | [pərmɐn'ẽtə] |
| personal (adj) | pessoal | [pəsu'al] |
| polite (adj) | educado | [eduk'adu] |
| poor (not rich) | pobre | [p'ɔbrə] |
| possible (adj) | possível | [pus'ivɛl] |

| | | |
|---|---|---|
| destitute (extremely poor) | indigente | [ĩdiʒ'ẽtə] |
| present (current) | presente | [prəz'ẽtə] |
| previous (adj) | prévio | [pr'ɛviu] |
| principal (main) | principal | [prĩsip'al] |

| | | |
|---|---|---|
| private (~ jet) | privado | [priv'adu] |
| probable (adj) | provável | [pruv'avɛl] |
| public (open to all) | social | [susj'al] |
| punctual (person) | pontual | [põtu'al] |
| quiet (tranquil) | tranquilo | [trãku'ilu] |

| | | |
|---|---|---|
| rare (adj) | raro | [ʀ'aru] |
| raw (uncooked) | cru | [kru] |
| right (not left) | direito | [dir'ejtu] |
| right, correct (adj) | correto | [kuʀ'ɛtu] |
| | | |
| ripe (fruit) | maduro | [mɐd'uru] |
| risky (adj) | arriscado | [ɐʀiʃk'adu] |
| sad (~ look) | triste | [tr'iʃtə] |
| sad (depressing) | triste | [tr'iʃtə] |
| safe (not dangerous) | seguro | [səg'uru] |
| | | |
| salty (food) | salgado | [salg'adu] |
| satisfied (customer) | satisfeito | [sɐtiʃf'ejtu] |
| second hand (adj) | usado | [uz'adu] |
| shallow (water) | pouco fundo | [p'oku f'ũdu] |
| | | |
| sharp (blade, etc.) | afiado | [ɐfj'adu] |
| short (in length) | curto | [k'urtu] |
| short, short-lived (adj) | de curta duração | [də k'urtə durɐs'ãu] |
| significant (notable) | considerável | [kõsidər'avɛl] |
| similar (adj) | similar | [simil'ar] |
| | | |
| simple (easy) | simples | [s'ĩpləʃ] |
| skinny | magro | [m'agru] |
| thin (person) | magro | [m'agru] |
| small (in size) | pequeno | [pək'enu] |
| | | |
| smooth (surface) | liso | [l'izu] |
| soft (to touch) | mole | [m'ɔlə] |
| solid (~ wall) | sólido | [s'ɔlidu] |
| somber, gloomy (adj) | sombrio | [sõbr'iu] |
| sour (flavor, taste) | azedo | [ɐz'edu] |
| | | |
| spacious (house, etc.) | amplo | ['ãplu] |
| special (adj) | especial | [əʃpəsj'al] |
| straight (line, road) | reto | [ʀ'ɛtu] |
| strong (person) | forte | [f'ɔrtə] |
| | | |
| stupid (foolish) | burro, estúpido | [b'uʀu], [əʃt'upidu] |
| sunny (day) | de sol, ensolarado | [də sɔl], [ẽsulɐr'adu] |
| superb, perfect (adj) | soberbo, perfeito | [sub'erbu], [pərf'ejtu] |
| swarthy (adj) | moreno | [mur'enu] |
| sweet (sugary) | doce | [d'osə] |
| | | |
| tan (adj) | bronzeado | [brõzj'adu] |
| tasty (adj) | gostoso | [guʃt'ozu] |
| tender (affectionate) | terno | [t'ɛrnu] |
| the highest (adj) | superior | [supərj'or] |
| | | |
| the most important | o mais importante | [u m'ajʃ ĩpurt'ãtə] |
| the nearest | mais próximo | [m'ajʃ pr'ɔsimu] |
| the same, equal (adj) | igual | [igu'al] |

| | | |
|---|---|---|
| thick (e.g., ~ fog) | **cerrado** | [səʀˈadu] |
| thick (wall, slice) | **grosso** | [grˈosu] |
| | | |
| tight (~ shoes) | **apertado** | [ɐpɐrtˈadu] |
| tired (exhausted) | **cansado** | [kãsˈadu] |
| tiring (adj) | **cansativo** | [kãsɐtˈivu] |
| transparent (adj) | **transparente** | [trãʃpɐrˈẽtə] |
| | | |
| unique (exceptional) | **único** | [ˈuniku] |
| various (adj) | **diverso** | [divˈɛrsu] |
| warm (moderately hot) | **quente** | [kˈẽtə] |
| wet (e.g., ~ clothes) | **molhado** | [muʎˈadu] |
| whole (entire, complete) | **inteiro** | [ĩtˈejru] |
| wide (e.g., ~ road) | **largo** | [lˈargu] |
| young (adj) | **jovem** | [ʒˈɔvẽj] |

# MAIN 500 VERBS

## 252. Verbs A-C

| | | |
|---|---|---|
| to accompany (vt) | acompanhar (vt) | [ɐkõpeɲ'ar] |
| to accuse (vt) | acusar (vt) | [ɐkuz'ar] |
| to acknowledge (admit) | reconhecer (vt) | [ʀɐkuɲəs'er] |
| to act (take action) | agir (vi) | [ɐʒ'ir] |
| | | |
| to add (supplement) | acrescentar (vt) | [ɐkrəʃsɐ̃t'ar] |
| to address (speak to) | dirigir-se (vp) | [diriʒ'irsə] |
| to admire (vi) | admirar (vt) | [edmir'ar] |
| to advertise (vt) | publicitar (vt) | [publisit'ar] |
| | | |
| to advise (vt) | aconselhar (vt) | [ɐkõsəʎ'ar] |
| to affirm (insist) | afirmar (vt) | [ɐfirm'ar] |
| to agree (say yes) | concordar (vt) | [kõkurd'ar] |
| to allow (sb to do sth) | permitir (vt) | [pərmit'ir] |
| | | |
| to allude (vi) | aludir (vt) | [ɐlud'ir] |
| to amputate (vt) | amputar (vt) | [ãput'ar] |
| to answer (vi, vt) | responder (vt) | [ʀɐʃpõd'er] |
| to apologize (vi) | desculpar-se (vp) | [dəʃkulp'arsə] |
| | | |
| to appear (come into view) | aparecer (vi) | [ɐpɐrəs'er] |
| to applaud (vi, vt) | aplaudir (vi) | [ɐplaud'ir] |
| to appoint (assign) | nomear (vt) | [numj'ar] |
| to approach (come closer) | aproximar-se (vt) | [ɐprɔsim'arsə] |
| | | |
| to arrive (ab. train) | chegar (vi) | [ʃəg'ar] |
| to ask (~ sb to do sth) | pedir (vt) | [pəd'ir] |
| to aspire to ... | aspirar a ... | [ɐʃpir'ar ɐ] |
| to assist (help) | assistir (vt) | [ɐsiʃt'ir] |
| | | |
| to attack (mil.) | atacar (vt) | [ɐtɐk'ar] |
| to attain (objectives) | alcançar (vt) | [alkãs'ar] |
| to revenge (vt) | vingar-se (vp) | [vĩg'arsə] |
| to avoid (danger, task) | evitar (vt) | [evit'ar] |
| | | |
| to award (give medal to) | condecorar (vt) | [kõdəkur'ar] |
| to battle (vi) | combater (vi) | [kõbɐt'er] |
| to be (~ a teacher) | ser (vi) | [ser] |
| to be (~ on a diet) | estar (vi) | [əʃt'ar] |
| | | |
| to be (~ on the table) | estar | [əʃt'ar] |
| to be afraid | ter medo | [ter m'edu] |

| to be angry (with ...) | zangar-se com ... | [zãg'arsə kõ] |
| to be at war | guerrear (vt) | [gɛʀə'ar] |
| to be based (on ...) | basear-se (vp) | [bɐzj'arsə] |
| to be bored | aborrecer-se (vp) | [ɐbuʀəs'ersə] |
| to be convinced | estar convencido | [əʃt'ar kõvẽs'idu] |
| to be enough | bastar (vi) | [bɐʃt'ar] |
| to be envious | invejar (vt) | [ĩveʒ'ar] |
| to be indignant | indignar-se (vp) | [ĩdign'arsə] |
| to be interested in ... | interessar-se (vp) | [ĩtərəs'arsə] |
| | | |
| to be lying down | estar deitado | [əʃt'ar dejt'adu] |
| to be needed | ser preciso | [ser prəs'izu] |
| to be perplexed | estar perplexo | [əʃt'ar pərpl'ɛksu] |
| to be preserved | ser preservado | [ser prəzɐrv'adu] |
| | | |
| to be required | ser necessário | [ser nəsəs'ariu] |
| to be surprised | surpreender-se (vp) | [surpriẽd'ersə] |
| to be worried | preocupar-se (vp) | [priɔkup'arsə] |
| to beat (dog, person) | bater (vt) | [bɐt'er] |
| | | |
| to become (e.g., ~ old) | tornar-se (vp) | [turn'arsə] |
| to become pensive | ficar pensativo | [fik'ar pẽsɐt'ivu] |
| to behave (vi) | comportar-se (vp) | [kõpurt'arsə] |
| to believe (think) | crer (vt) | [kreɾ] |
| | | |
| to belong to ... | pertencer (vt) | [pərtẽs'er] |
| to berth (moor) | atracar (vi) | [ɐtʀɐk'ar] |
| to blind (other drivers) | cegar, ofuscar (vt) | [səg'ar], [ɔfuʃk'ar] |
| to blow (wind) | soprar (vi) | [supr'ar] |
| | | |
| to blush (vi) | ficar vermelho | [fik'ar vərm'ɐʎu] |
| to boast (vi) | gabar-se (vp) | [gɐb'arsə] |
| to borrow (money) | tomar emprestado (vt) | [tum'ar ẽprəʃt'adu] |
| to break (branch, toy, etc.) | quebrar (vt) | [kəbr'ar] |
| to breathe (vi) | respirar (vi) | [ʀəʃpir'ar] |
| to bring (sth) | trazer (vt) | [trɐz'er] |
| to burn (paper, logs) | queimar (vt) | [kejm'ar] |
| to buy (purchase) | comprar (vt) | [kõpr'ar] |
| | | |
| to call (for help) | chamar (vt) | [ʃem'ar] |
| to call (with one's voice) | chamar (vt) | [ʃem'ar] |
| to calm down (vt) | acalmar (vt) | [ɐkalm'ar] |
| can (v aux) | poder (v aux) | [pud'er] |
| | | |
| to cancel (call off) | cancelar (vt) | [kãsəl'ar] |
| to cast off | desatracar (vi) | [dəzɐtʀɐk'ar] |
| to catch (e.g., ~ a ball) | pegar (vt) | [pɐg'ar] |
| to catch sight (of ...) | avistar (vt) | [ɐviʃt'ar] |
| to cause ... | causar (vt) | [kauz'ar] |
| to change (~ one's opinion) | mudar (vt) | [mud'ar] |
| to change (exchange) | trocar, mudar (vt) | [truk'ar], [mud'ar] |

| | | |
|---|---|---|
| to charm (vt) | fascinar (vt) | [feʃsin'ar] |
| to choose (select) | escolher (vt) | [əʃkuʎ'er] |
| to chop off (with an ax) | cortar (vt) | [kurt'ar] |
| to clean (from dirt) | limpar (vt) | [lĩp'ar] |
| to clean (shoes, etc.) | limpar (vt) | [lĩp'ar] |
| | | |
| to clean (tidy) | arrumar, limpar (vt) | [ɐʀum'ar], [lĩp'ar] |
| to close (vt) | fechar (vt) | [fəʃ'ar] |
| to comb one's hair | pentear-se (vp) | [pẽtj'arsə] |
| to come down (the stairs) | descer (vi) | [dəʃs'er] |
| | | |
| to come in (enter) | entrar (vi) | [ẽtr'ar] |
| to come out (book) | sair (vi) | [sɐ'ir] |
| to compare (vt) | comparar (vt) | [kõpɐr'ar] |
| to compensate (vt) | compensar (vt) | [kõpẽs'ar] |
| | | |
| to compete (vi) | competir (vi) | [kõpət'ir] |
| to compile (~ a list) | fazer, elaborar (vt) | [fɐz'er], [elɐbur'ar] |
| to complain (vi, vt) | queixar-se (vp) | [kɐjʃ'arsə] |
| to complicate (vt) | complicar (vt) | [kõplik'ar] |
| | | |
| to compose (music, etc.) | compor (vt) | [kõp'or] |
| to compromise (reputation) | comprometer (vt) | [kõprumət'er] |
| to concentrate (vi) | concentrar-se (vp) | [kõsẽtr'arsə] |
| to confess (criminal) | confessar-se (vp) | [kõfəs'arsə] |
| | | |
| to confuse (mix up) | confundir (vt) | [kõfũd'ir] |
| to congratulate (vt) | felicitar (vt) | [fəlisit'ar] |
| to consult (doctor, expert) | consultar ... | [kõsult'ar] |
| to continue (~ to do sth) | continuar (vt) | [kõtinu'ar] |
| | | |
| to control (vt) | controlar (vt) | [kõtrul'ar] |
| to convince (vt) | convencer (vt) | [kõvẽs'er] |
| to cooperate (vi) | cooperar (vi) | [kuupɐr'ar] |
| to coordinate (vt) | coordenar (vt) | [kuurdən'ar] |
| | | |
| to correct (an error) | corrigir (vt) | [kuʀiʒ'ir] |
| to cost (vt) | custar (vt) | [kuʃt'ar] |
| to count (money, etc.) | calcular (vt) | [kalkul'ar] |
| to count on ... | contar com ... | [kõt'ar kõ] |
| | | |
| to crack (ceiling, wall) | rachar-se (vp) | [ʀɐʃ'arsə] |
| to create (vt) | criar (vt) | [kri'ar] |
| to cry (weep) | chorar (vi) | [ʃur'ar] |
| to cut off (with a knife) | cortar (vt) | [kurt'ar] |

## 253. Verbs D-G

| | | |
|---|---|---|
| to dare (~ to do sth) | ousar (vt) | [oz'ar] |
| to date from ... | datar (vi) | [dɐt'ar] |

| | | |
|---|---|---|
| to deceive (vi, vt) | **enganar** (vt) | [ẽgɐn'ar] |
| to decide (~ to do sth) | **decidir** (vt) | [dəsid'ir] |
| | | |
| to decorate (tree, street) | **decorar** (vt) | [dəkur'ar] |
| to dedicate (book, etc.) | **dedicar** (vt) | [dədik'ar] |
| to defend (a country, etc.) | **defender** (vt) | [dəfẽd'er] |
| to defend oneself | **defender-se** (vp) | [dəfẽd'ersə] |
| to demand (request firmly) | **exigir** (vt) | [eziʒ'ir] |
| | | |
| to denounce (vt) | **denunciar** (vt) | [dənũsj'ar] |
| to deny (vt) | **negar** (vt) | [nəg'ar] |
| to depend on ... | **depender de ...** (vi) | [dəpẽd'er də] |
| to deprive (vt) | **privar** (vt) | [priv'ar] |
| | | |
| to deserve (vt) | **merecer** (vt) | [mərəs'er] |
| to design (machine, etc.) | **projetar, criar** (vt) | [pruʒɛt'ar], [krj'ar] |
| to desire (want, wish) | **desejar** (vt) | [dəzeʒ'ar] |
| to despise (vt) | **desprezar** (vt) | [dəʃprəz'ar] |
| to destroy (documents, etc.) | **destruir** (vt) | [dəʃtru'ir] |
| | | |
| to differ (from sth) | **ser diferente** | [ser difər'ẽtə] |
| to dig (tunnel, etc.) | **cavar** (vt) | [kɐv'ar] |
| to direct (point the way) | **direcionar** (vt) | [dirɛsiun'ar] |
| to disappear (vi) | **desaparecer** (vi) | [dəzɐpərəs'er] |
| | | |
| to discover (new land, etc.) | **descobrir** (vt) | [dəʃkubr'ir] |
| to discuss (vt) | **discutir** (vt) | [diʃkut'ir] |
| to distribute (leaflets, etc.) | **distribuir** (vt) | [diʃtribu'ir] |
| to disturb (vt) | **perturbar** (vt) | [pərturb'ar] |
| to dive (vi) | **mergulhar** (vi) | [mərguʎ'ar] |
| | | |
| to divide (math) | **dividir** (vt) | [divid'ir] |
| to do (vt) | **fazer** (vt) | [fɐz'er] |
| to do the laundry | **lavar a roupa** | [lɐv'ar ɐ ʀ'opɐ] |
| to double (increase) | **dobrar** (vt) | [dubr'ar] |
| | | |
| to doubt (have doubts) | **duvidar de ...** | [duvidar də] |
| to draw a conclusion | **tirar uma conclusão** | [tir'ar 'umɐ kõkluz'ãu] |
| to dream (daydream) | **sonhar** (vt) | [suɲ'ar] |
| to dream (in sleep) | **sonhar** (vi) | [suɲ'ar] |
| to drink (vi, vt) | **beber, tomar** (vt) | [bəb'er], [tum'ar] |
| | | |
| to drive a car | **conduzir** (vt) | [kõduz'ir] |
| to drive away (scare away) | **afugentar** (vt) | [ɐfuʒẽt'ar] |
| to drop (let fall) | **deixar cair** (vt) | [dejʃ'ar kɐ'ir] |
| to drown (ab. person) | **afogar-se** (vp) | [ɐfug'arsə] |
| to dry (clothes, hair) | **secar** (vt) | [sək'ar] |
| to eat (vi, vt) | **comer** (vt) | [kum'er] |
| to eavesdrop (vi) | **escutar atrás da porta** | [əʃkut'ar ɐtr'aʃ dɐ p'ɔrtɐ] |
| to emit (give out - odor, etc.) | **emitir** (vt) | [emit'ir] |

| to enter (on the list) | inscrever (vt) | [ĩʃkrəv'er] |
| to entertain (amuse) | divertir (vt) | [divərt'ir] |
| to equip (fit out) | equipar (vt) | [ekip'ar] |
| to examine (proposal) | examinar (vt) | [ezemin'ar] |
| to exchange (sth) | trocar (vt) | [truk'ar] |

| to exclude, to expel | expulsar (vt) | [əʃpuls'ar] |
| to excuse (forgive) | desculpar (vt) | [dəʃkulp'ar] |
| to exist (vi) | existir (vi) | [eziʃt'ir] |
| to expect (anticipate) | esperar (vt) | [əʃpər'ar] |
| to expect (foresee) | prever (vt) | [prəv'er] |

| to explain (vt) | explicar (vt) | [əʃplik'ar] |
| to express (vt) | expressar (vt) | [əʃprəs'ar] |
| to extinguish (a fire) | apagar (vt) | [ɐpɐg'ar] |
| to fall in love (with ...) | apaixonar-se de ... | [ɐpajʃun'arsə də] |

| to feed (provide food) | alimentar (vt) | [ɐlimẽt'ar] |
| to fight (against the enemy) | lutar (vt) | [lut'ar] |
| to fight (vi) | bater-se (vp) | [bɐt'ersə] |
| to fill (glass, bottle) | encher (vt) | [ẽʃ'er] |
| to find (~ lost items) | encontrar (vt) | [ẽkõtr'ar] |

| to finish (vt) | terminar (vt) | [tərmin'ar] |
| to fish (angle) | pescar (vt) | [pəʃk'ar] |
| to fit (ab. dress, etc.) | servir (vi) | [sərv'ir] |
| to flatter (vt) | lisonjear (vt) | [lizõʒj'ar] |

| to fly (bird, plane) | voar (vi) | [vu'ar] |
| to follow ... (come after) | seguir (vt) | [səg'ir] |
| to forbid (vt) | proibir (vt) | [pruib'ir] |
| to force (compel) | forçar (vt) | [furs'ar] |
| to forget (vi, vt) | esquecer (vi) | [əʃkɛs'er] |

| to forgive (pardon) | perdoar (vt) | [pərdu'ar] |
| to form (constitute) | formar (vt) | [furm'ar] |
| to get dirty (vi) | sujar-se (vp) | [suʒ'arsə] |
| to get infected (with ...) | contagiar-se com ... | [kõtəʒj'arsə kõ] |

| to get irritated | irritar-se (vp) | [iʀit'arsə] |
| to get married | casar-se (vp) | [kɐz'arsə] |
| to get rid of ... | livrar-se de ... | [livr'arsə də] |
| to get tired | ficar cansado | [fik'ar kãs'adu] |
| to get up (arise from bed) | levantar-se (vp) | [ləvãt'arsə] |

| to give (vt) | dar (vt) | [dar] |
| to give a bath | dar banho, lavar (vt) | [dar b'ɐɲu], [lɐv'ar] |
| to give a hug, to hug (vt) | abraçar (vt) | [ɐbrɐs'ar] |
| to give in (yield to) | ceder (vi) | [səd'er] |
| to go (by car, etc.) | ir (vi) | [ir] |
| to go (on foot) | ir (vi) | [ir] |

| | | |
|---|---|---|
| to go for a swim | ir nadar | [ir ned'ar] |
| to go out (for dinner, etc.) | sair (vt) | [se'ir] |
| to go to bed | ir para a cama | [ir p'ere e k'eme] |
| | | |
| to greet (vt) | saudar (vt) | [seud'ar] |
| to grow (plants) | cultivar (vt) | [kultiv'ar] |
| to guarantee (vt) | garantir (vt) | [gerãt'ir] |
| to guess right | adivinhar (vt) | [ediviɲ'ar] |

## 254. Verbs H-M

| | | |
|---|---|---|
| to hand out (distribute) | distribuir (vt) | [diʃtribu'ir] |
| to hang (curtains, etc.) | pendurar (vt) | [pẽdur'ar] |
| to have (vt) | ter (vt) | [ter] |
| to have a try | tentar (vt) | [tẽt'ar] |
| to have breakfast | tomar o pequeno-almoço | [tum'ar u pek'enu alm'osu] |
| | | |
| to have dinner | jantar (vi) | [ʒãt'ar] |
| to have fun | divertir-se (vp) | [divert'irse] |
| to have lunch | almoçar (vi) | [almus'ar] |
| to head (group, etc.) | encabeçar (vt) | [ẽkebes'ar] |
| | | |
| to hear (vt) | ouvir (vt) | [ov'ir] |
| to heat (vt) | aquecer (vt) | [ekɛs'er] |
| to help (vt) | ajudar (vt) | [eʒud'ar] |
| to hide (vt) | esconder (vt) | [eʃkõd'er] |
| to hire (e.g., ~ a boat) | alugar (vt) | [elug'ar] |
| | | |
| to hire (staff) | contratar (vt) | [kõtret'ar] |
| to hope (vi, vt) | esperar (vt) | [eʃper'ar] |
| to hunt (for food, sport) | caçar (vi) | [kes'ar] |
| to hurry (sb) | apressar (vt) | [epres'ar] |
| | | |
| to hurry (vi) | estar com pressa | [eʃt'ar kõ pr'ɛse] |
| to imagine (to picture) | imaginar (vt) | [imeʒin'ar] |
| to imitate (vt) | imitar (vt) | [imit'ar] |
| to implore (vt) | implorar (vt) | [ĩplur'ar] |
| to import (vt) | importar (vt) | [ĩpurt'ar] |
| | | |
| to increase (vi) | aumentar (vi) | [aumẽt'ar] |
| to increase (vt) | aumentar (vt) | [aumẽt'ar] |
| to infect (vt) | infetar, contagiar (vt) | [ĩfɛt'ar], [kõteʒj'ar] |
| to influence (vt) | influenciar (vt) | [ĩfluẽsj'ar] |
| | | |
| to inform (~ sb about ...) | informar (vt) | [ĩfurm'ar] |
| to inform (vt) | informar (vt) | [ĩfurm'ar] |
| to inherit (vt) | herdar (vt) | [erd'ar] |
| to inquire (about ...) | informar-se (vt) | [ĩfurm'arse] |
| to insist (vi, vt) | insistir (vi) | [ĩsiʃt'ir] |
| to inspire (vt) | inspirar (vt) | [ĩʃpir'ar] |

| to instruct (teach) | instruir (vt) | [ĩʃtru'ir] |
| to insult (offend) | insultar (vt) | [ĩsult'ar] |
| to interest (vt) | interessar (vt) | [ĩtərəs'ar] |

| to intervene (vi) | intervir (vi) | [ĩtərv'ir] |
| to introduce (present) | apresentar (vt) | [ɐprəzẽt'ar] |
| to invent (machine, etc.) | inventar (vt) | [ĩvẽt'ar] |
| to invite (vt) | convidar (vt) | [kõvid'ar] |
| to iron (laundry) | passar a ferro | [pɐs'ar ɐ f'ɛʀu] |

| to irritate (annoy) | irritar (vt) | [iʀit'ar] |
| to isolate (vt) | isolar (vt) | [izul'ar] |
| to join (political party, etc.) | juntar-se a ... | [ʒũt'arsə ɐ] |
| to joke (be kidding) | fazer piadas | [fɐz'er pj'adəʃ] |

| to keep (old letters, etc.) | guardar (vt) | [guɐrd'ar] |
| to keep silent | ficar em silêncio | [fik'ar ẽ sil'ẽsiu] |
| to kill (vt) | matar (vt) | [mɐt'ar] |
| to knock (at the door) | bater (vi) | [bɐt'er] |
| to know (sb) | conhecer (vt) | [kuɲəs'er] |

| to know (sth) | saber (vt) | [sɐb'er] |
| to laugh (vi) | rir (vi) | [ʀir] |
| to launch (start up) | lançar (vt) | [lãs'ar] |
| to leave (~ for Mexico) | partir (vt) | [pɐrt'ir] |

| to leave (spouse) | deixar (vt) | [dɐjʃ'ar] |
| to leave behind (forget) | deixar (vt) | [dɐjʃ'ar] |
| to liberate (city, etc.) | libertar (vt) | [libɐrt'ar] |
| to lie (tell untruth) | mentir (vi) | [mẽt'ir] |
| to light (campfire, etc.) | acender (vt) | [ɐsẽd'er] |

| to light up (illuminate) | iluminar (vt) | [ilumin'ar] |
| to love (e.g., ~ dancing) | gostar (vt) | [guʃt'ar] |
| to like (I like ...) | gostar (vt) | [guʃt'ar] |
| to limit (vt) | limitar (vt) | [limit'ar] |

| to listen (vi) | escutar (vt) | [əʃkut'ar] |
| to live (~ in France) | morar (vt) | [mur'ar] |
| to live (exist) | viver (vi) | [viv'er] |
| to load (gun) | carregar (vt) | [kɐʀəg'ar] |
| to load (vehicle, etc.) | carregar (vt) | [kɐʀəg'ar] |

| to look (I'm just ~ing) | olhar (vt) | [ɔʎ'ar] |
| to look for ... (search) | buscar (vt) | [buʃk'ar] |
| to look like (resemble) | parecer-se (vp) | [pɐrəs'ersə] |
| to lose (umbrella, etc.) | perder (vt) | [pərd'er] |

| to love (sb) | amar (vt) | [ɐm'ar] |
| to lower (blind, head) | baixar (vt) | [bajʃ'ar] |
| to make (~ dinner) | cozinhar (vt) | [kuziɲ'ar] |
| to make a mistake | errar (vi) | [ɛʀ'ar] |

| to make angry | zangar (vt) | [zãg'ar] |
| to make copies | tirar cópias | [tir'ar k'ɔpiɐʃ] |
| to make easier | facilitar (vt) | [fesilit'ar] |
| to make the acquaintance | conhecer-se (vp) | [kuɲes'ersə] |
| to make use (of …) | utilizar (vt) | [utiliz'ar] |
| | | |
| to manage, to run | dirigir (vt) | [diriʒ'ir] |
| to mark (make a mark) | marcar (vt) | [merk'ar] |
| to mean (signify) | significar (vt) | [signifik'ar] |
| to memorize (vt) | memorizar (vt) | [məmuriz'ar] |
| to mention (talk about) | mencionar (vt) | [mẽsiun'ar] |
| | | |
| to miss (school, etc.) | faltar a ... | [falt'ar ɐ] |
| to mix (combine, blend) | misturar (vt) | [miʃtur'ar] |
| to mock (make fun of) | zombar (vt) | [zõb'ar] |
| to move (to shift) | mover (vt) | [muv'er] |
| to multiply (math) | multiplicar (vt) | [multiplik'ar] |
| must (v aux) | dever (vi) | [dəv'er] |

## 255. Verbs N-S

| to name, to call (vt) | denominar (vt) | [dənumin'ar] |
| to negotiate (vi) | negociar (vi) | [nəgusj'ar] |
| to note (write down) | anotar (vt) | [ɐnut'ar] |
| to notice (see) | perceber (vt) | [pərsəb'er] |
| | | |
| to obey (vi, vt) | obedecer (vt) | [ɔbədəs'er] |
| to object (vi, vt) | objetar (vt) | [ɔbʒɛt'ar] |
| to observe (see) | observar (vt) | [ɔbserv'ar] |
| to offend (vt) | ofender (vt) | [ɔfẽd'er] |
| to omit (word, phrase) | omitir (vt) | [ɔmit'ir] |
| | | |
| to open (vt) | abrir (vt) | [ɐbr'ir] |
| to order (in restaurant) | pedir (vt) | [pəd'ir] |
| to order (mil.) | ordenar (vt) | [ɔrdən'ar] |
| to organize (concert, party) | organizar (vt) | [ɔrgəniz'ar] |
| | | |
| to overestimate (vt) | sobrestimar (vt) | [sobrəʃtim'ar] |
| to own (possess) | possuir (vt) | [pusu'ir] |
| to participate (vi) | participar (vi) | [pərtisip'ar] |
| to pass (go beyond) | passar (vt) | [pɐs'ar] |
| to pay (vi, vt) | pagar (vt) | [pɐg'ar] |
| | | |
| to peep, spy on | espreitar (vi) | [əʃprejt'ar] |
| to penetrate (vt) | penetrar (vt) | [pənətr'ar] |
| to permit (vt) | permitir (vt) | [pərmit'ir] |
| to pick (flowers) | colher (vt) | [kuʎ'ɛr] |
| | | |
| to place (put, set) | pôr, colocar (vt) | [por], [kuluk'ar] |
| to plan (~ to do sth) | planear (vt) | [plɐnj'ar] |

| to play (actor) | desempenhar (vt) | [dəzĕpəɲ'ar] |
| to play (children) | brincar, jogar (vi, vt) | [bɾĩk'ar], [ʒug'ar] |
| to point (~ the way) | indicar (vt) | [ĩdik'ar] |

| to pour (liquid) | verter, encher (vt) | [vərt'er], [ĕʃ'er] |
| to pray (vi, vt) | rezar, orar (vi) | [ʀəz'ar], [ɔr'ar] |
| to predominate (vi) | predominar (vi, vt) | [prədumin'ar] |
| to prefer (vt) | preferir (vt) | [prəfər'ir] |

| to prepare (~ a plan) | preparar (vt) | [prəpər'ar] |
| to present (sb to sb) | apresentar (vt) | [eprəzĕt'ar] |
| to preserve (peace, life) | preservar (vt) | [prəzərv'ar] |
| to progress (move forward) | avançar (vi) | [ɐvãs'ar] |
| to promise (vt) | prometer (vt) | [prumət'er] |

| to pronounce (vt) | pronunciar (vt) | [prunũsj'ar] |
| to propose (vt) | propor (vt) | [prup'or] |
| to protect (e.g., ~ nature) | proteger (vt) | [prutəʒ'er] |
| to protest (vi) | protestar (vi) | [prutəʃt'ar] |

| to prove (vt) | provar (vt) | [pruv'ar] |
| to provoke (vt) | provocar (vt) | [pruvuk'ar] |
| to pull (~ the rope) | puxar (vt) | [puʃ'ar] |
| to punish (vt) | punir (vt) | [pun'ir] |
| to push (~ the door) | empurrar (vt) | [ĕpuʀ'ar] |

| to put away (vt) | arrumar, guardar (vt) | [eʀum'ar], [guerd'ar] |
| to put in (insert) | inserir (vt) | [ĩsər'ir] |
| to put in order | arranjar (vt) | [eʀãʒ'ar] |
| to put, to place | pôr, colocar (vt) | [por], [kuluk'ar] |

| to quote (cite) | citar (vt) | [sit'ar] |
| to reach (arrive at) | chegar a ... | [ʃəg'ar ɐ] |
| to read (vi, vt) | ler (vt) | [ler] |
| to realize (a dream) | realizar (vt) | [ʀiəliz'ar] |
| to recall (~ one's name) | recordar, lembrar (vt) | [ʀəkurd'ar], [lĕbr'ar] |

| to recognize (identify sb) | reconhecer (vt) | [ʀəkuɲəs'er] |
| to recommend (vt) | recomendar (vt) | [ʀəkumĕd'ar] |
| to recover (~ from flu) | recuperar-se (vp) | [ʀəkupər'arsə] |
| to redo (do again) | refazer (vt) | [ʀəfez'er] |

| to reduce (speed, etc.) | reduzir (vt) | [ʀəduz'ir] |
| to refuse (~ sb) | recusar (vt) | [ʀəkuz'ar] |
| to regret (be sorry) | lamentar (vt) | [lemĕt'ar] |
| to reinforce (vt) | reforçar (vt) | [ʀəfurs'ar] |
| to remember (vt) | lembrar (vt) | [lĕbr'ar] |

| to remind of ... | fazer lembrar | [fez'er lĕbr'ar] |
| to remove (~ a stain) | remover (vt) | [ʀəmuv'er] |
| to remove (~ an obstacle) | remover, eliminar (vt) | [ʀəmuv'er], [elimin'ar] |

| | | |
|---|---|---|
| to rent (sth from sb) | alugar (vt) | [ɐlug'ar] |
| to repair (mend) | reparar (vt) | [Rəper'ar] |
| to repeat (say again) | repetir (vt) | [Rəpet'ir] |
| to report (make a report) | reportar (vt) | [Rəpurt'ar] |
| to reproach (vt) | censurar (vt) | [sẽsur'ar] |
| to reserve, to book | reservar (vt) | [Rəzərv'ar] |
| | | |
| to restrain (hold back) | refrear (vt) | [Rəfrj'ar] |
| to return (come back) | voltar (vi) | [vɔlt'ar] |
| to risk, to take a risk | arriscar (vt) | [ɐRiʃk'ar] |
| to rub off (erase) | apagar (vt) | [ɐpɐg'ar] |
| | | |
| to run (move fast) | correr (vi) | [kuR'er] |
| to satisfy (please) | satisfazer (vt) | [sɐtiʃfez'er] |
| to save (rescue) | salvar (vt) | [salv'ar] |
| to say (~ thank you) | dizer (vt) | [diz'er] |
| to scold (vt) | repreender (vt) | [Rəpriẽd'er] |
| | | |
| to scratch (with claws) | arranhar (vt) | [ɐRɐɲ'ar] |
| to select (to pick) | selecionar (vt) | [sələsiun'ar] |
| to sell (goods) | vender (vt) | [vẽd'er] |
| to send (a letter) | enviar (vt) | [ẽvj'ar] |
| | | |
| to send back (vt) | devolver (vt) | [dəvɔlv'er] |
| to sense (danger) | sentir (vt) | [sẽt'ir] |
| to sentence (vt) | sentenciar (vt) | [sẽtẽsj'ar] |
| to serve (in restaurant) | servir (vt) | [sərv'ir] |
| to settle (a conflict) | resolver (vt) | [Rəzɔlv'er] |
| | | |
| to shake (vt) | agitar, sacudir (vt) | [ɐʒit'ar], [sɐkud'ir] |
| to shave (vi) | barbear-se (vp) | [bərbj'arsə] |
| to shine (gleam) | brilhar (vi) | [briʎ'ar] |
| to shiver (with cold) | tremer (vi) | [trəm'er] |
| | | |
| to shoot (vi) | atirar (vi) | [ɐtir'ar] |
| to shout (vi) | gritar (vi) | [grit'ar] |
| to show (to display) | mostrar (vt) | [muʃtr'ar] |
| to shudder (vi) | estremecer (vi) | [əʃtrəməs'er] |
| to sigh (vi) | suspirar (vi) | [suʃpir'ar] |
| | | |
| to sign (document) | assinar (vt) | [ɐsin'ar] |
| to signify (mean) | significar (vt) | [signifik'ar] |
| to simplify (vt) | simplificar (vt) | [sĩplifik'ar] |
| to sin (vi) | pecar (vi) | [pək'ar] |
| | | |
| to sit (be sitting) | estar sentado | [əʃt'ar sẽt'adu] |
| to sit down (vi) | sentar-se (vp) | [sẽt'arsə] |
| to smash (~ a bug) | esmagar (vt) | [əʒmɐg'ar] |
| to smell (scent) | cheirar (vi) | [ʃejr'ar] |
| to smell (sniff at) | cheirar (vi) | [ʃejr'ar] |
| to smile (vi) | sorrir (vi) | [suR'ir] |
| to snap (vi, ab. rope) | romper-se (vp) | [Rõp'ersə] |

| | | |
|---|---|---|
| to solve (problem) | **resolver** (vt) | [ʀəzɔlv'er] |
| to sow (seed, crop) | **semear** (vt) | [səmj'ar] |
| | | |
| to spill (liquid) | **derramar** (vt) | [dəʀɐm'ar] |
| to spill out (flour, etc.) | **derramar-se** (vp) | [dəʀɐm'arsə] |
| to spit (vi) | **cuspir** (vi) | [kuʃp'ir] |
| to stand (toothache, cold) | **suportar** (vt) | [supurt'ar] |
| to start (begin) | **começar** (vt) | [kuməs'ar] |
| | | |
| to steal (money, etc.) | **roubar** (vt) | [ʀob'ar] |
| to stop (please ~ calling me) | **cessar** (vt) | [səs'ar] |
| to stop (for pause, etc.) | **parar** (vi) | [pɐr'ar] |
| to stop talking | **calar-se** (vp) | [kɛl'arsə] |
| | | |
| to stroke (caress) | **acariciar** (vt) | [ɐkɐrisj'ar] |
| to study (vt) | **estudar** (vt) | [əʃtud'ar] |
| to suffer (feel pain) | **sofrer** (vt) | [sufr'er] |
| to support (cause, idea) | **apoiar** (vt) | [ɐpoj'ar] |
| to suppose (assume) | **supor** (vt) | [sup'or] |
| | | |
| to surface (ab. submarine) | **emergir** (vi) | [əmərʒ'ir] |
| to surprise (amaze) | **surpreender** (vt) | [surprièd'er] |
| to suspect (vt) | **suspeitar** (vt) | [suʃpejt'ar] |
| to swim (vi) | **nadar** (vi) | [nɛd'ar] |
| to turn on (computer, etc.) | **ligar** (vt) | [lig'ar] |

## 256. Verbs T-W

| | | |
|---|---|---|
| to take (get hold of) | **pegar** (vt) | [pəg'ar] |
| to take a bath | **lavar-se** (vp) | [lɛv'arsə] |
| to take a rest | **descansar** (vi) | [dəʃkãs'ar] |
| | | |
| to take aim (at …) | **apontar para …** | [ɐpõt'ar p'ɛrɐ] |
| to take away | **levar** (vt) | [lɛv'ar] |
| to take off (airplane) | **descolar** (vi) | [dəʃkul'ar] |
| to take off (remove) | **tirar** (vt) | [tir'ar] |
| | | |
| to take pictures | **fotografar** (vt) | [futugrɛf'ar] |
| to talk to … | **falar com …** | [fɐl'ar kõ] |
| to teach (give lessons) | **ensinar** (vt) | [ẽsin'ar] |
| | | |
| to tear off (vt) | **arrancar** (vt) | [ɐʀãk'ar] |
| to tell (story, joke) | **contar** (vt) | [kõt'ar] |
| to thank (vt) | **agradecer** (vt) | [ɐgrɐdəs'er] |
| to think (believe) | **achar** (vt) | [ɐʃ'ar] |
| | | |
| to think (vi, vt) | **pensar** (vt) | [pẽs'ar] |
| to threaten (vt) | **ameaçar** (vt) | [ɐmiɐs'ar] |
| to throw (stone) | **jogar, atirar** (vt) | [ʒug'ar], [ɐtir'ar] |

| to tie to ... | atar (vt) | [et'ar] |
| to tie up (prisoner) | amarrar (vt) | [emɐʀ'ar] |
| to tire (make tired) | fatigar (vt) | [fetig'ar] |
| to touch (one's arm, etc.) | tocar (vt) | [tuk'ar] |

| to tower (over ...) | elevar-se acima de ... | [eləv'arsə ɐs'imɐ də] |
| to train (animals) | adestrar (vt) | [ɐdəʃtr'ar] |
| to train (sb) | treinar (vt) | [trejn'ar] |

| to train (vi) | treinar-se (vp) | [trejn'arsə] |
| to transform (vt) | transformar (vt) | [trãʃfurm'ar] |
| to translate (vt) | traduzir (vt) | [treduz'ir] |
| to treat (patient, illness) | tratar (vt) | [tret'ar] |

| to trust (vt) | confiar (vt) | [kõfj'ar] |
| to try (attempt) | tentar (vt) | [tẽt'ar] |
| to turn (~ to the left) | virar (vi) | [vir'ar] |

| to turn away (vi) | virar as costas | [vir'ar ɐʃ k'ɔʃtɐʃ] |
| to turn off (the light) | desligar (vt) | [dəʒlig'ar] |
| to turn over (stone, etc.) | virar (vt) | [vir'ar] |
| to underestimate (vt) | subestimar (vt) | [subəʃtim'ar] |

| to underline (vt) | sublinhar (vt) | [subliɲ'ar] |
| to understand (vt) | compreender (vt) | [kõpriẽd'er] |
| to undertake (vt) | empreender (vt) | [ẽpriẽd'er] |

| to unite (vt) | juntar, unir (vt) | [ʒũt'ar], [un'ir] |
| to untie (vt) | desatar (vt) | [dəzet'ar] |
| to use (phrase, word) | usar (vt) | [uz'ar] |
| to vaccinate (vt) | vacinar (vt) | [vesin'ar] |

| to vote (vi) | votar (vi) | [vut'ar] |
| to wait (vt) | esperar (vi, vt) | [əʃpər'ar] |
| to wake (sb) | acordar, despertar (vt) | [ɐkurd'ar], [dəʃpərt'ar] |

| to want (wish, desire) | querer (vt) | [kər'er] |
| to warn (of the danger) | advertir (vt) | [ɐdvərt'ir] |
| to wash (clean) | lavar (vt) | [lev'ar] |
| to water (plants) | regar (vt) | [ʀəg'ar] |

| to wave (the hand) | acenar (vt) | [ɐsən'ar] |
| to weigh (have weight) | pesar (vt) | [pəz'ar] |
| to work (vi) | trabalhar (vi) | [trebɐʎ'ar] |

| to worry (make anxious) | preocupar (vt) | [priɔkup'ar] |
| to worry (vi) | preocupar-se (vp) | [priɔkup'arsə] |
| to wrap (parcel, etc.) | embrulhar (vt) | [ẽbruʎ'ar] |
| to wrestle (sport) | lutar (vi) | [lut'ar] |

| to write (vt) | escrever (vt) | [əʃkrəv'er] |
| to write down | anotar (vt) | [ɐnut'ar] |